MODERN SOCIAL REFORMS

Solving Today's Social Problems

The choice you'll never know is the choice you'll never make. Many Americans are not sufficiently informed of the alternatives to make an intelligent choice of the life they most want.

—Nicholas Johnson

Live the questions now.
Perhaps you will then . . .
live along some distant day
into the answer.

—Raine Maria Rilke

We are called to play the Good Samaritan on life's roadside, but that will be only the initial act. One day the whole Jericho Road must be transformed so that men and women will not be beaten and robbed as they make their journey through life. True compassion is more than flinging a coin to a beggar; it understands that an edifice which produces beggars needs restructuring.

—Martin Luther King, Jr.

MODERN SOCIAL REFORMS

Solving Today's Social Problems

Arthur B. Shostak

DREXEL UNIVERSITY

MACMILLAN PUBLISHING CO., INC.
New York
COLLIER MACMILLAN PUBLISHERS
London

Printed in the United States of America

Macmillan Publishing Co., Inc.
866 Third Avenue, New York, New York 10022

Collier-Macmillan Canada, Ltd.

Library of Congress Cataloging in Publication Data

Shostak, Arthur B
Modern social reforms.

Bibliography: p.
1. United States—Social conditions—1960–
2. Social problems—Addresses, essays, lectures.
I. Title.
HN65.S54 362'.973 73–10694
ISBN 0–02–410190–7

Printing: 1 2 3 4 5 6 7 8 Year: 4 5 6 7 8 9 0

For my sons, Scott Elliot and Mark Judah,
whose lives strengthen my conviction
that the New America profiled in this volume
will soon be earned by us all.

Acknowledgments

Although as author I assume responsibility for this book's full range of shortcomings, I would share any credit with a team of collaborators, confidants, and kibitzers as insightful, constructive, and loving as any I have been privileged to work with across twelve years of publishing and a half a dozen previous books.

From the very start, in 1971, Elaine Axelrod, a student research assistant and treasured friend, believed in this project and gave it unflagging support. Gale Katz, who succeeded Elaine as my research assistant, located reams of backup material and gently volunteered long weekend days to help type the manuscript. Mark Friedman, another research assistant, specialized in uncovering foreign innovations that deserved inclusion in this book and helped calm the writer with his low-keyed example of "the examined life." Eric Vlam, a student friend, made helpful comments on several chapters, as did Jerry Pocius. Along with Heather Reeves, Jerry assumed large responsibility for the book's annotated bibliography. Lalita Balasubramanian, a graduate student from India, served as a full-time research assistant in the final five-month phase of this two-and-a-half-year-long writing project. For her craft in locating readings and data, as well as her patience with my forgetfulness and "artistic liberties" (incorrect citations of material I asked for, and so on), I owe deep and lasting appreciation—as well as for the generous assistance rendered on several occasions by her husband, Moni.

Drexel typist Susan Gershuni began the manuscript in the fall of 1972 with a quality of enthusiasm for the project and personal good cheer that helped make the difference when abandonment of the entire "impossible" undertaking was still a very real temptation. Phyllis Krieger, a neighbor, helped finish the typing, giving long evenings and inviting spring days over to that enervating task. Additional indispensable typing was graciously done by Ruby Walker, the secretary of my editor at Macmillan.

Ken Scott, the college editor who signed this book and sweated out its tortuous, confusing, and nerve-wracking completion, gave indispensable encouragement throughout. He also arranged for the considerable editorial assistance of two consulting sociologists, Paul Campanis and Donald Bylsma. At every important juncture, Ken smoothed the way and helped me believe that the book would really soon be finished, even when my fatigue and moments of depression argued otherwise.

William Goldbeck, administrator for "Choices for '76," and Kathy Howard, a staffer with People's Bicentennial Commission, both went out of their way to respond speedily and fully to my request for information on their projects—and have my deep gratitude in return.

Throughout the summer and fall of 1972 a very close friend, Michelle Pruyn, lent encouragement and protection against the distractions that everywhere tempt one as curious as myself from the task at hand. Another personal friend, Susan Marker, in the especially trying closing months of the project, worked very hard to keep me human and earthbound, indispensable aid without which the project might have finished off an author as well as a book. Finally, my two sons, Scott Elliot and Mark Judah, lovingly and in good humor, gave up at least six months' worth of leisure-style weekends that I might complete this project—for which they have my thanks and respect in amounts I am always inadequate in expressing.

As I said at the beginning, a pennant-winning, Stanley Cup, gold-medal collection of associates . . . without whom there would be nothing to acknowledge, and despite whom the book often falls short. Theirs, the credit; mine, the resolve to do it all still better, next time.

A. B. S.

Contents

MODERN SOCIAL REFORMS

Solving Today's Social Problems

Introduction: What You May Expect of This Book and What It Expects of You

Our task is to discover what everything in the universe, from electrons upwards, could, to its betterment, become, but cannot become without our help.

W. H. AUDEN

We need rising before us real present evidence of man's ability to act positively: not just to remove what is wrong, but to supply what is missing.

BENJAMIN THOMPSON

This book is a kind of cookbook of reform, a recipe collection of "better ideas" on how to resolve our change-resistant and time-honored social problems. Name several such problems, and the chances are good that you'll find some interesting answers for them somewhere in this volume. Partial answers? To be sure, and certain therefore to generate additional challenges. Expensive? Perhaps, and destined accordingly to tax our economic standard of living in discomforting ways we may not want to accept in exchange for the promise of social gains. Novel? In many cases, for example, educational parks, hydroponics, or the arguments in favor of bans of ads on children's TV and reversion to penal colonies. All of which is certain to raise eyebrows, furrow foreheads, and compel a quality of soul searching and assumption questioning all too rare in our "make-no-waves" climate.

This book deals in answers, in short, dozens of them, that point up the interconnectedness of things, the "dues" we must pay if our social gains are to prove just and substantial, and the boldness we must show both in analysis and in action, lest we increase the risk we run of losing not only what we have but all we hope for.

So Who Cares? We do care—you and I! I find us weary, many of us, of the "same old things" in the way of social reforms. Reflecting some of the boredom that dominated the 1972 Presidential campaign we are restless and ask impatiently, even plaintively, "What can we *do* about it? I mean, what can any of us be expected to do about it? Don't just push us to realize how messed up it all is, but help us to figure out ways to straighten it all out!"

Many who ask are something of a new breed; they know more about "how it really is" than did their counterparts in the somnambulistic 1950's. They also know less, in the sense that they do not believe in the snake-oil panaceas that were common in the ideology-ridden 1960's. Instead, drawing on the goodwill of the one decade and the new dream of the other, this new breed presses to learn how we can get on with the job. How can we stir again to the task of remaking America? Many, far more than we sometimes realize, are eager to join in a common effort, in Stewart Udall's words, "capable of restoring a vision, of reframing an American dream powerful enough to enlist our minds and persuasive enough to revive our ancient faith in the future of our country."[1]

And Then What? How do you get started? Where can you turn for alternative agendas, for pragmatic options you can arrange into a formidable and sophisticated campaign against the major social ills that so try us? Where can you look for the nitty-gritty, something beyond the loose inspirational rhetoric of naïve optimists and pious hopesters? Among other printed sources, *here;* the desire to centralize in one place, between two book covers, a high-quality collection of proposals for needed contemporary reforms essentially explains the origins and the ultimate product of a project that I have pursued with a research assistant for several years.

I realized with dismay some time ago that most texts and courses in "social problems," "American society," "American studies," and the like fail to follow up their analysis of contemporary social dilemmas with an imaginative and useful assessment of competing modern remedies. I was also perplexed by our failure to make enough of relevant experiments with social reforms in other countries (such as the Danish suspension of censorship, the long-time European reliance on midwives, and the occasional South American endorsement of homes and communities built by the poor themselves). Finally, I was chagrined by our general reluctance in the classroom to consider social reforms in a value-charged political framework. To pussy-foot around this subject because it is explosive (and has us trespassing on the academic turf of the political science crowd) seems ever less acceptable with every passing major election, as laymen (including most college students) in the voting booth were being earnestly called on to decide exactly what we on campus were carefully refusing to discuss.

On Meeting the Need. Accordingly, this book departs in three major ways from other texts in the field.

First, it tries to meet the call from students for blueprints for reforms, for how-to-do-it guides to solving the real-life problems that tax us all. Second, it tries to lend additional impetus to a steadily building campus curiosity about how problems are met elsewhere, about foreign remedies for social problems that nations share. Third, it advances a productive political framework, a comparison of four schools of political thought, and locates many of the reforms discussed—whether native or foreign in origin—inside that framework. In this way this book compels attention to the integral relationship of social policy, social problems, and political philosophy, however much disputation concerning them it may also unapologetically engender.

Why this attention to foreign answers to our domestic problems? Not only because our chauvinism restricts reflection on reform, but also because reflection on foreign ways enables us to stand outside of our own society. Too often we take much about us for granted. We must be challenged to question unexamined assumptions and thereby identify the forces within our society (such as its guiding interpretation of man's human nature or its distribution of political privilege) that can be channeled to assist in its rededication, its renewal, or its transformation.

And why this attention to political schools, to the conservative, liberal, radical, and visionary orientations that are behind the scores of reforms discussed hereafter? Because an unsparing examination of American realities will help us abandon the false idea that social reforms are derived from some sort of partisan unity game (Forward Together!), a transparent ruse that emphasizes ideological differences by cloaking them in fluff. As Benjamin DeMott explains,

> Until . . . [we have] specific demonstrations of the human power at least to grasp how the opposition came into being, why it is what it is, where the growing points in its understanding can be found—reconciliation will remain a fantasy and men will go on plotting their Enemy's instant destruction with stolen dynamite in secret cellars.[2]

Four types of political opposites, or schools of political philosophy, will therefore occupy us in a major section of the book, our grasp of their very competition paradoxically enhancing our always uncertain prospects of making real gains against social ills.

Methodological Aides. To lend diversity in style, tone, and emphasis to the volume, and also to spotlight some of the major contributors to the field, I have included over a dozen reprinted essays. Chosen from three hundred or more located and evaluated by student aides over two years, these essays by specialists offer the exacting reader much that may not be available in my more general efforts. I have also included an annotated bibliography of recent books that will increase the reader's depth of understanding in any of the many areas touched on. The inclusion of a bibliography points up a critical feature of the project that cannot be stressed enough: The full worth of this book can be realized only through the ensuing effort *you* put into reform analysis, assessment, endorsement, implementation—and reanalysis.

Objectives. The book that follows, then, is predicated on my assumption that reforms *can* be made. On this assumption, I have undertaken:

1. To expose for assessment a broad range of fresh solutions to social problems.
2. To stimulate new thinking about the personal part any of us may play in social reforms.
3. To call attention to relevant foreign gains and losses in responses to the social problems common to industrial nations.
4. To locate solutions inside a political framework and thereby to heighten recognition of the critical interrelationship of social policy, social problems, and political philosophy.

5. To appraise the current climate for social reforms.
6. To advance some guidelines for reform assessment by nonspecialists like ourselves.

Especially during a period like this one, a period of neglect of large-scale, broad-visioned social reforms, we should be sharpening our insights and plans for action. For the time will soon come when we will want to be ready with alternatives for assessment by fellow citizens who ask anew what *more* we could all be doing—for ourselves, for one another, for the nation, and for the community of all mankind. Only as our fundamental interdependency is finally grasped by everyone is fundamental social progress really possible. And only as we both—you and I—dare to venture out onto hazardous limbs will we contribute to the exasperatingly slow, yet continually exhilarating social progress we all seek.

Your Contribution to the Book

Certain aspects of your "homework" are so obvious as to require only brief mention. It should be clear that a limited-purpose book like this one will of necessity be incomplete (an unknown and probably awesome number of suitable reforms are excluded from review), superficial (teams of experts on each topic would have treated them in far more depth than this one writer can possibly muster), and outdated (the book's writing ended on September 1, 1973, long and eventful months ago). Note, however, that with the aid of your course instructor, your classmates, and interested others you can readily search out overlooked reforms, deepen your knowledge of them all, and update relevant data, research findings, political nuances, and so on. This book intends to serve as a prod to such action, a strong beginning, an unabashed stimulant . . . and no more, though certainly no less.

Far more demanding is the challenge set by five *special* aims of this project that are not necessarily included in books of this sort. The first aim is for you to gain familiarity with the history of social reform here and abroad. The second is for you to reassess the basic image of man that currently underlies our reform values and ideology. The third is for you to sharpen your "mind-blowing" powers when it comes to assessing *and* inventing better solutions to persistent social problems. The fourth is for you to intensify your appreciation of the part that anticipation of the future must play in contemporary affairs. And the final aim is to challenge you to leave the book more closely identified than heretofore—in action as in word and thought—with a reform position of considerable personal importance.

Reform History. How well can you do with the following imaginary headlines?

"Great Debate" Begun: Is Man His Brother's Keeper? [Bible lands, n.d.]

Amos Attacks Privileged Classes for "Oppressing the Poor" [Bible lands, circa 750 B.C.]

Subsidies for Poor Instituted to Thwart Social Reform: Plato and Aristotle Disagree on Issues—Plato Advocates "Prevention"; Aristotle, Higher Relief Standards [Athens, fourth century B.C.]

Relief Offices and Hospitals Ease Rigors of Chandragupta Reign [India, circa 300 B.C.]

Caesar Gives Free Land to Veterans Threatening His Regime [Rome, circa 35 B.C.]

Increase of Relief Giving by Monasteries Seen Threat to Parish Relief [Europe, circa A.D. 600]

Begging Prohibited to Relieve Labor Shortage Resulting from Black Plague: Employers Chalk Up Notable Victory [England, 1394]

New War on Poverty—Begging Prohibited Despite Charges of Undermining Christian Virtue of Charity [Ypres, circa 1525]

Henry VIII Takes Over Monasteries, Secularizes Relief Giving: Church–State Issue Sharpened [England, 1531]

Revolutionaries Transfer Relief Responsibilities from Religious Bodies to Cities [Paris, 1789][3]

Your ability to get all that is possible from the considerable material ahead depends in no small part on your facility with the historic ideas and time-honored issues capsulized in these hypothetical headlines.

Coming closer to home, what do you *really* understand of the history of recent American social reform? My focus in later chapters is exclusively on here-and-now matters. You will find it very difficult to grasp the full import of the material and to make an adequate assessment of the alternative, competitive reforms seeking endorsement unless you know how and why we have arrived where we are.

Our failures because of lack of such historical understanding are legion and costly. Of the past decade a social commentator, psychologist Kenneth Keniston, remarks,

> During the 1960's, it was the lot of Americans to live in mounting historical crisis, but not to understand it. The symptoms of the crisis were everywhere: deepening involvement in a war most Americans believe we should never have entered; poverty and urban deterioration in the world's richest nation; persistent racism in a society committed for two centuries to human equality; the growing disaffection of the best-educated generation in history. But when it came to defining what was the matter, most have not even tried. As a result, the symptoms of the crisis have constantly been confused with its causes, while the best efforts of both young and old have been wasted in episodic attacks on these symptoms.[4]

The task, then, is to unravel how "inevitably" America is what it is. We must work at understanding the shadow America's past casts over our times, if we would make a proper analysis of the present and develop a basis for clear prediction. Sociologist Evan Vlachos gently contends in this connection that "it is only by keeping the past available through memory and conquering the future in advance through anticipation that men may remain free."[5]

A Model of Man. What do you make of "human nature" and how are you inclined to represent mankind—as inherently unreliable, possibly even base?

Or as fundamentally sound, possibly even suprahealthy, if given half a chance? Your answer will reveal much about the interpretation you are likely to place on the social reform material in this volume and will explain why I urge you even *now* to get in better touch with your own position on this critical and controversial matter of man's basic nature.

The ancient Greek view of man—the one advanced by Aristotle though not by Plato—was as a cerebral, rational creature. This view, along with the early Christian conception of man as a creation in God's image and even the secular Renaissance ideal of man as a modern Odysseus set out on a lifelong voyage of adventure, has lost its following. Instead, many men today see themselves as biologically determined, as economically formed and restricted, and as politically motivated.[6] The Enlightenment image of man as a social animal liable to outbursts of irrational aggression has given way in our post-Freudian times to the image of an irrationally aggressive animal liable to outbursts of sociability. Robert Ardrey, for one, represents man as a depraved animal who requires stable social hierarchies, strong leadership, and a liberal dose of xenophobia.

Since Freud, then, we have begun to grasp the idea that our animal nature is our basic part. Whether curse or blessing, however, remains unclear. As Alex Comfort says,

> The paradox still remains that while our culture traditionally views the life of the senses as "lower" and antipathetic to the strenuous discomfort required by virtue, the facts all point the other way—to a correlation between the senses and our more benevolent and social force, and between repression and denial of the senses and our more murderous side.[7]

Modern man resembles one in whom, "as it were, directives and messages come to the Head Office from a clandestine department that the staff do not realize is there, with its own logic, its own aims, and the solidified inner attitudes of a child of three."[8]

This extraordinary evolution in viewpoint has been accompanied in America by the simplistic reduction of views of human nature to essentially two. The first suggests that life is really a war with intermittent, deceptive quietude. Very little goodness can be located in man's heart of hearts. Rather, men exist in perpetual, destructive conflict, and inner and social harmony are, at best, possible temporary states. Emphasis is placed on self-control and self-discipline, on the control of others, and on the idealization of the past. Man's intrinsic nature is selfish, his good conduct suspect, and his prospects slim. The contrary point of view assigns a more positive valuation to conflict and a brighter reading to man's prospects, provided that the welfare of all is advanced, that we learn to live with change, and that fresh currents in all things—ideas, art forms, and creative thought—are nourished.

How vital is all of this? Your view of man and his future will be *decisive* in your interpretation of the ideas in this book.

In my own view, if you basically distrust man (that is, you and me alike), you may have an excessive need for order and regularity and a deepset fear of the mutually destructive possibilities of men. And as one unsympathetic theorist, Philip Lichtenberg, warns, "The problem with this approach to life is that there is no escape from it; distrust leads to antagonism which leads to distrust which aggravates the antagonism."[9]

On the other hand, you may find yourself drawn to an ideology of uncertainty, potentiality, and trust of others. The uncertainty may be compensated by the unique rewards possible when you are willing to take chances. Trust is thought to foster an increased productive harmony and thus still greater trust.

Really so? Necessarily so? Unquestionably so? Beside the point! It is for *you* to conclude how reliable these insights are and to do so as part of a lifelong grappling with the issues involved.

Mind Blowing. How does mind blowing figure in your preparation or mental exercising for the material in this volume? An explanation is available in the abstract musing of celebrated architect Louis Kahn:

> In Venice, not long ago, I was discussing with students the preservation of the city from the destructive effects of its necessary industry. Among other ideas, I suggested the construction of smoke eaters, chemical eaters. They could be magnificent structures; I don't care if you make them out of brass.
>
> Now, do I know what a smoke eater is? I do not.
>
> But there ought to be one. This is what I mean by inspired technology.[10]

Similarly, architect Edward Durrell Stone works in a fanciful way toward an attractive goal that is possibly beyond attainment but, then again, possibly not:

> The automobile is the enemy of the city. We need more places where pedestrians can be free from vehicles. What New York really needs is a whole new pedestrian level one story above all the streets. I'd like to raise the whole level of the city and leave pedestrians on their own up there.[11]

The merits and demerits of such pie-in-the-sky schemes to one side, the more relevant point is that mind-blowing efforts are wonderfully productive. They help us to go places we might otherwise never have dreamed of, much less achieved on our own!

Now what does this have to do with my expectations of you as a user of this volume? Simply this: if you approach everything as Kahn and Stone do, their example of free-wheeling, mind-blowing creativity will stand you in very good stead—both in and outside of this joint mind-stretching venture of ours.

Time Tripping. Something of what I am trying to convey in this section is suggested by a description of an actual college course now being taught from the perspective of A.D. 2003:

> TIMESPAN: 2003 A.D. MINUS 30.
>
> Beginning with manspecies' first serious steps in the early 1970s to control his life-environ, the world has evolved into today's Quasi-Utopia. The contemprobs of what were then called "pollution," "population explosion," "institutionalized religion," "families," "linear learning," and "warfare," gave way to late-stops and transformed "people" headed toward extinction into provita on the threshold of ultimastate.
>
> This communiseries traces the development of the past 30 years to show how manspecies recog-dealt with early contemprobs and achieved his pres-

> entime. Besides converspeak and electronications, scholartists should be prepared to use such terms as cyborg, synergy, cloning, dystropia, cybernetics, communiversity, dymaxion. This communiseries will not be on satelliteach or brainset.[12]

Currently offered at the School of Continuing Education, New York University, the course attracts those who wish to "study the future in terms of the past."

And that is what I am driving at. It is not enough to pursue a strong grasp of the past and the present. It is vital that we also muse on the many alternative futures we can help promote, for only in this way can we really meet our critical responsibility to as-yet-unborn generations—as well as to ourselves in the future that is even now unfolding about us. Sociologist John Staude urges in this connection that we "begin to view men as builders and users of social structures rather than simply as receivers and transmitters."[13] This view can be furthered through the sensitivity I now ask you to adopt toward futuristics, utopia building, science fiction, occult exploration, and other time-tripping auxiliaries.

Accordingly, what sorts of concepts of the future should we be familiar with? Philosopher Oliver Reiser urges attention to at least those that appear in Table I–1.

TABLE I–1. Future Concepts

Data-processing Research	Parapsychology
Decision Theory	Pattern Recognition
Digital Computers	Physical Chemistry
Electroencephalography	Probabilistics
Electronics	Quantum Mechanics
Feedback Controls	Radar and Sonar
Guidance Systems	Radiobiology
Heuristics	Radiochemistry
High-pressure Physics	Radiophysics
Information Processing	Relativity Theory
Lasers	Self-organizing Systems
Linear Programming	Semantics and Semiotics
Logic Machines	Semiconductors
Low-temperature Kinetics	Servomechanisms
Machine Translation	Spectroscopy
Magnetohydrodynamics	Speech Compression
Masers	Solid-state Physics
Mathematical Synthesis	Stellar Evolution
Memory Systems	Surface Physics
Microwave Research	Theory of Games
Models and Theories	Thin-film Physics
Neurophysiology	Thinking Machines
Nomic Theory	Ultrasonics
Nonlinear Controls	Unidentified Flying Objects
Optics	Vibration Systems
Operations Research	Wave Mechanics
Organic Chemistry	[Etc., etc.]

Reiser concludes by urging men to accept fully the validity of two axioms: "Not one of us is without the power to contribute to the making of the future,"[14] and "Not one of us is free from responsibility for making the future."[15]

Why then do I urge you to bring a futuristic orientation with you in reading this book? Over and above Reiser's reasons are two additional gains suggested by Alvin Toffler:

> We can turn the time-mirror around and use a coherent image of the future to provide valuable insights into the present; and we can at the same time nurture personal change in ourselves in a subtle yet significant sense; for "successful coping with rapid change will require most of us to adopt a new stance toward the future, a new sensitive awareness of the role it plays in the present."[16]

Toffler adds that the basic thrust of his book is diagnosis, for "diagnosis precedes cure, and we cannot begin to help ourselves until we become sensitively conscious of the problem."[17]

Apropos the special focus of this book, then, we might mull on the possibilities raised in Table I–2. This is not the place to argue the pros and cons of any particular subscenario we might trace through the table; I include it only to help sensitize you generally to the various issues that a reform-oriented student can read into renderings of alternative futures.

TABLE I–2. Social Change Agenda: A Benign Scenario

Concern	*Present*	*1980–2000*	*2001+*
Key Issue	Redistribute Wealth and Power	Humanize the Planning and Control Process, Ecological Balance	Redefine *Wealth* and *Life*
Actors	State, Corporations, Unions, Political Parties	Cybernetic State and Extended Families	World Government and Self-actualizers
Locus	Renewed Cities, Opened Suburbs, New Towns	New Cities	Archologies and Communes
Conflict Focus	Egalitarianism	Planning	World Order
Key Hazard	Perennial Backlash	Technocratic Totalitarianism	Benign Fascism
Allies	Liberal Community and Planners	Human Potential Movement	Federalists and Humanists

Position Taking. Finally, you might pay specific attention to *you,* to where you personally fit into this entire bewildering matter. To claim and maintain a personal position on social reform issues requires at least three kinds of effort on your part: empathy with distant others, imaginative involvement through irregular pathways of research, and bold personal judgments where the crowd may think otherwise.

To begin with, then, there is the heady matter of daring to immerse ourselves completely in the problems and prospects of the others we are concerned with. (The others? Which "others"? I thought we were talking of ourselves!) A prison superintendent suggests:

> *if* people think that they can produce change for the better, what they should do is lock themselves in their own bathroom for about 24 hours and have somebody bring 'em their meals three times a day, and then you'll eat where you shit. Do that for a while and get some idea that things are not what they should be in institutions.[18]

This suggestion, of course, points out the indispensability of empathy. As Andrew Kopkind, a young theorist of the New Left, explains: "It is useless to pretend that we can deal with social class if we do not comprehend the feelings engendered by privilege; or deal with sexism if we cannot feel the pain of sexual oppression; or organize others if we can only hear ourselves talk."[19]

Second, there is the matter of daring to seek a hazardous, novel, and somewhat reckless approach to the subject at issue; of leaving the tried-and-true pathways for those less often trod in pursuit of a quality of insight distinguished as much by rarity as by reward. Some dare to turn and follow Jean Piaget into the mind of the child, Carlos Castaneda into the mind of the sorcerer, John Lilly into the mind of the dolphin, or Carl Sagan into the mind of an extraterrestrial being. Intellectuals like Claude Lévi-Strauss are often fascinated by primitives ("Man takes with him all the positions that he has occupied in the past, and all those he will occupy in the future"[20]). Others may prefer the way of R. D. Laing and the celebration of the schizophrenic as the culture hero of an alienated society: "The cracked mind of the schizophrenic may *let in* light which does not enter the intact mind of many sane people whose minds are closed."[21] Moving in a new direction these explorers take risks that contain the possibility of survival; there is always the chance that their explorations may reward in very special ways.

Some of what I am struggling to suggest here is conveyed with characteristic craft by Theodore Roszak in these thoughts on the built-in limits of the behavioral science tools we cling to:

> Behavioral sciences are a dubious project rather like making maps of imaginary landscapes that change by the hour and are recreated afresh by their inhabitants in the light of what every new map reveals. . . . We forget that to map a forest means less than to write poems about it; to map a village means less than to visit among its people; to map a sacred grove means less than to worship there.[22]

To plan, champion, help secure, and later to assess a social reform might entail forms of poetry writing, visiting, and worship . . . if we would really let go, take hold, and get into what we are about. (Critic George Steiner has said, "A linguistic that cannot handle a poem is on the wrong track. . . . It is very naive to claim that one can handle the simple but not the complex."[23])

Third, there is the scary matter of daring to judge a particular reform by our *own* values, almost regardless of how others judge that reform. Guided here by what? Possibly by quality-of-life maxims that content that bigger is *not* better, slower *is* faster, and less *is* more. Or as Mitzi Cunliffe says, in an extension of architect Mies van der Rohe's "less is more," "Less detritus for more austerity, less bombast for more simplicity, less pretentiousness for more modesty, less bureaucracy for more flexibility, less permanence, even, for more imagination."[24] Similarly, a heady source of values is available in the various meanings of the concept *natural* as defined by counterculture spokesmen:

1. To stress cooperation rather than competition.
2. To reject mastery over nature.
3. To reject hypocrisy, "white lies," and other social artifices.
4. To devalue detachment, objectivity, and noninvolvement as methods for finding truth; to arrive at truth, instead, by direct experience, participation, and involvement.
5. To emphasize the community rather than the individual.
6. To reject the mores and rules that interfere with natural expression and function (e.g., conventional sexual morality).
7. To preserve the environment, at the expense of economic growth and technology.[25]

The issue for our purposes, of course, is not the merit or shortcoming of any of these ideas but rather the case they make for the existence of readily available guides to personal value-construction.

I am calling on you to find in yourself the courage of passions, of caring deeply for something, of risking passionate mistakes. This is not a light matter, as Susan Brownmiller's pen portrait makes clear:

> The adjectives applied to liberals from the left and right are wrong, all wrong. Liberals per se are not wishy-washy, knee-jerk, bleeding heart, or limousine. They can be tough as nails, courageous and thoughtful as anybody else, and class has little to do with it. But they are not very interesting. The best of them are too busy being fair to allow them to come down hard on any side. Their passion must perforce be shallow. Their most admirable virtue is optimism, and for this I love them dearly.[26]

What I am urging on you is passion as well as optimism, and passion of a very special quality.

The idea has again been put especially well by Roszak: "Unless the eye catch fire, the issue will not be seen; unless the ear catch fire, the issue will not be heard; unless the tongue catch fire, the issue will not be named; unless the mind catch fire, the issue will not be known."[27] This is *not* to counsel impetuosity, impatience, or zealotry; it *is* to call on you to find it in yourself, in your own good time and for reasons you can live with and grow healthy on, to come out of your public policy "closet" and go public with a position this to you! Finally to "give a damn" and stand proudly for something! To move up to a declaration of self that helps to make a constructive difference!

Summary

In a sentence, this book is meant to help you claim and improve on your role as an active, constructive, and knowledgeable citizen where alternative and cosmopolitan social reforms are concerned. Toward this end, and having never promised you anything remotely resembling a rose garden, I have no compunctions about having laid out as much "homework" for you as I have in this trying chapter.

The material ahead is complex, demanding, and frustrating. It will try you! As the complexity and the density of social behavior have increased, so have the competing systems of behavioral explanation and prescription. Facts now come to us through screens of ideology, and the layers of ambiguity have increased considerably as the facts have become more numerous, the motivations of social actors more obscure, and the vested interests of the explainers more obvious.

Some *special* effort on your part is necessary if this trip together is to prove to be all that we might wish. Specifically, I urge you to gain new personal strength in the subject's historical background, in your musings on human nature, in creative mind-leaps, in futuristic time-trips, and in the elements of individual position-taking.

Am I asking a lot of you? Yes, and I recognize that, though I ask no more than is reasonable for any who would earnestly and maturely set out to guide the evolution of twenty-first-century America, to help resolve whether we will finally prove ourselves, as William Irwin Thompson says, "aborigines of another fall or the adepts of a new civilization beyond matter."[28] Is this a lot to ask? Probably . . . but nothing that you are not really equal to, especially if, as I suspect, you are another of those who has "lived with his top down all his life."[29]

FOOTNOTES

1. Stewart L. Udall, *1976: Agenda for Tomorrow* (New York: Harcourt, 1968), p. 5.
2. Benjamin DeMott, "Stone Men to the Contrary, the Time to Argue Is Now," *Life* (April 17, 1970), p. 28 B.
3. Donald S. Smith, *Social Welfare: Values, Means, and Ends* (New York: Random, 1969), p. 7.
4. Kenneth Kenniston, book review essay, *New York Times Book Review* (July 25, 1970), p. 26.
5. Evan Vlachos, "Icons of the Future and Scenarios of the Apocalypse," unpublished paper, undated, pp. V–61, 62 (Colorado State University, Department of Sociology).
6. Helpful here is J. C. Cooper, *A New Kind of Man* (Philadelphia: Westminster, 1972).
7. Alex Comfort, *The Nature of Human Nature* (New York: Harper, 1967), p. 104.
8. Ibid.
9. Philip Lichtenberg, *Psychoanalysis: Radical and Conservative* (New York: Springer, 1969), p. 121.
10. Hans Knight, "Architect Kahn Is Avid Reader of Fairy Tales," *Philadelphia Evening Bulletin* (June 24, 1971), p. 3.
11. Paul Goldberger, "Edward Durrell Stone Finds the 'Universal' Pays," *New York Times* (September 10, 1972), p. 8, Section 1.

12. As reprinted in *Saturday Review,* Education Issue (February 1973), p. 56.
13. John Staude, "Theoretical Foundations for a Humanistic Sociology," paper delivered at the 1971 Annual Meeting of the American Sociological Association, Denver, Colo.
14. Oliver L. Reiser, *Cosmic Humanism* (Cambridge, Mass.: Schenkman, 1966), p. 8.
15. Ibid., p. 10.
16. Alvin Toffler, *Future Shock* (New York: Bantam, 1972), pp. 4.
17. Ibid., p. 487.
18. J. Shalleck, *Prison* (New York: Grossman, 1972), p. 20.
19. Andrew Kopkind, "The Sixties and the Movement," *Ramparts* (February 1973), unpaged.
20. Claude Lévi-Strauss, *Tristes Tropiques* (New York: Atheneum, 1970), p. 7.
21. R. D. Laing, *The Divided Self* (Baltimore, Md.: Penguin, 1970), p. 31.
22. Theodore Roszak, *Where the Wasteland Ends* (Garden City, N.Y.: Doubleday, 1972), p. 410.
23. Elizabeth Hall, "The Freakish Passion: A Conversation with George Steiner," *Psychology Today* (February 1973), p. 66.
24. Mitzi Cunliffe, "Townscope: Pocket Parks," *Journal of the Royal Town Planning Institute* (September 10, 1971), p. 351.
25. Daniel Yankelovich, "The New Naturalism," *Saturday Review* (April 1, 1972), p. 35. The original list contains eleven additional items.
26. Susan Brownmiller in *New York Times Book Review* (July 25, 1971), p. 3.
27. Roszak, op. cit., p. 211.
28. William Irwin Thompson, *At the Edge of History* (New York: Harper, 1971), p. X.
29. Ibid., p. 18.

READING

Helpful even this early in our joint deliberations are speculations about the special nature of the social problems and the social reforms we can expect in the second half of the 1970's. In this reading, revised somewhat from the original version that I prepared for a Summer 1973 issue of The Futurist *(published by the World Future Society), I trace out some of the implications of the dramatic shifts in our national population profile and some of the host of related contradictions in unresolved public policy where social reforms are concerned. Whether you finally concur with some or all of my reasoning is quite secondary to the goal of spurring your* own *speculation* now *about the years—and reforms—immediately ahead.*

Reform Possibilities Through 1980, or, 1984

Arthur B. Shostak

The solutions to our social problems in the years immediately ahead promise to prove very different from anything that has ever gone before. The population heat is off, and the planning heat is on; the public's thirst for novelty is great, but the taxpayer's appetite for further costly programs is small; and the pressure to centralize reforms in the federal government via the computer is enormous, though some political forces favor radical decentralization of reform management through big business cost-plus involvement. Everywhere the reform agenda is in flux, and what the outcome will be is anything but clear.

Central to this turmoil are five basic questions that may determine the chances of many reforms in the second half of the 1970's: What is the reform significance of the dramatic shifts in our population trends? What is the American public seeking? What is it resisting? What part will the potential of the computer play in reform? And how are the public and private sectors likely to divide the action? Each of these questions is discussed in this article, with forecasts advanced to help you formulate your own answers—and better appreciate the novelty and the related peril of the reform challenge ahead.

My first forecast is that *the social reform agenda in the 1970's will differ substantially from any social reforms of the recent past.*

Up until very recently we have been influenced by the inadequacy of social expenditures in every conceivable field. As a result, we have focused on quantities—how many new relief programs costing how many billions or millions of dollars could we create immediately to meet this or that emergency? However, as a consequence of "probably the most important social fact in America today—the decline in population growth,"[1] our focus is now changing. After the immense post-World War II exertion to meet the basic needs of a baby-boom population, much of the pressure for quantity-oriented remedies is relaxing. There were fewer children under five in 1970 than in 1960, and the birth rate in 1972, a record low, was below the zero-population-growth level. Note also that immigration in 1972 was the smallest since 1964 and that the overall population growth rate was the lowest since 1937.[2]

As a direct result we already have unused seats in many public schools, production at less than capacity in many manufacturing industries, a striking decline in population density in many city neighborhoods, unused space on many trains, planes, and so on, and an unwelcome "softness" in consumer spending patterns. With the lag characteristic of a planless society we persist in old habits, seemingly oblivious to these new developments; for example, we are producing two units of housing for every new household formed.

Our social problems in the late 1970's will cease to be of the Malthusian variety we have grown accustomed to since 1945. We will no longer be called upon to plug holes in the dike with emergency millions. Instead, our social problems will steadily become *contra*-Malthusian. Instead of extreme population pressures, our problems will stem from unexpectedly rapid success in population containment and curtailment. We are about to trade one set of difficult problems for another set that is no less complex and demanding. Despite their seeming accessibility at first glance, they are likely to prove difficult to get at, hard to resolve, and exceedingly trying of our limited political energies and economic resources. For example, we will be called on to provide meaningful vocations, and not simply gainful work, for millions seeking places in a slow-growing, increasingly automated economy. And we will be challenged to respond imaginatively to the population's call for income redistribution, an issue likely to dominate the 1970's.

With no baby boom to feed, house, or educate, the emphasis of our task shifts radically from quantity to quality. No longer how much, but how. Not how many programs, but what particular programs, where, for how long, and how administered. The task now, Daniel P. Moynihan explains, is "to be selective. If, for example, we are going to have a guaranteed income at an adequate level without setting off an inflation that will quickly wipe out our gains, we simply have to learn to be prudent about other programs."[3]

To achieve a high level of productive selectivity and prudence will require a far-reaching development in social reform that could prove to be the signal accomplishment of the 1970's. At issue is our maturing beyond our past and present practice of racing pell-mell after first this and then that emergency with first this and then that piece of crisis programming. Instead we must attempt to move significantly ahead of potential or emerging social needs with preventive measures. At the very heart of this move, of course, is a radical switch from government-by-program (or crisis) to government-by-policy (or planning).

Consistent with the far-reaching change from population crisis to containment, my second forecast is that *the social reform agenda in the late 1970's will be more varied and eclectic than any that has ever gone before.*

This change will not result only from our shift from a Malthusian to a contra-Malthusian challenge, nor from the growing impact of volatile 18-year-old voters and the existence of the best-educated electorate in the nation's history. We must add to these influences several other related elements. The first consists of the many radical reform proposals—for example, the local community control of schools and police—that we carry over unresolved from the angry 1960's and that must finally be assessed.

The mid- and late-1970's further promise a new international flavor in reform considerations. Our haphazard exploration to date of the revamped British drug system, the Israeli child-care approach, the extraordinary Japanese psychiatric techniques, the Canadian children's allowance, and the like may give way to a stepped-up investigation of and experimentation with these ideas. For our electorate increasingly includes more well-traveled Americans with fond memories of clean and inexpensive trains abroad, modern "new towns" in England and Scandinavia, and inexpensive subsidized art programs on the Continent. Others less fortunate in their travel allowances have nonetheless traveled via the television tube, and a TV special on a foreign social reform innovation (parole for murderers in Scandinavia or sanctioned shanty towns in South America) can set our whole nation pondering. These foreign innovations, when coupled with the generally more permissive and novelty-hungry culture that steadily evolves around us, encourage the consideration, if not the adoption, of ever more diversity in reform.

Counter tendencies, however, are plainly evident, with a nationwide retreat from the "frills" of creative schoolroom innovation now leading the list. A powerful attempt to turn the clock back on proabortion and anti-death-penalty reforms, along with our dismal lack of imagination in designing alternative pathways for non-college-matriculants, haunts the scene. Despite this evidence of persistent reactionary sentiment there is reason to believe we will increasingly weigh exciting and exotic alternatives in social reforms—and like it.

Consistent with this turmoil, my third forecast is that *fewer reforms will probably be adopted in the near future than have been adopted in the recent past.*

There are two major explanations for this expected slowdown. First, there is considerable public disillusionment with the apparently slim returns on the dizzying flurry of social experimentation under the Kennedy, Johnson, and Nixon administrations. Whether or not well founded, there is a politically compelling body of conservative public opinion that is increasingly antagonistic to any more large-scale innovations in social reform—before unimpeachable evidence of sure rewards can be demonstrated. Because this demand appeals to liberals as well in its call for lay participation in governmental decision-making and in its challenge of rule-by-experts, the call for proof grows in bipartisan support and in its ability to slow the rate of social change.

Second, there is considerable taxpayer and business community pressure now building to use exacting cost-benefit ratios in making hard-headed choices among alternative social reforms. More progress for the dollar, more constraint, and more careful choice-making, the critics insist. Believing that there is apt to be no fiscal surplus for years to come (the Vietnam cessation notwithstanding), the economy-minded are zealously opposed to our doubling reform costs without any prospect of doubling benefits, a process that economist James Kuhn sarcastically dubs "doing good badly."[4]

Among its various sensitive responses to the call for economy in reform, the Nixon Administration has dramatically altered the role of the OEO and replaced its program-administration function with one of project testing and verification. For example, OEO's recent field test of performance contracting in education and its ongoing test of guaranteed annual incomes for welfare families address both public suspicion of new proposals and expert suspicion of actual cost-benefit ratios in matters of social reform.

Overall, however, the message seems clear. More reforms are going to find the going harder, the tests tougher, and the chances of adoption smaller than in the more generous, bolder, and possibly more idealistic and compassionate years just past.

As much more than a footnote to the aforegoing, my fourth forecast is that *nearly all proposed reforms will have to meet unprecedented computer-based tests.*

If one word had to be chosen to characterize the differences between social reform affairs before and after 1975, that word could be *selection* or *planning* or *creativity,* but it will more likely be *computer.* Nothing again will ever be the same, for the new generations of amazing high-speed electronic idiots write their own rules and set us new demands that alter the "game" of social reform in very substantial ways. Three brief examples should suffice. First, any proposed social reform taken seriously by power holders will be subjected to computer simulation tests more precise, revealing, and exacting than any before-the-fact hurdle ever previously set up (note the new discretionary tactic available to opinion molders: they can simply decline to bother with the computer simulation and evaluation of a proposed reform). A harbinger of things to come was the novel effort that econometric-model builders put into tests of the McGovern economic reform proposals in the summer of 1972. As difficult as various computers found the "radical" McGovern program to run, the unprepared public was left no easier task in picking and choosing among the many different "judgments" produced.

Second, any proposed social reform will have to meet the new test of its "social accounting" evaluation. Throughout the late 1970's progress will be made in the gathering, storage, linkage, and reportage of facts, with the computer undergirding the entire previously impossible effort. Whether or not we soon endorse a national data inventory, a five-year census (with annual sample polls), and the like, we will know more and more about one another in the years ahead. Accordingly, a system of social accounts, or factual measures of social needs, gains, lags, and incipient problem areas, is likely to develop among city, state, and federal bodies. What they measure and report on, and how, when, and where, will go far in helping policy makers to set priorities and to choose among alternative modes of social reform.

Finally, any proposed social reform will have to meet the creative, imaginative possibilities presented by a "wired society" like ours or be dismissed as hopelessly behind the times. The computer sets new standards for reform architects. It can do things we have yet to conceive of and do them accurately in milliseconds. If, for example, we sought to establish a nationwide system of labor credits as described in Edward Bellamy's 1896 classic *Looking Backward,* we could do so, though before the existence of present-day computers such an idea would have been hopelessly impractical. Similarly, if we desired to keep daily tabs on employment opportunities everywhere in the nation, we could do so—and are even now moving steadily toward this goal. The computer has expanded our vistas enormously, and no reform will hereafter be taken seriously that does not appear to take advantage of them.

I do not wish to minimize the considerable hazards posed. Computer programs, as the public comes steadily (and painfully) to appreciate, are only as good as their human programmers. Many of the humanistic values we seek to promote through complex social reforms do not readily lend themselves to "computerese." And even the most sophisticated machine simulations or evaluations are only as valid and thoroughgoing as the field-collected data fed into the machines. Allowing for all of this and for the ever-more-necessary controls on computer uses—and abuses—it remains clear that the machine and its corollaries (data-collection systems, new "logics" in policy making, and so on) will recast the whole of social reform.

Finally, there is the vital issue of reform management. Will the public or the private sector of the society direct the action? My fifth forecast is that *the lion's share of the evolving social reform agenda will go—for the first time—to the private sector.*

Basic to this statement are three underlying assumptions. First, a Republican administration opposed to enlarging government's role wherever industry might substitute instead will serve through 1976. Second, public antipathy will continue toward enlargement of the distant, bureaupathic "monster" it begrudgingly acknowledges as its federal government. And third, industry's need for alternative employment opportunities, especially those diversification opportunities backed up with cost-plus contracts, will continue unabated.

The record to date, to be sure, is uneven. At the fringes there are successful, if miniscule efforts by private enterprise to offer alternatives to public mail, fire-fighting, and police services. Of considerably more interest is the steady movement of major corporations into the enormous market represented by early-childhood centers and nursing-home management. Topping them all, however, are the multi-million-dollar joint ventures of the OEO and corporate America. Although the record in the case of industry direction of certain Job Corps centers is apparently a fine one, the OEO found much to fault in a major 1972 "performance contract" trial of industry's ability to succeed in the remedial education of poor youngsters. Taken in isolation this OEO criticism might appear to dim the chances of further, more extensive collaboration. But we must not ignore the three political assumptions cited earlier, and we must also consider the related arguments that productivity and dynamism are greater in private than in government efforts and that the nation's aversion for creeping socialism is easily aroused by the party out of power. Daniel P. Moynihan probably speaks for many when he urges that the private sector be protected against the effects of the indefinite growth of government: "It is not sufficiently seen that the stability of American politics has derived from the persistent growth of wealth deriving primarily from private enterprise."[5]

Although all of us are conscious of the many hazards of entrusting private industry with public concerns, of the enormous challenge of policing contracts, assuring quality, protecting clients, and so on, the trend continues to gain momentum. It is part of a larger movement that includes support for revenue sharing (giving power back to the states and the cities), community corporations (giving power back to the grass roots), and guaranteed minority representation, as in state slates to the 1972 Democratic Convention. It is as American as apple pie, this move to let creative business corporations rather than Uncle Sam enlarge their share of the reform "market."

Summary. Predictions of which particular social reforms will finally be adopted are risky. More reasonable are forecasts of the influences that are likely to dictate the choice of future social reforms.

Five such forecasts have been discussed. They suggest that future social reforms will be most likely to focus selectively, rather than broadly, on a new contra-Malthusian set of human needs. These reforms will be fewer in number than in years past and will meet unusually rigorous field and cost-accounting tests. These reforms will be drawn, however, from a wider and more exotic range of alternatives than ever before considered. Nevertheless, they will all be held to one set of tests, the set dictated by the peculiar abilities (and shortcomings) of modern high-speed electronic computers. And they will be managed to a greater degree than ever before by private enterprise rather than by governmental units.

The tasks set you and me are both dismaying and exhilarating. They dismay when we soberly consider how much each of us in the lay public must set out to learn lest we grow slavishly dependent on so-called experts in social planning, social accounting, and social-reforms-through-electronics. At the same time our tasks exhilarate when we contemplate the breathtaking possibilities in social reform now available to us.

The challenge is in deadly earnest, for we dare not lose our campaign to humanize social reforms to our morally indifferent computer "allies." The world of our five forecasts can go either way. It can reward us with a society closer to our heart's desire or punish us with one closer to Orwell's warning of a mere thirty years ago. Ten years, five forecasts, and *our* contribution will see it all out.

FOOTNOTES

1. Daniel P. Moynihan, "Emerging Consensus?" *Newsweek* (July 10, 1972), p. 23.
2. "Nation's Fertility Rate Hit Record Low in 1972," *Wall Street Journal* (May 17, 1973), p. 25.
3. Moynihan, op. cit. See also Daniel P. Moynihan, "Equalizing Education—in Whose Benefit?" *The Public Interest* (Fall 1972), pp. 69–89, and Robert Lekachman, "The New American Tories," *Dissent* (November–December 1969), pp. 471–476.
4. Moynihan, "Emerging Consensus? " op. cit., p. 23. See also Ben J. Wattenberg and Richard M. Scammon, "Black Progress and Liberal Rhetoric," *Commentary* (April 1973), pp. 35–44, and Richard Flacks, "Strategies for Radical Social Change," *Social Policy* (March–April 1971), pp. 7–14.
5. Moynihan, ibid. See also Richard C. Cornuelle, *Reclaiming the American Dream* (New York: Random, 1965), and Staff of the White House Conference on the Industrial World Ahead, *A Look at Business in 1990* (Washington, D.C.: Government Printing Office, 1972).

PART I

On Evaluating Alternative Reforms

How might we go about evaluating the many contradictory reforms that beckon for support from this book's chapters and selected readings? Perplexed by this question, students may ask, "How can *you expect us to evaluate these crazy, compelling, and complex ideas? We are novices—at best—in many of these areas! We can't figure out whom to believe, and we are afraid of winding up confused and demoralized. Your self-promoting experts, whether proponents or critics, regularly 'snow us,' and all of this hurts!" For my part, I patiently insist that we* can *struggle together to develop new and rewarding evaluation skills. Convinced of this I ask your careful attention to six guidelines that may reduce the "hurt" somewhat and can help minimize "snow"-related hazards.*

Note carefully that I say "guidelines" and not firm "standards" or hard-nosed "criteria." Evaluation, which is a rudimentary art still in its flat-earth stage, can only be hinted at in the brief compass of our short discussion. My restricted goal is to sensitize you to certain broad and helpful measures of real worth in alternative and competitive reform proposals. The best of you will take advantage of this general introduction to pursue the entire matter to far more depth and scope, lest as babes in the evaluation woods you continue to risk being hurt by animals you did not even know were out there.

CHAPTER 1

Six Guidelines, Sixty-six Cautions, and a Gentle Reminder

I am tempted to be generous because these people are on the right side. But if our vision is distorted by the well-known principles that virtue is often accepted as a substitute for competence, and that indignation is a sure sign of virtue, we debase the problem being attacked. The consequences of diverting reformist energies into unproductive courses of action on the basis of faulty diagnoses and self-defeating action proposals are too tragic for us to applaud careless work.

RALPH H. TURNER
Sociologist

How could everybody involved have thought such a plan would succeed? How could I have been so far off base? All my life I've known better than to depend on the experts. How could I have been so stupid, to let them go ahead?

PRESIDENT JOHN F. KENNEDY
(*After the Bay of Pigs invasion*)

To begin with I recommend that we ask of every reform we encounter: Does it address itself to *the* question we really want to wrestle with?

Before we get caught up in the particulars of the alternative reforms proposed for a social problem, we should step back and ask ourselves if we really have the correct problem in front of us? At issue here is Peter Drucker's insistence that the most common source of mistakes in management decisions is the misguided emphasis placed on finding the *right answer* rather than the *right question.* Our failure, for example, to include population controls in the questions we have asked about health reform measures has left us badly shaken by the results. Paradoxically, as Stewart Udall says, "in the last ten years we have increased human hunger by feeding the hungry. We have increased human suffering by healing the sick. We have increased human want by giving to the needy."[1] Similarly, Udall urges us to stop "solving for" autos rather than for a balanced transportation system; for houses, in place of close-knit communities; and for school buildings, instead of superior instruction. By this shortsighted preoccupation of ours with private satisfactions over public needs, Udall concludes, we only ensure the persistence of the shabby, the soiled, and the second rate in our overall living environment.

J. Robert Oppenheimer may have had this outcome in mind when he stated shortly before his death that the whole world was quite obviously going to hell, adding, however, that the one slim chance of its *not* going to hell was that we do absolutely nothing to stop it. Practically, this means that we must stop *crusading*—that we must turn away from reforms that supposedly support such abstracts as love, righteousness, peace, and freedom, and stop fighting such equally vague bogies as communism, fascism, racism, and the imaginary powers of darkness and evil. Instead we must choose reforms with goals that can be secured; we must direct our energies, as Alan Watts recommends,

> from abstract causes to specific material undertakings—to farming and cooking, mining and engineering, making clothes and buildings, traveling and learning, art, music, dancing, and making love. Surely, these are excellent things to do for their own sake and not, please not, for one's own or anyone else's improvement.[2]

Whether or not this is the right course, the thought does sharpen the evaluation issue: What are we really after to begin with? In the background keen ears might discern an ancient Chinese curse that softly threatens, "May you get what you think you want!"

Unanticipated Consequences? Over and again we must ask: Is this reform attractive in its entirety, and what should we make of its possible unplanned-for consequences? In this connection, for example, I have some deep-set qualms about the hazards of imposing penalties on individuals in areas where we have previously chosen instead merely to levy fines on institutions. Individual penalties, Ralph Nader insists, are finally necessary as a supplement to inadequate civil and criminal penalties if we are to eliminate corporate malfeasance. For example, a coal mine executive whose mine consistently evades safety legislation might be sent down into the pit with his men for five or six weeks.

Similarly, there is considerable doubt in my mind that we really want to reinstate a reform option popular in the 1800's, the payment of bounties for exceptional citizen behavior, as cited by David Bird:

> In August, 1972, the Federal Government paid $10,000 to a New Yorker who had pressed authorities for over 30 years to investigate toxic and illegal discharges by Anaconda into the Hudson River. The Government, fining the company $200,000, said it hoped the bounty would encourage others to report polluters.[3]

The hazard of such action was tersely described by the New York office of the American Civil Liberties Union: "What you need to avoid is encouraging irresponsible gossip or a kind of 1984 situation with everyone spying on his neighbor."[4]

In short, we must ask ourselves whether a proposed reform will truly solve the problem we would address, or whether it perhaps contains new and even nefarious hazards that will require reform of the reform in an endless and costly cycle.

A minimum test of a proposed reform is whether *you* are prepared to live as an object of your own reform project. If not, the likelihood is great that there is a basic failing in your favorite proposal. Note, however, that even if you are prepared to live under the rules of your project, we cannot conclude that the project has worth for others. For example, a reform project described by Marcus Raskin sought to turn the San Quentin prison into a four-year liberal arts college with the same problems and quasi-freedoms as a college. Although the reformers may have been prepared to live as objects of their own scheme, the project was at that time impracticable. What was clear, however, was that the reform could probably *not* have made the situation worse for the inmates.[5]

Indeed, in the entire matter of reform we would do well to remember the old obstetrical adage: *"Primum non nocere"* ("First, do no harm").

Comprehensibility? Assuming that we have chosen the right question to pursue, I recommend that we ask next of every reform we encounter: Does it lend itself to clarification and specification so that we can actually know what we are talking about?

Definitions, for example, ought to be assessed with special care. Does the proposed reform really move with appropriate clarity and caution toward a clear-cut population and a specifiable goal? As Herbert Packer has pointed out, for example, one searches the federal Organized Crime Control Act (1971) in vain for a definition of *organized crime,* which is an operative term in this criminal statute. When asked about the omission the drafters explained that it was impossible to define but that everybody knew what it was.[6]

At the same time, however, we must be wary of conventional or pat definitions that persist despite their vacuity. The "success" of educational institutions, for example, is often defined arbitrarily in terms of pupil-teacher ratio, the number of Ph.D.'s on the faculty, and so on. This definition actually rests on very little, especially where a clear and direct relation is brashly alleged to exist between quantifiable "input," like the pupil-teacher ratio, and the quality of the end product.

As another case in point a seventy-five-year-old Chicagoan offers an explanation for the attendance of the elderly at a federally funded neighborhood nutrition center: "What's really important for us is that we can get three really wholesome meals a week here and, above all, have a little companionship with them. . . . We've been eating together for three years, so we're really sort of a family now."[7] To define and evaluate this nutrition-aid program only in terms of caloric-intake goals would plainly be to overlook much of its value.

A Fighting Chance? If we find that the problem itself is worth addressing and after its obvious and less-than-obvious components have been isolated, we might next ponder the question: Does a particular reform have a ghost of a chance? As our time and energies are limited, we must spend them only on reforms that have some chance of being adopted.

What should guide our evaluation of the chances of adoption of any particular reform? Four attributes appear to merit special attention.

First, attention is quickly won when a "new" development seems to pose a readily apparent threat; for example, persistent heavy smog and the real hazard of a lethal warm-air inversion, or the daily poisoning of beach water and the occasional wash-ups of countless diseased and destroyed fish. The greater the jeopardy and the more vivid its dramatization, the more public support its reform is likely to receive. Second, the public especially responds to an issue that seems to threaten almost everyone and not just a small percentage of the population. For example, school bussing antagonizes the many who prefer to protect their children's educational privilege rather than to eliminate the unfair disadvantage to a minority of others. Third, a problem gains attention if its ills can be traced to, and blamed on, a small number of excessively privileged others. Then we can aim our pious outrage at this over-privileged group, such as the profiteering rich, without having to face up to the need to alter our *own* behavior or to pay higher personal taxes or both. Finally, we are drawn to problems that seem highly responsive to hard-nosed technological solutions, for once again we prefer to leave *our* basic human attitudes, expectations, and behavior patterns unchanged while bulldozers. computers, and other machines deliver us from all evil.

Translated into terms Archie Bunker would readily grasp, reforms stand a chance of adoption to the extent to which they are as plain as day, threaten us all, can be pinned on a few heavies (pinkoes, bosses, lazy welfare bums), and lend themselves to machine-dominated answers that do not cost good people like us very much at all.

This is *not* to argue that attitudes toward various reforms cannot or will not be changed. Campaigns, concerted effort, PR ballyhoo—all this and more *can* change the adoption prospects of any particular reform. But at any moment in time the various reforms that court your approval are unevenly attractive to the rest of the public—and that ponderous fact ought to be worth something in your comparative assessment.

Backup? Having wrestled with what it is you want done, on what terms, and with what likelihood of adoption, you are ready to ponder the quality of the supporting data available.

A good example is a new federal criminal law reform that stands or falls on our present-day ability to predict the future behavior of one another—a power we do not, after all, possess. The new (and possibly unconstitutional) provision of the Organized Crime Control Act holds a twenty-five-year jail sentence over the head of a two-time felony offender who appears to be a top-level, professional, hard-core criminal likely to offend again. Not only do such long sentences demoralize prison inmates, but they require a judge to make a determination extraordinarily beyond his predictive ability. One expert, Norvell Morris, warns that our statistical equipment for diagnosis and prediction is so primitive at present that for every true prediction of "dangerousness" (twenty-five years!) there will be two persons so condemned who would probably not have committed a crime. Clinical predictions, he insists, should be regarded as futile unless they can be effectively tested statistically. And until you have a sound statistical foundation for interference with liberty, you should not interfere—especially if only on an intuitive presupposition of danger.[8]

Capability? Finally, over and above the importance of the reform, its definition, its adoption possibilities, and the data support, there remains the all-important matter of whether or not the proposed reform is likely to do the job we think we want done.

That we often traffic only in the shopworn is pointedly made clear by our reliance on the seamy old social aid we know as the blacklist:

> The Chicago Crime Commission has been publishing for many years now lists of businesses in which crime-syndicate money is the predominant major investment. The lists are given extensive press publicity. But then what does a community like Chicago do? If there is a margin of fifty cents on a fifth of Scotch, why, the community buys there.[9]

Similarly, there is growing reason to suspect that another old tool, the rent strike, which was dramatically revived briefly in the late 1960's, has also played itself out. As Garry Brewer says,

> As a pathological indicator of little sustained utility, what alternative response mechanisms to the rent strike are possible, probable, and desirable? Would cooperative ownership of slum dwellings relieve the short-term stresses manifest in the strikes? In the longer run, what future does nonprofit or other institutional ownership of slum dwellings have? . . . Rent strikers lack "cohesiveness" and staying power; what might be done and what possible incentives can be imagined to unionize tenants? . . . Why should a policy-maker really be concerned, knowing as he now does that rent strikes are not very effective and can be managed with token, symbolic gestures?[10]

Before I slip away from the larger point, I hasten to restate it: The issue is not the strengths or weaknesses of rent strikes, blacklists, and so on; rather it is whether or not any proposed reform is really likely to accomplish the goals we have set for it. And *that* assessment responsibility should profitably try every strength you command.

Summary. My primary goal in this deliberately brief and cursory chapter has been to suggest some directions that your evaluation of contradictory and competing reforms might take. In reverse order I have urged you to assess the relative ability of competitive reforms to deliver on their claims, to find necessary data support, to earn a significant following among relevant publics, to achieve conceptual clarity, to survey the development of unanticipated consequences, and to isolate the problem before attempting to formulate a solution.

If space permitted, I would go on to discuss at length the additional points I only summarize here:

1. Be especially exacting when you assess and compare reforms offered by your favorite political school, lest your partisanship undermine your integrity and your responsibility for fairness.
2. Do not attempt to assess exclusively on rational grounds. However dismaying you may regard the fact, allocative problems in society involve fundamental value choices for which there is no simple rational

calculus; for example, there is no rational way of weighing investment in education against investment in health.

3. Be especially wary of the many proposed reforms that have not yet passed field tests of merit, as they may fall considerably short of the necessary practicality.
4. Do not assume that a given reform, or its competitors, will work equally well under different economic, political, and social conditions.
5. Be especially wary of assessing according to "what the system needs," except as you recognize the conservative political bias inherent in such a concept. You must step outside the functionalist frame of reference if you are to transcend a status quo political orientation and avoid "serving" a social system that fairly begs instead for social change.

Clearly, there is no gainsaying the complexity and difficulty of the task that remains. Indeed, an especially keen insight here from Benjamin DeMott could not be more sobering: "One of the several reasons for not judging is that the minute it's done, the judge is judged, stands fully visible in his own fatuity and self-congratulation, beyond sympathy, ripe for sentence himself."[11] If we will strain in our assesments after humility and not excessive pride, after co-creation and not caustic carping, we can prove imaginative, skeptical, and constructive appraisers of support-seeking reforms. Indeed, lest we over-emphasize the difficulty of it all, and thereby court paralysis, we ought gently to remind each other every so often that where assessment is concerned people do do it everyday, and do it rather well.

FOOTNOTES

1. Stewart L. Udall, *1976: Agenda for Tomorrow* (New York: Harcourt, 1968), p. 43.
2. Both the Oppenheimer and the Watts material are from Alan Watts, *Does It Matter?* (New York: Vintage, 1971), pp. 23, 24.
3. David Bird, "Bounty for the Accuser," *New York Times* (August 6, 1972), p. E-5.
4. Ibid.
5. Marcus G. Raskin, *Being and Doing* (New York: Random, 1971), pp. 230–231.
6. Herbert Packer, as quoted in *The Center Magazine* (May–June 1971), p. 9.
7. Seth King, "Nutrition Centers Prove a Boon to the Elderly in Chicago," *New York Times* (September 10, 1972), p. 80.
8. Norvell Morris, as quoted in *The Center Magazine* (May–June 1971), p. 39.
9. Ibid., p. 27.
10. Garry D. Brewer, book review in *Policy Sciences* (June 1971), p. 205.
11. Benjamin DeMott, *Super-grow: Essays and Reports on Imagination in America* (New York: Dutton, 1969), p. 90.

READING

How would you go about evaluating a nation's effort to effect social change by remodeling its schools? In this engaging report Verne Moberg covers a lot of material trying to answer this question about a post-1962 Swedish educational reform. As she does so, we learn much about a "(relatively) en-

lightened culture," a country at once the most anti-American and the most Americanized of all European nations, and a nation that is "not a bad school these days." And at the same time we gain new insights into the process of evaluating a major social reform.

The Great Swedish School Reform: Can You Really Make Social Change Happen by Remodeling the Schools?

Verne Moberg

I keep going back to Sweden without really knowing why. The place certainly isn't what it's made out to be. The official PR image of an immaculate utopia, diligently dispensing social justice for all is by now a cartoon. Marquis Childs's notion of Sweden as a "Middle Way," a cross between socialism and capitalism, was a tourist's tale.

But after having lived in the States, I always feel relieved to get back to Sweden. The air is cool, and the thinking is clear: people have an uncanny gift for gut-level common sense. Another awesome national trait of theirs is a sort of stolid, point-blank, flat-footed honesty—Swedes are pitifully poor at hustling but are good at hard work. (It is the same quality that has been caricatured in the classic Scandinavian stereotypes in the United States: the blue-eyed blockhead, the Dumb Swede you read about in Hemingway and Sandburg and Sinclair Lewis and Stephen Crane. What was virtue back home was the object of ridicule in America.) It is that quality of innocence, it seems to me, that explains how Swedes have been able to evolve the (relatively) enlightened culture they have today: they simply didn't feel in their bones that it couldn't be done.

Most Americans I try to explain this trait to immediately grow indignant. "But *Sweden* is *different*. Sweden is a socialist country!" But, to say the least, it is misleading to classify this place as simply "socialist" when only 5 per cent of the industry is government owned and practically without interruption for the past forty years the country has been ruled by the Social Democrats. These pragmatic politicians are certainly not pushing very hard to change Sweden's economic profile. Of course, the government does regulate a number of services and industries (radio and TV, for example), and Sweden may be the most anti-American country in Europe. Nevertheless, it's probably also the most American*ized* country there—the influence of U.S. corporate strength is apparent everywhere.

Moreover, it does not look as if Olof Palme, the forty-six-year-old former education minister elected prime minister in 1969, is about to speed up the pace. He is himself a product of American schooling (Kenyon College, 1948) and has managed to win a reputation outside Sweden as a meticulously articulate and progressive politician, a kind of Swedish version of Jack Kennedy, shifted 40 degrees to the left. What Americans also have to remember about Sweden today is that these people still have a king. In 1920, when the Social Democrats formed their first government, King Gustaf V laid down certain rules: no socialism, no large military cutbacks, and no getting rid of the king. Right? Yes, right. The Social Democrats promised.

Ever since then they have been trying to figure out how to do away with the monarchy, but this is a touchy issue. The present king, Gustaf VI Adolf, has just celebrated his ninetieth birthday and is a terribly nice old man whom a large portion of the population is fond of. But the political prognosis for his grandson, Crown Prince Carl Gustaf, is definitely on the gloomy side.

One thing I was wondering about when I went back to Sweden this time was whether there is evidence there today that you can really effect social change by remodeling the schools.

Prime Minister Palme and an army of school-board bureaucrats claim that they are counting on schools to provoke social change, to restructure a small and rather monolithic capitalist country into a genuinely modern democracy. The comprehensive school reform that Sweden began planning back in the forties and inaugurated in 1962 is designed, they say, to do just this.

What it boils down to is a total integration of the public school system into a single comprehensive system offering (theoretically) a good general, basic education to everybody from the age of seven to sixteen. Previously, students were channeled at an early age into either college-preparatory or vocational programs. In effect, parents made this choice for the children, who by the time they reached university level had little opportunity to make up the work (often including a mastery of Greek and Latin). Now, in the new comprehensive system, the choice of specialization comes at a much later stage; and even if students do "major" in vocational subjects in the upper grades, they may still enter the university (which now operates on essentially an "open enrollment" basis). Under the new system uniform programs of study are closely regulated (including not only requirements but also "compulsory electives"). Much of the inspiration for the new plan came from the United States.

Despite its obvious advantages over the system that preceded it, the Great School Reform is apt to sound tragicomic to many American observers. You don't democratize a school system just by standardizing the various game plans for graduation. And allowing students to pick their major fields of concentration certainly doesn't mean that they're liberated from the high-power pressures of family or class or sex-role stereotypes.

According to critics on the right of the Social Democrats, the Great School Reform is indeed bringing change, but not in the direction of democracy: the school system is becoming increasingly centralized and homogeneous, they say, and there's no longer room for a variety of styles of education—including, for instance, *Christian* education. (Some people have even threatened to start, as it were, religious free schools for this purpose.)

In the view of the leftist critics, the name of Palme's game is repressive tolerance; the subsidies to student government and all the talk about school democracy are parliamentary safety valves to make the Social Democrats look good—which they very much need to do with a new prime minister in the midst of a painful period of inflation now several years old.

Coming to Sweden from the outside, an American will find it hard to judge who the enemy (if there is any) might be. After having visited Sweden, Lenin once said that if there ever were a revolution there, the first act of the winners would be to invite the losers to lunch. It is a national ethic: the honor code of the North demands at least a pretense at cooperation, regardless of party affiliation.

But surely the comprehensive school means considerable improvement. In the past schooling was determined by class in Sweden, and in 1930 only a small percentage of the population went as far as the *gymnasium* (the next stage in school for the college-bound). In 1945 it was only 13 per cent, and by 1972 it had grown to 80 per cent.

Nevertheless, at the university level the percentage of the student population with working-class origins has not increased very much over the years, though nobody pays tuition and generous financial aid has been available for decades practically for the asking. Class prejudice, apparently, is more than a money thing: it's centuries of ingrained attitudes about who is supposed to be inferior, a conception of higher learning as a luxury reserved for the rich.

Even more significant than these statistics is the whole style of teaching in Sweden: rote learning in a master-slave relationship, all controlled by a supreme sovereign called a *rektor* (principal). In many classrooms in Sweden the teacher's desk is still perched upon a patform at the front of the class, and whenever visitors enter, pupils are required to rise and greet them. I'm told that a generation or two ago the situation was much worse (students did not even address each other, and never the teacher, with the informal *du* form), but by American standards it is abysmally authoritarian.

Few Swedes are pleased by the state of their schools, and no students I've ever talked with have been optimistic. But just now hardly anybody—with the exception of those few maverick rightists pining for Christian education—would think seriously of starting up free schools. In fact, many leftists will tell you that the idea is reactionary, because the government would never give you the money to run one and therefore a "free" school would be too expensive for anyone but rich kids to afford.

On Ascension Day (*Kristihimmelfärdsdag;* literally, "Christ's Heaven Trip Day") in 1968, not long after the barricades had begun to rise around the Sorbonne, young rebels in Stockholm staged their own revolution at the university—to the delight of onlookers who had never seen one and couldn't take time off to go down to Paris. Several buildings were occupied, and weekend-long meetings were held in protest against Olof Palme's new university reform: word was that it would render the universities somewhat more "American." Up until then it had been possible to remain an undergraduate ("professional student") for years on end, but the new plan would change all that. Sequences of "requirements" would be standardized to track for more "efficient" job placement. In Stockholm, which had scarcely seen a demonstration for decades (the trade unions' ritual May Day festivities no longer counted), thousands of people were marching down the street, yelling, *"Makt åt folket!"* ("Power to the people"), demanding completely different conditions in the universities. Trudging along in that parade, I had a hunch that Sweden might really change.

It did, very slightly, in the following ways:

The new university plan was processed through a number of further reforms until it emerged as a complex modification of the original plan, which everybody describes as even more hopelessly complex and unsatisfactory. So now not even the rightists are pleased with the universities and nobody can do much about them.

A few students (especially the ultramilitant "Double Maoists") dropped out of college to "join the workers," and these days it is considered chic among young leftists to study welding or other apparently useful skills.

Anders Karlberg (Red Anders, Stockholm's Rudi Dutschke) led one of the movements to splinter the Communist Party; he's since dropped out of sight, but cynics say he'll emerge at any time as a minor leftist bureaucrat.

Participating in demonstrations has become a respectable way of life for thousands of Swedes, especially in Stockholm, and the May Day ceremonies have emerged as a meaningful platform for a wide spectrum of political groups, who turn out in large numbers.

Education is established as a political issue, discussed as such even among students on the high school level—who are by now talking about striking for better textbooks. In 1968 Gören Palm, an important poet and activist, published a book analyzing the capitalist, pro-NATO content of textbooks, and when it became a best seller, the journalists eagerly set to work criticizing what the Swedes were teaching their children in school.

By the time of my last visit to Stockholm the excitement of the 1968 student revolution had faded to fond memories, and the country was suffering from a surprisingly high level of unemployment, especially among teachers. Over the past decade, now that more students were entering the universities from the comprehensive schools, "too many" had majored in education, and, as a result, about half of all the Swedes who graduated from the pedagogical institutes (i.e., certified teachers) were out of work. Perhaps Palme's plan for the regimentation of university studies made some sense after all. Or, more likely, the crush of the present economic system had simply become intolerable: to expect humanistic educational reform at a time when teachers are begging for jobs—and housewives are picketing supermarkets to protest the constant inroads of inflation—would be simply absurd.

Moreover, the high idealism of the master plan (*läroplan*) of school reform, however elegantly phrased, seemed ridiculously remote from reality. For instance, one reform specified in the National School Board's detailed curriculum guide is the discussion of sexual stereotypes and sex roles in virtually all areas of the humanities, at all levels of elementary and secondary school. The sad fact is, of course, that extremely few teachers actually *know* anything about the history and politics of sex roles: there are no women's studies programs in the institutions of higher learning. One scholar, Karin Westman Berg in Härnösand, taught a course on the image of women in literature for five years at the University of Uppsala Extension Division, resulting in the founding of radical women's groups throughout the country. But credit has never been given for such courses. This year, because of budget cuts, Westman Berg is unemployed. Yet the government and education schools continue to require comprehensive school teachers to teach what they do not know.

On the other hand, *sex education* has had a full-fledged place in Swedish schools and education colleges for some years, and yet it remains the laughingstock of many students. This past year one of the popular songs in Sweden and Finland was a jazzy blues number called "What a Young Man Should Know," the lyrics of which are said to be quoted from a sex-education text. M. A. Numinen, a pop singer, crooned (literally):

> The young man should keep in mind that . . .
> his wife may well require more foreplay,
> as well as verbal expressions of endearment,
>   than he himself.
> The woman may not be able
>   to experience entirely satisfying
>   intercourse until after months,
>   indeed, even years of marriage. . . .
> What is crucial is that
>   neither partner place demands on the other
>   but rather enter into the new intimacy
>   in as liberated a fashion as possible.

It boggles the glands to speculate what grotesque effects such sexist counsel must have when delivered from the podium of an authoritarian Swedish classroom.

As for textbook indoctrination, the situation hasn't changed much since 1968. During a visit to one of Stockholm's better schools, when I asked a group of students what they were learning about Vietnam, there were guffaws. One student eagerly opened his history book to the page on Vietnam: the photo showed South Vietnamese women protecting their babies from grimacing Liberation Front guerillas, and the caption read simply, "The United States supports the government of Vietnam." Considering Palme's reputation abroad for militancy on the question of U.S. intervention in Southeast Asia, this, in the midst of the school reform, is pretty ironic.

The country's large and ubiquitous student-government organizations, subsidized by acts of Parliament, have taken positions on many general issues: there is much talk and writing about what is called "school democracy," as well as "family democracy" and "industrial democracy." Ironically, at the same time many Swedes are questioning whether the word *democracy* has any meaning at all.

Most of the cultural excitement in Sweden, it seems to me, comes from the writers and people around them. Of course, this trend may be true everywhere, but in Sweden people—and I mean all kinds of people—read a lot more. (According to UNESCO ratings a few years ago on the number of books published per capita, Sweden ranked near the top while the United States placed about twenty-third.) These days writers are trying hard to get in closer touch with the population, and publishers, in a financial bind, are naturally also eager to see more people read.

When you are printing books for a small population (eight million Swedes), editions are relatively small, no matter how much reading people do, and technical costs, proportionately, are therefore high. Hence, book prices in Sweden have always been astronomical, and at the end of the sixties, when inflation caused them to soar even higher, authors started to complain. People, even poor people and especially students, they said, have to be able to afford books; also, writers have to live. So it was clear that prices had to drop at the same time as royalties were raised.

As a result of the debate over book pricing—and over "author power"—a new publishing firm was founded by the Authors' Union. It is called *Författarförlaget* (the Authors' Publishing House) and is controlled by authors. Prices are about one third to one half of what other publishers charge, while authors get a royalty of 16 per cent (instead of the standard 7 to 10 per cent). Since 1970 *Författarförlaget* has brought out about a dozen books a year, including works by the very best writers—members of the union who have all agreed to offer a manuscript to *Författarförlaget* every once in a while.

Several Swedish publishers and especially the smaller ones have been promoting a new literary genre known as the political children's book, the product of an ongoing debate on the rights of children. The issue came up in the last half of the sixties in a number of books: *Scrap-Culture for Our Children* by Gunilla Ambjörnsson and a manual on how to talk to kids, by Francis Vestin; the Danes' *Little Red Schoolbook* was also popular. At the same time other authors were questioning the entire idea of a separate children's culture: Why should books be categorized as juvenile or adult titles? Was this classification simply another dangerous by-product of capitalist publishing? Several writers suggested publishing "family books," and Clas Engström, the founder of the Authors' Publishing House, actually wrote one: his generation gap comedy, called *Are Adults Out of Their Minds?* (on youth and drugs versus middle age and liquor), was popular both in book format and on TV. And the children's books then available were raked over the coals: Astrid Lindgren's best-selling Pippi Longstocking series was charged with racism (remember her absentee father, the South Seas cannibal king?). Gradually, a number of new "political" books began to appear, including a kids' book on Vietnam and another on Cuba; *Why Chand Works,* about the exploitation of children in India; stories of single-parent families, children with alcoholic fathers, retarded kids, etc.

Siv Widerberg, the editor of the children's news page on Stockholm's largest daily, is my favorite author of political children's books. She writes poems and short stories for children, often with a kind of interior monologue. Usually there's a political point, and the pieces work so well they're just plain good reading—adults as well as children think so. Widerberg has also recently written a novel for retarded adults. One rarely thinks of it, but retarded children grow up to be retarded adults, and there are virtually no books for them.

In the past five years a number of other activist authors have been writing in an interesting new form: *skolteatern* (school theater).

Theater folks—actors and directors and producers—are increasingly interested in working for kids. Rather than putting on fixed performances in expensive metropolitan theaters that only affluent adults can afford, they are traveling about the countryside in very small troupes, giving little political plays in school gymnasiums, hospital waiting rooms, and library auditoriums. There is street theater as well, of course, and most of these groups (à la Open Theater) will get into discussions with the audience afterwards about the politics of the play. Sven Wernström's *Ett Spel om Plugget* (*A Play About School*) was one of the most popular works. It urged students to call their teachers *du,* among other things, and got banned by a number of principals.

One uniquely Swedish institution you hear a good deal about these days is *Författarcentrum* (the Authors' Center), founded by two radical poets in 1967 and now, of course, subsidized by the government.

The premise of the center was that artists, especially writers, were too isolated from the people and vice versa; there should be more firsthand encounters between writers and readers. So a kind of speaking bureau was set up to send writers out to meet people in hospitals, libraries, schools, nursing homes, and prisons, among other places. The center also printed pamphlets full of poems that sold for a crown (20 cents) each to try to get people to read more modern poetry. On several occasions a "culture bus" full of writers has toured the country, giving readings on highways and byways.

The Swedes love new ideas, the more radical the better, especially if they don't have to be put into practice. And if Swedes are not always so clever at making up their own ideas, well, they are superb at importing them.

A few days before I left Stockholm a friend of mine told me about a meeting she had been to where "some crazy Dane" had been talking up the idea of what sounded very much like free schools—or rather, deschools. The most intriguing things she said he talked about were some notions from a book called *Hvis skolen ikke fantes* (*If There Were No School*). Doing a little checking, I discovered that the author is Nils Christie, a Norwegian sociologist. His book has been written up in the papers and promoted by a number of radical school-reform people in Denmark. From their description, he sounds like a Scandinavian Ivan Illich.

According to Christie, there are two main reasons why we'd be better off without schools:

1. Even though schools systematically track students by economic status with startling efficiency, people still regard schools as a means to social mobility, and that illusion itself preserves the status quo.
2. Because the knowledge explosion is progressing at such a rapid rate, people know (relatively) far less about their world than ever before in history. By now no one can possibly get a good "general" education in either the natural or social sciences; moreover, all that we really need to know and are capable of learning are certain very basic humanistic principles.

Ideally, then, what we really require is a "school-less society"—or a world in which the society itself is the school and all its adults are the teachers.

I wouldn't be surprised if a number of Swedish radicals eventually do take Christie seriously. Meanwhile, there are many other exciting learning places for young and middle-aged and old people to be. In fact, as a country, Sweden is not a bad school these days. Even for foreign students.

PART II

Four Major Reform Approaches

Knowing "who the players are" and what their strengths and limitations are is indispensable—and is therefore the preoccupation of this lengthy and fundamental section of the book. The four perspectives discussed—conservative, liberal, radical, and visionary—are important to the rest of the book. They also shape and explain many of the political and philosophical realities of us all.

Listening to University of Pennsylvania urbanologist Edward Banfield conclude a Fall 1972 seminar paper on the nature of social reform, I leaned forward and asked him for a specific example of the power of social theory to shape political action. He patiently explained that a view that found the root of labor market inadequacies in the job candidate himself would probably focus on the supply side of the equation (as in most OEO and MDTA job-training projects), whereas a view that instead faults the larger society would probably focus on the demand side of the equation (as in calls for the government to operate as an employer of first and last resort, a guarantor of adequate jobs for all!). In other words, a theory that highlights the inadequacies of the actor will focus reforms on changing the actor, whereas another view might be that the actor is perfectly fine and that it is the situation itself that is in need of reform!

Nodding agreement, I added to his illustration the less popular view that the root of inadequacies lies in the ownership of the means of production. And the relatively fresher view that faults the quality of the jobs themselves and would thoroughly overhaul the very meaning of work itself in preference to mere tinkering with the mechanics of work distribution.

The illustration points out that we can choose among four alternative basic *perspectives when we move in on any and all social problems. To the extent that we choose consciously, carefully, and out of (conditional) conviction we are probably the stronger for it. Too often, however, our selection process is rife with unexamined assumptions, weak with careless reasoning, and taxed by unsupportable ideological rigidities. In the labor market illustration, the four major schools of political philosophy, and therefore social policy, are made clear: the conservative focuses on the inadequacies of the job seeker, whereas the liberal leans toward faulting the societal system as a whole; the radical raises questions about the economic foundation of everything, and the visionary calls attention to the psychic and cultural foundations of it all. Thus we have C-L-R-V, which I shall use to stand for all four perspectives in the pages that follow.*

Four Major Reform Approaches

CHAPTER 2

Leading Schools of Reform

Ideology shakes when it no longer convincingly interprets reality—whereupon it must change to account for the new reality, or die.

TODD GITLIN

The ground plan of this chapter is as follows. I begin with a general discussion of the four basic schools of thought, stressing especially their dissimilarities. I focus next on the policy approach of each, stressing this time their nitty-gritty practical proposals for modern social reform. I turn finally to some of the complexities of the subject, the better to ground the preceding discussion in reality. My purposes are to draw you into the framework of this book and to challenge you to take a stand.

A Fourfold Typology

Going directly to a real-world illustration, let us examine the four possible approaches to the nation's health crisis that are outlined in Table 2–1. Although the table grossly oversimplifies people's attitudes and probably offends enthusiasts of all four approaches, it nevertheless replicates the determined narrow-mindedness that an impartial witness can often observe in a heated discussion among spokesmen for the C-L-R-V positions.

Pulling back a bit from a specific question to more academic and basic matters, let us examine Table 2–2 for the responses of the four approaches to three heart-of-the-matter inquiries.

Note how all four perspectives draw initially on an implicit and critical image of man. Conservatives see us as tragically flawed and irascible, ever in need of external constraints. Liberals see us as understandably human, neither saint nor sinner by destiny, but as causing problems when subject to inferior social structures and culture(s). Radicals represent us as unknown both to ourselves and to them, so "crippled" are we by the "false consciousness" engendered in us by capitalistic personality exploitation. Although confident that we have the innate stuff to manage our affairs after the (distant) "withering away of the State," they feel that we will probably require an indefinite period of tutelage under the "Dictatorship of the Proletariat" (as represented by a radical cadre). Visionaries, on the other hand, have poetic, romantic, and unyielding confidence in us and in themselves. Some go so far as to insist that we are not only ready for, but have already begun the exhilarating effort to transform and surmount realities that otherwise seem formidable constraints on human unfolding, freedom, and joy.

TABLE 2–1. Four Approaches to the Nation's Health Crisis

	Conservative	*Liberal*	*Radical*	*Visionary*
1. *Is there a health crisis?*	No! Best health care anywhere!	Probably. Care is planless! Cries for control!	Yes! Care is too damn expensive! Cries for collectivization!	Without doubt! Care is merely remedial; should be both preventive and expansive!
2. *Who is responsible?*	Malingerers and malpractitioners!	Archaic medical formats.	Exploitative capitalist medicine!	Scientism's tyranny over the modern psyche.
3. *Who can help?*	AMA traditionalists.	Medical planners and concerned statesmen.	Socialized medicine architects; the movement.	Demystified and decentralized paramedics and concerned laymen.
4. *Goals?*	Lower bills and moralistic self-control! Pride in real attainment.	Power to a health planners protectorate!	Power to a health-savvy cadre! Free care now!	Power to healthy humans! Away with the mystique of professionalism.

Table 2–3 shows the interpretation of *the* major themes in man's history as given by C-L-R-V.

Not surprisingly conservatives regularly rely on the metaphor of "disease" when pressed to rationalize a controversial program they champion. Challenged, for example, about urban renewal efforts that are actually efforts to remove poor people, conservatives will uncomfortably explain that the city is sick and requires hard-boiled and ruthless "surgery." Cloaking their ideas in an impressive medical metaphor, they go on to argue that such pathologies as the unworthy poor—like cancers—must be "cut out" before the social body can regain its health.

Liberals, on the other hand, are given over to the equally cold-blooded metaphor of the errorless machine. Challenged about planning fiascos that have uprooted entire urban communities for puny material gains clearly incommensurate with the ensuing human losses, liberals will patiently explain that the fault is *not* in planning. Rather, the fault lies in the fact that the city is fragmented and overly timid in its planning. Total and bold planning is required!

Radicals, in turn, are doctrinaire about a metaphysical model of history, one that combines elements of both the body and the machine metaphors. Challenged, for example, about their ruthless dismissal of the sensitivities and even the civil liberties of the bourgeois enemy ("pigs," and so on), radicals will heatedly retort that larger issues than an individual's hurt feelings or tem-

TABLE 2–2. Four Approaches to Three Basic Questions

	Conservative	*Liberal*	*Radical*	*Visionary*
1. *Where do social problems originate?*	Disregard for tradition, custom, and verities.	Societal roots, organizational inefficiencies.	Economic exploitation as part of end-of-capitalism stage of dialectic.	Failure to grasp the truly valuable; misguided psychic consciousness; absence of self-actualization.
2. *What might solve problems?*	Growing disillusionment with macro-change fiascos of distant bureaucrats.	Rising aspirations and educational levels; growing respect for planning.	Popularism; rise of new class alliances; revolutionary fervor; rage in the oppressed.	New recruits to new forms of consciousness; relentless search for antidote to materialism and unhappiness.
3. *What is there for us to do?*	Restore the laissez-faire and grass roots orientation of old; rededicate ourselves to traditionalism.	Make adjustments within the present order; stay in touch with reality; promote social reconciliation.	Stir class consciousness and correct grasp of exploitation; provide cadre leadership to the masses; midwife the revolution.	Reorder the entire works; redefine reality; promote social reconstruction; help the "pioneer" and public alike to a still more enlarging vision of the good life.

TABLE 2–3. Four Approaches to Man's History

	Conservative	*Liberal*	*Radical*	*Visionary*
1. *What does history pinpoint as man's basic fate—to date?*	Contest: survival is the reward of the fittest in tooth-and-claw conflict.	Caring: a person's better side often triumphs over gross self-interest.	Calumny: we are robbed of life by illicit expropriators of the economic means of production.	Collaboration: mankind grows only when authentic and communal, only when all work together for the transformation of each.
2. *What is the nature of wealth?*	Scarce, irreplaceable, and only divisible; if you gain, I lose.	Scarce; substitutable; subject to slight expansion; if you gain, I may gain somewhat.	Scarce; captured by exploiters; if they gain, we all lose.	Illusionary, except as nonmaterial; therefore, infinitely expandable; I gain only as you gain.
3. *What should motivate us?*	Self-interest; being for the actor.	Self-renewal; being for the system.	Selflessness; being for the collective.	Self-actualization; being for the individual psyche.
4. *When should reforms be implemented?*	Over the years, cautiously, after reflection.	Over the months, with calculation and prior testing.	Within weeks (or otherwise years), with wrath and craft.	Now . . . with love and courage.

porary loss of freedom are entailed in the midwifing of a total economic revolution. They go on to argue that you either grasp it all and agree or remain a disgraceful and dangerous captive to "false consciousness."

Visionaries, for their part, are turned on to the psyche and the soul as the metaphor of poetic preference. Challenged about the airy irrelevance of these to the real issues of today, they are likely to respond as does Theodore Roszak:

> The world cries out for revolution—for the revolutions of bread and social justice, and national liberation. Not for a moment do I deny that fact (though my own pacifist and anarchist instincts make me dubious that violent militancy can for a certainty achieve those ends). But it needs the *next* revolution too, which is the struggle to liberate the visionary powers from the lesser reality in which they have been confined by urban-industrial necessity.[1]

Arming themselves with an alluring and yet perplexing utopian metaphor, the visionaries go on to assure one and all that their preoccupation, "dream thieving and idolatrous worship, the privation of the senses and the metaphysics of science—belong to the radicalism of the next revolution"[2] and that the possibilities for ultimate victory are clear to see. (Roszak: "But I trust to nobody's optimism, nobody's despair. Not yet."[3])

Pulling this all crudely together Table 2–4 lays it out.

TABLE 2–4. Four Approaches to Reform

	Conservative	*Liberal*	*Radical*	*Visionary*
1. *Where should reform focus?*	On lessons available in "the good old days."	On postindustrial lessons suggested by meritocratic scenarios.	On the radical struggle for social justice and sweeping change.	Inside; on the truth we experience in our own liberated essence.
2. *Who can help?*	Responsible royalists, rugged individualists.	Principled planners, moralistic managers.	Have-nots, cadre.	Those who are self-aware and tuned in.
3. *Goal?*	Autonomy.	Assimilation.	Action taking.	Self-actualization.

Note especially that the contemporary conservative accents control and our responsibility to police our own latent savagery. The liberal accents communications and our responsibility to keep the channels open among us, lest silence lead to brooding and brooding to apathy or revolution. The radical accents confrontation and our responsibility to lay our lives on the line—if need be—in the good fight. And the visionary accents communion along with our responsibility to strain to free ourselves from unexamined spiritual bondage to all that grinds us down.

Finally, as might be expected, the four perspectives differ profoundly in their definition of the primary tension that dominates the future unfolding about us. Conservatives peer into a crystal ball that suggests a Hobson's choice between firm control *or* irrational chaos. Liberals interpret the message in terms of planned democratic order *or* archaic dehumanized statism. Radicals believe the choice is between either egalitarian justice (a historical "inevitability") *or* meritocratic totalitarianism (a historical abomination). And visionaries see a choice between a new consciousness *or* the further encroachment on man's nature by technocratic scientism.

This is as far as I care to go in general commentary. I propose that we move on to focus more sharply on each of the four schools and to identify some of the real-world policy particulars of each.

Alternative Agendas for Action

Hereafter, when I use the term *conservative* I will be referring to a cluster of attitudes, values, and action patterns that emphasizes the restoration of firm social controls and harsh penalties as the best possible means to defeat a disastrous social entrancement with sentimentalism, socialism, and sin. (Commentators explain some of the 1972 McGovern defeat in terms of a successful conservative effort to link him to "acid, amnesty, and abortion"). The conservative also emphasizes the preservation of individual autonomy and social privilege as the best antidote to the massification, crowd culture, and "Big Brother" governance that threaten us all.

Connecticut's Republican Governor Thomas J. Meskill, a forty-five-year-old self-avowed political conservative, helps make this theory more practical and meaningful with his 1972 advocacy of the following:

1. *Restoration of Capital Punishment* "for premeditated murder; for the killing of a police officer, even accidentally in a jailbreak or something of this nature; for rape, and . . . for illegal selling of drugs."
2. *Minimization of Taxes.*
3. *Austerity in Government Spending.* "Within our own priorities we'll spend more where we feel more is warranted. But I don't think there is any area of government where economies cannot be effected."
4. *Harsher Criminal Laws.* The Governor supports a law providing for mandatory three-day jail terms for drunken drivers in a first-offense case: "We're not trying to fill our jails, but we are trying to convince people that it's very hazardous to drive when you've been drinking." The Governor does not favor the use of wiretaps in domestic matters: "But I think in any case where a criminal is using the telephone in the furtherance of his criminal activity, I think there's no right of privacy that's guaranteed there."

Overall, the Governor is deeply impressive in his reading of social trends that he believes explain today's alleged ground swell in favor of conservatism: "whenever problems arise that threaten people's homes, threaten their personal safety, or threaten their jobs, then I think they become more conservative. I think that they are the same people. It's just that they are a little more sensitive to the possibility of losing something."[4]

Now, how does such a position differ from the one I identify as *liberal?* Helpful in this connection is a clarification advanced recently by a leading conservative theorist. Liberals, he explains, are

> more apt to see the world in its specific reality; they experience the sights and sounds and smells of poverty; they empathize with the actual victims of injustice and therefore have a more naturalistic understanding of what injustice means. . . . Even if they *do not believe* in robbing the rich to feed the poor they may be willing to do so if they see someone going hungry.[5]

The conservative, on the other hand,

> becomes more incensed because his *theories* are not being put into operation than he is because somebody's baby was bitten by a rat. He knows that there is discrimination in the world, that some people are denied decent housing and adequate employment, but he is more annoyed at the "irrationality" of this condition than he is by its real-life effect on human beings. Not only is [he] usually unconcerned about the specifics of injustice, he will denounce all sympathy for the misery of others as immoral altruism.[6]

The differences, in short, are profound and compelling, with enormous and readily apparent implications for controversy in every aspect of social policy formulation, implementation, and assessment.

By *liberal,* then, I refer to an emphasis on the promotion of equality of opportunity, social justice, and cultural assimilation as the best possible counteraction to malignant discrimination, undue privilege, and intercultural hostility. That society is worthiest that offers the fullest and most identical membership to all. That government is best that is most humane and most ambitious in its planned guidance of the nation's destiny.

A recent statement of the liberal position is found in the writings of sociologists S. M. Miller and Pamela Roby. As a result of their interpretation of America's most pressing needs they promote this seven-part agenda:

1. *Expand the Economic Pie;* if we can learn how to overcome our stop-and-go economic policy, we can generate the kind of surplus that will make redistribution possible;
2. *Reduce Economic Insecurities;* if we choose to guarantee employment and earnings we can remove obstacles to the cooperation of men in social change;
3. *Lessen Inequalities;* we should change our regressive taxation system; accent a progressive federal income tax and Family Assistance Plan, among other reforms;
4. *Share the Burden of Racial and Class Integration;* if we insured homes to cover any related depreciation in value, and insured compensatory social services to reward affected neighborhoods we could substantially reduce "backlash" resistance to integration;
5. *Universalize Services;* we should expand and improve such demonstrably worthy programs as Headstart, and the Neighborhood Youth Corps., even while initiating a National Health Service, and other such overdue reforms;
6. *Promote Educational and Job Mobility;* we should reexamine the Credentials Requirements for postschool success; offer scholarships to any who desire additional schooling (especially manual workers); overhaul vocational education; and revamp public schooling at every level;
7. *Increase Participation and Power;* if we encouraged the establishment in bureaucracies of Review Boards and Ombudsmen, along with European-style Worker Participation in shop and union, we will have gained much in our struggle to invest democracy with meaning.

Overall, Miller and Roby conclude on an optimistic note:

> What we have heard are revolutionary tactics without revolutionary goals, and the reiteration of liberal objectives without recognition of their failure. What we are suggesting is a radical restructuring capable of appealing to a large number of voters who feel the need for change and do not see the possibility of a politically viable program.[7]

A third major claimant on the loyalties of a large number of voters is the school I identify as *radical,* a cluster of attitudes, values, and action patterns that emphasizes the fostering of a steadily building, inevitable, total transformation of capitalism that will finally make possible some variant of socialism in America. The radical perspective, whether socialist, Marxist, or syndicalist, takes capitalism and imperialism as variables rather than as givens. It declines to assume that the social order in the United States (and capitalism in general) is essentially just, harmonious, and timeless. Rather, the radical sees this social order as historically changing, temporal, and as likely as other social orders to be transformed by emerging economic and social forces and by the activities of rational and creative human beings.

Although radical agendas differ widely among themselves (as do *also* those of various conservative and liberal factions), the program set out recently by journalists and political activists Jack Newfield and Jeff Greenfield is illuminating:[8]

> the real division in this country is not between generations or between races, but between the rich who have power and those blacks and whites who have neither power nor property.
>
> . . . .
>
> a unifying populist platform might include:
>
> stricter industrial safety laws;
>
> a 90 percent tax on inheritance and estates—and tax reforms to help the workingman;
>
> free medical care for everyone;
>
> public ownership of utilities;
>
> limits on land ownership by individuals and corporations;
>
> new antitrust laws to go after industrial concentration as well as monopoly;
>
> expanded Social Security benefits, including a decent income base for those who cannot work;
>
> cable television franchises for civic groups;
>
> free and equal access to television for all politicians;
>
> strict controls on the profits of banks; and
>
> an end to corporate power and control of both market and the regulatory agencies.

Such a platform is thought capable of turning racial antagonists into allies: "With the added weight of the burgeoning consumer, environmental, and women's movements, and the millions of new voters between eighteen and twenty-one, an effective political coalition could take power."[9] Overall, then, the new populist movement pins its hopes on a hard-headed attack on economic privilege that rests neither on conservative fears, nor on liberal or visionary dreams, but on an uncompromising demand for fairness in competitive matters and justice in all things.

We come now to the fourth and last of the political and philosophical schools that concern us in this volume, the *visionary* approach. When I use this term, I refer to a group of people who emphasize the practical and attainable aspects of all that others dismiss as utopian and hopelessly romantic. Just as the radical cuts through the fog of unexamined assumptions to question the tenability and inevitability of capitalism, so does the visionary, but he cuts deeper yet:

> properly, urban-industrialism must be regarded as an *experiment* . . . a failed experiment, bringing in its wake every evil that progress was meant to

> vanquish. . . . What *is* to blame is the root assumption which has given the machines and desires a demonic animation: that the transcendent aspirations of mankind can be, *must* be translated into purely secular equivalents; that culture—if it is to be cleansed of superstition and reclaimed for humanitarian values—must be wholly entrusted to the mindscope of scientific rationality.[10]

Deeply convinced of the very opposite, the visionary urges us all to press beyond the spell of Science, to replace Science with new sacred values lest all our other revolutions leave our cultural framework insidiously intact. The fate of the soul, the visionary concludes, is the fate of the social order: "Like inside, like outside." Until we deliberately regain a psyche of wholeness and fulfillment, the world about us will steadily wither.

As for offering a set of programmatic visionary reforms, Theodore Roszak's earlier writings located the following on the far side of the urban-industrial wasteland:[11]

1. A proper mix of handicraft labor, intermediate technologies, and necessarily heavy industry.
2. The revitalization of work as a self-determining, nonexploitative activity—and as a means of spiritual growth.
3. A new economics elaborated out of kinship, friendship, and cooperation.
4. The regionalization and grass roots control of transport and mass communication.
5. Nonbureaucraticized, user-developed, user-administered social services.
6. Labor-gift and barter exchange systems in the local economy.
7. The commune and neighborhood as a basis for personalized welfare services.
8. The role of neighborhood courts in a participative legal system.
9. The societywide coordination of worker-controlled industries and producers' cooperatives.
10. Credit unions and mutual insurance as an alternative to the big banks and insurance companies.
11. Deurbanization and the rehabilitation of rural life by way of an ecologically diversified organic homesteading.
12. Noncompulsory education through free schools, folk schools, and child-minding cooperatives.

These and countless other proposed solutions to the tangled problems of decentralism and communitarianism have—as Roszak wryly notes—suffered from his own amateurish efforts at social invention. And, he adds, they have also received some attention from far more gifted minds.

Of late, however, and for reasons that set the visionary position strikingly off from all others, Roszak has come to the conclusion that such theoretical conjecture is all but meaningless politically. Like Marcuse before him, Roszak now draws back from planning for others. Instead, he stresses that it is those who are *doing*—people in the process of changing their homes, neighborhoods, cities, and regions—who are most apt to know best what they need and what works. Their resourcefulness and their practical and experienced on-the-scene judgment are to be relied on far more than the most prestigious expertise and the presumptions of those who have a general but not a personal knowledge.

Which is not at all to suggest that a visionary perspective leaves us no action agenda to help us move forward. On the contrary, the possibilities for each of us are both demanding and exhilarating. For one thing, we can dare to experiment with commune-style living ("the one place in all the fierce, foolish world where men and women may call their souls their own"[12]). And we can each strive to exemplify an ideal of life by which the many may judge themselves and the world. Finally, Roszak suggests that we live in the motivating belief that urban industrialism is a failed cultural experiment and that the time is at hand to replace it with the visionary commonwealth.

Clarifications—and Complexities

As I reread once again, for the zillionth time, what I have written in this chapter to this point—and puzzle over it all anew—it seems important to me to wrestle here with three subsidiary matters.

For openers, I trust you understand that each of the four schools houses *many* internal variations. In the visionary school alone one profits from the following distinct but interrelated insights—to mention only a few of many contributing elements:

Astrology	Human potential movement	Sufi
Bioresonance	Theosophy	Gurdjieff Study
Biofeedback	Spiritism	Hare Krishna
Scientology	Synanon	Zen
Macrobiotics	Tibetanism	Taoism
Witchcraft	Buddhism	Sokagakkai
Rosicrucianism		I Ching
Peyote Cult		

Accordingly, when elsewhere in the book I use the term *visionary,* you may well be curious about which is the particular focus of the reform I am discussing; that is, do I mean *visionary* in the human potential way, or according to the Buddhist model, or in terms of the bioresonance orientation? I expect you to approach my overly bold labels (C-L-R-V) with much caution and concern, for we both know they are a hazardous form of shorthand, a tricky kind of gross identification that glides over considerable internal variation within each school.

Second, I would have you note that the existence of the many subsidiary components inside each of the four schools helps explain an otherwise startling phenomenon, the steady growth of important forms of interschool convergence. Although the discussion thus far has stressed the many dissimilarities among the four perspectives, the rest of this book will suggest the tentative, fragile, and slowly growing points of agreement among the four belief systems —a most provocative matter!

Certain members of the radical/populist camp, for example, are unabashed admirers of conservative perceptiveness concerning the menace of violent street crime, the failure of the welfare system, and the limits human nature places on the abilities of centralized government—along with sensing the need to reestablish contact with those human values the workingman prizes most: family, hard work, pride, loyalty, and endurance. Similarly, from the conservative right comes news of the growing strength of "radical libertarians," whose left-sounding platform includes:

1. Sharp criticism of recent U.S. genocide in Vietnam.
2. Opposition to the immense power of state-corporate fascism that in their view is the current form of government in this nation.
3. Defense of individual liberty in the black community against what they consider the mindless oppression of the white policeman.
4. Support for Supreme Court decisions of recent years that favor the rights of the individual against the authoritarianism of the state.

Such right-wing conservatives, one of their number explains, are now doing everything the New (populist) Left is doing, for different reasons, perhaps, with different emphasis on the various issues, perhaps, but nevertheless acting to reduce the power of the state.[13]

Politics makes strange bed fellows? It always has—and will for indefinite long years ahead! But in terms of our limited purposes here the point is that there is an exciting turbulence on the C-L-R-V scene where social reforms and social policy are concerned. Both acrimony *and* alliances, dissimilarities *and* similarities across C-L-R-V lines infuse our reform dialogue with fresh vitality, invaluable criticism, and boundless creativity—however much they compound my problem of accuracy and fairness in using the C-L-R-V pigeon holes to sort out the hundred or so reforms I would call to your attention.

Finally, there is a delicate point I would strain to make about dynamism in reform agendas. For example, the change agenda I will link to a visionary perspective in the later chapters should be respected as tentative and time bound. It will probably look quaint and possibly even conservative to visionaries living in the year 2073 (provided, that is, that the 1973 visionary agenda has flowered in the interim). Across the intervening hundred years visionaries are likely to reassess and enhance their 1973 orientation. And it is the very temporary, tangled, and volatile nature of the reform process that I would highlight here: Do not "judge" a school by its immediate reform particulars; look far deeper, lest you confuse situational nitty-gritty with real substance and undervalue the critical dynamism of all four turbulent schools. Grasp where each is coming from, to be sure, and struggle to understand its present-day "face," but strain also to discover where it can go and seems to be going—for flux and growth are basic hallmarks of all four schools.

Afterthoughts

Friends so often raise the following four questions about this chapter that I am convinced of the reasonableness and usefulness of sharing my answers with you in lieu of a more conventional summary of the chapter's contents.

First, they ask where the visionary school comes from and what makes me think it reasonable to treat it as an equal of the more readily recognized, time-honored C-L-R perspectives? Although it can be traced back to the Old Testament prophets (Isaiah, Amos, and so on) and can be linked as well to the bohemian ethos evident throughout history, the visionary perspective is especially significant as a post-1960's phenomenon on the American cultural scene. Crudely labeled the counterculture, Consciousness III, and the new culture, it seems to me fully as important now as the other three schools, both in its own terms and as a new standard against which we are obliged to assess the other three alternatives. Believing this, I am especially anxious to help readers make the acquaintance of this relatively new, media-abused school of social thought. With a certain calculated amount of brashness then, I elevate it to equality with the C-L-R schools, confident that time will confirm the permanent post-1960's significance of the visionary school of thought.

Second, and not surprisingly, I am asked if I am provisionary, anticonservative, or what? With some exasperation I insist that my effort in this chapter, and throughout the entire book, is to be as fair as possible to all four schools. I have my own biases and values, but I strain to minimize their significance in this book. So I would have you waste little energy in trying to analyze *my* position as you work your way through the volume. Put all of your energy instead into getting in touch with your *own* position in these matters.

Third, I am asked if I am not letting the four schools off too easily. Some wonder if I do not unduly accent the positive, and they ask therefore if I could lay out some of the negative qualities of each of the schools even this early in the volume, with the attendant risk of prejudicing the case somewhat against one or another of the points of view. With this in mind I invite them and you to peruse the material tersely set out in Table 2–5.

TABLE 2–5. Negative Qualities of the Four Schools

	Conservative	*Liberal*	*Radical*	*Visionary*
1. *Preoccupation and peril?*	With restoration; a backward task?	With pacification; a temporizing task?	With revolution; a devouring task?	With renaissance; an ill-fated task?
2. *Chief motive force.*	Fear of further losses; desire to repeat history.	Fascination with possibilities of applied science; desire to remake history.	Rage to redress grievances; desire to midwife history through revolution.	Dream of enlarging gains; desire to help mankind rejoin history.
3. *Aura?*	Timid and yet fierce; firm and unyielding.	Plaintive and puzzled; ever ready for better solutions.	Fierce and yet warm; firm and unyielding.	Earnest and eager; every ready for further enlightenment.
4. *Flaw?*	Distrust of man and men.	Overemphasis on science and technology.	Overemphasis on economics and ideology.	Distance from men and machinations.

Now the task of assessing these less-attractive dimensions of the four schools and incorporating them into a fair overall judgment of each school is a heavy one and requires a large volume of further information, some of which I hope the rest of this book will provide. Any but a very tentative judgment *at this time* is patently premature!

Finally, my friends are curious about my expectations of the reader at this point. How much do I expect you to grasp of the four-school "lesson" this early in the book? I urge you to relax. If successful, the book will enable you to build slowly and steadily an increasing sophistication in and mastery of the material. An astute reader may gain:

recognition of how unevenly he grasped the full import of a school he thought he identified with;
eagerness to assess freshly an old, favored school against the new allurement of a school he has seldom considered before, and
mature and sobering recognition of how much there really is to learn and to consider before advocating one social reform or another.

Relax, and yet dig in! The book *can* help you make substantial gains as a thinking, feeling, vision-perfecting citizen and human being—which is, after all, much of what the C-L-R-V schools are finally about, however differently they may seem to define this goal.

For Further Reading

A very small sample of the various writers and sources to whom you *must* refer if you are to mitigate against my own interpretive shortcomings includes:

Conservative	*Liberal*	*Radical*	*Visionary*
Irving Kristol	Seymour M. Lipset	Gary Marx	Edger Z. Friedenberg
William F. Buckley, Jr.	Daniel Bell	Richard Flacks	Norman Brown
William Chamberlain	John Kenneth Galbraith	Michael Harrington	R. D. Laing
Theodore Hess	Herbert Gans	Eugene D. Genovese	Abraham Maslow
Russell Kirk	Irving Howe	Paul Goodman	Theodore Roszak
Jerome Tuccille	Edward Kennedy	Paul Sweezy	Arthur Waskow
Ernst Van Den Haag	Bayard Rustin	Angela Davis	Alan Watts
Ayn Rand	Harriet Van Horne		Germaine Greer
	Nathan Glazer		
The National Review	*The New Republic*	*The Nation*	*The Mother Earth News*
The New Leader	*Harper's*	*Monthly Review*	*Manas*
The Public Interest	*America*	*Ramparts*	*Commonweal*
Time	*Saturday Review*	*New Society*	*Futures Unconditional*
Commentary	*Atlantic*	*Telos*	
	The Progressive		

FOOTNOTES

1. Theodore Roszak, *Where the Wasteland Ends* (Garden City, N.Y.: Doubleday, 1972), p. xxvii.
2. Ibid., p. xxxii.
3. Ibid., p. xxxiv.
4. *New York Times* (May 4, 1973), p. 13.
5. Jerome Tuccille, *Radical Libertarianism* (New York: Harper, 1970), p. xvii.
6. Ibid., p. xviii.
7. S. M. Miller and Pamela Roby, *The Future of Inequality* (New York: Basic Books, 1970), p. 252.
8. Jack Newfield and Jeff Greenfield, *A Populist Manifesto* (New York: Warner, 1972), p. 21.
9. Ibid., p. 23.
10. Roszak, op. cit., pp. xxix–xxx.
11. Ibid., p. 432.
12. Ibid., p. 430.
13. See Tuccille, op. cit.

READING

How valid is the typology in this chapter? Having labored over it for several months I have little hesitation in admitting that I am not sure, that I would do parts of it differently if I could do it all over again. Helpful in this connection is this forceful essay by an exacting and constructive reader, a twenty-two-year-old senior in a class of mine and a personal friend, Gerald Pocius. Along with others he read chapters of this book in manuscript; unlike the others he made an effort to help me grasp a telling and substantial weakness in the fourfold typology as I originally developed it. I am pleased to reprint the unsolicited essay he turned in—and later polished for publication at my urging—both as an example of how susceptible to improvement are all *the ideas in these pages and as a high-quality example of the kind of constructive criticism you should begin to expect from yourself.*

Bedrockers: The Missing School

Gerald L. Pocius

After much thought and reflection, I still come away from your fourfold classification with a sense of incompleteness. I now believe that my difficulty here rests with your portrayal of the conservative school; their case, as I understand it, is misrepresented, and their ideology differs from that conveyed by the chapter. I feel that another school of thought exists, one that concerns

Reprinted by permission of the author.

itself not with the past or the future but with the present; not with change but with homeostasis. This school is finding an ever stronger voice in America and is attracting an ever-increasing number of followers.

Each of the four schools of your chapter is concerned with change of one kind or another, whether into a tranquil past or a transcendental future. This fifth school that I speak of concerns itself with the preservation of the present, with the glorification of the nation's greatness. To label this fifth school of thought, I would prefer the term *bedrocker:* it is marked by its opposition to change in *any form*. My choice of nomenclature, however, is arbitrary; other classifications are possible, as, for example, in Bertram Gross's writing on the "friendly fascism" that he sees on the rise. More recently, James Dickenson has noted the emergence of a related political school that he calls the "bedrocks."[1]

In order to describe the bedrocker school better, it will be useful to revise some of the tables found in this chapter, adding this fifth school to them. I shall start with Table 2–2. (See Table 1 on the next page.)

America, the bedrocker would especially point out, is the richest land in the world, one blessed with an abundance of wealth and happiness. We have placed a man on the moon and have fought the spread of Communist tyranny. America may have its problems, but they are miniscule when compared to the advantages that can be found in this great land.

Social problems arise, then, because we fail to see the greatness that fills this land. We fail to recognize that all of our problems could be solved if we would only utilize the resources we find around us. We needn't call for some drastic type of restructuring of society. To solve any particular problem, we should not blame others but focus instead on our own personal strivings. We must be careful not to become deluded by the rhetoric that claims to hold the real answer. In a strong and healthy America, we can point the finger only at ourselves, at our own weaknesses and lack of initiative.

America *is* a healthy and happy society, the bedrocker claims. We become deluded into thinking otherwise by deluded critics who find nothing right with the country. The television networks, for example, are controlled by left-leaning eastern intellectuals, and the major eastern newspapers present a greatly biased view of social problems. Demonstrators and criticizers fill the media, distorting our nation's true image. They call for change where none is needed.

The bedrocker looks upon dissent as a threat to the future of the country because social problems can *never* be remedied in an atmosphere of disorder and disturbance. The average American must be heard, for he is the backbone of the country: our leaders *will* respond to the plea of the "silent majority," and the demonstrators will be quieted. In this vein, Agnew when vice president suggested that protest leaders should be separated from society "with no more regret than we should feel over discarding rotten apples from a barrel."[2]

The basic differences between the bedrocker and conservative schools can readily be seen in this disagreement over the nature of man in society (see Table 2, my revision of Table 2–3 in the chapter). The chapter claims that conservatives "see us as tragically flawed and irascible, ever in need of external constraints." This Hobbesian view of man, I feel, belongs not so much

TABLE 1.

	Conservative	*Bedrocker*	*Liberal*	*Radical*	*Visionary*
1. *Where do social problems originate?*	Disregard for tradition, custom, and verities.	Ourselves; personal weaknesses and failings.	Societal roots; organizational inefficiencies.	Economic exploitation as part of end-of-capitalism stage of dialectic.	Failure to grasp the truly valuable; misguided psychic consciousness; absence of self-actualization.
2. *What might solve problems?*	Growing disillusionment with macro-change fiascos of bureaucrats.	Never blaming personal failings on external sources; restoring pride in the America of today.	Rising aspirations and educational levels; growing respect for planning.	Popularism; rise of new class alliances; revolutionary fervor; rage in the oppressed.	New recruits to new forms of consciousness; relentless search for antidote to materialism and unhappiness.
3. *What is there for us to do?*	Restore the laissez-faire and grass roots orientation of old; rededicate ourselves to traditionalism.	Silence dissent and criticism; display pride in our country; choose wise leaders who know best.	Make adjustments within the present order; stay in touch with reality; promote social reconciliation.	Stir class consciousness and correct grasp of exploitation; provide cadre leadership to the masses; midwife the revolution.	Reorder the entire works; redefine reality; promote social reconstruction; help the "pioneer" and public alike to a still more enlarging vision of the good life.

TABLE 2.

	Conservative	*Bedrocker*	*Liberal*	*Radical*	*Visionary*
1. *What does history pinpoint as man's basic fate—to date?*	Contribution: Each man, acting in his own self-interest, will promote his own good; a group acting thusly will promote general good.	Contest: Survival is the reward of the fittest in tooth-and-claw conflict.	Caring: Man's better side often triumphs over gross self-interest.	Calumny: Men are robbed of life by illicit expropriators of the economic means of production.	Collaboration: Mankind grows only when authentic and communal, only when all work together for the transformation of each.
2. *What is the nature of wealth?*	Scarce, irreplaceable, divisible; if you gain, we all gain.	Scarce, irreplaceable, and only divisible; if you gain, I lose.	Scarce; substitutable; subject to slight expansion; if you gain, I may gain somewhat.	Scarce; captured by exploiters; if they gain, we all lose.	Illusionary, except as nonmaterial; therefore, infinitely expandable; I gain only as you gain.

to the conservative as to the bedrocker school and touches on the major difference between them.

Conservatives are concerned with the individual, his inalienable rights, and his ability to succeed, provided external restraint is minimal. It is the individual that society must serve. Jerome Tuccille echoes this idea when he writes that

> Conservatives claim to be champions of individual freedom, advocates of limited government, organized strictly for the purpose of defending the individual from domestic violence and the country at large from international aggression, devoted passionately to the creation of a laissez-faire society with equal liberties for each and every individual.[3]

The propensities of man make it clear that he is good when left to himself. The restrictions of government must be few. Like Adam Smith and Jeremy Bentham before him, the conservative believes that "the market is a sufficient regulator and distributor if only it is left truly free to do its work."[4]

The bedrocker, on the other hand, feels that the government must take the necessary measures to ensure the success of those with initiative. Those who strive should be rewarded, whereas those on the fringes should be penalized. American society is geared to success and those who refuse to accept the rules should be willing to face the consequences. The bedrocker may take any measure that is necessary to ensure the greatness of the country. Traditions and precedents can be disregarded in situations in which drastic action is required. Laws may be reinterpreted, or even overlooked, if a threat to the nation seems imminent. Leaders will act as benevolent guides through a time of turmoil.

Bedrock reform (see Table 3, my revision of Table 2–4) would concern itself with the elimination of the "failures" who plague America, those who drag its name into the mud. Thus, we should reinstitute the death penalty and even extend its uses. Electronic surveillance should be used in the arrest and conviction of those who threaten the image of a great America. In the chapter, it was stated that conservatives would perform "ruthless surgery" on the poor in an urban renewal effort, removing them like a cancer so that the social body can regain health. This is clearly the bedrock solution. The poor have failed because of their own inabilities and they must be removed.

The conservative would insist that this attitude toward urban renewal is inaccurate. Each community should be controlled by its own people, not by a "surgeon" government. When William F. Buckley, Jr. announced his candidacy for mayor of New York City, he denounced the attitude that bedrockers hold in this area:

> The beauty of New York is threatened by the schematic designs upon it of the social abstractionists who do not look up from their drawing boards long enough to recognize what it is that makes for human attachments—to little buildings and shops, to areas of repose and excitement: to all those abstractions that so greatly inconvenience the big-think social planners. The obsession with urban renewal must, in due course, be tranquilized, before the City loses its hold on human sentiment.[5]

Finally, see Table 4, my revision of Table 2–5.

Table 3.

	Conservative	*Bedrocker*	*Liberal*	*Radical*	*Visionary*
1. *Where should reform focus?*	On lessons available in "the good old days."	On elimination of dissent; proper guidance of attitudes.	On postindustrial lessons suggested by meritocractic scenarios.	On the radical struggle for social justice and sweeping change.	Inside; on the truth we experience in our own liberated essence.
2. *Who can help?*	Responsible royalists; rugged individualists.	Leaders who recognize the "real America" of the "silent majority."	Principled planners; moralistic managers.	Have-nots; cadre.	Those who are self-aware and tuned in.

TABLE 4.

	Conservative	*Bedrocker*	*Liberal*	*Radical*	*Visionary*
1. *Preoccupation and peril.*	With restoration; a backward task?	With placidity; a destructive task?	With pacification; a temporizing task?	With revolution; a devouring task?	With renaissance; an ill-fated task?
2. *Goal.*	Autonomy.	Acceptance.	Assimilation.	Action taking.	Self-actualization.
3. *Chief motive force.*	Fear of further losses; desire to repeat history.	Fear of movement; pride in "American dream."	Fascination with possibilities of applied science; desire to remake history.	Rage to redress grievances; desire to midwife history through revolution.	Dream of enlarging gains; desire to help mankind rejoin history.
4. *Aura?*	Timid and yet fierce; firm and unyielding	Proud and outspoken; missionary-like zeal.	Plaintive and puzzled; ever ready for better solutions.	Fierce and yet warm; firm and unyielding.	Earnest and eager; ever ready for further enlightenment.
5. *Flaw?*	Overemphasis on the man of the past.	Distrust of man and men.	Overemphasis on science and technology.	Overemphasis on economics and ideology.	Distance from men and machinations.

I feel that the addition of the bedrocker as a fifth school would provide the perspective that seems to be missing from the chapter. With its addition, we can adequately examine any social issue that might face us. I hope this short essay will expose some of the difficulties I have found with the chapter and that my comments will prove useful for future dialogue and thought.

FOOTNOTES

1. See Bertram M. Gross, "Friendly Fascism: A Model for America," *Social Policy,* Vol. 1, No. 4 (November–December 1970). Also James R. Dickenson, "The Two Americas," *The National Observer,* Vol. 12, No. 10 (March 10, 1973).
2. Henry Steele Commager, "Is Freedom Dying in America?" *Look,* Vol. 34, No. 14 (July 14, 1970), p. 37.
3. Jerome Tuccille, *Radical Libertarianism: A Right Wing Alternative* (New York: Bobbs, 1970), pp. 1–2.
4. Kenneth M. and Patricia Dolbeare, *American Ideologies: The Competing Political Beliefs of the 1970s* (Chicago: Markham, 1970), p. 210.
5. William F. Buckley, Jr., *Quotations from Chairman Bill,* compiled by David Franke (New Rochelle, N.Y.: Arlington House, 1970), p. 285. On the question of urban renewal, see also Richard Sennett, *The Uses of Disorder: Personal Identity and City Life* (New York: Vintage, 1970), and Norman Mailer, "Why Are We in New York?" *New York Times Magazine* (May 18, 1969).

CHAPTER 3

Day Care: "And a Little Child Shall Lead Them"

. . . if men were mothers—or at least agreed to take a full share in the responsibility for rearing children—my guess is that this country would come to care in a meaningful sense for its future generations much more quickly and happily.

PATRICIA G. BOURNE

When we fully value children and spend our important dollars on them, we will not only provide society's offspring with quality child development services; but also guarantee families adequate housing, good health care, recreation and a decent, secure income; and offer each child a future toward which he or she may look forward.

PAMELA ROBY

Conservatives anxious to protect the American family, liberals eager to help everyone, radicals intent on gaining a head start for the children of have-nots, and visionaries excited about redirecting American family life altogether—this unique constellation of forces keeps day care prominent on our national reform agenda.

Some see day care as an ominous peril; others as potentially rewarding in the extreme. Some focus on it as only a means; others as a worthy end in itself. All that the disputants seem able to agree about is the explosive nature of the current fragile moratorium on sweeping new federal legislation on day care. Still reeling from an unexpected Presidential veto in 1971 of a massive federal breakthrough, the pro-child-care forces are only slowly regaining momentum. None doubt, however, whatever their partisan position in this heated matter, that we will see renewed public and professional debate, legislative turmoil, and a nationwide pressure for you and me to take a concerned and considered position in the matter.

What Is It All About?

The day-care controversy in America can be capsulized in our historic progression:

1. Stigmatized day care (babysitting) for the welfare poor.
2. Low-budget day care (babysitting) for the working, as well as the welfare poor.

3. Subsidized day care (child development orientation à la the OEO Getset Model).
4. Nationwide day care, proposed as a right of all and predicated on a novel development model of the child, its parents, and the state.

Over time a limited-function, custodial, low-level child care for the nuclear family has grown into a widely heralded response, even a potential panacea (in the minds of some partisans), to a wide spectrum of current social ills.

A modest list of claims or hopes for a well-organized, nationwide system of child care commonly includes five major items, which have been listed as follows by Marvin Bloom and Frank J. Hodges:

1. For many children, particularly those from poor or working-poor families, day care could provide relief from a drab, dispirited and possibly deleterious home environment.
2. The day care experience might be socially enhancing, psychologically maturing, educationally invigorating, and culturally stimulating.
3. For the mothers of these children, it might provide relief from a cycle of childbearing to childrearing that seems continuous and, at times, hopeless.
4. Further, the free time gained by day care would provide these mothers with an opportunity to pursue education or career interests.

   It would allow them time to spend in the company of their peers, engaged in activities of their choice, unencumbered by on-going child-care demands.
5. A system staffed with competent personnel would enhance earlier recognition of many developmental, psychological, and social problems. . . .

   Problems causing educational difficulties, (such as in learning to read), problems leading to psychological disfunction, problems inhibiting socialization or maturational processes—all of these, if recognized earlier, could be more successfully coped with or ameliorated.[1]

No wonder, then, that a broad group, including professional social workers, welfare rights organizations, women's liberation spokespeople, and key HEW members of the Nixon Administration, encourage the adoption of this reform, the establishment of a national network of subsidized, quality child-care centers.

Nevertheless, with all of its heady potential this reform has experienced the fate of every other social issue today in America; namely, it has come to have four major, and very different, "realities." As Table 3–1 suggests, and as this chapter will further elucidate, child-care centers are seen by conservatives as some kind of collectivist plot to destroy the family and mold a conformist simp of a child; liberals are drawn to the welfare-relief and women's liberation linkages; and radicals find much to welcome in personality-shaping and counterinstitutional possibilities. Visionaries, in turn, wonder if child-care centers are a costly detraction or a critical supplement to a total social transformation that will see children belonging to, and being cared for by all of us.

States righters and decentralists alike are against the federal government's taking charge of day care as that erodes local autonomy. Indeed, John Birchers

TABLE 3–1. C-L-R-V Views on Child-Care Centers

	Conservatives	Liberals: Patchwork	Liberals: Realization	Radicals	Visionaries
Position:	Against	For: limited	For: total	Partially for	Mixed
Target Group:	Welfare "chiselers"	Poor families	All families	Poor parents	All parents
Goal (General):	To protect the family; hold down "outsiders"	To bring the poor into the mainstream	To extend the logic of the status quo	To advance the course of the revolution	To promote imaginative variations on old forms
Subgoals:	To help keep young children and mothers at home	To use work requirement and "head start" to help make the poor more like everyone else	To direct attention to the potential of every child; call for new gains	To use day care to help mold the anticapitalist new man and to generate counterinstitutions	To loosen up or even dissolve the family unit
Means:	To oppose all day-care legislative moves; to promote private industry franchise operations as alternative to "big government"	To support workcentric, welfare-provoking day-care legislation	To support child development orientation and mental health concerns	Independent neighborhood-conducted day-care operations	Commune and kibbutz model; utopian goals
Problems:	Growing public interest in optional aids to nuclear family child-rearing	High cost of using day care as a welfare reform measure	Stiff public skepticism over wisdom of developmental model	Public and private disdain for "brainwashing" of children	Public dislike of challenge to family as central cultural institution

and radicals alike are against any level of government's moving in here as that would erode individual freedom. As if this opposition were not enough, some groups on the right urge the state to supervise child rearing for the welfare poor so as to ensure the development of a docile and "domesticated" lower class. Certain minority groups eager to help their children move up insist that the state provide "head start" institutions for this purpose. Other minority groups just as strongly reject any inculcation of WASP middle-class values into their children. Some parents prefer programs of enlarging play and wondrous exploration for the very same youngsters that other adults want to have taught only traditional classroom manners, reading, and other basic cognitive skills. And always, on the left, radical groups hover about, insisting that it is the responsibility of the state to provide free child-rearing institutions for everyone who wants them.

In short, when we first think about day care we are misled by what seems to be a rough consensus about its goals, as itemized by Patricia Gerald Bourne:

> It should, of course, care for and protect our children.
>
> It should connect the child's world of home and day care.
>
> It should provide an environment that fosters his development of a sense of self, self-worth, and security, and his ability to get what he wants and needs from the environment around him; and one which stimulates and develops his cognitive and sensory abilities.[2]

When we look closer, however, we discover that we are *not* at all close to a policy-relevant agreement on what day care ought to be—and this is all the conservatives, liberals, radicals, and visionaries concerned with day care can agree about.

Could it be otherwise—if we so desired—and could we move with dispatch and skill? Possibly. For we have done so once before: the creation, within a twenty-four-month period in 1941–1942 filled with wartime pressures, of government-financed nurseries and child-care centers for working mothers that enrolled over 1.5 million American youngsters suggests that the task, although difficult, is not impossible . . . if we once again resolve to do it.[3] To get there from here requires first a consideration of the respective positions of our conservative, liberal, radical, and visionary day-care specialists.

The Conservative View

Few vetoes in modern times have cheered conservatives as much as the Nixon defeat in 1971 of the Comprehensive Child Development Bill. Behind their pleasure with the veto is the unyielding conservative opposition to any institutional alternative to the American family "as we know and love it."

To help explain—and illustrate—this stance, I have reprinted at the end of the chapter a far-sighted essay on the subject from a distinguished conservative journal, *New Guard*. Written by C. P. Sarsfield before the President's veto, the essay sets us the challenge of four fundamental questions in this controversial matter:

1. How reasonable is it to regard such legislation as a "foot in the door"? ("Ultimately, those parents who do not want their children to benefit

from psychological testing and treatment will discover that they have nothing to say in the matter.")

2. How reasonable is it to contend that such legislation is not necessary? ("If the working mothers of the nation were satisfied with their child care arrangements, and told federal inquirers so, they were not exactly clamoring for federal day care, were they?")
3. How reasonable is it to suggest that the hidden goal of such legislation is to mold personalities more suited to slavish dependency on big government?
4. And how reasonable is it to conclude that the stakes entail the very survival of the family itself, replaced now by an unholy trinity of state-parents-child?

Note also, as you carefully assess both the thesis and the way it is developed, the deep dedication of the writer to local state-level over federal-level activities, the antipathy toward anything that smacks of experimenting with people, and the unsparing indictment leveled at sociologists and their imitators.

The stakes could not be higher. The family is represented as "the last, as it is the first, force in defense of Western civilization." So feelings naturally run high, and hyperbole runs even higher, as in the example of OEO sterilization ("Later, if citizens of 'inferior merit' are still reluctant to be sterilized, the government, in the interest of the rest of society, will eliminate the voluntary element altogether"). Such drastic expectations to the side, the article is a compelling and provocative testimony to some of the real dangers inherent in the expansion of government social services as well as to the workings of the conservative heart and mind.

Ethnic Conservative Variation. Six months after Sarsfield's article appeared, philosopher Michael Novak, author of the best-selling book *The Rise of the Unmeltable Ethnics,* developed a comparably provocative argument in a leading Catholic periodical, *Commonweal.*

Child-care programs, Novak insisted, are needed because the old extended family has broken up. The family that wants to stay together, three generations in the same household, is penalized economically. They are penalized emotionally, too: rewards no longer reinforce the old patterns. In this context, child care rapidly becomes too much for two parents alone. Child care, Novak contends, is a social matter, for "children need more than two adult models: they penetrate the defenses of two far too quickly." In addition, in the families that especially interest Novak, those in the working class and the lower-middle class, the wives must work or the husbands hold two jobs if the family is to survive economically.

The liberal solution here, the creation of a state child-care bureaucracy, fails in Novak's view to meet the issue directly. Far more preferable is a plan that would deliberately and generously reward families and neighborhoods that take better care of their *own* children:

1. Elderly family members could receive tax rewards for the time spent in child care.

2. If members of a neighborhood took turns watching the children, they too could be rewarded.

In this way, Novak promises, links between children and neighbors would be strengthened. The morale of the elderly would be bolstered, and the economic burdens of all in the family would be lightened.

Why this pay-for-care tack? To help reverse the atomization ravaging American life. To help reduce alienation through the pouring of resources into local networks among ordinary people. To help use government aid to strengthen families and neighborhoods rather than to take more and more of their functions from them. Above all, perhaps, to help "prevent the interposition of new bureaucracies, based on castes of experts, into the routines of ordinary life." For wherever there are experts, there is arrogance. And ordinary people tend to lose their social skills, tend to grow not stronger but weaker and more dependent. Accordingly, the primary test for a day-care proposal, and every other political idea for that matter, must become whether it helps or penalizes families and neighborhoods.[4]

Private-Enterprise Variation. Still another alternative to no-child-care-at-all or to subsidized family and neighborhood care that appeals to certain conservatives involves the recent entry of business into the field of franchise day-care operations, sometimes sarcastically referred to as "Kentucky Fried Children." Boldly based on business's ability to make a profit, franchise centers reach out to a population of white-collar women—teachers, executives, professionals. The high fees charged are attributed in part to the use of the "latest" in early-learning techniques, a popular item with an upwardly mobile clientele.

On a much smaller and far less-publicized scale, certain industries, like KLH in Cambridge, Avco in Boston, and Tioga Sportswear in Fall River, Massachusetts, have opened day-care centers on the premises for their employees. Should these pioneers succeed in proving that corporate day-care facilities can substantially reduce employee turnover, tardiness, and absenteeism, as well as increase production, such centers could become as commonplace in factories and office buildings (as now at the HEW headquarters) as are industrial cafeterias today, provided, however, that a way is found to accommodate the demand of WITCH, a highly militant woman's liberation group, to have "mothering breaks, say for an hour, along with lunch and coffee breaks."[5]

Certain conservatives welcome such viable alternatives to government encroachment, even though they mean a strange extension of the concerns of the business firm. They are especially taken with those day-care reforms that additionally offer some possibility of helping to shape productive, compulsively achieving, and skillfully competitive adults . . . a kind of ideological bonus for endorsing the "Kentucky Fried Children" approach to the entire child-care dilemma. Private enterprise, anyone?

The Liberal View

Day care is an idea whose time has come, liberals insist, even though they can agree on little else about the subject. Two major views, those of "patchwork" and of "realization" advocates, contend inside the liberal camp, the seesaw going first this way and then that, depending on the momentary degree of liberal sympathy for, or hostility toward, the status quo in mainstream styles of life.

When sympathy for conventional American traditions has the nod, day care is seen by liberals as a means of bringing those unfortunates who have fallen behind the Average American up to the normative achievements of that mythical individual. From the realization perspective the pro-day-care campaign is seen as part of a larger drive to fulfill the "American dream" or to extend the technical rationality of our industrial order into the sloppy areas of our private lives that have thus far eluded it. "Well-being and national planning for all!" the realization motto might energetically read, whereas the motto of the hard-nosed patchwork liberal would probably be "First aid and the status quo for everyone!"

The patchwork orientation has dominated the rationale for day care since the establishment of the first day nurseries a century ago. Adherents today, however, are divided on what it is they primarily hope to patch:

1. The tax rolls, touched and often severely strained by unpopular welfare costs.
2. The economic duress of welfare families.
3. The emotional and intellectual deprivation of children in have-not households.

Accordingly, certain patchwork supporters have been sympathetic with reforms that:

1. Force welfare mothers even of preschool children either to take jobs or to care for the children of other welfare mothers who are working.
2. Give children a "head start" in their primary school years, compensating for the apparent inability of public schools to educate or understand the non-Anglo or non-middle-class child.

Liberals so oriented find much to discourage them, however, in the high costs of day care (estimated at $2,330 per child). They are perplexed as well by the serious problems of family rights as well as the quality-of-child-care issues raised by pressure-to-work tactics. And they are cowed by the antagonism of have-not activists. The latter, not surprisingly, resent the patchwork assumption that the lower-class family is a defective socializing agent for children.

Critics also contend that the patchwork enthusiasts exaggerate the value of freeing mothers, especially welfare mothers, for employment. This reasoning is thought by Peggy and Peter Steinfels to be based on some very questionable assumptions:

> That there are employable skills possessed by mothers on welfare; or—
> That they can be quickly trained to acquire these skills, and—
> That the economy in the face of newly emerging employment patterns can absorb a significant number of such newly available workers.[6]

Patchwork advocates reply lamely that demonstration projects support their line of reasoning, that many welfare mothers prefer work to home life, and that the labor market has infinite capacity . . . if only bad-mouthing pessimists will stop undermining consumer confidence in the marketplace, with the resultant artificial decrease in the creation of new jobs.

However uneven the fortunes of the patchwork crowd, the position of the realization camp is not much stronger, for its more modern goal of liberating *all* women to work and helping *all* children to develop to their fullest sets it apart from large numbers of Americans quick to judge such objectives as undesirably radical (although today we have more working mothers than ever before, more than twice as many as in 1950, and the figures are expected to double in the next decade). In truth, however, these day-care advocates fundamentally accept the values and direction of the present society; their argument is simply that these national goals are far from realized today.

Typical of the realization supporters are members of the National Organization for Women (NOW), the woman's liberation group with the broadest consensus of any in the movement. NOW's three major goals (twenty-four-hour free day care, equal pay for equal work, and abortion on request) are directly related to freeing women from their sex-role occupations and would allow them to participate equally with men in the contemporary labor market. Their prorealization stance is based on their view of day care as crucial in the integration of economic structures *in our present society*.

Overall, the day-care blueprint of realizationists, whether NOW members or others, includes two basic components. The first is to expand the accessibility of day care and enhance its character so that women of *all* social classes will consider such *public* (or tax-subsidized private) care an attractive alternative to home care. This goes far beyond the preoccupation of the patchwork crowd with welfare mothers. Second, the realizationists also go beyond the work-promoting orientation of the patchworkers to offer a fresh and controversial concept for day care, namely, child development. As explained by Maya Pines, the dream is a large one:

> The pioneers of early learning want to give every child a chance to develop his capacities to the fullest. Their techniques will increase man's variety, not reduce it. If they succeed, middle-class children will no longer be held back to some comfortable average—and poor children will no longer be crushed before they can learn to learn. Both will be allowed to find their own intellectual identities. Both will come closer to reaching their potential. This should make each human life more interesting, more productive, and more rewarding.[7]

Realizationists concede that this represents an extreme departure from a hundred previous years of narrow public and government attitudes toward early-childhood services. But they insist that their agenda for nurturing is "as American as apple pie," consistent with our tradition of public education, and a natural next step in the evolution of American society.

President Nixon strongly disagreed when, with his 1972 veto of the Comprehensive Child Development Bill, he struck hard at the realization viewpoint:

> For the Federal Government to plunge headlong financially into supporting child development would commit the vast moral authority of the National Government to the side of communal approaches to child-rearing over against the family-centered approach.[8]

Anxious lest the child development orientation "diminish both parental authority and parental involvement with children,"[9] the President made plain his own strictly patchwork view of day care as an unfortunate but necessary deviation from American norms that involves a minimal effort associated with the welfare poor.

Day-care critics have been quick to make much of a central dilemma that undermines the realization approaches and divides its advocates. Once one leaves the highly rarefied level that calls for the fullest possible development of a child's potential, it becomes clear that there is actually *no* consensus on such real-life issues as operational particulars and subsidiary values. Many parents, for example, do not believe that their children can or should determine their own actions or decide what to believe. Nor is developing intellectual capacities to the fullest necessarily a clearly held ideal in a situation in which other capacities—social, athletic, and so on—may compete for attention. Child development, in short, much to the confusion and chagrin of certain over-simplifying realizationists, is a concept that is interpreted very differently from class to class and ethnic bloc to bloc.

Even where consensus may exist locally, the necessary funding often does not, this lack constituting a second and telling weakness in the realization program. The national average cost of day care is about $800 per child per annum, but this figure is based in part on a ratio of one adult to thirty children for each hour of contact. The government now requires one adult with a degree for every five children (Israeli programs operate on a one-to-four ratio), and this requirement promises to double or triple the average cost. An OEO study, for example, of "exemplary" day-care programs shows that those that maintain a ratio of one adult to five children for each hour of contact and that have first-rate educational, developmental, health, and parent-involvement components cost between $2,500 and $3,500 per child per annum.[10] And opponents of the vetoed Comprehensive Child Development Bill never tire of pointing out that the legislation would have cost as much as $2 billion in its first year alone (proponents retort that overruns on defense contracts cost $29 billion in 1972).

Lest you be left here with a false impression of liberal immobility, please note that for all of their otherwise basic differences liberals *do* agree that something has to be done . . . and now! By which they mean, at the barest minimum, that rationality *must* be brought immediately into the "nonsystem" in federal day care.

Few inside or outside of the sixty or so child-care programs run by the federal government deny that they have contradictory goals, little exchange of information, different categories of eligible clientele, separate supervising agencies, distinct procedures and guidelines, and nonmatching geographic boundaries defining local communities for planning and service delivery. Weakened by competition and conflict among agencies, this chaotic, uncoordinated "non-system" serves children poorly, if at all.

Liberal reformers naturally urge extensive consolidation and coordination of agencies. They hold out the promise of such related gains as:

1. Reduction of per-child costs through broader sharing of services, joint purchasing, and elimination of overlap.
2. Matching of geographic boundaries by which local communities are defined so that community boards may develop, oversee, and coordinate the programs of the various agencies.

Politically, however, as one student of the subject, Pamela Roby, wryly concludes, "the task will not be easy for although each agency and interest group recognizes the need for coordinated child care programs and policies, each wants to be the one to coordinate the others."[11]

The Radical Perspective

If the conservatives want to go forward with day care very slowly and the liberals want to raise up the poor (patchwork) or raise up the child (realization), the radicals take a still different tack with their dual concern for character molding and parallel-institution building.

Radicals are taken with the possibility that a generation of children reared beyond the influence of oppressed, brainwashed women might prove open to anticapitalistic thoughts and might well adapt to a noncapitalist style of life. Collective child-rearing, modeled perhaps on Chinese and Cuban models, is seen as one way to mitigate undesirable character traits, including those mainstays of the market mentality—competitiveness, selfishness, violence, acquisitiveness, and intolerance. Children in radical day-care centers will be changed by their cooperative, nonauthoritarian experience. As they learn to share and be tolerant, they are expected to grow up to change the society, whatever its initial ethos.

Of special interest in this connection, because they are better developed and less downgraded than the Chinese and Cuban efforts, are the child-care systems of Israel and Russia. The kibbutzim and children's houses of the latter two nations are cited often because they illustrate the group rearing of children and multiple mothering. Such methods are psychologically helpful and effective sources of socialization and of intellectual stimulation. Above all, however, these models excite as a positive and relatively fast means of instilling radically new values.

Radicals find the majority of our day-care centers glorified baby-sitting services. They condemn them for teaching children to be passive, for programming them through routine, and for instructing them in an invisible, proconformist curriculum: toward work (subservience), race (superiority/inferiority), sex roles (dominant/submissive), competition (valuable), and cooperation (problematic). Or, as two young women explain, with the "hidden curriculum" of most centers:

> by the age of four, children are assimilating the idea that a woman's place is in the home. . . . They are learning to follow directions without asking

> why. They are learning how to deny their own feelings and needs in order to win approval from adults.

The writers urge their audience to conclude with them that "as radicals . . . our goals for children are in conflict with those of the institutions . . . corporations and universities."[12]

In this same vein the Radical Education Project (REP), for example, has distributed a pamphlet attacking government and industrial day care as a deceptive means of enticing women into low-paying jobs: "If the need for child care is isolated from other needs, women will be caught in limited reforms that will also train children to be docile, obedient workers that the system needs." From still another angle, Rosalyn Baxandall, a New York founder of the pioneer Liberation Nursery, adds additional doubts:

> Too often it ties women to lousy jobs. The industries that are setting them up are the ones that can't keep employees; they're bribing the women. Day care centers should be in the neighborhoods where people live. It's not a good idea to drag a child to work with you on the subway.

Wrapping it all up, the day-care practitioner adds: "Besides, parents ultimately don't have too much to say about day care when a big corporation is controlling it."[13]

Similarly, the pet reform of the realization liberals, the developmental focus in child day care, has come in for scathing radical review. The radicals maintain that like the earlier Head Start the developmental orientation promises far too much and only sets the poor up for still another disappointment. As class-oriented radicals see it, the issue is helping all children begin with *equal* conditions . . . and this, in turn, requires income redistribution, the democratization of privilege, and similar radical efforts that extent far beyond the mere provision of eight hours of good developmental child care plus good health care and nutrition. As an article in *Ramparts* says, "To condemn (poor) children for not flourishing in school or on the job after attending a child development program which is only a fraction of their total experience only reveals our insensitivity to their real life circumstances. True equality of opportunity can only be achieved by the creation of equality of conditions."

What with their very particular dream of character molding, then, and their enormous differences with nonradical efforts in practice and in theory (as with the liberal deemphasis on the proequality campaign), the radicals go it alone. The day-care enthusiasts among them press on the establishment a demand for only space and money and insist on the authority to run their own centers themselves. Typical is a situation in the District of Columbia that *Ramparts* reported on:

> Women, family groups, black churches all have begun their own day-care centers, many of them unlicensed, in an effort to avoid paying the outrageous prices charged by organized nursery schools. In effect these underground centers could represent the beginning of a new school system outside the public schools and the existing school systems. They are staffed by volunteer labor of mothers and fathers and charge as little as $60 per year per child.

That contrasts with HEW day-care guidelines which call for spending $2348 a year per child, most of which goes to pay professionals.[14]

These parallel or counterinstitutions are unique in the stress placed on the presence of male teachers, the role reversals encouraged in the "housekeeping corner," and other aids to the installation of radically new values and ideas.

The Visionary Perspective

As in the case of the liberal rift among patchwork and realization supporters, a sharp division taxes the strength of the visionary camp and dilutes the visionary's impact on the entire day-care dialogue.

On the one hand, there are feminists like Shulameth Firestone who roundly condemn all day-care centers. As they are now constituted, they are simply a means of taking pressure off women and thereby undermining women's revolutionary consciousness ("Day-care centers buy women off"). She urges a redirection of energy instead toward the feminist and the cybernetic revolutions. This redirection will make possible three remarkable goals:

1. the freeing of women from the tyranny of their biology by any means available (including artificial reproduction), and the diffusion of the childbearing role to the society as a whole, to men and other children as well as women;
2. the economic independence and self-determination of all (including children); and—
3. the total integration of women and children into the larger society.[15]

From this point of view our families will soon become superfluous; children will belong to everyone and will be cared for by everyone.

From a related perspective there is much sadness—and anger—over the stress being placed in day-care centers on early-learning gains. Writer Eda J. LeShan explains:

> Unwilling to make long-range plans, unwilling to commit ourselves to the cost of saving our world, we have latched onto the insane notion that early training in cognitive skills will solve our human dilemma. We want so desperately to believe that filling our children's heads with facts will remove the decay of cities, the pollution of our air and water, and the involvement in immoral, psychotic wars. In the absence of decent nutrition for millions of children, in the absence of anything but token, windowdressing programs for job training and employment of masses of our population, in the absence of a communal willingness to give up greed and self-interest or a kind of nationalism that may end in a nuclear holocaust, we have become obsessed with a gimmick—the simple fact that young children can memorize all sorts of irrelevant facts if we force them to.

Such a preoccupation is traced back to an extraordinary indictment:

> we are a nation which has come to hate children—to live in terror of nature and childhood—because we are so desperately frightened by the dangers in our lives.
>
> We are desperately frightened because we do not know how to make

> people care about each other or how to be less violent and warlike; we feel paralyzed by the enormity of the social problems we face, and in our panic we search longingly, hysterically, for easy answers.[16]

Day-care centers with anything less than an effective and total commitment to helping us all overcome the self-centeredness of the individual and the nationalism of groups are dismissed as "easy answers."

On the other hand, there *are* visionaries who have much more use for child-care centers. For one, Eva Figes, a feminist and the author of *Patriarchal Attitudes,* looks forward to a day when children must be treated as primarily the property of the state: "This means fairly substantial child allowances for all children, and sufficient state and/or industrial nurseries for children."[17] At issue here is the utility of day care as an instrument for helping to modify the whole family structure. The nuclear family is roundly condemned as a poor place both for women to spend their lives and for children to grow up in. Or as writer Susan Edmisten explains:

> From whatever quarter and point of view, the same message seems to be coming through: people no longer want to raise their children alone, in the isolation of the nuclear family. If the thinking of the flourishing psychotherapeutic profession has any validity at all, one conclusion is inescapable: our parents messed us up. Thoughtful people are now saying they don't want to be on the other end of the destruction. For many parents and children, the new notion of day care promises a solution.[18]

The nuclear family is not especially healthy, one might say, for children or for other living things. So, day care to the rescue!

But not just any kind of day care. Rather, the kind most closely attuned with the vague colorful goals of children's liberation . . . the kind that features men teachers, consciousness-raising sessions, and the exhilarating like. According to Eda LeShan,

> A nation that really gives a damn about the learning potentials of young children would be providing decent housing, parent-education programs in all child-health-care centers and schools, and rich nursery-school experiences with loving, sensitive, insightful adults. Such a nation would create a climate of life in which every child would be told, in deeds as well as words, "How beautiful you are. What a wonder of nature! What a joy it is to watch your own special and unique flowering. Let me re-experience the wonders of childhood, the pleasures of learning and growing, as I watch your unfolding, and in that sharing, help us both to become more profoundly human—and ourselves."[19]

Communes come readily to the minds of certain visionaries as a natural locus for such a "climate of life." But overall, enthusiasm for such small-scale experimentation in child care is regularly qualified by the insistence that liberation ultimately requires the *total* transformation of society.

Summary

What is one to make of all of this? According to Bettye M. Caldwell, that not even day care itself is sure:

> it does not know whether it should serve the child, the parent, or the family. It cannot make up its mind whether it is a service for families with social pathology or for all families, whether it should be limited to children from economically underprivileged families, or be offered to all children, whether it wants to change children or preserve cultural styles from one generation to the next.[20]

It is precisely in this area of planning for our children, of saying much about the kinds of children we want, that we are most timid in this country. (Rebecca Smith of the Child Welfare League of America observes, "We cannot name one community in the United States with services sufficient to meet the needs of its children."[21])

When all is said and done there is only *one* common national denominator in the matter of the *kind* of child care we seem to want (and how much we are willing to spend for it): the coalition that has formed around day care is really a coalition based on the needs of the 11.5 million women in the labor force. It is only thereafter, and quite secondarily, a coalition interested in the special developmental needs of all children. There is, of course, "no reason why the needs of adults and the needs of children cannot be complimentary—no reason, that is, until the question of our individual and national willingness to pay is faced."[22]

To pursue such unsettling and unflattering controversy further, let us ponder the following:

> What is local control? Is it governance by persons living within an area served by an individual child care center or perhaps two or three such centers? Is it direction by communities of 5,000 or more, 50,000 or more, or over 100,000?[23]

> What characteristics are child care workers to have? Should they be required to meet specific professional standards? Set by whom, and consisting of what? Should they reflect the racial and ethnic characteristics of the population? If so, how can this representation best be obtained?[24]

> if middle-class women can work, why should welfare participants be relieved of the need to work? Despite this, however, would society be willing to pay for another program so that the American "work ethic" may be fulfilled?[25]

> Should day care be available to all, or only to low-income and welfare recipients? If it is made available to only the welfare recipient and working poor, it may acquire the stigma attributed to present public assistance programs. If, on the other hand, it is available as a subsidy to all classes, the costs would be trebled or quadrupled.[26]

> in the light of pressing social welfare needs—for example, health-care services, housing, education, income maintenance, and so on—what is the importance of day care? . . . how great a resource investment should be made when there are alternative social welfare programs currently competing for funds.[27]

And these, of course, are only a few of the nettlesome questions to be answered. Money questions are among them, and assuming that high-quality developmental care can cost as much as $2,500 per child, a host of difficult questions clamor for attention:

> Will those in favor of getting welfare women out to work be willing to pay $5,000 for care for a woman's two children in order to save $2,400 on her AFDC grant?
>
> Will a woman whose earning power is $6,000–$8,000 be willing to spend $5,000 of it for child care in the private market?
>
> If she isn't, can the franchisers now entering the business with enthusiasm make a profit?
>
> Will industry and labor unions be willing to provide that magnitude of fringe benefit?[28]

Provocative in this matter is the warning of sociologist Pamela Roby: "In coming years, the importance of cost as a child care issue will vary with the political priority given to children and mothers. . . . The creation of adequate funds for child development services will require the creation of a political priority for children and mothers."[29]

If this is so, then in conjunction with all the quandaries and controversies cited throughout this chapter it would seem that in the short run the prospects for day care in America are very uncertain . . . at best. And yet, the need has one expert, Mary Dublin Keyserling, issuing the following ambitious call:

> We should set a goal for the provision, over the next five years, of developmental day care services for at least two million additional children, merely to catch up with the worst of current backlog. At least half these places should be fully subsidized and the rest partially subsidized, with fees charged according to income. Federal appropriations of at least $3 to $4 billion a year would be needed for this purpose.[30]

This same expert also warns that "until very substantial amounts of public funds become available, the gap between need and available good care will remain shocking."[31]

Now, *if* you were interested in seeing high-quality public-aided day care expand beyond the 900,000 places we presently license in this country for the use of 6 million children of working mothers, you can still work for short-term, feasible, and incremental gains toward this goal. Typical of the sort of strategies that warrant your careful consideration is Patricia Gerald Bourne's hard-headed plan for securing piecemeal advances:

1. To help with the deterrent of building costs we could create an FHA-style, long-term guaranteed mortgage arrangement. This could provide large-scale capital for day care center construction at a very low cost to the government, and might have considerable appeal to the nation's bankers.
2. To spur interest in center enrollment we might give tax credits to employers if they pay for day care services for the children of their employees, especially if such people are hired off of the welfare rolls.

3. Similarly, we might grant any day care program, including those geared to profit-making, credits on their building mortgages if they take welfare or near-welfare children.
4. Adult education funds might be linked to a kind of instruction in "child development" that includes the operation of nursery or day care.
5. Less energy might be spent pressuring the legislative branch for new appropriations, and more on ferreting out and combining existing federal and private funds.

Perhaps most promising, the plan's designer concludes, is a maneuver that would seek to link our growing national concern over wage stability with child care. Like the Scandinavians before us we could choose to substitute social benefits that generate activity in the economy *without* inflationary stress in place of wage increases. Free or subsidized child-care services, if once seen by wage earners as a constructive substitution for (inflationary) wage increases, just might be politically acceptable.

This strategy of "piecemeal picking and poking" at the present system, according to the plan's author, is about all that our national ambivalence over desirable styles of child care and our reluctance to pay for more than "baby-sitting" currently permit:

> [It] may strike those who have hoped for a bold and straightforward initiative as incredibly depressing. I would argue simply that a politically acceptable bold initiative at this point in history would have to take such a form that it would be a genuine disservice to the nation's children.[32]

Our attitudes toward day care reveal much about us . . . and may reveal much also to our children.

Too much, perhaps, if we do not soon move to ensure for *every* child a childhood not one iota inferior to that which we want or dream of for our own.

> . . . children have the greatest need of all. Our goal should be free, universal, consumer-(this means parents) controlled child care, where children, even rich children, have the daily companionship and learning opportunity of being with peers as well as their parents. . . . (MAUREEN ORTH)

FOOTNOTES

1. Marvin Bloom and Frank J. Hodges, "Day Care Centers?" *The Humanist* (July–August 1971), p. 33.
2. Patricia Gerald Bourne, "What Day Care Centers Ought to Be," *The New Republic* (February 12, 1971), p. 22.
3. Judy Kleinberg, "Public Child Care: Our Hidden History," *The Second Wave,* Vol. 1, No. 3 (1971), p. 24.
4. Michael Novak, "A Politics of Family and Neighborhood," *Commonweal* (May 19, 1972), p. 257.
5. Jacquin Sanders, "Day Care Centers—Who Needs Them?" *Philadelphia Daily News* (January 25, 1971), p. 15.
6. Peggy and Peter Steinfels, "Day Care: Patchwork, Realization, or Utopia?" *Soundings,* Vol. 55, No. 1 (Spring 1972), p. 52.

7. Ibid., p. 52.
8. Ibid., p. 47.
9. Ibid., p. 48.
10. Bourne, op. cit., p. 22.
11. Pamela Roby, "Young Children: Issues and Goals for the Next Decade," *Child Care—Who Cares? Foreign and Domestic Infant and Early Childhood Development Policies,* Pamela Roby, ed. (New York: Basic Books, 1973), p. 21.
12. L. Gross and P. MacEwan, "On Day Care," *Women: A Journal of Liberation,* Vol. 1., No. 2 (Winter, 1970), pp. 27–29.
13. Quoted in Susan Edmisten, "The Psychology of Day Care," *New York Magazine,* (April 5, 1971), p. 45.
14. "Underground Day Care," *Ramparts* (October 1971), p. 19.
15. Shulameth Firestone, *The Dialectic of Sex* (New York: Morrow, 1971), pp. 238–240.
16. Eda J. LeShan, "The Sesame Street Syndrome," *The Humanist* (November–December 1972), p. 9.
17. Eva Figes, *Patriarchial Attitudes* (Greenwich, Conn.: Fawcett, 1970), p. 179.
18. Edmisten, op. cit., p. 46.
19. LeShan, op. cit., p. 11.
20. Bettye M. Caldwell, "A Timid Giant Grows Bolder," *Saturday Review* (February 20, 1971), p. 49.
21. As quoted in Grace W. Weinstein, "Communities That Care," *Parent's Magazine* (May 1972), p. 113.
22. Ibid.
23. Roby, op. cit., p. 11.
24. Ibid., p. 21.
25. Bloom and Hodges, op. cit., p. 34.
26. Ibid.
27. Ibid.
28. Bourne, op. cit., p. 22.
29. Roby, op. cit., p. 5.
30. Mary Dublin Keyserling, "Day Care: Crisis and Challenge," *Childhood Education* (November 1971), p. 64.
31. Ibid., p. 66.
32. Bourne, op. cit., p. 22.

READING

Another Step Toward 1984

C. P. Sarsfield

In Brigham City, Utah, there is a school for 2,000 students run by the federal government. Its most unusual feature is that, within its wire fence, it provides living and sleeping facilities for the students—and necessarily so, since all the students are Navajo Indians from New Mexico. They are bussed a thousand

Reprinted with permission from *New Guard* (January–February 1972), 1221 Massachusetts Ave., N.W., Washington, D.C. 20005.

miles to Utah to school. Every fall, the federal government charters Greyhound buses to take them away from their families, homes, and culture.

Most of the children are older than average for their grade level, because, while young, the mothers often hide them in order to keep them home. But even twelve or thirteen is too early to be jerked away from the roots which nourished one and to be thrown into a sterile environment. Navajo religion is highly animistic—the elements of nature are endowed with divinity and are worshiped. Ordinarily, the tribe gives support to this religion, and community religious celebrations and prayer nourish the blossom, though small, of faith. Thirteen-year-olds do not know the rituals; they cannot remember the difficult prayers. And they are not allowed to remember any divinity for the months they are at school. The federal government is so happy with its project that it has now decided that all children should be entitled, as a matter of their "right," of course, to similar "care" to shelter them from the unhealthy influences of their families. It has created the Child Development Act. At this writing, the bill, passed easily by both Houses, is in conference, shortly to be sent to the President. Efforts are underway to obtain a Presidential veto. By the time this goes to press, that effort will have been successful or will have failed: if the former is the case, this article will serve to clarify one more threat of centralized government in preparation for a battle on a later day. If the veto is not obtained, this article may stand to remind its readers of yet another lost opportunity to conserve something valuable in America.

The Child Development Bill moved effortlessly through both Houses of Congress disguised as an antipoverty measure. Legislation dealing with poor and minority groups of the nation is always easy to get through Congress. All that is needed is a huge sob-story publicity campaign on the wretched condition of their lives, their inability to help themselves, their neglected state, their desperate need for the only help available to them: the bureaucratic largess from the federal coffers. And such a campaign is easy to sell most people: it appeals to the slumbering guilt nerves so sensitized by the liberals, it appeals to the dormant impulses of Christian charity; the execution of such schemes is relatively painless to most citizens: the responsibility for action is simply shifted to the government's shoulders. A few conservatives, or thoughtful men endowed with basic good sense, may object and complain, but they are discounted as "insensitive."

So this was an antipoverty measure. Those sections of the bill calling for its programs to be "universally available . . . to all children as a matter of right" and stipulating a mixture of "all socioeconomic levels" were overlooked. The sponsors of the bill said it was merely a federal subsidy of day-care centers (nothing exactly new, by the way), so that welfare mothers could get to work and off welfare. Somehow, it didn't strike anybody as extraordinary that $100 million for the first fiscal year and $2 billion for the next was a little expensive for hiring nurses and nursery school teachers, or that in five years it might be $10 billion. The provisions requiring only 65 per cent of the funding initially to be used for the economically deprived were glossed over.

The statistics of the Women's and Children's Bureaus of the Department of Health, Education, and Welfare do not support the theory of the supposedly desperately needed day-care centers, either.

In 1950, 22 per cent of the labor force in the United States was composed of mothers of children under eighteen years of age. In 1970, that had risen to 42 per cent of the labor force, totalling 11.5 million women. A significant increase, one might think. But more statistics should focus the matter. A 1970 federal survey found that 70 per cent of such children had been receiving free care—in their home by another family member or relative. Only 30 per cent of working mothers had to pay for their children's care. On July 30, 1971, a Finance Committee report could state. "In summary, then, most working mothers . . . express satisfaction with their present child care arrangements."

Yet two months to the very day after this report was published, the House passed the Child Development Bill. Apparently few had bothered to read the committee report. If the working mothers of the nation were satisfied with their child-care arrangements, and total federal inquiries so, they were not exactly clamoring for federal day-care, were they?

It is not as if the federal government were not doing anything for children now. An Appalachian Regional Commission report discovered 310 federally funded early childhood programs currently administered by 18 different federal agencies. This included some 480,000 children in Head Start programs costing $1,050 each and approximately 35,000 children in Follow Through programs, with an expected cost of $800 each. Most federally funded programs are established at local levels, and without any coordination with state governments—a bureaucratic idiosyncrasy, making for duplication of efforts and services, loss of money, and inefficiency of administration. For example, in South Carolina alone, 40,000 more children could be served by Head Start if it were allowed to be administered by the state. But no, federal bureaucrats are highly jealous of their power over human affairs. And H.R. 1, the Family Assistance Bill, passed earlier in the session, had provisions of its own for day-care programs.

No, the day-care veneer of the Child Development Bill is pretty thin. The Senate Committee on Labor and Public Welfare report reveals more between the lines of the intent of the bill: "During the past decade there has been national recognition of the importance of child development processes for education, pediatrics, family development, mental health, and artistic endeavors." The interest in mental health begins to be visible: "Currently, research has focused primarily on the cognitive development of the child. Little attention has been paid to . . . moral development, use of aggression . . . emotional development, socialization. . . ." Current research has informed only on cognitive development. Such language as this seems to reek of the desire for research into other types of development. The statement of the purposes of the bill itself suggests what these may be, as it explicitly abandons the day-care justification for broader realms: "millions of children are suffering unnecessary harm from lack of adequate day care services."

"We must see to it," said Dr. Edward Zigler, Director of the Office of Child Development, "that . . . centers are institutions where our nation's children . . . can enrich one another." A tender-sounding idea, one that would gladden the heart of a kibbutz director. Alas, it flies in the face of reality in that children's abilities to "enrich one another" are sharply limited, practically by definition. Children cannot teach one another virtues. Charity, decency, and other moral qualities do not arise spontaneously—they are learned from the emulation of moral adults.

Children subjected to a communal situation become excessively responsive to peer pressure, which, in turn, is easily created by adult hands. Communally raised children grow up to be anxious conformists, slavishly obedient to the authorities they are told to respect.

Yet such a collectivism of child rearing seems to be precisely what certain advocates of the bill have not too far in the back of their minds. The bill has all the practical potential to be a grand-scale social experiment with the nation's youth.

The privately sponsored and initiated propaganda used for background support further clarifies that hidden intent. *Look* magazine devoted most of its January 26, 1971, issue to cheerfully propagandizing the decline and imminent fall of the American family. Women's magazines have for a long time been telling women how downtrodden they are in having to care for their children.

Donald Fraser, by some irony the successor to Walter Judd's Congressional seat, is one of the most enthusiastic supporters of government-supported children's collectives. France, Sweden, and Russia have all been extolled within the pages of the *Congressional Record* as Mr. Fraser has explained how these countries have found alternatives to child rearing.

"It is unreasonable to demand that the parents should meet all the child's needs, still less that the mother should accept responsibility for the child's upbringing to the extent she does now. This responsibility must be shared by both parents, both of whom need outside support." The old triangle relationship that supported Western civilization was father-mother-child. (Only a few despicable reactionaries even think of another Trinity, which created all these people and keeps them in existence.) The new one will be state-parents-child.

"The purpose of upbringing is to promote the development of children's personalities and their social adjustment," states a Swedish expert on child development.

And that, perhaps, is the crucial attitude. Social adjustment is not the purpose of upbringing. Psychology has long recognized that the stability provided by a loving mother is the most important influence on emotional development; without it, insecurity, hatred, self-doubt, and the antisocial consequences of delinquents and deviants arise. The purpose of upbringing is to guide a child to the most complete development and full maturity that he as an individual is capable of realizing, with careful respect for his distinct human nature. For such purposes the family is the ideal, close-knit, profoundly mutually interested nurturing body.

In today's otherwise increasingly standardized world, the family is the last bastion of individualism. In an emotionally rich situation, a child learns that he is different from all others. He has a sense of his own intrinsic value—because he is what he is, he has a dignity apart from his intelligence, from his social class, from his tangible accomplishments. The prevailing sociological view would deplore such "maladjustment." To sociologists or their imitators, only an identity conglomerate with one's peers is desirable. The achievement of some socially approved, communally beneficial, material goal is the only exaltation they would allow the human spirit.

Discussion of the importance of the family unit and of the dangers of personality standardization did not occur in the Congressional hearings on the Child Development Bill, however. The House Committee on Education and Labor held a mere three hearings, with only five main witnesses, two of them Congresswomen from New York, who praised the bill as a "modest, conservative" step toward liberating women from the sufferings created by insufficient child services. Two governors and a former governor testified as well. Their conversation dealt with the fine points of bureaucracy and administration: the ramifications of bypassing state authority in administration, the waste of money and efficiency.

That federally established local programs are better suited to the needs and desires of local circumstances than state programs is a misconception fostered by the planners of federal schemes, one argued against by the governors at the hearings, to the exclusion of more substantive examination.

A state-initiated research group, The Education Commission of the States Task Force on Early Childhood Education, issued a report supporting the adoption of child development services, to be administered, of course, with state participation in planning and execution. The Commission's vision of child development was different in essence from that of the framers of H.R. 6748 and S.2007. The first priority of the state commission was "strengthening the role of the family as the first and most fundamental influence on child development." No mention of the need to produce "well-adjusted" children, or of relieving intolerable burdens of motherhood. The difference is significant to note, perhaps because it indicates that the ECS report was written by individuals closer to the "people" of the nation than Federal City ideologues who are notorious for living in a world of their pet illusions.

The bill under consideration provides for the establishment of Child Development Centers, Child Development Councils, and a Model Federal Government Child Development Program. The program calls for complete services of "mental, physical, and social examination, diagnosis, identification and treatment" of all children. In addition, it would establish Child Advocacy Officers and Neighborhood Offices of Child Advocacy.

The Child Advocates are to supplant the parents as guardians of a child's welfare. That is not the stated purpose of the office—such blatancy is not necessary; but the outlines of the trend are here laid out. The Child Advocates would function in neighborhoods as itinerant troubleshooters, searching for deficiencies or abuses in the care or environment of children, and proceed to "take such actions as may be appropriate" with the child or family. Powers of decision will rest entirely with these Child Advocates—they will operate subject only to their own discretion once they are hired by a Council on Child Development.

These Councils are the supposed "local supervision" bodies. Great amounts of space are consumed in defining the composition of the Councils: ten members, half of whom must be parents of children served by Child Development Programs, the rest of whom are to be "broadly representative of the economically disadvantaged," and one who might be (but is not required to be) specifically skilled in child service. The Councils, however, are figurehead bodies. Hidden away in a later section of the text is the provision that after six months, suggestions are to be culled for the purpose of promulgating federal standards for day-care programs. The *Encyclopaedia Britannica Dictionary* definition of promulgate is "to put into effect by public proclamation, as a law or dogma." Federal standards might supposedly be guidelines—but they are effective law. Governor Moore of West Virginia, speaking of experiences with the Model Cities Program before the House Committee on Education and Labor, testified that ". . . local policy boards soon discovered that the policy was really made in Washington."

It would be comforting, but nonetheless somewhat rosy-eyed to maintain that the federal standards are sure to be good. Like the woman in the supermarket who, when told of the health hazards of the preservative BHT, which has been banned in Germany and the United Kingdom, exclaims: "Why, I'm sure our government wouldn't let anything *bad* be given to us!" the American people trust the intentions and actions of their government. That is actually the ideal arrangement: citizens are naturally entitled to that measure of security. But in a revolutionary age natural orders are disrupted. Trust of the government is a luxury that can be afforded only at dire peril. And this is a revolutionary age.

Trusting, docile citizens were confident that the Office of Economic Opportunity would take all necessary and proper steps to alleviate poverty and make life in America more perfect for everyone. They trusted that, if created by the federal government, it would be good. Now the OEO is providing free sterilizations to the people of Anderson County, Tennessee. Just as the Child Development Centers, established as amendment to the OEO Extension Act, will provide free medical, mental, and emotional testing and treatment. A small beginning is all that is needed.

When OEO finds voluntary sterilizations (so far about twenty people have presented themselves for this service) to be contributory to the health and happiness of Appalachian hillbillies, the programs will expand. OEO will decide not to limit the opportunities for such health and happiness to only those enlightened who seek them out: it will, in its all-encompassing concern for the people, gently chide all of a certain social strata to explore the possibilities further. Later, if citizens of "inferior merit" are still reluctant to be sterilized, the government, in the interest of the rest of society, will eliminate the voluntary element altogether. Likewise Child Development mental care will initially be available to all youngsters and all will be invited to participate in it. Ultimately, those parents who do not want their children to benefit from psychological testing and treatment will discover that they have nothing to say in the matter. In the children's interests, of course, as a matter of their right to a good life. If the children object, well, that's simply proof of their need for these services.

And suddenly, those who today approve of voluntarily sterilizing the hillbillies in eastern Tennessee with federal money might find that it might not be such a good idea, after all—not for them. And when parents find their children removed from them by government command, they might realize that the Navajo Indians in Brigham City, Utah, are not exactly privileged by the federal help which equals federal intervention in their lives. The acquiescent middle classes are the ones whom this realization is suddenly going to strike with a mighty force. Just as bussing became an issue when it affected middle America, so child control will be resisted only when its effect is painfully felt. The ire of a righteously indignant populace will be glorious to behold, and its effects may be incalculable—if only the brainwashing has not been too complete by that time so that, complaisantly, we sacrifice what is most dear to us for the sake of being "well-socialized."

And that danger is a real one to fear. Daily, it seems, our nation sacrifices—or allows to be sacrificed—more and more principles and ideals that constitute her nature. Like fine cloth fraying from all sides, becoming merely the naked threads that used to hold together a magnificently variegated design, our traditions are being eroded and torn away. By law we are violating our human natures, refusing to do what is natural and good for us. We have allowed ourselves to be deprived, as a nation, of our recognition of God. We have permitted governments or their agents to care for us, to educate us, to tell us what we will do and what we will not do. Our children are standardized by mass-produced public education, by television, by movies, by magazines, by the popular pressure for "peer-group" cohesiveness. The family—unique, woven around itself, charged with emotionalism and loyalties—is the last, as it is the first, force in defense of Western civilization.

CHAPTER 4

Alternative Prescriptions for a Healthier America: Conservative and Liberal Viewpoints

All indications are that within the next few years "medical politics" will become every bit as central to life in these United States as black politics and women's politics.

M. G. MICHAELSON

Asked to assess the profession of which he is an angry young member, Dr. Thomas Levin does not hesitate to identify "an archaic health delivery system, reinforced by an atavistic guild system, serviced by a barbaric health education system."[1] Similarly, Rick J. Carlson, a lawyer with a keen interest in medical matters, identifies our health-care industry as "formidable, fragmented, and complex at the point of entry; swathed in mystique during the treatment process; and haughty about the results of its performance."[2]

On the other hand, Harry Schwartz, an influential editorial and medical writer for the *New York Times,* insists that "American medicine is now at the height of its capability, providing more—and more effective—help to a larger number of our people than ever before. . . . American medicine is probably, on the whole and with exceptions in particular areas, the best in the world."[3]

Perhaps. But at least one liberal specialist on the subject, Senator Edward Kennedy, thinks it critical to put eight telling questions to what may or may not be the best health-care system in the world:

1. Should good health care cost an American everything he owns?
2. Should good health care mortgage a family's future?
3. Should Americans be denied good health care because they cannot pay?
4. Should Americans seek out health care or should health care seek out those in need?
5. Should Americans organize their health care or should the health care system organize itself?
6. Should Americans be left to find high-quality care or should the health care system guarantee quality?
7. Should hospitals and doctors be both businessmen and healers?
8. Should health insurance be big business?[4]

The Senator's own research and answers leave him "shocked to find that we in America have created a health care system that can be so callous to human suffering, so intent on high salaries and profits, and so unconcerned for the needs of our people."

To which judgment conservatives rush to take sharp exception—calling instead for applause, for new recognition of the remarkable achievements of the world's most modern and scientific medical system. The United States, they proudly point out, has:

More doctors per capita than all but three or four other nations.
The greatest number of first-rate hospital beds.
The most advanced medical technology.
The largest pool of skilled manpower.
A decisive lead in nearly all phases of health research.
A higher quality of medical education than anywhere else in the world.

Not surprisingly, we spend a higher percentage of our Gross National Product on health than does any other nation (7 per cent, or $75 billion in 1971; this amounts to $358 per person)! It is plainly time for patriotic pride and hardly for petty carping!

But we are getting too far ahead of the chapter's material. Suffice it to say here that the C-L-R-V controversy in this entire matter could not be sharper or more acerbic.

To facilitate understanding I have organized our four-school comparison of health-care reforms around four major questions:

1. What is at the heart of our so-called health crisis?
2. What is central to successful reform?
3. What can we expect from the health-care professionals?
4. What particular reforms should we press for?

Coursing through the entire discussion is my underlying conviction—made plain as the chapter unfolds—that we *are* going to get significant change in health-care policies in the near future. Whether the change will take the form of benign neglect, national health insurance, or a radical or visionary change of extraordinary character is far from clear at this time. But on this expectation of change, and possibly on this alone, the four schools agree: We are going to have to do *something* about the way our medical care is distributed, priced, paid for, and culturally defined. Our task in this chapter is to struggle toward some sort of personally satisfying answer to the critical question of exactly what that something should be.

Conservatives and Our Health-Care System

The Conservative Heart of the Matter. Because of their preoccupation with our complicity in our own social problems conservatives readily indict you and me as culprits in explaining the weaknesses in the nation's health-care system. Their argument is that we seem to have some perverse inborn zest for gaining medical attention. For when we are offered new, more technologically refined medical services, we go out of our way to develop still more subtle ailments "requiring" more refined forms of treatment. In a variation on

Parkinson's Law, supply seems to determine demand: build new hospitals and we will fill them!

Hence it follows that we have no irreducible, objectively measurable health needs, only vague, culturally defined desires for care. So we will endlessly bitch and gripe about health-care inadequacies. Honest but futile attempts to generate a greater supply of health-care services to allay consumer complaints will only elicit a greater demand and greater dissatisfaction in an endless and self-defeating cycle.

Central to Reform. If pushed to identify one issue more basic perhaps than any other, many conservatives might characteristically point to fiscal accountability. In their cost-conscious view American medical care is too cheap! The system is overtaxed by malingerers, symptom collectors, and lonely souls looking for sympathetic attention, drawn by a fee structure that grievously errs on the side of generosity!

Waxing nostalgic, cost cutters conjure up half-mythical memories of a Golden Past when patients were firmly kept from their own base impulse to exploit health care by the expedient of direct fee-for-service billing. If we would only return to our senses and charge the cost of health care directly to most patients (the "worthy" poor would receive subsidization, of course), we might get far more adult, circumspect, and responsible behavior from all the parties involved. (Exactly *how* the poor would be protected is sometimes lost sight of in the advocacy of laissez-faire.)

Similarly, a return to direct billing in place of third-party billing (e.g., Blue Cross, and so on) should force nonaffluent hypochondriacs out of the doctor's office. And if patients knew they had to pay out of their own pockets for the "overdoctoring" (extra hospitalization, extra tests, extra consultations, and so on) they force physicians to prescribe out of fear of malpractice suits, patients themselves might exert a new and effective pressure for economizing.

Professional Contribution. Health-care professionals are expected to set their house in order, lest the "medicrats" in government take advantage of the "crisis" situation to stake out a still-more-outrageous claim to power over the industry.

Central to this issue is the position taken by many conservatives on the alleged doctor shortage. Conservatives urge the medical profession to adopt five major reforms:

1. The profession might create a new tradition of national service that would obligate every physician to serve for some specified time period—say, at least three months every decade—in some part of the country in special need.
2. The profession might establish a three-year moratorium on training in overcrowded specialties, thereby directing new students into understaffed roles.
3. The profession might make several years as a general practitioner a requirement for specialty training.
4. The profession might undertake to assure adequate coverage for all at

all times, as through requiring membership by doctors in coverage "pools."

5. The profession might designate certain geographic areas of "doctor surplus" and attempt to discourage other physicians from practicing there.

As well, the government might offer tax incentives to attract medical personnel into the ghettos, might expand its chain of OEO neighborhood health centers, and might put more money into the Public Health Service's National Health Service Corps (it is now providing health-care personnel for more than a hundred communities).

Overall, however, there is an irresistible ideological inclination to dismiss as flamboyant and exaggerated most claims about an alleged doctor shortage. Scorn is freely heaped on impractical schemes for rapidly increasing the number of medical school graduates (a "lesson" is cited in the expanded number of new Ph.D. scientists who find themselves a glut on the market, albeit only a few years ago there was great national alarm about shortages of scientific manpower). Indeed, certain conservatives predict that we will be faced with a doctor *surplus* by 1980.

Conservative Reforms to Pursue. Where do we—as conservatives—go from here? Possibly to a defensive stance that insists that the best course is no reform action whatsoever! An extreme view combines a disbelief in the efficacy of medicine altogether with fierce opposition to any governmental infringement on the freedom of (worthless?) physicians.

For example, conservative economist Eli Ginzberg insists that there is no health crisis because health services have very little to do with people's health: "disease is largely self-limiting. People who are ill, even seriously ill, will generally get well without the active intervention of a physician." Ginzberg's further contention is that medical care is actually a somewhat self-indulgent alternative to cutting back on "too much alcohol, too many drugs, and promiscuous sexual relations."[5] Similarly, though in a far less extreme view, economist Victor Fuchs concludes that as large a reduction in mortality can be achieved by the expenditure of one more dollar for education as by an additional dollar for medical care.[6] Medicine, as we practice it, remains focused on repairs of the human machinery at a time when theoretical and empirical evidence suggests that health may be determined more by socio-environmental factors (such as the "culture of poverty") than by health-care delivery services.

However this may be, there is no final solution for the health "crisis" because, in the end, every solution is unacceptable. For to make our health-care system more equitable would require drastic limitations on the personal liberty of physicians, tantamount to conscription (for example, ordering doctors to practice in urban ghetto areas). Improved medical services, of dubious value in themselves, are plainly *not* worth the price (conscription) they entail in the erosion of democratic principles.

If this stand-pat position does not suit, there is a related but more progressive conservative reform program that takes grim account of the considerable lobbying that makes some sort of national health insurance scheme a strong likelihood. Facing directly into this possibility conservatives strain to make the best of it by championing two changes that can actually alter substantially all such national health insurance schemes.

The first of these changes puts pressure on the individual consumer to become an active seeker of more economical care. It does so by prohibiting total-coverage health insurance, thereby giving us ample monetary reasons to cut down on the medical bills we pile up (a precedent exists in our $52 deductible provision for hospitalization under Medicare). Going farther, it is proposed that a family that has Blue Cross coverage should confront a $100 deductible provision to help discourage unnecessary hospitalization; a family with a $6,000 income might be fully responsible for the first $300 of medical expenses and half of the next $600, a maximum total payment of $600.[7]

Typical of this approach is the proposed National Healthcare Bill, sponsored by conservative Senator Thomas J. McIntyre of New Hampshire and endorsed by the Health Insurance Association of America. The bill would make comprehensive *private* health insurance policies available to all through a system of federal income tax credits. Although the costs to the poor and the uninsurable would be covered by taxation, all who could afford to pay for their health insurance would do so.[8] (The liberal schemes, in contrast, would add to everyone's income taxes and Social Security taxes as well. Liberals, however, regard waiting for the health-care industry to correct itself as comparable to "waiting for the oil industry to request a reduction in depletion allowances."[9])

The second change sought in national health insurance schemes has conservatives urging adoption of compulsory catastrophic illness insurance. At issue is the kind of case that Dr. Michael Crichton, author of *Five Patients,* relates of an unfortunate who spent two weeks in a Boston hospital for a high fever that was never diagnosed—and received a bill seventeen feet long that equaled the patient's yearly earnings. Or the case of a Minnesota farmer who had to mortgage his farm and spend the last four years of his life paying for one thirty-seven-day hospital stay for ulcer surgery.[10]

Stung by such (atypical?) horror stories, conservatives urge complete insurance coverage for the 90 per cent of us vulnerable to high medical expenses incurred by catastrophic illness. (Such coverage, by the way, might entail a rather minor overall tax expense, because although every working-class and middle-class family lives in dread of bankruptcy from catastrophic illness, the incidence is actually quite low.)

Encouraging in this connection is the 1972 adoption of a kidney ailment provision in the new Social Security Bill. Intended to help ten thousand Americans blunt the $5,000 average annual cost of dialysis (an artificial means of cleansing the body of impurities after kidney functions have ceased), this provision has been hailed by some as opening up the Medicare program to the coverage of many whose ailments are extraordinarily costly to treat.

Summing Up. What is the conservative position? Essentially, it is that there is no health crisis; that there is no solution for it anyway; and that, besides, we wouldn't want to try most of the flamboyant solutions that have been proposed.

What, then, do conservatives want? Respect for the health industry's real accomplishment, reinstitution of its traditional components (direct billing, self-policing, and so on), more self-control over our hypochondria, and fewer unrealistic expectations of medicine's power to remedy social problems; all of this—and our unyielding opposition to any kind of legislation that would "collectivize" the health industry under a national health insurance scheme!

Stressing the delicate, complex, and little-understood nature of the health-care challenge, conservatives finally urge the nation to stay loose and to experiment only in a go-slow fashion. For only increased reliance on cost-conscious choices and on the market mechanism will provide students of the nation's health-care system with keen insight into what we, as consumers, are *really* willing to finance.

Preserving as wide an area of choice as possible for both health professionals and patients, we can protect what is in many respects the world's best medical system. Great danger threatens, however, from the politicians. As Marvin Henry Edwards warns, "in an age when more and more people have become accustomed to the government handout—to receiving more from society than they have contributed to it—the promotion of social programs has become politically the thing to do."[11] Hungry power-grubbers among the politicians promote the phony myth that government can produce "magic answers . . . despite debacle after debacle in education, housing, mail service, military production, and other areas." And they refuse to recognize that it is *not* to changes in the medical system but in our life styles that we must look for the quickest results in improving the nation's health over the next decade. All of which leaves anxious and sometimes discouraged conservatives to ask, with Edwards, "Must American medicine become another disaster area before the lesson is learned?"[12]

Liberals and Our Health-Care System

Unlike the conservative, who is preoccupied with our accomplishments in health care, the Liberal begins with a keen anger that, although it may never reach the white-heat level of the anger of the radical, nevertheless dominates the entire ensuing analysis.

The indictment ranges widely over various fundamental issues. Americans, the liberal bitterly charges:

Find that health care is taking a bigger and even more outrageous share of our incomes.

Have little assurance of the quality of care we are receiving.

Are forced to accept care at a time and in a manner and a place more suited to the convenience and profit of the doctor and the hospital than to the needs of the patient.

Are vulnerable, regardless of income, to financial ruin because of health-care costs.

Are paying (circa 1972) over 170 per cent of the daily hospital service charges we paid in 1960.

> Are astonished to find out too late how little real protection our costly health insurance actually provides.

Liberal Senator Abraham Ribicoff sums it up in terms of "high costs, not enough doctors, nurses, or other health professionals, too many people receiving poor care or no care at all, inadequate health insurance, and most medical care organized and operated in a manner that rewards inefficiencies and perpetuates inequities."[13]

The Liberal Heart of the Matter. The heart of the matter is actually a forced choice between the interpretation of health care either as a privilege (the conservative contention) or as a right (the liberal postulate). Because of their preoccupation with our failure of nerve where a vigorous interpretation of health care as a right is concerned, liberals are quick to indict you and me for moral cowardice and political confusion.

Liberals contend that health is so basic to a man's ability to prosper that we should *guarantee* the best possible health care to *every* American at any cost he can afford. With the groans of cost-conscious and contrary-minded conservatives as a backdrop, liberals insist that we have the knowledge, the wealth, and the ability in America to assure that every American will get the health care he needs and not be faced by financial ruin in the process. The big question, they dramatically conclude, is not ability but resolve: Do we have the will to do it?

As for the conservative fear that a policy shift from health care as a privilege to health care as a right necessarily means a tidal wave of claimants, the liberal insists otherwise. People certainly have tended to make use of new medical services as well as their new purchasing power to get help as it has become available. But this does not "prove" any inborn greed for medical attention! Rather, our apparently infinitely expandable demand for medical care is viewed by liberals as peculiar to our society at this time: Our long history of a widespread, severe limitation in the supply of adequate medical services has built up a temporary backlog of unmet health-care needs.

Once this pent-up demand is met, we can escape the endless, self-defeating cycle of seemingly inadequate supply and unsatiable demand engendered by our conservative health-care policies. Health writers Barbara and John Ehrenreich hold out an appealing prospect:

> As a result of the artificial shortage created by the medical professions and insurance companies, an American enters the health system, when he can, with a vast backlog of unmet needs and unattended complaints. Lift the present financial and logistic barriers to care, provide services which are both technically excellent and socially acceptable, and people will use them, perhaps initially even overuse them. But, after a while, with quality care routinely and easily available, they may well . . . need and demand *less* care.[14]

Health services, in short, interpreted anew as a right rather than a privilege threaten little havoc and promise substantial social gains—at least as liberals understand it.

Central Issues in Liberal Reform. If pushed to single out the most basic reform issue of all, liberals might characteristically point to the absence of clear-cut governmental social policy in this matter. As many as twenty-three different federal departments, agencies, and commissions operate uncoordinated programs relating to our health, with HEW alone overseeing nearly three hundred health-linked projects. With refreshing candor, HEW explained to Senator Ribicoff in 1970, "up to and including the present there has never been a formulation of national health policy as such. In addition, no specific mechanism has been set up to carry out this function."[15] How then, liberals ask, are we to solve the health-care problems of cost, quality, and equality of access? Only an overall, policy-guided approach can secure fundamental changes in public and private financing mechanisms, manpower supply and use, medical education, regional planning, and so on.

Judging our present lack of significant national health-care policy an "intolerable situation," Senator Ribicoff gravely observes,

> If there is no policy, there can be no goals. If there are no goals, there can be no strategies. This is what we have today, and the result is that medical care, instead of being a public responsibility, is a private business. It is operated more for the convenience of its practitioners than according to the needs of the sick.[16]

This abject absence of national policy understandably rankles cool-headed, superrational, and planning-conscious liberals.

One of the results is the liberal's fervid conviction that the reliance in other countries on crisp central policy explains how it is all done better elsewhere. Britain's National Health Service, for example, is often hailed as providing the large-scale, centrally controlled framework within which British society can decide rationally what it wants to spend on medicine and where it wants to spend it. Without such central direction, decision making in our country is obscured amidst a million private transactions.

Professional Contribution. If the public is expected to take to heart the liberal's scathing indictment of health-care malpractices, the professionals inside the system are at the same time sharply challenged to redefine their roles and regroup their forces. Reform advocacy among liberals centers about a new definition of the "good" doctor and the adoption of a new model—the health management organization—to heighten the satisfaction of *all* parties in the health-care system.

To begin with, liberals reject a narrow and pristine definition of the doctor's role (à la the conservative model) in favor of a far more humanistic orientation. For example, the April 1972 issue of *Medical Economics* contained a heated debate on the appropriate stance of doctors toward "nuisance" patients with "trivial" complaints. A liberal physician, George Brown, wrote as follows:

> The fact that our patients are not reluctant to bring us their problems is what HIP prepaid practice and preventive medicine are all about. People go to a doctor because of a need, which is very real to the patient even if it's

> neurotic. If it is indeed a neurotic need—and we all draw our share of hypochondriacs—it is the doctor's job to relate to it, even if only as a good listener.[17]

Conservatives, preoccupied with "immoral" demands on the very scarce time of highly trained and highly paid professionals, could not disagree more.

Second, the "good personal doctor" is located by his liberal supporters not working for a fee, alone in his solo office, but working instead for a salary in group practice or in a health maintenance organization (HMO). In such an arrangement an individual's health becomes the concern of a group of doctors in a novel kind of large-scale medical organization and not merely that of a single doctor in a "cottage industry" setting. Organized *systems* of health care, the HMO's provide comprehensive services for a fixed, prepaid annual fee. Although set up in various patterns, all HMO's provide a mix of out-patient and hospital services through a single organization and a single payment mechanism, in the fashion of first-rate community health services.

HMO critics dwell on an anonymous, unsubstantiated collection of "horror stories" of the long waits, the mixups over lost records, the hospital admissions requested but refused, and so on—the inconveniences and indignities that many patients in group practice are alleged to suffer. They ask if the HMO is not insensitive to the spirit of the times. In the words of Harry Schwartz,

> The call everywhere in America today is for decentralization, for breaking large units into small units, for reducing giant bureaucracies to human size so the individual can feel at home with them. But in medicine—where the individual doctor working on a fee for service basis does provide a decentralized, human-sized, non-punchcard directed service—the political pressure is all the other way toward repeating the errors of bureaucratic gigantism that have gotten us into the present mess in so many fields of American life.[18]

Millions today enjoy better care—in terms of free choice—than they would if forced to use the group practice of HMO's, conservatives conclude.

Undaunted by such carping and fully confident that it can all be worked out, liberals, led by Senator Edward Kennedy, propose two extraordinary reforms:

1. HMO's will be required to accept *all* individuals who seek membership during a once-a-year, thirty-day grace period. This will ensure HMO coverage of many individuals now barred from insured care, people whose care is certain to be expensive and cost more than the individual will pay in his premium.
2. HMO's will be required to deliver the largest and most detailed range of health services imaginable, including physical, mental, dental, alcoholism, and drug abuse care.

Anticipating the anxiety this proposal must create in cost-conscious conservatives, liberals take to the offensive. They point out that instead of shifting the onus of cost cutting to the consumer, as in conservative proposals, the HMO concept intelligently places full responsibility on the dispenser—and therefore provides the strongest possible incentive to keep enrolled patients healthy and to cure them quickly when ill.

Hampered at present by legal barriers in some twenty-two states, HMO's have in thirty-five years managed to enroll only some 4 per cent of the American population, or 125 groups with about 8 million members. Backed now, however, by a Republican administration plan to have 90 per cent of the population enrolled by 1980, the HMO bandwagon includes ever more medical schools, hospitals, and even some insurance companies. Many in and outside of the health-care industry have no doubt that some form of group practice is the medicine of the future.

Liberal Reforms to Pursue. As the liberal understands it, we can either wait for the health-care industry to correct itself (a conservative preference), or we can strengthen the ability and resolve of government to nudge medical reforms along. Many believe that there is a set of essential requirements without which no real change can occur. These include:

1. Universal, tax-financed national health insurance that will provide a basic package of medical care benefits to all citizens.
2. Basic care financed on a prepaid basis to motivate cost control.
3. Federal, state, and local quality controls, established for the medical profession but with significant review from outside the profession.
4. Federal, state, and local means, perhaps through a combination of franchising and financial inducements, established to provide appropriate distribution of health-care facilities and personnel and to eliminate needless and costly duplication.
5. Financial and other incentives by government that stimulate health-care providers to offer services of a uniformly high quality.
6. Individual consumers' being offered a reasonable choice of providers, including the right to purchase their care from any source they desire—national health insurance, however, to be applied only to providers who meet minimum standards of quality.[19]

Conceding that temporary dislocations of special interests will result, liberals insist that such turmoil is a reasonable price for the extraordinary benefits entailed.

Focusing more specifically on three major concerns, liberals offer crisp and controversial blueprints for cost controls, hospital reforms, and universal health-care insurance, where care is a right.

1. In the matter of cost controls, many liberals seem to favor the imposition upon individual health-care professionals of strict economic controls. In 1971, for example, almost half of all physicians' Medicare claims were cut by the government agencies responsible for screening and paying claims; the cuts averaged nearly 12 per cent. Earlier, in 1969, a price freeze on physicians' fees was adopted by the Bureau of Health Insurance of the Social Security Administration, and the government moved in 1970 to curtail payment for the use of nursing homes and to reduce both hospital admissions and the length of patient stays in hospitals.

Success in the campaign is clear—and leads to liberal calls for still more vigorous efforts. In fiscal 1971, for example, the nation's health-care expenditures rose 10.7 per cent, a substantial increase but still the smallest annual percentage rise since the 1966 adoption of Medicare and Medicaid. Similarly, after Phases I and II of economic controls in 1971 the medical care component of the Consumer Price Index increased only 2.2 per cent, well under the 6.5 per cent average annual figure for 1966 to 1970. By mid-1972 it was indisputable that President Nixon's price control program had stopped the medical cost explosion.

At present (early 1973) health-care prices are actually rising less rapidly than the overall cost-of-living index. There is no question but what this successful containment of medical price rises serves to ease off the inflation-rooted pressure for a drastic restructuring of the entire medical system. Although this development may cheer conservatives and certain liberals alike, it also sharpens the challenge of how to keep the lid on.

2. Hospital reform is another major liberal preoccupation. At a price tag of $30 billion in 1971, and as the most expensive of all health-care components (it consumes nearly 60 per cent of the health-care dollar), the hospital at the same time has more potential clout than any other health organization (it is the only institution the good doctor and the very sick patient believe they cannot do without). To attempt to rationalize health services and cut the $105-a-day average hospital cost (1972; almost double the 1966 figure) while ignoring far-reaching hospital reforms is probably to confront eventually a harsh choice between perpetuating the hospital status quo (a conservative preference) or succumbing to total federal control (a radical preoccupation).

All the more appealing to middle-of-the-road liberals, therefore, is a hospital reform plan predicated on *shared* authority among the federal and state governments, the health professions, and the hospitals themselves. Bold in its proposed use of federal power, the plan also strives to preserve a large degree of professional, institutional, and state responsibility. The three proposed operational steps are the following:

a. Enfranchise most general hospitals—perhaps 5,000 of the existing 7,000—as public utilities or public service corporations. Unlike the traditional utility, however, they would not only be regulated but would become key elements in the regulatory apparatus, responsible either for providing or assuring provision of the whole spectrum of comprehensive health services, at reasonable cost, to all persons in a defined community or service area. In multihospital communities, overlapping franchises would probably be necessary.
b. A hospital that chose not to take on the burden of the franchise could become a nursing home or some other type of health-care facility, or could continue to operate as a hospital but without certain financial advantages—for example, participation in Medicare and Medicaid—that could be reserved for the franchised institution. If necessary, tax-exempt status could be limited to the latter.
c. Require all essential health-care providers, both individual and institutional, to affiliate with a franchised hospital. Physical decentralization would be encouraged. All would share a single, computerized, hospital-based patient-record system. This would not only promote continuity

of care but would enable the hospital's professional staff to extend its present in-patient utilization and quality controls to all community health services.[20]

Proponents are cheered by the fact that about a third of the states have already enacted hospital rate-review laws and/or "certificate of need" programs for approval of new hospital facilities. It should be only a short step to full utility regulation.

The utility regulation of hospitals, in turn, would facilitate just the kind of central policy guidance that liberals espouse. A 1972 government study of hospitals, for example, made dozens of the kinds of budget-paring recommendations that only central direction can secure:

Regional groups of hospitals should share services, which would, for example, reduce the 90,000 obstetrical beds in American hospitals by 38,000, which are unneeded.

Expand home health care programs, which, in turn, would reduce nationally the need for 20,000 hospital beds.

Place patients needing long-term, as opposed to acute care in special facilities that would not only be less expensive but would also reduce the need for 126,000 beds in general hospitals.[21]

What is crucially missing, then, and amounts to an inexcusable abnegation of responsibility, is a clear and positive indication of federal interest in the hospital "crisis"—an interest that liberals define in terms of helping the health industry and the states together to assume new responsibility in reform.[22]

3. National health insurance plans have been proposed unsuccessfully for nearly sixty years and have been introduced periodically in Congress for almost thirty years. Two recent developments, however, raise new hope in supporters:

a. The adoption since 1966 of Medicare and Medicaid has helped accustom Americans to accepting federal money for private health care.
b. The ensuing inflation in health-care costs (as demand outstripped supply in a "cottage industry," high-profit situation) lends support to a massive and largely successful campaign to undermine confidence in the health-care status quo.

Together these developments are hailed as paving the way for the vast new programs now being introduced to an uncertain and skeptical Congress. Indeed, a plethora of health schemes is available from which to choose, including bills from Senators Jacob Javits, Claiborne Pell, and Edward Kennedy and from the AMA and the Nixon Administration itself.

The strongest of these—the "Health Security" Bill proposed by the late Walter Reuther's Committee of One Hundred and introduced by Senator Edward Kennedy—would provide so-called European-style cradle-to-grave health-care coverage for almost every resident in the country. Compulsory in membership for all Americans, the Kennedy bill offers:

a. Comprehensive health benefits (beyond anything envisioned in rival bills).

b. Unlimited coverage for physician visits and care (including surgery) and hospital care.
c. Hospital psychiatric care (with a 45-day limit).
d. Skilled nursing home care (120-day limit per spell of illness).
e. Up to twenty visits (per spell of illness) to a fee-for-service physician for psychiatric care.

Straightforward about its intent to be a substitute for private insurance plans, the Kennedy bill would also promote:

The formation of prepaid group practice (HMO's, for example).
The enticement of doctors into rural and ghetto practice.
The subsidization of continuing education for physicians.
The imposition of strict new controls on drug prescribing.

Costs would be met by employer-employee contributions (two thirds) and general tax revenues (one third). Overall, the bill reflects the Senator's considered belief that "we can create a unique American health care system that will preserve free enterprise for doctors and still offer patients the financial support and adequate care they need."

Indeed, so zealous is the Senator in assuring others that he does not want to see American medicine socialized that he regularly spotlights four special features of his own bill, namely:

a. The federal government would not own hospitals or employ physicians.
b. The government would not try to assign doctors to areas where they are scarce, nor would it tell medical students what specialty they would study.
c. The government would not interfere in the doctor-patient relationship.
d. The government would not create an overarching federal agency in Washington, telling every area and community in this nation exactly how they must offer health care.

Instead, the Senator wants to promote "the doctor's right to be both businessman *and* healer by taking actions which make sure that it is good business to respond to the needs and demands of the people for healing."[23]

Summing Up. What do liberals want in the way of health-care reform? Conservatives charge them with promoting illusory frauds that aim to make expensive medical care seem more freely available than it is at present. All of the proposed bills, Kennedy's included, represent an ill-advised flight from the market regulation of demand and supply and are designed without adequate realization of the new difficulties that arise as the market is weakened and its regulatory functions fall increasingly into the clutches of Washington "medicrats." To a man, of course, conservatives utterly reject the imposition of this mode of health care on unwilling Americans and insist that it can exist only in a pluralistic medical system as one possibly viable form of medical care delivery among a host of voluntary others.

Radical critics line up to take their own special swipes at liberal plans; much is made of the fact that:

1. They do not ensure that all forms of care will be absolutely free at the point of delivery.
2. They rest on a relatively regressive ("soak-the-poor") tax base.
3. They shy away from a call for the nationalization of the notoriously exploitative American pharmaceutical industry.

What is even worse, except for the inconvenience of having to report their true incomes to the Internal Revenue Service, under liberal plans American doctors remain much as they are at present, arrogantly unaccountable to the American public.

The visionaries, in turn, have their own disagreements with the major thrust of liberal health insurance reform plans. For the kind of unprecedented personal, informed health-care autonomy that the visionary seeks is touched hardly at all by the conventional administrative and structural changes the liberals seek. Indeed, visionaries see with special clarity that in fundamental and exasperating ways the enactment of national health insurance plans might actually increase the mystique and power of health-care professionals by placing them at the top of an inaccessible, impersonal national health system bureaucracy. Dedicated to bringing all such structures down and to helping us learn how to share knowledge across artificial divisions, visionaries finally regard the liberal program as just another misguided, if well-intentioned, plan.

In a very special way, the liberal dilemma is captured here in microcosm, and the discomfiture of the change-agent-as-liberal-realist can be keenly felt. When first proposed in 1970, the Kennedy bill was widely hailed as a broad liberal program for financing, reorganizing, and, to some measure, regulating the nation's health industry. Today, with Congressional support for strong liberal measures very hard to secure, compromise is the rule and conciliation the strategy. A revision of the 1970 bill is now carefully promoted as a responsible, "free enterprise" financial arrangement for paying for health services and no longer as a broad blueprint for far-reaching and value-challenging change. Was this switch reasonable? Necessary? Pragmatic? Deceptive? It offers, in very sharp relief, a cameo of the would-be health-care reformer who, like liberal Senator Edward Kennedy, believes in "maintaining the free enterprise system in this country and in American medicine"[24] and has to grapple with the internal contradictions of his own strategy.

FOOTNOTES

1. As quoted in David Hapgood, "The Health Professionals: Cure or Cause of the Health Crisis?" *The Washington Monthly* (June 1969), p. 60.
2. Harry Schwartz, *The Case for American Medicine: A Realistic Look at Our Health Care System* (New York: McKay, 1972), pp. IX–2.
3. Ibid.
4. Ibid., pp. 20–21.
5. Eli Ginzberg, "The Outlook for Educated Manpower," *The Public Interest* (Winter 1972), pp. 100–112.
6. Victor Fuchs, as quoted in Nathan Glazer, "Paradoxes of Health Care," *The Public Interest* (Winter 1971), p. 76.
7. For impressive detail and advocacy, see Martin S. Feldstein, "A New Approach to National Health Insurance," *The Public Interest* (Spring 1971), pp. 93–105.

8. Charles A. Siegfried, "The Private Sector," *New York Times* (August 14, 1972), p. 27.
9. Robert E. Tranquada, "Rx for a Sick Health Care System," *Long Island Press* (June 25, 1972), p. 23.
10. Both cases are drawn from William A. Nolan, *A Surgeon's World* (New York: Random, 1972).
11. Marvin Henry Edwards, *Hazardous to Your Health: A New Look at the "Health Care Crisis" in America* (New Rochelle, N.Y.: Arlington House, 1972).
12. Ibid., p. 196.
13. Abraham Ribicoff, "The 'Healthiest Nation' Myth," *Saturday Review* (August 22, 1970), p. 20.
14. Barbara and John Ehrenreich, "The Medical Industrial Complex," *The New York Review* (December 17, 1970), pp. 14–22.
15. Ribicoff, op. cit., p. 20.
16. Ibid.
17. Quoted in Schwartz, op. cit., p. 271.
18. Ibid., p. 194.
19. Tranquada, op. cit., p. 23.
20. Anne R. Somers, "Remedy for Hospitals," *New York Times* (November 24, 1972), p. 37.
21. "U.S. Study of Hospitals Charges Poor Designs Spur High Costs," *New York Times* (November 23, 1972), p. 24.
22. Somers, op. cit., p. 37.
23. Nancy Hicks, "Kennedy Assures Doctors on Bill," *New York Times* (September 28, 1972), p. 21.
24. Ibid.

READING

Again and again throughout this volume we want to look abroad and ask how they meet the same challenges in other countries. Especially helpful in this vein is this essay by A. Peter Ruderman, a searching and balanced assessment of lessons we Americans might import from Canadian experience with a comprehensive health-care system. Note especially the cautions recommended against an overly simplistic transfer of plans across national boundaries and the writer's sobering conclusion that the prospects for Medicare here "are just as good or bad as the prospects for consensus." Even as you read carefully for knowledge of medical matters, you can gain all the more from keen attention as well to the author's high-quality assessment of the possibilities of transferring a program from one country to another.

Canadian Medicare: Can We Use a Plan That Good?

A. Peter Ruderman

As proposals to set up a comprehensive medical care system go forward in the United States, more and more Americans look to Canada as a model. The

Reprinted by permission of *The Nation* (October 23, 1972).

U.S. government has subsidized American university research to study different aspects of the Canadian health-care system, and at its November meeting in Atlantic City, the American Public Health Association will devote a session to "issues arising from the experience of the Canadian health insurance programs."

Why is Canada singled out from the vast number of countries whose health services are available for the United States to emulate? Mainly, I suppose, because it is a nearby, familiar place that has been supplying doctors and nurses to the American market for years. People south of the border naturally wonder whether Canadian Medicare can be imported too.

But Americans who set themselves to learning how and why the Canadian health-care system works must also bear in mind that with respect to its politics and the temper of its people Canada *is* different. It isn't just the spelling or the fact that schoolchildren learn "a pint of water weighs a pound and a quarter" instead of "a pint's a pound the whole world round." The differences are big enough to make me wonder whether the Canadian health-care system, admirable as it may be, could exist in an American context.

Canada is a confederation of ten provinces, plus the Yukon and Northwest Territories. Whether or not it is a loose confederation depends on who is Prime Minister at the time and which province we are talking about. The British North America Act of 1867, which serves as a Constitution, explicitly identifies health as a provincial responsibility and—as in the United States—the national government deals itself in by providing money. Federal-provincial revenue-sharing is the key to the political structure in all areas. The national government levies income taxes, roughly one third of which are earmarked for the provinces. The provinces also receive federal grants for specific programs and can raise revenue independently with sales taxes and fees of various kinds; in the case of health, they may collect insurance premiums if they so wish. Sharing out the revenue involves federal-provincial conferences, at which the national leaders try to jockey the provincial ones into line. Premiers of poor provinces are usually docile; those from provinces that put more into the national treasury than they receive from it tend to go their own way. There is usually a "special arrangement" for Quebec.

If by Medicare we mean out-patient or physician care, organized government programs were pioneered by the old Socialist (CCF) government of Saskatchewan in the 1940's. The present-day system results from soundings taken by a Royal Commission on Health Services that was appointed by a Conservative Prime Minister (Diefenbaker), and reported to a Liberal (Pearson), with final legislation coming from another Liberal (Trudeau). The national legislation permitted the provinces to set up Medicare programs and provided for federal cost-sharing when they did. The provinces came into line in the usual order—Saskatchewan had its program off and running five years before the national legislation was passed; Ontario came in after the fact, and with obvious reluctance that it could not do its own thing instead; Quebec, after something of a confrontation between the government and the doctors, entered last and with a set of radical proposals for organizing health care that will be described below.

Even in the larger cities, Canadian politics is a participatory matter. The provincial constituencies (ridings) are small, and anyone who really wants to can know his member personally. Sometimes the ordinary member of parliament (national or provincial) finds that he has little to do except act as a sensor of local opinion. As a backbencher he has no real say in deciding policy, nor is he free to vote against his party's position on major issues. From the point of view of executive decision-making, it is a convenient system. It could be brutally undemocratic in the wrong hands, but that is where the nature of the people comes in. No law forces a Prime Minister to resign if he loses a vote of confidence, but he usually does. A government with a heavy majority does not really have to worry about public opinion until close to election time, but nonetheless it does. A few months ago, the Ontario government (elected with a big majority and no election in sight for three or four years) decided to drop a $150 Ontario scholarship that was given to certain outstanding students. There was a howl in the newspapers, and within days the minister in question performed a rapid about-face, postponing the cut to the following year.

At the administrative level, rules and regulations never seem to be as tightly construed in Canada as in the United States, and more concessions are made for the sake of goodwill or convenience. People who go out of their way to be nice can be found as clerks in Medicare offices, or working in hospitals, as elsewhere in Canadian society. They are no more efficient or diligent than their opposite numbers in other countries, but they are more accommodating. Perhaps they can afford to be, in a country where people are fairly apt to be law-abiding and not out to "beat the system."

Even organized interest groups show this accommodating tendency. Despite the continuing rise in the cost of living, the Ontario Medical Association at its meeting last May decided to postpone any discussion of increases in the fee schedule to 1974. A surprising number of doctors actually feel a bit uncomfortable about the amount of money they have been making (as much from harder work as from higher fees) since Medicare came in.

Here is how the Canadian health-care system works. A few weeks ago I had to consult a doctor. I might have gone to a family doctor (the number of general practitioners, though declining, is still large), but I am a patient of the Family Practice Service at the Toronto General Hospital, mainly because it is a four-minute walk from my office. The doctor examined me (the clinic gives an appointment every fifteen minutes, which is a more leisurely pace than is maintained in most office practice, and as a first visit this one lasted a half hour), took some blood samples, and wrote a prescription.

No money changed hands, except that I paid the hospital pharmacy 65¢ for an item that would have cost $1.50 at retail. The doctor submitted a claim for this visit in his monthly statement to the Medicare plan. If it had happened to be included in the sample audit, I would have been asked to verify the service provided. Computerized "practice profiles" are also used to identify errors and cheating, and disciplinary sanctions include payment of the doctor at a reduced rate. The fee for each procedure is set in a schedule prepared by the Ontario Medical Association. By "opting in" to the Medicare plan, doctors agree to accept 90 per cent of the fee schedule as payment in full. Doctors who "opt out" face collection problems, since the province then pays the patient directly, and most doctors prefer the 90 per cent. Fee schedules, originally promulgated unilaterally by medical societies, are increasingly matters for "collective bargaining" with provincial ministries of health.

The cost of the laboratory work indicated for me was met out of the hospital budget. That is approved each year in advance by negotiation between the hospital and the province, and in recent years the province has used a "global budget" in which they give a lump sum of money to each hospital to cover increased costs, new services, etc., and the hospital administration decides how it is to be spent. If I had gone to a private laboratory, the pathologist would have billed Medicare at the rate set for these tests in the OMA fee schedule. The fee separates the "technical" and "professional" components; the pathologist, for example, would be paid the entire amount if all the work had been done in his office, but only the "professional component" if all he did was produce a report on a test made elsewhere.

For all physician and hospital services (there is no ceiling on medically indicated treatment) a single individual in Ontario pays a premium of $132 per year and a family twice that amount. Roughly one half of the actual cost is met by the federal government (poorer provinces get more and the richer ones less) and the remainder comes from provincial tax sources. Premiums are lower in most provinces than in Ontario and the tax contribution is consequently higher. The total cost per capita is probably a bit more than $250 per year now; the 1972 figure is not yet available. The premium in Ontario is high enough so that a surplus is accumulating; this, under the name of the Health Resources Fund, helps to support medical education in the province. In aggregative terms, Canadians are devoting 5.5 to 6 per cent of gross national product to health care, compared with perhaps 0.5 per cent more in the United States, though it's hard to be precise because the definitions vary.

When an affluent country like Canada undertakes to provide its people with comprehensive health care, the first flush of enthusiasm tends to result in overspending. Canada may have slightly fewer physicians per capita (one active, practicing physician per thousand) than does the United States, but there is no acute sense of shortage in most of the country, although nurse-practitioners are being trained for service in remote and sparsely populated areas. There are, if anything, too many general hospital beds, and bed targets are being lowered rather than raised. This involves the closing of small and uneconomical institutions and a general rise in standards of care offered by the remainder.

In an attempt to rationalize the operation of the health-care system and control the inevitable rising costs, a number of shifts are taking place. Nursing homes are being taken into the hospital-care system in more and more provinces; home-care programs are being developed. Hostels are being put up to lodge patients in experimental programs of day surgery and for other types of care. There is also a growing feeling that an organized system of outpatient care (patterned somewhat after existing community clinics) may be able to handle a still greater number of patients on an ambulatory basis, and further reduce the hospital bill. Such economies, of course, can be realized only when unneeded hospital facilities can be shut down or converted, in phase with declining demand.

Canadian Medicare can still be viewed as in a transitional period, with public financing, but with traditional kinds of health-care institutions and styles of practice persisting. Reorganization and consolidation of the system is beginning, however, and perhaps the proposals for Quebec give a foretaste of the future. The Quebec plan is based on establishing a provincial network of local health centers where it is felt that primary physician care on an out-patient basis, under the same roof with social and family services, will meet 85 per cent of all health-care requirements. These centers are linked with hospitals for specialist services, and finally with the university hospitals in Montreal, Quebec City, and Sherbrooke, for "superspecialty" service.

About a dozen centers are already in operation, staffed largely by enthusiastic younger doctors who have accepted "sessional payments" rather than a fee-for-service arrangement. The planners hope that all general practitioners will be practicing on a salaried basis in health centers within fifteen years.

Local administrative boards, with professional and community representation, report to regional boards that cover both health centers and hospitals. The old religious and voluntary hospitals, with their independent boards of trustees, have "gone public," though not without a struggle. The more prosperous medical specialists (particularly the English-speaking ones, who would have no trouble finding jobs elsewhere) are resisting the pressure to change their style of practice, and Quebec Medicare still makes provision for fee payment on the traditional basis. The new program, while comprehensive so far as medical care is concerned, has been criticized for making insufficient provision for public health activities.

In the Canadian system of "unity in diversity" no province can go it alone, and the federal government has recently tried to control rising costs by limiting its financial commitment for health. Basically, the proposal is to freeze the federal contribution in an early year, and thereafter to tie increases to (*1*) growth in population; (*2*) ability to pay, as measured by increases in gross national product; and (*3*) a modest additional "thrust fund" that can be concentrated on specific programs which the Department of National Health and Welfare wishes to stimulate in the provinces. After considerable discussion, and the adoption of a compromise formula whereby no province will receive less than it gets under present arrangements, it looks as if this formula will be accepted.

While medical and hospital care have been made widely available, there are still worrisome gaps in coverage. In provinces that collect premiums—even in token amounts—those of the poor are paid by welfare (Ontario also charges no premium to persons over sixty-five), but some people still are not covered. These may be healthy young adults employed in firms too small to come under the formal collection mechanism, who gamble on continuing good health by not paying their premiums. Some may let their payments lapse because of forgetfulness or senility. The administrative tendency is to "forgive and forget" and to grant coverage provided that individuals able to do so pay their delinquent premiums. After all, the system was set up to provide benefits rather than to show a profit.

Out-patient prescription drugs are a sore point because, for many individuals, they are the only out-of-pocket expense for health care. Drugs for hospital in-patients are covered by the hospital budget, and hospital pharmacies sell to their registered out-patients at or near cost, but the average person who sees a doctor in his own office must pay for the prescription either directly or through membership in a voluntary insurance program. Deductible drug insurance of 25¢ and 50¢ has become a popular fringe benefit in collective bargaining.

Finally, dental care is not covered. The dental profession in Canada is much more wedded to free enterprise than is the medical profession, and there is a scarcity of dentists—only one for more than three thousand Canadians. Also, geographic disparities are severe. Toronto, Montreal, Vancouver, and other big cities may approach the U.S. ratio of dentists to population, but some communities of fifteen thousand or twenty thousand receive no dental services except for the periodic visits of the Northern Ontario dental train or similar peripatetic practitioners. Despite the shortage, dentists have shown reluctance to grant hygienists greater responsibility or to accept intermediate-level personnel on the lines of the New Zealand dental nurse. Since dental schools are few and have high professional standards, the personnel to deliver mass dental care will have to come from the ranks of hygienists and technicians, and for the present "denticare" cannot be considered because the work load could not be handled. There has also been a recent flap in Ontario over "denturists," who bypass the dentist and sell false teeth directly to the public at lower prices; this practice is now to be legalized.

The other major gap is posed by geography. Some communities are too small to keep even one doctor fully employed, and current opinion would base medical services on catchment areas of five thousand to six thousand, the minimum that could justify a medical group of three doctors and supporting staff, plus a small community hospital. Nurse-practitioners and nurse-midwives are being trained for outpost duty in areas where public health nurses have served for many years. But when the weather is bad and planes cannot land, when communities cannot be reached during breakup in the spring and freeze-up in the fall, when auroral disturbances knock out the radio link, there are limits to what even the best-trained nurses can do unsupported. Finally, at the periphery of settlement, there are small clusters of Indian or Eskimo families whose access to medical care is limited to the drug chest administered by their chief or possibly by a clergyman, a storekeeper, or a Mountie.

The arrival of Medicare in the different provinces provides a fascinating spectrum ranging from painful confrontation to painless transition. In Saskatchewan, when provincewide Medicare was proposed in 1962 after two decades of buildup, there was substantial physician opposition to some of the government's proposed regulations. This culminated in a doctors' strike. Before the dust had settled, a lot of ill will had been generated. However, the final system was not so far removed from the proposals that had provoked the strike, and a community clinic movement had been pioneered by doctors who refused to join the strike.

Eight years later, the province of Quebec seemed to be moving toward very much the same kind of showdown, with the government sticking to every clause of its original proposal. A strike of medical specialists, in this case without the support of many general practitioners, ended abruptly when the flurry of FLQ violence occurred—proving once again that nationalism is a very efficient distraction from the gut issues.

In Ontario, the old physician-sponsored plans were liquidated when Medicare came in, and the provincial government was deprived of their accumulated experience. Private insurance companies were used as carriers on a temporary basis, and administration was not consolidated in a single provincial program until April 1972. By contrast, when Medicare started in Nova Scotia, the physician-sponsored plan (Maritime Medical Services, Inc.) simply began to report to a provincial medical care commission rather than to its previous board of directors, and the main problem was the mechanical one of shifting from the manual processing of sixty thousand claims per month to the computer processing of four times that number.

In most provinces that transition was relatively painless, and a number of reasons may be adduced. In the first place, the physical effect of the change was small. People had already been covered by provincial hospital plans for at least ten years, and when Medicare was introduced through national legislation a number of provinces already had comprehensive Medicare (as in Saskatchewan), a limited public program (as in the Cottage Hospital system of Newfoundland), or flourishing schemes sponsored by the medical profession or private insurance companies. This meant that the physician work load did not rise inordinately, although doctors are somewhat busier today. The need for additional physicians that did arise was met by expanding medical school enrollment, building new medical schools, and attracting physicians from abroad—mainly from other Commonwealth countries. In general, immigration requirements for doctors are less stringent in Canada than in the United States, and the provinces that feel the greatest need make it relatively easy for a qualified foreign physician to set up practice.

The emotional adjustment of the medical profession was not particularly difficult in most cases. Doctors were already accustomed to the billing requirements and control measures of insurance companies and professionally sponsored medical care plans. Comprehensive Medicare was generally viewed for what it was—a change in the payment mechanism rather than a threat to the professional independence of practitioners, though there were inevitably a few holdouts.

By and large, organized medicine proved amenable to reason. Physicians took their responsibilities for health care seriously and learned early that there was more to be gained from cooperation with government than from blind opposition. Some provincial medical societies are clearly stuffier and more conservative than others, but the Canadian Medical Association is a far more progressive body than its American counterpart.

Group practices and community clinics have been around too long to be called experimental, but innovative changes continue to crop up. The typical Canadian medical group—more common in the west than in the east—comprises from five to nine doctors, usually general practitioners, or some combination of general practice with internal medicine, and one or two other specialties. The group is usually physician sponsored, and the original members put up the capital (or borrow) to set up a small management company that owns the premises. A partnership agreement specifies how the income of the group is to be distributed—most commonly in some relation to the billings generated by each member but sometimes a flat sum like an annual salary. Groups are popular among doctors because they provide more leisure time and the chance to get away for vacations and refresher courses, and among patients because they usually maintain a duty roster so that a doctor is always available in case of need.

The most common type of "community clinic" differs from the physician-sponsored group mainly in the existence of a board that owns and manages the premises. The medical practice is much the same as with other groups, although community clinics are more likely to undertake health education and preventive work and to provide ancillary staff such as social workers or psychologists.

Occasionally consumer-sponsored groups have been started on the American "prepaid group practice" model. These have found it hard to maintain membership loyalty, and thus to raise capital, because the "members" are free to go to any other doctor they wish, since the bill will still be paid by Medicare. Experiments are currently going on with formulas whereby the provincial government pays such groups a "capitation" amount per member. The group then contracts to provide total medical care for its members and to meet their outside doctor bills. This, it is hoped, will result in savings because the consumer-involvement groups have been found in a number of studies to have lower hospitalization rates than other forms of practice.

A few medical practices have taken the form of true community enterprises offering a range of medical and social welfare services, with the entire operation under the control of consumer-directors. Problems have arisen when low-income consumers were confronted with the cost of hiring physicians at six or seven times their own income level and when the physicians felt that the consumers were not competent to make technical judgments.

Other experiments that are being tested include the use of nurse-midwives and nurse-practitioners not only for outpost service but in settings where they either screen cases for physicians or share their practices. Public health nurses have in some areas been attached to solo or group practices for follow-up and home-visiting assignments. Hospital-based practices and home-care programs are other approaches. There have been experiments that get double mileage out of psychiatric institutions by running day-care programs for one group of patients and night care for those who "work out but sleep in."

Canadian experience shows that a country can provide medical and hospital care for its population through public financial mechanisms while at first leaving the structure of private fee-for-service medical practice largely untouched. The same could be said for a number of countries in Western Europe.

Canada, among other countries, is now entering a period of administrative consolidation and reorganization of health-care services, stimulated by the politicians' apprehensions about rising costs. New questions are being raised about traditional structures like hospital boards of trustees, local boards of health, and fee for service. It cannot yet be forecast whether this second transition will be painless or will involve another round of confrontation in some provinces. Once again, Canada is not alone; rethinking and reorganization of service is going on in Britain, Denmark, Sweden, and a number of other countries.

As to whether the Canadian, or the more general Western, model of Medicare can be adopted in the United States, some questions remain to be answered. Canadian political parties have all, to a substantial degree, espoused the welfare state. In the parliamentary system of government, the party in power typically commands the votes necessary to pass legislation that has been drafted as a "complete package," with technical considerations in mind. The vast majority of voters of all parties support the health-care system, and that has been the indispensable factor. Has anything approaching this voter or politician consensus been reached in the United States? Could a technically satisfactory Medicare plan be adopted under the adversary system of a contending legislature and executive?

Canadian experience shows that some restraint can be placed on hospital costs through budget control. The freedom provided under "global budgeting" is mainly the freedom of the hospital to choose where it will cut back when the financial situation is tight. Would American state and voluntary hospitals be willing to give up their autonomy to operate under similar constraints?

Canadian experience shows that physicians' fees can also be restrained. It is possible because the medical societies had detailed fee schedules in the first instance, because fees are now discussed or actually negotiated with public authorities, and because both sides are reasonably cooperative and continue to communicate with each other. If the doctors did not go along with the system, it could not work; if it were open ended the cost would be prohibitive. Are American doctors and their professional associations similarly disposed?

The major Canadian insurance companies lost a lucrative field of business when Medicare came in. They did some advertising and some lobbying for their side but failed. (Incidentally, in Manitoba and Saskatchewan the government has also taken over automobile insurance, and the new NDP government in British Columbia will presumably do so soon.) What is the relative bargaining strength of insurance companies and government in the United States?

Of all these points, I think that the need for consensus is the most important. Consensus was achieved in Canada, as it was in other countries around the world. The prospects for Medicare in the United States are just as good or bad as the prospects for consensus.

CHAPTER 5

Alternative Prescriptions for a Healthier America: Radical and Visionary Viewpoints

We particularly ask you—
When a thing continually occurs—
Not on that account to find it natural
Let nothing be called natural
In an age of blood confusion
Ordered disorder, planned caprice,
And dehumanized humanity,
lest all things
Be held unalterable!

BERTOLT BRECHT

The Radical Heart of the Matter

Given their preoccupation with betrayals predicated on private gain-making, radicals are instantly ready to indict our unconscious or possibly even conscious complicity in America's health-care scandal. Among other things we can be condemned for impressionable complacency, ignorant callousness, and self-centered craftiness.

Our complacency, for example, has us willingly dazzled by the mystification and puffery that accompany the alleged breakthroughs of Merlin-like health researchers, by the expensive and stainless glitter of new "gee whiz" medical apparatus, and by the contrived and seemingly infallible wisdom of countless TV nurses and Welby-like doctors. We overlook "facts" that soundly condemn American medicine, expose its hypocrisy, and excoriate its practioners. Two examples popular with health radicals allege that:

1. We often get too much health care, rather than too little: American doctors, for example, perform twice as many operations as do their British counterparts.
2. Approximately one-fifth of the surgery performed in America is unneeded; some three million people annually suffer pointless and expensive surgery.[1]

Radicals urge us, accordingly, to go beyond a simplistic view of imperialism that merely has the haves keeping the goodies from the have-nots. Rather, we are challenged to recognize that the supposed goodies are themselves often poisonous!

We are callous in our ignorance of or indifference to the very special casualities of our health-care system. Radicals point to a fact made plain by dozens of government studies in the 1960's: The poor, the blacks, and the aged are often sick, and, conversely, the sick are often poor, black, and/or aged. Infant mortality rates for the poor are twice those of the national average; life expectancies are years shorter. Dr. Martin Cherkosky asserts,

> The principal cause of the low ranking stems from the fact that we are just not delivering our medical services adequately to all segments of society. The poorer elements in our society—the blacks, Puerto Ricans, and other poor population groups—die at significantly earlier ages than the more affluent whites.[2]

Radicals never cease railing against this injustice, many insisting that private exploitation of health-promoting care is a crime against humanity.

Finally, we can be indicted for rather unbecoming craftiness in protecting our *own* privileged health-care status. With certain conservatives we are condemned for being confused about just how much medical care is a human right. Is a person entitled to visit a doctor every time he has a headache or a stomach ache, we ask with our liberal friends, or does his human right to medical care begin only when he has a genuinely serious illness? Radicals impatiently sweep aside all such efforts at making economic or rational distinctions and settle the matter emphatically in favor of our placing no conditions on the absolute right of all to free, high-quality medical care!

Radical Reform Focus. If pressed to identify one central issue more revealing than any other, many radicals often point to the alleged existence of a (criminal?) conspiracy in our health-care system.

Liberals, you will recall, insist that our health industry is near chaos because it is a nonsystem dominated by small, inefficient, and uncoördinated enterprises—simply adrift, with no one to blame. Liberal solutions seek to put the health industry on a more "rational"—that is, businesslike—basis, as through the use of national health insurance, HMO's, and so on. Radicals insist there is only one thing wrong with this analysis of the health-care crisis: it is based on a false assumption. If the function of the American health industry is to provide adequate health care for you and me, we might conclude that there is no American health *system*. But this is like assuming that the American automobile industry has as a high priority safe, cheap, efficient, pollution-free transportation, or that the TV networks take seriously their function of giving comprehensive, penetrating, and meaningful information to their viewers. Like the auto and TV industries, however, the American medical industry has many items on its agenda, and patient health-care simply does *not* take the top priority. Instead, profit making, research, and staff training loom much larger—and have the covert, conspiratorial allegiance of hospitals, doctors, medical schools, drug companies, the AMA, health insurance companies, and others. Analyzed, then, in terms of healthy industry functions (patient care being the least significant of them all), the medical industry emerges as a coherent, highly organized system.

Accordingly, the system *can* be faulted (it is not "just drifting"), and it cannot be salvaged by "more of the same," however deceptively appealing the liberal reforms, predicated as they are on a false assumption of nonsystem ills. Conspiracy is the crux of the matter, and gaining control of a covert, exploitative system is the central reform issue.

Professional Contribution. Radicals are torn between their bitter animosity toward the AMA and their fervid trust in the promise of young mavericks among doctors and nonprofessionals alike. Although insistent that much reform can be wrested painfully from the plutocrats in the health industry, many radicals remain finally persuaded that only *total* change—including but not limited to the nationalization of the industry—will *really* do the job.

In the interim, however, four particular reforms are asked of health-care professionals. They are advised to expose the conspirators in their own ranks. They are also to promote a new definition of the "good" radical doctor. They are expected to support the creation of new paraprofessional posts in medical care. And they are advised to search eagerly abroad for contracapitalistic clues to better ways to tend to our health needs.

1. Ripe for exposé in the demonology of health-savvy radicals is the stately, plump, and seemingly monolithic American Medical Association. Long the unchallenged voice of organized medicine in the United States, the AMA is denounced for its rigid record of archconservatism in the political and social fields. According to Gwen Gibson, in fifty years of protecting the rights of the private physician and "the sanctity of the American home," the AMA has opposed:

> public health vaccinations against diphtheria, public venereal disease clinics, the mandatory reporting of tuberculosis cases to public health agencies, federal grants for mother-and-child welfare programs, low-interest loans for medical students, Social Security, group practice of any kind, and even Blue Cross and Blue Shield plans.[3]

Radicals now toll the bell of decline for the monolith, citing its failure to hold onto its membership in recent years (down 8 per cent in the last ten years), its steady losses to the rival American Hospital Association, and its considerable loss of public credibility. Linked to the age of the guild-dominated, individual craftsman, an age now clearly past, the AMA's rear-guard stance exasperates and draws the steady fire of radicals insistent that "insiders" of integrity hasten the demise of the "dinosaur."

2. The second expectation of practioners concerns a new role prescription, one that attempts to redefine *professionalism* and *professional roles,* to change their nature and our understanding of them. Central here is a disavowal of the moral cynicism of conventional medical practice cited by H. Jack Gieger: "Too many of us still treat the rat-bites and ignore the rats; treat the lead poisoning and ignore the plaster on the crumbling tenement walls; treat the

napalm burn and ignore the war."[4] Recommended instead, is rapt attention to the following:

> What are the radical health professionals saying? In general, that our social order is a dehumanizing corporate state, dominated by an exploitative capitalism at home and a militaristic imperialism abroad, and characterized by socialization of the individual away from individuality and toward conformity, adaptation to the system and to the needs of technology. That this system creates (indeed, requires) poverty, racism, inequity, oppression, and indignity, and trains us to ignore it, accept it, or profit from it. That the system has little or no capacity for basic change. That our institutions, including our health institutions, function not to serve the consumer or the community, but rather to serve the interests of this exploitative social order and the interests of those who run the institutions; thus hospitals are run not for the patient or the community but, in crucial ways, for the benefit of ourselves, the professionals, and the other institutions we control or share in. That the very nature of our "professional role" is reactionary and oppressive.[5]

Accordingly, the key challenge here is to promote the power of the people in all health-related matters, initially through selfless professional service in community-dominated alternatives (the "free clinic" movement, health collectives, and so on) and, ultimately, through winning control of major medical institutions for the men and women who work in and utilize the services of such "liberated" institutions.

To this end doctors and medical students have participated in the civil rights programs of the early Medical Committee for Human Rights, the area work of OEO-funded neighborhood health centers, and the antipoverty efforts of the Student Health Organization. As well, in 1970 students, faculty members, and the deans of several eastern medical schools founded the Medical Alliance for Political Action (MAPA) and began a well-publicized lobbying effort for an end to the war in Vietnam.

On the local level, as, for example, at Yale, a MAPA chapter has chosen to:

> Pressure a New Haven nursing school to recruit more black students.
> Help to set up a free Panther clinic.
> Begin an extensive investigation of local health conditions in jails and prisons.

On the national level MAPA prepares analysis of federal health programs and pending legislation (impact upon the poor, for example) and has compelled HEW officials to grant it representation on important health advisory committees. In all, MAPA members understandably earn radical kudos for breaking with their profession's political conservatism and seeking to revive its life-affirming and humanist traditions.

3. Radicals also urge the health profession to welcome paraprofessionals into its ranks, laymen with limited but useful skills who can save lives, relieve doctors for unconventional tasks, and help reduce the crushing burden of health costs.

Despite ingrained thinking that holds that only traditionally trained doctors can be entrusted with the health of a patient, it is plain that alternative routes to medical proficiency exist and should be used to save lives and money. Former military medics or high school graduates trained in health care, for example, are being hailed as one of the keys to solving the nation's shortage of physicians: "They are not doctors, but they're the next best thing—trained personnel who know how to deal with emergencies, perform basic medical tasks, and meet on-the-spot needs of patients." Similarly, a new class of paraprofessionals, the qualified nurse-midwives, are trained at ten schools in America to give expectant women prenatal care, deliver babies, and then offer follow-up counseling for mother and child, thereby meeting a critical doctor shortage in all these areas.

As might be expected, the medical profession and the public have been slow to accept such radical changes of the status quo. But the pressure for acceptance is substantial, and the AMA in 1971 finally endorsed the use of certified ex-medics, even as the stuffy American College of Obstetricians and Gynecologists finally extended its official recognition to the nation's seventeen hundred nurse-midwives.[6]

These paraprofessionals are looked to by radicals to help humanize American medical practice. For example, as Judy Klemesrud notes:

> Although they generally must follow the maternity procedures of their hospitals, several nurse-midwives said they thought they would probably be more liberal than a doctor about letting the patient decide for herself whether she wants a member of the family with her in labor; whether she prefers to have the baby in a sitting position or lying down; with or without her legs in stirrups; and with or without the enema and the shave and the episiotomy (the surgical cutting of the perineum).[7]

It is not surprising, therefore, that this new style of medical practice is upsetting time-honored conventions:

> "Some middle-class women in the wards have seen us teaching a new mother how to breast feed," said Marilyn Schmidt, 25, nurse-midwife at Cumberland Hospital in Brooklyn. "They've also overheard our family planning talks and seen us teaching postpartum exercises. Afterwards, some of them have asked why they're not getting the same care."[8]

Understandably, then, radicals expect much to follow from their uncompromising advocacy of ever greater reliance in health care on paraprofessionals.

4. Finally, in the area of in-service reforms radicals urge everyone in health care to look abroad for "clues" to a better health system. For example:

a. In Sweden, which has the lowest infant mortality rate in the world, mothers are routinely turned over to the care of midwives early in pregnancy.
b. In China, paramedics, known in the countryside as "barefoot doctors" and in the cities as "workers' doctors," learn in five months of formal training enough to treat minor complaints and common illnesses, issue medications (penicillin, tranquilizers, birth control pills, and so on), and

accent preventive medicine (immunizations, sanitation, and health education)—all of which they perform while continuing to farm the land or work in factories.

c. The Chinese hospital functions very differently from ours, what with the doctors' being liable to criticism from all employees and patients, administrators' being expected to work one day a week at manual labor, patients' being consulted in all aspects of their care, and so on.

Other examples—often drawn from Cuban, Eastern European, and Soviet health-care experience—are commonly cited with barely qualified enthusiasm.

Of course there is disagreement on the superiority of other systems over ours. Conservatives, for example, delight in "exposing" shortcomings in the much-vaunted British socialized health-care system. Focusing sharply on Britain they find that:

British hospitals are overcrowded to an extent unknown here.
From 1948 to date, only three new hospitals have been built.
The average length of hospital confinement is many days shorter here.

Similarly, it is claimed that in comparison with European doctors our own are much more active in preventive medicine and, on the average, spend more time with each patient. Overall, the infamous "waiting lists" of the overseas nationalized health-care systems are grimly cited as "the best indicator of all as to what changes may be expected if government health programs are adopted here."[9]

Similarly, the radical boasts, for example, that a hospital room in socialistic Sweden (in 1970) cost only $1.40 a day, a doctor's visit $1.35, and drugs only a minimal sum when they are not free. Conservatives will heatedly retort that Swedes pay over 20 per cent of their taxes—the highest such rate in the world—for health care! Undaunted, the radical internationalist may argue that Sweden still devotes 1 per cent less of its GNP and $45 less per person for health than we do—in return for far more than our "care-as-a-privilege" system seems inclined to provide.[10] And so the debate in international comparisons, endless in its possible combinations and permutations of data and rhetoric, rages on and on.

Radical Reforms to Pursue. Radical strategies vary all the way from break-the-system to infiltrate-and-remake, and they cover most points in between as well. At one pole is this terse verdict of a disillusioned health planner in San Francisco: "I'm pinning my hopes on chaos—only when conditions become sufficiently chaotic will there be genuine reform."[11] At the other pole is a more calculating and far more patient call for "a long march through the institutions" from radical change-agents whose clarion call is "Power to the people!"

A host of reform particulars are unique to the radical health campaign, including a provocative insistence that we soon reorder our priorities in medical research. In Howard Levy's words:

> The unquestioning acceptance of the justifications for expending scarce research dollars on esoterically rare diseases, such as cystic fibrosis (a genetic

disease almost always limited to white people), as opposed to, let's say, sickle-cell anemia (a common and often fatal genetic disease affecting predominantly Black people), is but a reflection of prevailing racist attitudes and institutions in American society.[12]

Similarly, the high earnings of doctors prompt a bitter call for a legal limit on "profiteering." No longer should our disorganized, fee-for-service system of health-care delivery, by virtue of the enforced scarcity of physicians, make many if not most doctors rich.

Although radicals advocate more use of paraprofessionals, free clinics in poverty neighborhoods, more recruitment of minorities into medical schools, neighborhood control over the boards of local hospitals, and the adoption of overseas medical advances, these recommendations pale alongside the major radical prescription, the nationalization of the entire American health empire.

At issue is the single-minded radical preference for the "political economy" type of health service common in East Europe and Great Britain, over our own traditional "market economy" model. Both models, of course, are basically systems for distributing or rationing scarce resources. Each answers the critical question of who makes the decisions about who gets what resources, and each does so in a fundamentally different way. (All other questions—for example, whether doctors are salaried or not, whether the service is free or not—are thereby rendered secondary.)

Our market economy model holds that the distribution of resources is best determined by capitalist forces. We rely on cash payments by the consumers of medical care for services rendered, though there are a variety of ways in which market forces can be rigged and the consumers repaid (for example, through state or private insurance schemes). On the other hand, the political economy model rests on the distribution of resources by centralized political means. In practice this usually means that services are wholly or largely free, though theoretically and logically this model is perfectly compatible with payments for services.

Calling for the nationalization of the American health industry, radicals promise that the political economy model will open the public purse to a revamped health-care system and remove (immoral) economic obstacles to the use of medical services. Abolishing the market role of the consumer, the nationalization model (like that of the British National Health Services, a leading example) will replace the role of consumer-as-buyer with the role of consumer-as-voter. Although the details remain to be worked out, the radical reform will essentially "draft" medical personnel across the nation into a new federal "army" in the war on ill health, this army being no mere rhetorical metaphor but a vast new government bureaucracy of medical people.

Why nationalization? Because nothing short of it, nothing less than a radical change in the ownership of the means of (health) production is thought equal to the challenge. The critical issue in reform is, and has always been, *control:* How are we to achieve decisive power?

Until control is wrested from the health-care plutocrats and returned to community health projects the poor will continue to get sick, the sick will get poorer, and the medical-industrial complex will wax rich. (In this connection, it helps to understand that radicals press the collectivization issue *very* hard. Cornering their liberal cohorts, they persistently ask, for example, if you are willing to regulate the doctors and the hospitals, why not the drug companies and the companies that sell hospitals everything from commodes to catheters to computers?)

Going farther and deeper than the liberal critic, the radical insists on demolishing any naïveté we might have about the "novelty" of our health crisis. As Michael G. Michaelson puts it,

> Today we know that the painfully earned tax dollars of "middle Americans" are certain to be dropped as mines and bombs in Southeast Asia or launched as space shuttles and modules to the moon. Today we know that millions of our fellow citizens are unemployed or chained to heroin or to an apartment squeaky with rats; we know that millions cannot feed their children or clothe them properly or send them to college or even send them out to play in the grass. (There is sparkling cut glass out there, broken bottles, dope, and air thick with exhaust and gasoline.) Is it really possible for anyone to see in the medical mess an exception rather than a reflection? Is it possible, really, to be surprised?[13]

It would seem that in America today, it is not only our health-care industry, but our entire social, political, and economic order that is distorted and unwell.

The drift of the argument is clear. Control and power deficiencies inside any particular social institution are impossible to remedy except as the entire social order is revolutionized. More specifically, health-care reforms without sweeping social reforms are *not* acceptable. Radicals want to see health reform used as a launching pad for a broad range of tangential social changes. They are utterly disinclined to be paralyzed by conservative arguments (and liberal acquiescence!). And they utterly reject the notion that the health-care industry should have a smaller rather than a larger socially supportive function (conservatives, you will recall, want to "free" medicine for a far more limited role, a far less flamboyant vision, and a far "realer" kind of accountability).

Instead, radicals insist that health reforms be accompanied by massive correctional efforts aimed at malnutrition, auto accidents, war, pollution, and the grisly like. They are especially derisive of the government's decision to spend millions on a new crash program to cure cancer at the very same time that it condones the spewing into the air of tons of cancer-causing industrial pollutants. Good health, they conclude, absolutely requires freedom from occupational hazards, poisonous drugs and food, and bad housing—which freedom in turn necessitates new forms of radical control in America.

Not surprisingly, then, the paultry efforts by liberals to preserve the private-profit, free-enterprise character of health care while introducing more rationality, planning, and system into it, only derisive scorn from health-knowledgeable radicals. The Kennedy bill, for example, would dare to counter seriously the stranglehold power of doctors with the puny counterdevice of advisory boards (albeit with consumer majorities). Advice is *not* control, radicals snort, and power would clearly remain in the hands of the medical profession:

> The only way to effect fundamental change in the health system so that it will provide adequate, dignified care for all is to take power over health care away from the people who now control it. National health insurance would *not* be a move in the direction of a national health *system;* it would be more of a shuffle sideways.[14]

The liberals, stung by this rebuff and unimpressed with the radical prescriptions ("hopelessly romantic," "unlikely of attainment," and so on), have parted ways with the radicals by mutual consent, at considerable cost to the entire uncertain campaign for health-care reform.

As for the chances of the radical platform, the obstacles could not be more formidable. According to Barbara and John Ehrenreich, to secure radical reforms is to:

> ask our big city medical empires to turn their priorities from research, teaching, and institutional expansion to the care of sick people;
>
> ask the health products industry to favor the consumer over the stockholder; and—
>
> ask a growing sector of American industry to come into health as a public service, or not to come at all.[15]

Clearly, fundamental improvements in health care can be achieved only through a head-on confrontation with our political and economic system.

Even relatively minor matters like proposed limits on the earnings of doctors provoke heated argument. Not only are high earnings thought fair by conservatives in light of the many low-income years spent in training and as a reflection of the high degree of skill, knowledge, and responsibility expected of physicians, but also as a relative matter. Harry Schwartz argues,

> When a Muhammad Ali and a Joe Frazier can command millions of dollars for a single fight and a Ralph Nader can charge $2,500 for a single hour-long speech, it is not surprising that some outstanding physicians can and do earn annual incomes in excess of $100,000.[16]

Similarly, the radical call for more extensive use of paraprofessionals, especially indigenous personnel in ghetto areas, confronts an unexpected opposition from certain ghetto activists. These spokesmen suspect a plot to provide only "second-class people and second-class care" for the poor and deprived. Although the suspicion is groundless, it feeds into a larger and more difficult matter, the feeling many people have that when they feel sick they want to see a full-fledged doctor and not some less-well-trained substitute.

Still more telling, however, is critical opposition to the key matter of nationalization. Conservatives are especially attentive to the stubborn fact that any sweeping reform will have to be delivered primarily by today's physicians. Although their counterparts in Britain, China, Chile, Cuba, and Scandinavia have demonstrated remarkable adaptability, resiliency, and patriotism in comparable change situations, conservatives take a strange delight in hinting at sabotage and resistance if radical reform is imposed upon the nation's physicians, dentists, and other health service personnel against their will and without consideration of their ideas and legitimate interests.

Conservatives also point to our postal and public school systems as proof of their contention that nationalization does not mean efficiency, even as our telephone system teaches that even a private system can develop serious flaws. Furthermore, although the reorganization of medical services into larger units could integrate services and offer increased efficiency, larger health-care institutions are in themselves no more a guarantee of a break for the public than the replacement of the corner grocery store with a Safeway or an A & P. Grimly the critics conclude that if "revolutionary proposals for transforming American medicine are adopted and implemented, medical care in this country will cost more while providing less satisfaction and poorer treatment for millions."[17]

"Social surgery" of the nationalization variety that radicals propose is emphatically dismissed by many as a cure worse than the disease. Even to consider it is to ignore the critical fact that the American medical care system, with its 4,000,000 workers, its 7,000 hospitals, its 20,000 nursing homes, its 356,000 physicians, and its incredible array of specialized skills and equipment is "quite simply *the* most complicated industry in the United States. To suppose that we know enough to improve it through radical changes imposed upon this system in a brief period is fantasy more appropriate to an LSD 'trip' than to sober legislative deliberation."[18] Accordingly, any expectation that a radically persuaded Congress is equal to the enormous challenge of creating new and effective reforms to alter our health-care system substantially must give way to pessimism—especially when one honestly contemplates the runaway costs and enormous waste of Medicare and Medicaid to date.

To which unending argument certain increasingly exasperated radicals are inclined to reply softly, but firmly: "Revolution, anyone?"

The Visionary Heart of the Matter

Whereas many liberals insist that effective health-care action will require organization on the part of the victims, many radicals urge us not to beg favors of criminals (health-care plutocrats). Conservatives, disbelieving and utterly dismayed by the other schools, are likely to call down a plague on both houses, whereas visionaries might regard the wrangling of all three with a wry and patient tolerance. From the very special perspective of the visionary school there are no criminals, we are all victims, and still more organization is the last thing needed if we are to gain significantly new strength in health matters.

As you would expect from their preoccupation with our total failure to comprehend what is *really* at issue, visionaries fundamentally indict all of us as misguided complicators in explaining supposedly temporary weaknesses in the nation's health-care system. At the very heart of our problem is our definition of *health*. Unlike the conservative, who defines health as the absence of disabling illness; or the liberal, for whom it means feeling okay; or the radical, who identifies it with community togetherness, the visionary expects remarkably more from the notion. *Health* is taken to mean an extraordinarily heightened sense of self-realization, self-liberation, and self-actualization.

Conservatives, liberals, and radicals accept the popular notion that all illnesses have physical causes and are therefore properly the subject of medical responses. Visionaries quietly ask if the opposite might not be true: Could it be that all illness is initiated by changes in consciousness? If so, then the heart of the matter is to be found in grasping that *all* illness is largely psychosomatic! Visionaries propose, accordingly, that the physical manifestations of illness are always effects and that much of the real cause actually lies within the realm of the mind and the psyche.

Illness, from this very special and controversial perspective, is believed to be caused by a breakdown in the dialogue between the conscious and the unconscious. As Andrew Weil explains,

> In the case of infectious illness, the initial causative change is not that germs appear to attack the body but that something happens in the person that permits a breakdown in the normal harmonious balance between the body and the microorganisms surrounding it.[19]

It follows, then, that the key to healing does not lie in dealing with the superficial external manifestations that are currently the object of conventional health care. Rather, the key is in helping the patient himself to restore his own equilibrium. The goal becomes the restoration of the natural state of openness between the conscious and unconscious minds.

Taking the reintegration of consciousness as their focus, visionaries naturally identify the key agent in the health restoration process as the patient-as-physician, for the responsibility for achieving a reintegration of an ill (or disintegrated) consciousness rests ultimately with the sick person: the power to heal, like the power to make ill, resides in the patient.[20]

Basically, the issue here has far wider currency than is commonly recognized, though few are willing to face up to its full implications. Even some liberals, represented here by Senator Edward Kennedy, sometimes grasp this visionary point:

> the people have been given less say in the area of health care than in almost any other area of American life. In no other area do they have so little choice or control. In no other area is the provider of services given such total freedom and authority.[21]

But few, including the Senator, press further to grasp the provocative critical insight that it is we ourselves who can actually threaten the medical plantation far more profoundly than does anything else, the radical call for nationalization notwithstanding. Ignorance of one's body, one's health, and one's mind-body-world unity cuts across class, race, sex, and age lines. Reform requires that we redefine our concepts of doctor and patient and even of good health. And as health writer Michael G. Michaelson gently but firmly points out, "These least tangible tasks are the most urgent."[22]

Central to Visionary Reform. No other concept may capture as much of the revolutionary potential inherent in the visionary health movement as does the concept of cooperative care. With their call for cooperative care visionaries press for a completely new health system, one in which self-knowledge replaces mystery, in which self-help is regarded as a matter of common pride and not of stubbornness, and in which decisions are made by all involved. Designed to help free all of us from our crisis-care and doctor-as-elitist system, the visionary plan focuses instead on mass health education, self-help, patient participation, and the rejection of all that is currently authoritarian in our health-care system.

Revealingly, the other three schools persist in viewing medicine not as a service but as a product, with financial incentive thought necessary to induce the providers to give decent care. Even the term *health consumer,* originated by liberal reformers and now used regularly by nearly everyone from the AMA to the most radical critics of health care, perpetuates the notion of health care as a product.

Visionaries reject the very term *health care* and the insulting and tired politics that it implies. A parent and child relationship is called to mind by this old notion, one complete with a carer and a cared-for, a strong and a weak party, a giver and a recipient, an active and a passive partner. In its place the visionary reform urges making the person central and providing cooperative care. (Typical is Joan Haggerty's exasperated assertion that even the terminology in conventional obstetrical practice is damaging: "The doctor is said to 'deliver' the baby. Damn it, the *woman* delivers the baby, the doctor *receives* it."[23])

Apropos the path-breaking demands of the woman's health movement, Mary Costanza, a woman doctor, explains:

> These women demand that they not be talked down to. They demand health education and self-help programs. They demand safe abortions. They demand an active role in controlling what happens to their bodies. They demand to do for themselves medically what they believe is reasonable for them to do.[24]

Over and over again the visionary movement poses what this same sympathetic physician characterizes as "very fundamental and startling questions: Shouldn't the people be active participants in decision-making concerning health matters? Shouldn't the patient be regarded primarily as a thinking, responsible person?"[25]

These questions, of course, challenge a precept dear to the hearts of conservatives and liberals alike. Labeled by political scientist Robert Dahl the "criterion of competence," this precept insists that it is not necessarily rational for you to insist upon participating in all decisions that affect your interests in a vital way. Dahl's examples ask, "Would you want the passengers to vote on the plane or the ship's course? Would you want the patients to vote on the methods or criteria of surgery or the training of surgeons?"[26]

Condemning these as traditionally stultifying examples, visionaries expose the trap of extending these analogies too far into the sphere of social decisions in general. One *does* have the right, they insist, to know the assumptions of the experts, to be aware of clashes among them, to challenge them, and to choose other experts whose assumptions are more palatable.

Professional Expectation. Health-care professionals are challenged by visionaries as by no one else. Against the visionary call for cooperative care I believe that the conservative call for industry self-regulation, the liberal dream of rationalization, and the radical demand for a new concept of government service all pale. Visionaries counsel nothing less than heresy. As Mary Costanza says,

> They imply that health professionals have no intrinsic expertise about the moral, social, and political wisdom of a given health care system.
>
> They imply that given the facts and an honest explanation of them, the American public can decide, as well as the Establishment, what a reasonable national health care system should be.
>
> They imply that patients could actively decide about their medical treatment, as they decide whether to accept the advice of counsel.[27]

Heresy! Imagine! To contend seriously that given the facts and an honest explanation of what the problem is patients can decide for themselves, for example, whether the risks involved in a particular procedure are acceptable ("How many unnecessary D & C's, hysterectomies, radical mastectomies, and every other kind of -ectomy could surgeons so freely perform if women were better informed of the facts before they consented to have their insides cut up?"[28]).

Impatience with the human targets of change is considerable, and impassioned calls for the demystifying of medicine are increasingly common. The indictments are far-reaching:

1. The medical profession guards information with all the effectiveness of a patented copyright.
2. We are duped into believing that information about our bodies is beyond the scope of our comprehension.
3. Medical training uses the Prussian army as its model, a system that degrades, humiliates, and makes infantile all it touches.
4. The fear of many patients that they will be punished unless they are totally submissive reveals a profound distrust of the people in control of their bodies.
5. Because of their mystique, doctors feel impelled to behave as if they have all the answers.

Visionaries of this persuasion are especially aggrieved by the growing evidence that American medical care focuses narrowly on symptomatic relief and medication designed to calm patients. Much of the daily work of physicians deals with tension headaches, intestinal complaints, or vague feelings of anxiety with little or no demonstrable organic basis. Many patients really seek reassurance, elementary psychiatric care, and simple human companionship. They get some of this, along with mood-conditioning drugs, pain relief, sleep ensurers, and a bottomless supply of placebos. What they do *not* get is any new grasp of the sources of their symptoms, any new notions of how to fight back, any new reason to believe they can finally break their incapacitating patterns—and strike for a new and better life.

Not surprisingly, therefore, the less hopeful among the reformers like Ellen Frankfort can see the Way, but not a way:

> If all drugs had a listing of their ingredients, pregnant women now on antidepressants . . . could check to see if a suspect ingredient were present. . . . of course, that would give women the autonomy to stop taking a drug without consulting their doctor first, something that neither doctors nor drug companies are about to encourage.[29]

Overall, then, some of the reformers are grimly convinced that "so long as the profit motive exists, doctors will not exhibit the kind of medical accountability consumers need. Until the fee-for-service is eliminated, consumers will have to keep constant checks on doctors."[30]

Less grim visionaries choose to focus on the many open-minded and reform-eager people inside the ranks of the health-care professions who seem to be intrigued by, if not yet entirely convinced of, the merit of the cooperative care approach. One concerned physician explains:

> The issue comes down to whether each individual health professional is willing to accept the patient as an equal and not as a helpless inferior.
>
> When shall this miracle of cooperation and mutual respect occur? No one knows. But it is coming.[31]

Elsewhere, the journalist Norman Cousins gently points out that "the ultimate art of the good doctor is to make good patients. He does this by making the patient a full partner in his recovery."[32] From this special perspective some visionaries are confident that professionalism in health care, scrutinized this time by activists who reject the Olympian qualities and mystique of any class, will be enhanced.

Visionary Reforms to Pursue. Basically there are two related types of reforms at issue, one set explicitly designed to help us examine those who until now have been sacrosanct in examining us and a second set concerned with helping us take over some of the more basic functions of the medical-Brahman caste. The two sets of reforms are often conjoined, of course, as in the recommendation that women ask to look through the doctor's microscope at the smear slide just taken from them. A woman medical journalist, Ellen Frankfort, notes in this connection, "By looking, as I did when I had trichomonas and seeing the fast-moving creatures darting back and forth, the disease and my own body became less mysterious. So, of course, did the doctor."[33] Comparably bold, if somewhat less novel, is the compilation by the Woman's Center in New York City of its own list of good and bad doctors, rated by women who have used them, the latter list especially targeted for adverse publicity.

Also in the way of helping the health-care consumer gain new leverage it is recommended that:

1. Lay activists translate professional jargon into language any person can comprehend.
2. Patients be given a copy of their medical records, X-rays, and test results.

3. Hospital patients be allowed to participate in their own treatment, sit in on medical conferences, and help make medical decisions.

These and a large number of other recommendations are meant to ensure not only dignified and nonpatronizing care but also medically sound help that takes into account the latest scientific knowledge.

Over and over visionaries strain to explain that it is not that the freedom and authority of medical professionals must be limited so much as it is that the freedom and authority of all of us laymen to learn medical principles and to have useful access to medical tools must be enhanced. In operational terms this can mean a general call for more support of preventive health education programs. According to Nancy Hicks,

> Only $30-million of the $18,200,000,000 budget of HEW goes to teach health lessons, and most of this is spent by the Bureau of Indian Affairs.
>
> Less than 1 per cent of the total $75-billion spent on health services goes for health education for laymen.[34]

In personal terms it can mean increasing resort to any one of a large number of new-style book-length guides to medical self-help. Typical is *The People's Handbook of Medical Care,* which is based upon two strong convictions:

> First, people can learn to be responsible for a substantial part of their own medical care, for such care is increasingly expensive, inadequate, or administered under such degrading conditions as to be of little value.
>
> Second, much information about medicine is couched in needlessly obscure terms. In order for the public to learn to take care of itself, medical information must be made accessible; it should be presented in informal language free of "mystery and awe."[35]

Special attention, as you might expect, is paid to a patient's medical rights and privileges. Similarly, provoked by propatient court decisions the American Hospital Association in 1972 adopted a twelve-point "bill of rights" for hospitalized patients.[36]

In the matter of joint or group activity the visionary perspective can generate the following kind of experiences (note that this case is not just incidentally focused on the nation's only home-birth center):

> Women Act To Control Healthcare (WATCH) is a Chicago based women's group composed of healthcare workers and consumers concerned about the institutional healthcare services available for women in Chicago.
>
> WATCH first got interested in the [Chicago Maternity] Center when we realized that it offered a unique, personalized maternity service for all women, regardless of their ability to pay; and that with its imminent incorporation into the Northwestern medical complex, home delivery might be phased out. We found that the Maternity Center treated all women equally and with dignity. For the population that now uses the Center (45% are Black, 40% Latin, 5% White Appalachian, 5% White middle class), home delivery is a need because: (1) these women cannot afford the fees of traditional hospital care, (2) there is no hospital to meet their ob/gyn

needs in their own communities (e.g. Loretto Hospital in Maywood recently closed its ob/gyn ward leaving Maywood without any services), (3) their culture has always regarded childbirth as a natural process to happen at home, or (4) it is disruptive to leave their families for a hospital stay as there is often no one to stay home with their children. Also, having a baby at home takes away from childbirth the mistaken notion of it being a disease, and makes it a natural process; hence, women have babies, doctors don't deliver them while women are passive and impatient. Healthcare in this way becomes a human right, as it should be, defined by the women who use the institution.[37]

Note how the conservative defense of business as usual is rejected out of hand, how the liberal call for still more rationalization is just as readily passed over, and how the radical stress on ownership of the means of (health-care) production is ignored for the time being.

Instead, the key in the entire matter is the way in which a patient perceives his or her body and health. Illuminating in this connection is a popular pamphlet, "The Gynecological Examination," prepared by the Health Organization Collective of the New York City Woman's Health and Abortion Project. Ellen Frankfort recalls the use a friend of hers made of the guide during her gynecological checkup:

> She took off her clothes, kept on her shoes and once in the stirrups, she continued to read: "Harvey," she said (since she has a doctorate she decided to call him "Harvey" since he calls her "Eve"), "have you checked out my blood pressure? And how about a smear for VD? The culture, not the gram stain?"
>
> Harvey was flabbergasted. Never before had any woman checked him out.[38]

Similarly, Frankfort recommends making a Christmas gift of a plastic speculum: "Along with a mirror, a lamp, and a red bow, it might just be the perfect gift for the feminist who has everything except an image of what she looks like inside."[39] If happiness is, as leading self-help women activists claim, "knowing how your uterus looks," then health, the journalist concludes, "may be using that knowledge to keep our uteri the way we like to see them."

Now it might seem to some of you that this visionary blueprint, with its focus on democratizing relationships in health-care matters, strays far from the poetry and romantic musing about mind-psyche epidemiology with which the discussion began. Perhaps. And then again, perhaps not. For these are only represented as *preliminary* reforms, the opening goals in a long and arduous, as well as compelling and enlarging program of personal and societal renewal. After cooperative care has been secured—and during the struggle for its attainment—laymen and professionals alike will be drawn naturally to still more basic questions about health and ill health.

Chapter Summary

With invigorating dissonance the four major schools of political thought generate a unique answer to just about every major question about health care. It does seem at times that the four schools are not talking about the same subject, what with the conservative endorsement of the status quo, the more critical liberal call for central government direction, the angry radical demand that we nationalize the entire mess, and the visionary's preoccupation with self-assertion and cooperative care in health matters.

Little seems agreed upon, even as far back as the fundamental question of whether or not the nation has a health-care "crisis":

1. *Conservative*—Hardly! Best care in the world, though its failure to bill patients directly overloads it with exploitive types.
2. *Liberal*—Probably! Care is almost as good as in nationally planned systems—such as in the Scandinavian nations—and can soar in quality with the use of rational planning!
3. *Radical*—Emphatically! Have-nots are victimized by a deliberate conspiracy of the privileged; only an extreme overhaul of the entire system can make a difference!
4. *Visionary*—Until *health* is defined in completely new ways—to accent its integration into a self-actualizing life order—piecemeal hysteria over health "industry" minutiae only misleads.

As shown in Table 5–1, the four schools differ on even the major ills and the preferable care sites.

TABLE 5–1

Conservative	*Liberal*	*Radical*	*Visionary*
Open-heart surgery	Coronaries	Infant mortality	Psychosomatic complaints
Part transplants	VD	Hunger	Natural childbirth
Leukemia and kidney treatment gains	Emergency care	Addictions	Personal and home care
Hospital care	Office and out-patient care	Sickle-cell anemia	
		Clinic care	

Indeed, every imaginable aspect of the situation is controversial, including even the very value of life itself. Conservatives crisply assign financial limits to intensive health care, whereas radicals would spare no expense, liberals would agonize over practicality, and visionaries would deny the very validity of the death-as-disaster scare itself.

Not surprisingly, when asked to define the position of the patient the four schools offer four different characterizations:

Conservative—the patient as plunderer.
Liberal—the patient as "patsy."
Radical—the patient as plundered.
Visionary—the patient as Prufrock, the would-be prince.

When asked to cite the critical agent or major party in the entire health-care drama the four schools produce four different candidates:

Conservative—the professionals, of course!
Liberal—the planners, when all is set right!
Radical—the change agents, as the cutting edge of mass protest and total reform!
Visionary—the people themselves, as claimants of a new private and collective consciousness!

Put another way, as in Table 5–2, the schools propose quite different expectations or goals—this finally is a major resolution of *yours* to make.

TABLE 5–2. Health-Care Goals of the Four Schools

Conservative	*Liberal*	*Radical*	*Visionary*
What should we press for?			
Catastrophe insurance Coinsurance element Deductable feature National health-care bill	Kennedy Plan HMO's Central planning Computer control	Neighborhood cooperatives Paraprofessionals Nationalization of all!	Self-help clinics Self-care aids Cooperative care ethos
Why? What is health care?			
A product!	A service!	A right!	An opportunity!
What can we gain?			
New pride in status quo	Rationalized status quo	Nationalized status quo	New definition of *health* and *self*

Which is to say, the quantity and quality of health-care questions you are left to puzzle over is impressive. Among other open issues, you may want to wrestle with these:

1. Are the conservatives persuasive when urging us to scale down our expectations of a health-care system? Should we endorse their stress on investing scarce tax dollars elsewhere, as in fundamentals like slum clearance, rather than in more OEO health centers?
2. Or should we trust in liberal notions that through more rational planning we can have both?
3. Or with our radical friends, should we champion the collectivization of the entire "cottage industry" itself?
4. Or should we join our visionary colleagues in encouraging a transformation of our mind-and-soul expectations to achieve suprahealth for the people?

Similarly, you may want to puzzle over these matters:

1. *Central cause?* What is it that goes to the very heart of the reform platform under scrutiny? All such proposals are incapable of achieving their

goals if the reasoning on which they are based ignores the central cause(s) of our health-care dilemma.

2. *Trade-offs?* We pay for improvements in health care by devoting a larger share of our productive resources to medical care and a lesser share to other (competitive) goods and services. How far should this trade-off be carried? How can we determine the optimum proportion of medical care to other goods, beyond which we would not wish to give up still more housing or education to obtain more medical care?
3. *Market forces?* We leave to the natural forces of supply and demand the answers to riddles that planners resolve in more socialistic health-care systems. For example, what is the "appropriate" charge for the services of different doctors? How much should doctors earn in different specialties? Should we soon relegate such decisions to our planners?

Pandora's box? Labyrinth? Perhaps. . . . Hard? Heavy? Of course! Else, why bother?

What, then, does this chapter ask of you? Above all, that you connect with the major piece of "homework," the challenge of attending in new ways to your *own* health and to that of others. You know more now about health-care issues than do many of your co-citizens, and it is incumbent on you therefore to act to promote the best interests of their health and your own. Exactly how is your own affair, but that you are obligated—and that the state of your "health" (self-esteem, social contract, and so on) is in the balance—is clear. "Is there a doctor in the house?" reads differently now. There *is* a "doctor" here, and he is *you* . . . and me. To paraphrase, we have met the health-care reformers, and they must be *us*.

FOOTNOTES

1. Charles Foley, "One-Fifth of U.S. Surgery Unneeded, Doctor Asserts," *Philadelphia Inquirer* (October 2, 1972), p. 23.
2. Quoted in Jack Kelley, "U.S. Ranks 25th in Male Life Expectancy," *National Enquirer* (January 29, 1973), p. 2.
3. Gwen Gibson, "Why Doctors Are Quitting the AMA," *New York* (May 31, 1971), p. 7.
4. H. Jack Gieger, "Hidden Professional Roles: The Physician as Reactionary, Reformer, Revolutionary," *Social Policy* (March–April 1971), p. 25.
5. Ibid.
6. Sid Ross and H. Kupferberg, "The 'Medex'—One Answer to the Doctor Shortage," *Parade* (May 23, 1971), p. 16.
7. Judy Klemesrud, "Midwives Carry a New Image into Hospital Delivery Room," *New York Times* (September 20, 1972), p. 46.
8. Ibid.
9. Marvin Henry Edwards, "Socializing Medical Care or Was Dr. Kildare a Medical Service Dropout," *New Guard* (March 1971), p. 7.
10. Abraham Ribicoff, "The 'Healthiest Nation' Myth," *Saturday Review* (August 22, 1970), p. 19.
11. "Americans Are Now Found to Be in Favor of a National Health Insurance Program," *New York Times* (August 9, 1971), p. 20.
12. Howard Levy, "Counter Geiger," *Social Policy* (May–June 1971), p. 51.

13. Michael G. Michaelson, book review, *New York Times Book Review* (July 9, 1972), p. 10.
14. John Ehrenreich and Oliver Fein, "National Health Insurance: The Great Leap Sideways," *Social Policy* (January–February 1971), p. 9.
15. Barbara and John Ehrenreich, "The Medical-Industrial Complex," *The New York Review of Books* (December 17, 1970), p. 14.
16. Harry Schwartz, *The Case for American Medicine: A Realistic Look at Our Health Care System* (New York: McKay, 1972), p. 99.
17. Ibid.
18. Ibid.
19. Andrew Weil, *The Natural Mind: Another Way of Looking at Drugs and the Higher Consciousness* (Boston: Houghton, 1972), p. 168.
20. Adapted from Weil, ibid., p. 170.
21. Quoted in Michael G. Michaelson, book review, *New York Times Book Review* (July 9, 1972), p. 10.
22. Ibid.
23. Joan Haggerty, "Childbirth Made Difficult," *Ms* (January 1973), p. 16.
24. Mary Costanza, "Introduction," in Ellen Frankfort, *Vaginal Politics* (New York: Quadrangle Books, 1972), p. xxvii.
25. Ibid., p. xxviii.
26. As quoted in Ehrenreich and Ehrenreich, op. cit., p. 14.
27. Costanza, op. cit., p. xxviii.
28. Ellen Frankfort, "For the Feminist Who Has Everything," *The Village Voice* (December 21, 1972), p. 80.
29. Frankfort, *Vaginal Politics,* op. cit., p. 116.
30. Ibid., p. 93.
31. Norman Cousins, "Can Doctors Cause Disease?" *Saturday Review* (August 22, 1970), p. 32.
32. Ibid.
33. Frankfort, *Vaginal Politics,* op. cit., p. 228.
34. Nancy Hicks, "Preventive Medicine Need Called Great," *New York Times* (November 16, 1972), p. 54.
35. Arthur Frank and Stuart Frank, *The People's Handbook of Medical Care* (New York: Random, 1972), p. 6.
36. L. K. Altman, "Hospital Patients' 'Bill of Rights' Backed," *New York Times* (January 9, 1973), p. 1.
37. "Midwifery," *Science for the People* (January 1973), pp. 16–17.
38. Frankfort, *Vaginal Politics,* op cit., p. 243.
39. Frankfort, "For the Feminist Who Has Everything," op. cit., p. 29.

PART III

Aspects of a Better Life

We turn now to some aspects of our life that meet three particular criteria. First, the need for immediate reform attention seems clear. Second, a large number of high-quality domestic and foreign reforms offer themselves for our consideration. And third, I believe that each has a special and personal relevance to the reader (as they do to the writer!).

This section of the book opens with a chapter-length exploration of available aids to our interpersonal relationships. Such items as renewable marriage contracts, the Masters-Johnson sex clinics, and zones for legalized prostitution are reviewed. The chapter that follows focuses on reforms in childbirth and child rearing, including "natural" delivery, abortion on request, male paternity leave, adventure playgrounds, educational parks, and the voucher plan, among many other possibilities. Together the chapters hold out the promise of a remarkable new start for all of us, whether as adult implementors of these changes or as members of the yet-unborn generations that will be fortunate to know them from the inside out.

CHAPTER 6

Partnering: Brave New Marriage

The same Americans who all these years blamed their bad marriages on themselves, now, if they seem less happy or good, blame themselves on marriage. Is marriage really necessary? At one time only Bohemians and socialists—people like that—asked the question. Now it has become the property of the middle class: the people who twenty years ago talked about togetherness; the people who ten years ago thought once you had her orgasm straightened out, that was that; the people who faithfully kept saying that marriage has its ups and downs and, you know, it's a compromise and you have to work at it but, taken all in all, it's still the best shot at happiness. These are the people who are now saying, "Marriage is hell"—and maybe the hell with it. It is "as obsolete as the piston-engine plane." It is "the triumph of hypocrisy." It is "a ghetto of lunacy." Suddenly priests seem to be the only people left who really want to get married.

MELVIN MADDOCKS

I don't think that there are more people with sexual problems than there were—they are just dealing with them now.

DR. JUDD MARMOR

Reforms for American Marriages

College students, to judge from a recent national survey, are more concerned about the crisis in family life than about any other social issue. And with good cause:

At least 48 per cent of the couples getting married this year will ultimately be divorced.

The divorce rate is increasing faster than both the steadily climbing number of marriages and the general growth of population.[1]

Of the couples who do not get divorced as many as two-thirds tell researchers their marriages are a sharp disappointment to them.[2]

More and more children are growing up in fatherless homes.[3]

At the same time, however, there are other facts worth pondering:

The rate of Americans entering their first marriages has declined for nearly 25 years—but, in the last 10 years, remarriages have shown an increase of 40 per cent.[4]

People who have *good* marriages enjoy better health and live longer than those who have discordant marriages or who remain single; and—

The children of parents who have good marriages are more inclined to have good marriages of their own.[5]

The conclusion, one marriage counselor suggests, "is obvious: a good marriage provides a very efficient, pleasant, and profitable way for most people to live. So let's save the institution and all those marriages."[6]

Taking this statement at face value, how might we make new progress in "saving" American marriages? In the section that follows, five reforms are singled out for discussion, each as promising as it is controversial.

Marriage Contracts. "What if we made the tough part of marriage getting in instead of getting out?" ask authors Norman Sheresky and Marya Mannes in their 1972 work, *Uncoupling: The Art of Coming Apart.* The writers (a lawyer and a journalist) speculate about the consequences of our requiring prospective mates to explore beforehand—and in writing—their motives for marriage, as well as their intentions with regard to children, property sharing, and future alimony should the marriage fail. Now if we require starry-eyed engaged couples to take a hard-nosed look at their motives and potential obligations, many may never go through with marriage at all. "But," exclaim the authors, "that, in part, is just the point!"[7]

Immediately following, abridged and altered from the original in the interests of clarity, is an unusual personal contract, or legal-style hypothetical agreement between a fictitious engaged couple, whom I will call "Arthur May" and "Susan Kan."

MEMORANDUM OF UNDERSTANDING AND INTENT

Article I. *Historical Representation. Arthur* hereby warrants to *Susan* and guarantees that she may act in reliance upon the following representations:

A. He still occasionally contributes to the support of his living parents and intends to continue to the extent that he is able during marriage.

B. *Arthur* was previously married in September 1958, and that marriage ended in divorce in April 1970. There are two children of that marriage, *Adam*, age 13, and *Kent*, age 11. The terms of divorce awarded custody of both boys to their mother, with visitation rights including an afternoon every week, a full weekend twice a month, and equal sharing of holidays and vacations. Other child-care terms include. . . . [A copy of the entire divorce decree has been shown to and read by Susan.]

C. *Susan* has been made privy to the character and history of mental illness treatment in *Arthur*'s family. There are no hereditary or other diseases prevalent in *Arthur*'s family and *Arthur* is in excellent physical health.

D. There is no history of any arrest or conviction of *Arthur* for any criminal behavior, nor is there any history of compulsive addiction to drugs, alcohol, or gambling.

E. *Arthur* is currently employed as an associate professor of social sciences at Maslow University at a salary of ______. His salary during the three previous years was as follows: __________.

F. The relationship of *Arthur* with his parents and his brothers and their families have been explained fully to *Susan*. *Arthur* and *Susan* have discussed at length his family's tradition of celebrating key religious holidays together and *Arthur*'s desire to continue that tradition. *Arthur* has agreed that he will make no arrangements for other familiar visitations without the consent of *Susan*.

G. There has been nothing in the past sex life of *Arthur* that requires further disclosure. There are no sexual acts that are important to him or an essential part of the sex life contemplated by him that are not presently practiced by the parties together. *Arthur* has been able to express himself sexually in all the ways important to the parties together, and such issues as frequency of intercourse, desire for periods of sexual abstention, positions of intercourse, and so on have all been explored to *Arthur*'s satisfaction.

[In the section that is inserted here as Article II, Susan warrants to Arthur representations that cover the same material as in Article I. Typical of the material Susan might cover is the following: (C) *Susan*'s relationship with her mother is unusually close, and she talks with her by phone as often as six times a month. *Arthur* and *Susan* have had many conversations concerning what *Arthur* has protested to be far too close a relationship between mother and daughter. Although *Susan* has agreed to limit her calls to four a month and not to pressure *Arthur* to make more than two visits a year with her to her mother, *Susan* feels such concessions should not have been asked of her. *Arthur* has expressed considerable hostility toward *Susan*'s mother and has openly displayed such hostility. For his part, he has agreed to discontinue such practices. Each party agrees that the mother-in-law issue has not been fully resolved between them, but they agree that their marital relationship should have priority over the relationship between *Susan* and her mother. (D) Between 1969 and 1973 *Susan* was married, that childless marriage ending in divorce in October 1973 under circumstances that have been fully disclosed to *Arthur*.]

Article III. Future Expectations

A. *Arthur* and *Susan* have discussed fully where they propose to reside during the course of their marriage. They agree that their primary consideration shall be proximity to *Arthur*'s place of business. That factor should govern regardless of where *Susan* may be employed and regardless of whose earnings are greater.

B. Neither party insists on, or has even expressed any preference concerning, the other's adherence to any particular religious belief. Neither will, without the consent of the other, impose any religious belief upon any children of their own or any children who come into their care.

C. It is the parties' present intention that *Susan* continue to matriculate at graduate school and work part time, health permitting, until such time as she may become pregnant. The parties have no exact intentions concerning the employment of *Susan* after the birth of any child or children, although *Susan* has expressed the feeling that simply caring for children would not be sufficiently stimulating to her.

D. Both *Arthur* and *Susan* have expressed opposition to adultery. Both parties have agreed that in the event either engages in any serious or prolonged affair with anyone else, he or she is under an obligation to disclose that fact to the other.

E. The parties intend to have two or three children of their own. It is their desire to have such children sometime after the next two years, and the possibility of having a child prior to that time causes them some anxiety.

Should *Susan* become accidentally pregnant, the parties are now inclined to have the child and not seek an abortion. The final decision will be a joint one, neither party dictating to the other.

F. *Arthur* and *Susan* have discussed and have rejected the following notions: marriage of limited duration, separate beds, a conventional sex-role division of household tasks, divorce by reason of the physical incapacity of the other, divorce by reason of their inability to conceive a child together.

G. Although the parties agree that the question of adopting a child may become important to them, they feel that it is better to leave it undetermined at this time.

Article IV. Future Support

A. In the event that either party desires a separation (by mutual agreement or legal degree) or a divorce during the first five years of marriage, provided there is no surviving child born of the marriage, neither party will request support from the other unless he or she is in dire need thereof, and then only for such temporary periods as may be deemed necessary. . . .

Article V. Division of Property

A. *Arthur* has a checking account at the First Pennsylvania Bank of Philadelphia, the balance (April 30, 1973) of which is ________.

B. *Susan* has a checking account at . . .

C. *Arthur* owns 200 shares of *M-reit* Corporation, having a present value of approximately ________; he owns no other securities.

D. Neither party owns any real property.

Article VI. Future Ownership of Property

A. In the event of a separation or a divorce the proceeds of a joint checking account and a joint savings account will be divided in the same proportion in which such funds were contributed by the parties.

B. All property now standing in the name of either shall continue to be held in that name.

C. In the event *Susan* is unable to work during a period of maternity, her contributions to the joint funds shall be deemed to have been during that period in direct proportion to the contributions previously made by her during the period immediately preceding such maternity.

ARTICLE VII. MATTERS OF ESTATE

A. After thirty-six months of marriage each party agrees to leave the other at least 40 per cent of his or her entire estate. . . .

In witness whereof, the parties hereto have signed their hands and seals this 30th day of April, 1973.

__________ Arthur May
__________ Susan Kan

Note that in the agreement the parties come through as struggling, honest, and somewhat self-contradictory types (see, for example, the seemingly sexist concession to Arthur made on place of residence and the lingering anger recorded in connection with Susan's concession on phone calls and visits to her mother).

Men and women equal to preparing—and regularly renegotiating—a contract of this sort are fallible, error-vulnerable humans like the rest of us, if somewhat braver and more open. Their contract is not meant to be a record of goals already achieved or a promise of future saintliness. Rather, it is a basic tool, an early contribution to an ongoing, dynamic, and realistic relationship that can honor us all.

Now the aforegoing is invalid under existing laws in every state in the union. Furthermore, as Sheresky and Mannes recognize:

> the very idea of such a contract goes against the grain of our romantic matrimonial tradition. Yet the notion of the fullest possible disclosure of relevant facts and viewpoints, the concept of the planned marriage, and the idea of facing the possibility of the dissolution of a union prior to entering into one should not threaten the institution of marriage in our society. . . . Indeed, such frankness might well guarantee its future.[8]

Videotape Marital Therapy. To help show couples the inadequacies of their joint behavior, a small number of adventurous therapists are exploring the potentialities of modern video equipment. One such pioneer, William J. Lederer, sets five conditions on his therapy process:

1. If there are children in the marriage, they must be completely involved in the videotape therapy.
2. All meet one hour a week at the home of the clients during dinner time (research suggests people tell fewer lies while eating together at home than they do in the therapist's office, where they tend to behave like strangers).
3. Every dinner meeting is recorded on a videotape for immediate post-dinner viewing and analysis.
4. If the couple really want to stay married, the therapy has to be accomplished within six weeks.

Especially novel is Lederer's insistence that the family under observation must do its *own* therapy—his only function is to guide them in a useful direction.

In a typical situation the first of the six dinners took place at the home of a couple who had tried everything else in a four-year-old last-ditch effort to save a seventeen-year-old marriage. Lederer recalls asking Adam, the husband, "At the beginning of your meal your wife asked you if you would take her to the opera on Friday night. Do you remember what happened?" To which Adam replied proudly, "You're damned right I remember. I tried to be pleasant, so I told her I'd be glad to take her." He smiled, winked, and added confidentially, "Personally, I think opera is a lot of junk." After letting Adam watch himself on the video-connected family TV set, Lederer was not surprised by the husband's reaction, "Turn the goddamned thing off! My God, I thought I was being nice to Ellen, but the look on my face could kill. I looked like bloody murder." His fifteen-year-old daughter volunteered at that point, "Daddy, that's the way you always look when you talk to mother." And his two sons, ages nine and eleven, nodded their heads in agreement.

Lederer turned the video on again, without the sound, and instructed each member of the family to look at himself carefully on the screen—to observe studiously his or her own facial expressions, body motions, and speech patterns. At the end of the hour, Lederer explained, he would ask each of them to evaluate objectively what kind of person he thought he presented to others. When the video playback ended, tears were rolling down Adam's face, and he asked, "How could Ellen have stood me all these years? I'm always scowling and clenching my fists. I look terrible." Ellen spoke up with shame in her voice, "I look at myself up there on the TV screen and I see a spoiled bitch. I have to have my own way—like when I asked Adam to take me to the opera on Friday." Their daughter added, "I saw on the screen that I was interrupting everybody. Now I know why mom and dad scream at me to shut up." The two younger boys, Lederer recalls, did not say anything, and didn't have to. Lederer then asked, "Is this the way you want things to continue?" Ellen shook her head and began weeping. Adam said, "Hell no! It's like a goddamn lunatic asylum." By the end of this first session Lederer felt confident they would make it.

At the end of the sixth and final meeting he let the family look at the playback of the first meeting. Everyone groaned. They could not believe that this hostile and sarcastic group on the TV screen had been their family, for by the sixth session they were treating each other, and reacting to each other, with dignity and respect.[9]

Everybody's "cup of tea"? Hardly! Expensive? Yes, but costs can be reduced through the substitution of tape-recording equipment for the (preferable) video materials. The larger point, of course, remains the telling one: we all need help in gaining new insights into our behavior and its meaning to others. This is still another exciting new option for you to keep in mind.

Open Marriage and Relationships. Central to much of the aforegoing is the emergence in certain sections of society and the espousal by many counselors of what is known as the open marriage:

Open Marriage	*Traditional or Closed Marriage*
"An honest and open relationship between two people, based on the equal freedom and identity of both partners."	"Jealousy means you care. Sacrifice is the true measure of love. Your mate will not change. You will not fight. You will share all your time together. You will have total security."

Helpful in an open marriage are such strategies as collaborative self-examination, a here-and-now orientation, grants of privacy, role flexibility, and bedrock trust—each of which will be tersely defined.

As anthropologists Nena and George O'Neill, authors of *Open Marriage,* explain, "good communicating means continuing re-evaluation of your self—who you are—and conveying it at gut-level to your mate, who hopefully will give you gut-level, equally honest feedback." Good relationships are also thought to depend on living in the immediate present: "Long range plans are good, but a house in the country, three cars, two and a half children orientation can stop you from living in the 'now.' " The granting of privacy is another essential, as each member of a marriage or a household requires private time for self-examination and psychic regeneration. And a flexibility or switching of roles—either part time or temporarily—helps: "Not until you start doing your spouse's work do you realize how much it takes."

Above all, however, open marriage requires open companionship, a pattern that need have nothing to do with sexual infidelity—despite the rantings of critics who see "open sex" lurking somewhere close offstage. (Weary of puritanical reactions to their book, which range somewhere between flinch and panic, the O'Neills sagely suggest that the open marriage concept is "like a Rorschach test. It tells you where people are at. They read the book and still go on understanding it their own way.") Open companionship, in turn, makes tenable your having close friendships in marriage with someone of the opposite sex other than your spouse ("No one person can fulfill all the needs of another all the time"). Of course, if the marital relationship is shaky, open companionship is ill-advised, as trust is a basic ingredient if open companionship is to enhance life rather than exacerbate tensions.

Plainly, this new model for marriage is an attitudinal rather than a "how-to" approach. Nevertheless, after insistent urging from readers and audiences (the book stayed on the best-seller list for a record forty-two weeks in 1972, and over 1.5 million paperback copies are now available), the O'Neills offer a few concrete suggestions:

> Tape-record your next argument. "It can be very helpful. You hear all the nuances. You hear much more. Each of you listen to the tape alone and then together. From the circumstances, the tone, you may realize what you've really been fighting about."
>
> Initiate a new kind of "happy hour," one like the O'Neills, married twenty-eight years, have. "One hour a day when you do what you want, and I do what I want. It might even take place with both of us in the same room."
>
> Write a contract. "Not an agreement to hold to like a legal contract for a construction job, with a penalty clause, but a statement of desires and wishes

that is negotiable and subject to change. Realize that you are a process—you are changing. Realize that you can direct that change."

Adopt a "modified Ginott pattern," as expressed in child psychiatrist Haim Ginott's book *Between Parent and Child.* This means "say what you see, tell what you feel, but don't criticize." Moving from a dented fender to "You're just like your mother" is a perfect "how not to" in this case.

When challenged about the likelihood of any of these suggestions' soon catching on in the general population, the O'Neills put most of the hope for open marriage and open companionship on young people, for whom the "really important issues of identity, roles, self-actualization, and improving relationships" are ever more important.[10]

Critics, and there are many, insist that the open marriage concept goes too far or else nowhere far enough:

> In the political spectrum of Brave New Marriage, the O'Neills are liberals rather than radicals. They are for small mercies: extending the permissible boundaries of proper conduct, raising the ratio of pleasure to sacrifice without disturbing the conscience. They want to ease the general strain by semantics, by redefinition.[11]

On the other hand, the charge is also made that few of us are really equal to the open marriage challenge:

> Brave Old Monogamy called for rather ordinary virtues—principally patience. Brave New Marriage, under the advertisement of reducing expectation, calls for a sort of Renaissance man of the heart, with apparently unlimited time and energy, the balance of a tightrope walker, and the tact of a diplomat.[12]

And you? What will *you* have?

Creative Adultery—for Women. Whereas men have for centuries used adultery as a way of handling their private lives, only recently have married women begun in a remarkably guiltless way to employ extramarital affairs as a deliberate method of hanging on, of seeking the best of two worlds. Possibly as many as a third to a half of city-dwelling middle-class wives have an extramarital love affair at one time or another to "help keep my marriage together." Brave new reform, or hypocritical old insanity? Cynthia Epstein, sociologist author of *Woman's Place,* urges caution in interpretation and judgment, as "the subject is not even being investigated."[13]

At the same time, however, Epstein does think the practice is increasing, and she attributes this to the fact that many such women are feeling themselves more liberated than ever before in the history of the American wife: "They're less afraid of the consequences should an affair go badly and result in a breakup of their marriages. It's not because they're sexier than before, but because they have more resources to fall back upon."[14] Similarly, Mimi Lobell, co-author with husband John of *The Free Marriage,* explains: "I had to come to realize that I was one finite person, and that my husband could like two people or five people or even ten people at the same time. I feel happy that he's happy because I'm not competitive with those women."[15] Dr. Warren Pomeroy, a Kinsey associate, contends in this connection that "it is possible to have extra-marital relations and not be unfaithful, and just as possible to be unfaithful without having extra-marital sexual relations."[16]

Critics are incensed over the moral confusion and the low incidence of guilt as opposed to the bravado, pride, or sheer joy evident in the revelations of those who advocate "creative adultery." Some critics refer cynically to "adultery as dishwasher," the city wife's latest appliance, an assist at keeping house. All that proponents and critics seem agreed upon is our need to learn more of substance about the phenomenon:

> So touchy and untouched is the subject that there isn't even a reputable literature. . . . Pop books abound, but they merely thrash about in the morality of the behavior. Psychiatrists publish conclusions about women's motivations based on patients who feel neurotic about their affairs, and not, since they don't come to call, on the ones who don't.[17]

And at the same time, as one hostile female commentator concludes, "all around us it goes on, barely documented—cocksure husbands naturally the last to know."[18]

Summary. What does it all mean? And how are we finally challenged? The quarrel over Brave New Marriage, writer Melvin Maddocks points out, is essentially a quarrel over Brave New World:

> Sexual ethics—the comic debates of reluctant prudes versus determined lechers—are the least of it. What is happiness? What even is pleasure? What dare one say is *real?* These are the ridiculously portentous questions that keep worrying their way into a reader's mind. Along with that other question: *Do these people know?*[19]

What we *do* seem to know is the direction, if not the justification, of our super-speed changes in marriage:

> The will to condemn has gone out of society in the matter of divorce and abortion. . . .
>
> People don't lose their jobs or even their [reputations] because of adultery, though they may lose their reputations now by indulging in too much chastity. . . .
>
> In practice, moderate Brave New Marriage is here, and the ideologues shouting "Repression!" are fighting a battle largely won.[20]

There is much, of course, that remains for you to pursue elsewhere, reforms precluded by severe space restrictions from more than citation here:

1. A new vocabulary in this entire matter is earnestly called for by sociologist Jessie Bernard. She uses concepts like "personhood," "temporarily permanent" relationships, and "pair-bound" (for "married"): "Once we have words for the new statuses," Dr. Bernard writes, "we can clarify their nature."[21]
2. A "national family policy" is also urged by Dr. Bernard: "Policy in the

future is going to make it possible for more and more people to achieve good marriages." This vision, however, has one critic caustically picture "the marriage of the guaranteed minimum: freedom and innocence gently nudged along by the 'social engineer', supervised no doubt by a U.S. Department of Pair-Bound Relations."[22]

3. Street communes as alternatives to families are recommended by South African psychiatrist David Cooper, a leader in the antipsychoanalytic movement. Cooper advocates an end to families rather than the treatment of family-induced disorders. His street communes are family-sized groups preoccupied with Cooper therapy: "training people to smoke marijuana, to take acid in their own time in their own right context, and to steal from supermarkets."[23]

The final challenge is the danger that we will fail to consolidate our gains and connect them to comparable breakthroughs in the social system. Writer George B. Leonard puts it tersely when he contends that "getting in or out of wars like Vietnam has less to do with logistics than with sex." Leonard goes on to explain that as all matters are interrelated,

> no matter is more central than our concept and feelings about what it means to be a man or woman.
>
> For example, the pride, aggression, hot competitiveness and desire for dominance summed up by the Mexicans as *machismo* contribute very directly to militarism and violence, racism, overpopulation, and the rape of the planet.
>
> It may be, in fact, that no new politics is possible without a new sexuality.[24]

Extraordinary . . . a *very* provocative idea.

New Attitudes Toward Sex

The New Sex Therapies. Sexual problems are probably one of the leading causes of marital discord and divorce today in this country, with possibly half of all couples afflicted in one way or another. For many what is called "the act of love" is commonly awkward and painful, often shameful and embarrassing, and sometimes completely impossible. Sex itself remains the source of more misinformation, misunderstanding, taboo, and tragedy than practically any other subject in our society.

Why? The nation's leading sex experts, William H. Masters and Virginia Johnson (Masters), blame the church, the state, and the medical profession itself. Many religions continue to equate sex with self-indulgence rather than recognizing it as a natural function like breathing, eating, and sleeping. Legislators, desperately trying to preserve shopworn norms of sexuality, often promote ignorance and taboo instead (as with laws prohibiting coitus before marriage or attempting to proscribe certain sexual acts). And the laggard medical profession is in far too many cases just as ill informed and ill equipped to deal with sex as is the general public.[25]

On a more personal level, one of the explanations for sexual dysfunction in America at this time is the fraud of our male "sex education." As Gail Sheehy puts it,

> The basic problem is that until recently the American man has had almost no reliable source of information about sex. First he is a little boy being told

> by the big boys, "When you're older, you'll know." Next he's an older boy telling another ignorant youth he'll know. Then he graduates from being a son into being a father, rarely asking the girls along the way specific questions because that would be to admit he still doesn't know.[26]

Similarly, there is a conspiracy of silence about the "bed and bored" syndrome that costs us dearly. As Francois Duyckaerts explains,

> After a few years together many couples still have sexual intercourse, but they no longer have any sex life with each other. They no longer play the childish games which allowed them to express unconscious conflicts, nor do they try to seduce one another . . . in short, they have forgotten the great secret of being in love.[27]

To which Masters and Johnson add:

> in a sexual interaction, when a partner does not express obvious appetite in the bedroom, the immediate question is, "What's wrong?" When an aggrieved sexual partner expresses these emotions, most men or women force themselves to undesired sexual performance to relieve the partner's frustration. It is under these circumstances of forced performance, of treating sexual interchange as anything but a natural appetite, that unrewarding sexual interaction or even sexual dysfunction frequently result.[28]

No wonder then that the situation of many of us is most tersely and poignantly captured in a one-sentence description a staffer recently offered of sex clinic clientele: "When they come here, they'd give anything in the world to be different."[29]

Historically, men and women took their "marital" (sexual) discontents to a clergyman or a family doctor who was usually ill prepared to help. For the very few who could afford it, financially and otherwise, there was the expensive and lengthy option of psychotherapy. In 1970 the situation changed dramatically with the publication by Masters and Johnson of *Human Sexual Inadequacy,* a detailed description of their pioneering techniques for treating such widespread sexual disorders as impotence, frigidity, and premature ejaculation.

The essence of good sex therapy, according to Wardell Pomeroy, a former Kinsey collaborator, is to exert authority over patients who are understandably reluctant to come to grips with their bodies and their emotions: "I get very explicit. I'll say, 'Take your clothes off, take a shower together. Make notes and tell me what happens. Think that I'm giving you a prescription at the drugstore that you have to go out and fill.' "[30] Similarly, the co-directors of a Long Island clinic deal emphatically with seemingly mundane but possibly deep-rooted "excuses" for inaction:

> We get patients in here who tell us everything's okay now, they know just what to do, but they can't do it because their mother-in-law is forever calling up, or they're afraid the kids will walk into the bedroom. We give them some directive therapy. Tell them to get phones with wallplugs so they can disconnect. Tell them to buy a lock for the bedroom door. Let the kids knock.

When questioned by a reporter about a similar case in which there might be a complicating emotional issue, a senior clinic therapist snapped back, "There may be. . . . Let's worry about it after he's learned to have good intercourse with his wife."[31]

Since 1970, the modern sex clinic has shown promise of becoming as vital a part of the modern hospital as the emergency room and the intensive care unit. Professionals, many trained by Masters and Johnson at their Reproductive Biology Research Foundation in St. Louis, have established clinics of their own across the nation, even as scores of physicians and psychiatrists have adopted the Masters and Johnson method, or some variant, in their own practices. Abroad, clinics have been established in Amsterdam, Geneva, Hamburg, London, and Stockholm (as of November 1972).

The co-directors of a Long Island clinic describe a typical help-seeking couple as follows:

> married about eight years. He ejaculates prematurely and she has orgasms only through manipulation, never during intercourse. They both feel robbed. They've withdrawn from one another physically and psychologically, have intercourse maybe once a month, watch a lot of TV, and, when they first come to see us, they sit on opposite sides of the waiting room and read magazines. We saw a couple like that yesterday. It was their seventh visit. Now they come in and sit alongside each other. They talk. Their whole relationship has opened up. They're having intercourse two times a week. He's delaying his ejaculation for five or six minutes. She hasn't yet had her first orgasm with a penis contained, so it isn't where they want to be yet, but they're getting there.[32]

At present, by the way, none of the clinics treat single people, or at least will not admit they do—for legal reasons and as a concession to their boards of directors.

Sexual therapy and couple counseling is usually directed by two therapists (co-trainers), one a man and one a woman, one oriented to the body and the other to behavior. Beginning with "sensate focus" exercises, the couple is instructed to stroke various parts of each other's bodies—carefully avoiding genital contact—so as to master the art of giving pleasure in order to be more available for receiving it. Once the partners have begun to shed their inhibitions about physical contact, stroking proceeds to the breasts and the genitals. When the therapists feel the couple is ready, sexual intercourse is assigned for homework.

A myth has sprung up that sex therapy is simply mechanistic treatment, a mere catalogue of techniques. Proponents insist otherwise, though they do not deprecate the many specific techniques used, for example:

1. Couples who hesitate at touching one another's genitals are advised to overcome their queasiness by using lotions that stimulate genital fluids.
2. Premature ejaculation is delayed by the female's learning exactly where and how to destimulate her male partner's penis by squeezing it.
3. The husbands of women who have orgasms only through clitoral manipulation brush up on the most orgasm-producing intercourse positions.

But these nostrums, proponents explain, are made available only along with a large dose of marital psychotherapy, albeit directed toward a specific symptom.

Masters and Johnson have always been very clear and emphatic about this: sex is communication:

> The basic means of treating the sexually distraught marital relationship is, of course, to reestablish communication.[33]

> Attaining skill at physical stimulation is of minor moment compared to the comprehension that this is but another, more effective means of marital-unit communication.[34]

> As professionals we must teach husbands and wives to communicate the waxing and waning of their sexual appetites.[35]

Not surprisingly, proponents of the new sex therapies make much of the claim that troubled partners can learn to convey to each other—in many cases for the first time in their lives—what kind of sexual contact is gratifying. For another thing, many couples are alleged to find it the first time that they have ever really worked together to solve a problem.

What does it cost? In the fall of 1972 a clinic on Long Island headed by a former member of the Masters and Johnson staff was charging from $1,800 to $2,000 for fourteen to twenty sessions, spaced over three or four months. This fee was reduced, however, if the income level of the couple and the number of dependents warranted the least expensive treatment fee, then set at $10 a session. Included in the bill were three-month and six-month follow-up visits and the right to call for advice at any time. Not surprisingly, the waiting list (forty-five couples were in treatment) required a delay of about six months.[36]

Critics, like existential psychiatrist Rollo May, worry about misdirections:

> while some clinics do free people for a better relationship, many undermine the fact that sex is connected with tenderness. Certainly nothing is wrong with technique as such, in playing golf or acting or making love. But the emphasis beyond a certain point on technique in sex makes for a mechanistic attitude toward lovemaking, and goes along with depersonalization.[37]

Others, such as Dr. Charles Socarides, another New York analyst, actually question the worthiness of the goals: "There's a tendency to assume that everyone should make love and well. Some people can lead perfectly normal lives without feeling they should be functioning like Don Juan."[38] Sex therapists respond to the first concern with their own emphasis on communication between the partners ("genitals don't have sexual intercourse, *human beings* do"[39]). Similarly, some, like Anthony R. Stone, respond to the second criticism by stressing the *real* goal involved: "Who says you have to have an orgasm every time? Sometimes the most beautiful thing can be just to lie quietly holding the other person and feeling their warmth."[40] Sex clinic proponents also point out that their patients are all volunteers—and their waiting lists are as long as Dr. Socarides's arm.

In any case, it is clear that the field is dynamic and that change comes very rapidly. For example, Dr. Don Sloane, a director of a sex-therapy unit at New York Medical College, urges a radical alteration in the restrictive focus of Masters and Johnson on married couples:

> I think it's rather judgemental to insist that the communication be between a married couple. Why not single people? Why not two women who want to communicate better? Why, for that matter, not a woman who wants to masturbate more successfully, to communicate with herself? It may be all she's got. Take old people. Why shouldn't we help the elderly widowed?[41]

Comparably provocative is the "vision" of Dr. Harold Lear, a urologist with psychiatric training who directs the sex clinic at New York's Mt. Sinai Hospital: "Our ultimate goal is to make sex therapy as readily available as any other health service."[42] Central is the intention of all sex clinics not only to evaluate the efficacy of their treatment but also to do basic sexual research ("What we don't yet know and may come to know is the most interesting aspect of sex therapy"[43]).

A final thought: social science writer Linda Wolfe, after investigating five clinics in the New York area in 1972, concluded a helpful essay on sex therapy with a terse and constructive assessment of its dangers:

> Are there dangers? Probably only the usual psychotherapy danger, the risk of falling into the hands of practitioners without sensitivity and training. It is likely that the field will shortly be deluged by newcomers who are at best mediocre, climbing aboard the racy bandwagon as fast as their feet will carry them. As always, they will outnumber the good ones. Fortunately, brief therapies designed to treat specific symptoms can probably do less harm than long-range ones designed to explore total personality, for the simple reason that if you don't find yourself cured of the symptoms within ten to twenty sessions you know you ought to quit and go elsewhere.[44]

On a more positive note a clinic director explains: "It's like learning to ride a bicycle. Once you get the hang of it, you never forget."[45]

Sex-Advice Columns. Although in the United States the two sisters who regularly help column readers with personal puzzlers ("Dear Abby" and "Ann Landers"), along with Dr. Joyce Brothers and others of this journalistic advice-rendering sorority, have become increasingly bold in range and ethos, a popular newspaper column in Scandinavia still leads the way. Authored by a married couple who call themselves "sex mechanics," the column seeks to create an atmosphere in which sex is regarded as natural and fun and sexual deviations are thought of only as different. The weekly column starts from the premise that we are born with the ability to reproduce but not with the ability to enjoy it; the journalists undertake to demonstrate that this need not be so.

Asked to explain the column's large following, one of the writers reflected on the considerable personal mobility made possible by an escape from debilitating and erroneous notions of uniqueness: "A person might have trouble eating with chopsticks, but if he sees that the fellow at the next table also has trouble, he feels better. With sex, you can't see the other fellow's problems. We try to tell people about their neighbors."[46]

Are we ready for such a column today in America? We come close with certain advice columns in *Playboy* and in women's magazines; we offer *Sexology* and *Sexual Behavior* for sale at numerous magazine stands; and we award high viewer ratings to late-night talk-show efforts of a sort at sexual enlightenment. Also, we have begun a similar column in the nation's oldest continuous newspaper, *The Philadelphia Inquirer*. To be sure, the American version is dour and delicate, authored by a husband-wife team of physicians. But compared to the prior evasions and euphemisms of the old advice columnists, the new feature ("Human Sexuality") is a welcome advance.

Sex Courses on Campus. In the opinion of columnist and academic Max Lerner, "eros has broken through": "to have sexuality discussed seriously in the established realm, in accepted as well as underground or marginal publications, and in college classrooms as well, is a long step toward social sanity."[47] Especially "on target" is the unusual course given by Gerhard Neubeck at the University of Minnesota, which I spotlight the better to challenge you with the question: Just what do *you* settle for on your campus in this connection?

Professor Neubeck's course, "Human Sexual Behavior," begins with a desensitizing exercise that has classmates exchange words with one another on cue from the teacher—much like a kindergarten word drill, except that the words include *clitoris, erection, vagina,* and so forth: "This idea that sex talk is dirty talk is deeply ingrained in us. . . . If you repeat 'vagina' often enough, it loses some of its threat."

Much of the course is given over to Neubeck's responses to student questions: "For the first time, many of my students find in this class an adult who is willing to openly admit that he is a sexual being. I'm not defensive about sex, and I don't want them to be." Married for thirty-two years to a woman with whom he fled the Nazis in 1939, Neubeck has three children, all of whom teasingly picketed his course on its initiation in 1967 with signs reading "Daddy is a dirty old man" (a reporter adds, "Perhaps because he barely escaped the Nazi horror, the sexual fears that preoccupy Americans seem small by comparison, and he is able to view the scene with detachment. Happy in his marriage, Neubeck brings an emotional security to the class").

Subjects touched on in class range from technical virginity to extramarital sex, from pornography to prostitution, from menstruation to menopause, from abortion to "abnormal" sex. Neubeck quotes from the poetry of e.e. cummings, Bertrand Russell's autobiography, and John Updike's *Couples* as well as Masters and Johnson's study of the physical aspects of sex. Reading assignments in 1969 included Vance Packard's *The Sexual Wilderness,* a book called *Sex and Love in the Bible,* and articles from scientific journals. "I don't have all the answers for you," Neubeck explains to his students, "but you should be aware of the confusion. Somewhere along the way, sexuality got separated from the rest of life. I want to integrate it again. . . . As I see it, sexuality is not a matter of whether you do or don't, but, rather, the nature of it. It isn't enough just to learn how to avoid problems and resolve conflicts. You should be able to learn to enjoy what life offers."[48]

"Free Zones." So long as there is no consensus on sexual morality, and so long as there are irreconcilable differences in judgment as to what constitutes erotica, pornography, obscenity, brutality, and so on, a separate-areas type of solution may offer society a far wider accommodation than any other currently contemplated.

At issue is our seeming choice between "cracking down" on sexual permissiveness (erotic advertisements, pop pornography, "XXX" movies, and so on) or doing nothing but hoping for the best. A third option, recommended as a "holding operation" by economist Ezra Mishan, would have us set aside a known place in the city for any form of erotica, pornographica, or what have you. Well policed to maintain order and prevent violence, these areas would house unmolested the avantest of avant-garde theaters; no literature, drawing, painting, or work of art would be proscribed; nude shows could flower; and exotic or adventurous groups of every sort could congregate and enact their fantasies.

Why bother? To avoid giving unnecessary offense to more traditional members of the public. Under such a plan no adult need feel aggrieved:

> Not only does each group have the freedom it desires—the permitters to indulge their tastes without restraint, the conservatives to enjoy without fear of being jarred or embarrassed—but, in addition, any grown person can both have his respectability and, on occasions, discard it. He can be sure of being able to avoid unwanted sexual stimulus without sacrifice of any convenience, and can be equally sure of obtaining it on occasions of his own choosing.

To be sure, there would be problems in implementing this "red-light-district" idea (such as location, size of area, and so on). But, as Mishan points out, "it is better to face such problems in a rational spirit, and while there is yet time, than to continue to drift on in perplexity."

For time does threaten to run out on us, so great are the contradictory and rapidly building pressures for an either/or response to the sexual liberation ethos of the present. There are still vital options open to society, Mishan counsels in closing, options other than just "Back up!" or "Forward!" But these options require us not to yield to momentums that would sweep us along in only *one* direction:

> Separate areas, in this and other contexts, are a means of both preserving variety and reducing conflict—or, put otherwise, of enlarging the area of personal freedom and amenity. It is one of the options open to a democratic society, one that we ought to start thinking about in all seriousness.[49]

Among others, the mayor of New York promised in 1972 to give all serious consideration to a recommendation that inadequate crackdowns on midtown prostitutes give way to the establishment of a city-controlled "free zone," one of the options still open to us.[50]

Summary. Overall, where sexual knowledge and craft are concerned we reach out for new insights, sensitivities, and power. Writer Rona Jaffe wistfully captures some of our new orientation: "It has always seemed to me a shame that we are a people who know more about heart transplants than we do about female orgasms, when we will probably have more need in our lifetimes to know about the latter."[51]

In the process of reaching out, of course, a number of shopworn misconceptions are being replaced by sounder insights, for example:

1. The goal of simultaneous orgasm is being sharply downgraded, and the "project" of helping one another attain orgiastic release is recommended instead as far more available and joyous.
2. The view that some kinds of orgasms are *more* normal, *more* natural, and *more* desirable is replaced by a pluralistic approach that explores the diverse ways males and females can achieve sexual release.
3. The fact that a full male orgasm, unlike ejaculation, does not happen at all without learning or training is recognized, demystified, and dealt with.

Albeit uneven, and subject itself to faddism and error, progress in improved sexual communication *is* one of our major reform accomplishments.

Much is probably contributed, although relevant data are scarce, by attitude-shaping, bias-taxing ads like this one:

> Kathy is 9. Her parents told her if she slept with her hands under the covers she wouldn't grow.
>
> Kathy will grow up of course, but she'll have bad feelings about doing something that many people do. And her parents will have passed an old guilt on to a new generation.
>
> But Kathy's parents can't take all the blame. When they were 9, they were probably told the same thing. And even though they know the folk tales about going blind and getting warts aren't true, they still believe it's bad for children to explore themselves.
>
> The odd thing is they probably couldn't even give you a good reason. Like most parents, they probably don't know about the recent figures that show that almost all men and a majority of women have masturbated.
>
> The truth is, even Kathy's parents didn't stop, though their parents told them to. They just felt more guilty about it. What they were doing was responding to the basic sexual desires which men and women have at all stages of life. And because it is not always possible to fulfill these needs through sexual intercourse, there are many times in life when masturbation becomes the only alternative.
>
> It may be too late for Kathy's parents to change their feelings. But once they realize how universal this activity is, they can learn to stop passing on these unnecessary guilt feelings to their children. And let Kathy grow up a happy woman with a healthy attitude about her body.

Sponsored by the Community Sex Information and Education Service, Inc., a private, national, nonprofit organization dedicated "to the prevention and solution of all sex problems," the ad is just one among a host of new and sensitive services that include telephone counseling, referrals for safe and legal abortions, and arrangements for free pregnancy and VD tests. Perhaps the point is best made in the organization's motto: "Sexual ignorance is not bliss." Or, to paraphrase George Santayana, those who do not know their puritanism are probably fated to repeat it.

A host of additional (if uneven and variously motivated) aids to personal growth also are newly available. A long-playing record, "Sexual I.Q. Test," offers one hundred intimate questions on sexual attitudes and experiences, along with convenient answer sheets and a rating guide: "Learn if you and others are superior, average, or below in your sexual awareness. . . . Your final score estimates your sexual I.Q., your sexual honesty, and your sexual adequacy. . . . An authenic test recommended for group participation as well as for the individual." Another aid, *The Joy of Sex: A Gourmet Guide to Love Making,* has earned wide critical acclaim, in part for its premise that lovemaking should be joyous, inventive, and carefree; for its incorporation of wisdom, tenderness, and affection beyond the traditional marriage manual; and for its ability, with relaxed humor, sound counsel on hang-ups, homely "household hints," and extraordinary illustrations, to promote an awareness of the profound relationship that sex is *for.* To which list could be added cassettes for car-driving listening, video TV cassettes for private home-instruction in sex and love issues, "programmed"-instruction books of a behaviorist learning orientation, and so on.

With all of this, of course, our progress remains uneven. For example, so-called sex education books for children ages three to thirteen are still, by and large, a keen disappointment. In Sheila Cole's assessment,

> Most avoid almost all discussion of sexual emotions, fantasies, pleasure, or how sex affects people's relations with one another. By the mere fact of their exclusion, such topics are rendered taboo. . . . Masturbation, the most common form of sexual activity for a child, is barely mentioned.
>
> Although many people now recognize that it is normal for children of the same sex to like each other, have crushes on each other, explore each other's sexual organs and even masturbate together, none of these books mention these facts. Nor do they take the opportunity to reassure the child that this kind of homosexual activity does no physical harm, and must not be used to make a child feel guilty.[52]

Similarly, Ellen Willis, a critic of "XXX" pornographic films, strongly dissents from any quick and favorable judgment as to their liberating and growth-aiding character:

> Today's porn is based on the conceit that taboos are outdated, that the sexual revolution has made us free and innocent—a fiction that can be maintained, even for the time span of a movie, only at the cost of an aggressive assault on all feeling. . . . they are so unimaginative, partly because they objectify women's bodies and pay little attention to men's—American men are *so* touchy about you-know-what—but mostly because they deliberately and perversely destroy any semblance of an atmosphere in which my sexual fantasies could flourish.[53]

In a misogynist culture in which male sexuality tends to be confused with dominance and to be corrupted by overt sadism, the sexual revolution can degenerate into a more advanced form of hypocrisy. Instead of saying one thing and doing another, the game can become one of saying and doing the same thing but feeling another, or not feeling at all.

Much remains to be accomplished, then, and mistakes made along the way (as with the discredited ideology of "porn liberation") require still more reform energy. At the heart of it all, and equal perhaps to directing and motivating the entire campaign, is recognition of the essential part the sexual revolution *can* play in a new politics. As writer George B. Leonard explains,

> Perhaps it is provocative to suggest that statesmen, scientists, administrators, and technicians bent upon influencing outside events look first at their own relationships with lovers and friends, wives and children. If so, let that be my chief provocation. For today every "solution" is personal, dwelling not entirely "inside" (as some humanistic psychologists now claim) nor entirely "outside" (as most managers and technicians have long assumed), but in the interaction of the two. To change the world, start with both.[54]

FOOTNOTES

1. Norman Sheresky and Marya Mannes, "A Radical Guide to Wedlock," *Saturday Review* (July 29, 1972), p. 33.
2. Betty Yorburg, *The Changing Family* (New York: Columbia U.P., 1973), p. 4.
3. "More and More Broken Marriages," *U.S. News & World Report* (August 14, 1972), p. 30.
4. *U.S. News & World Report,* op. cit.
5. William J. Lederer, "Videotaping Your Marriage to Save It," *New York* (February 19, 1973), p. 38.
6. Lederer, op. cit., p. 39.
7. Sheresky and Mannes, op. cit., p. 38.
8. Ibid.
9. Drawn from Lederer, op. cit., pp. 38–41.
10. All of the quotations of the O'Neills are drawn from Louise H. Lione, "Open Marriage: Does It Mean the Same as Open Sex?" *Philadelphia Inquirer* (April 8, 1973), p. 1-F.
11. Melvin Maddocks, "Brave New Marriage," *The Atlantic Monthly* (September 1972), p. 69.
12. Ibid.
13. Quoted in Linda Wolfe, "Can Adultery Save Your Marriage?" *New York* (July 3, 1972), p. 39.
14. Ibid.
15. Quoted in Judy Klemesrud, "Marriage: Everybody's View Had a Champion on the Panel," *New York Times* (April 14, 1973), p. 20.
16. Quoted in Wolfe, op. cit., p. 40.
17. Ibid.
18. Ibid.
19. Maddocks, op. cit., p. 69.
20. Ibid.

21. Jessie Bernard, *The Future of Marriage,* p. 69.
22. Maddocks, op. cit., p. 67.
23. Quoted in Linda Wolfe, "The Doctor's Dilemma," *New York* (February 28, 1972), p. 58.
24. George B. Leonard, *The Man and Woman Thing* (New York: Delacorte, 1970), p. 140.
25. Lloyd Shearer, "Sex: Back to Nature," *Parade* (July 30, 1972), p. 4.
26. Gail Sheehy, "Can Couples Survive?" *New York* (February 19, 1973), p. 35.
27. Francois Duyckaerts, *The Sexual Bond* (New York: Delacorte, 1971), p. 22.
28. Shearer, op. cit., p. 4.
29. Alice Murray, "Serenity and Respect Mark Sex-Therapy Project at Hospital on Long Island," *New York Times* (September 10, 1972), p. 103.
30. "All About the New Sex Therapy," *Newsweek* (November 27, 1972), p. 71.
31. Linda Wolfe. "The Masterses' Disciples: Sex Therapy in New York," *New York* (April 17, 1972), p. 70.
32. Ibid., p. 70.
33. Ibid.
34. Ibid.
35. Ibid.
36. Shearer, op. cit.
37. Murray, op. cit., p. 103.
38. "All About the New Sex Therapy," *Newsweek,* op. cit., p. 72.
39. Ibid.
40. Anthony R. Stone, letter to the Editor, *Newsweek* (December 18, 1972), p. 6.
41. Dr. Martin Shepard, psychiatrist, as quoted in Boyce Rensberger, "Clinics for Sex Therapy Proliferate over Nation," *New York Times* (October 29, 1972), p. 66.
42. Wolfe, op. cit., p. 74.
43. Wolfe, op. cit., p. 76.
44. Ibid.
45. "All About the New Sex Therapy," *Newsweek,* op. cit., p. 72.
46. John M. Lee, "Danes and Swedes Are Moving Toward Greater Sex Freedom," *New York Times* (November 6, 1968), p. 44.
47. Max Lerner, "The Realm of Eros," *New York Post* (November 27, 1972), p. 33.
48. The quotations of Neubeck are drawn from Nancy Gay Faber, "Sex for Credit," reprinted in A. Shostak, ed., *Sociology and Student Life* (New York: McKay, 1971), p. 75.
49. Ezra Mishan, "A Modest Proposal: Cleaning Up Sex Pollution," *Harper's* (July 1972), pp. 54–56.
50. "Lindsay Rejects a 'Red Light' Area," *New York Times* (August 9, 1972), p. 41.
51. Rona Jaffe, "Fair Sex for the Fair Sex," *New York Times Book Review* (August 13, 1972), p. 16.
52. Sheila Cole, "Goodbye to Birds and Bees," *Ms* (May, 1973), p. 72.
53. Ellen Willis, "Hard to Swallow," *New York Review of Books* (January 25, 1973), pp. 22, 23.
54. Leonard, op. cit., p. 140.

CHAPTER 7

Parenting: Childbearing and Child Rearing Reconsidered

Train up a child in the way he should go and when he is old he will not depart from it.

PROVERBS 22:6

The childhood shows the man,
As Morning shows the day.

JOHN MILTON

Symptoms of growth may look like breakdown or derangement; the more we are allowed by the love of others and by self-understanding to live through our derangement into the new arrangement, the luckier we are. It is unfortunate when our anxiety over what looks like personal confusion or dereliction blinds us to the forces of liberation at work.

M. C. RICHARDS

What might childbearing and child rearing be about? In a reading at the end of this chapter a medical doctor urges our looking at childbirth as a "transcendental trip, a trip to outtrip all other trips, one in which to be deeply and spiritually and completely involved."[1] Elsewhere educational critic Jonathan Kozol urges a reorientation in child rearing toward a conception of the human personality as a "full or organic or continuously living and evolving firmament rather than as a filing cabinet of acceptable traits."[2]

Signs of progress in both matters, albeit slow and uneven, are seen by the discerning. Socialization in the 1970's is increasingly understood as an interaction that involves the child as an active partner rather than as a unilateral manipulation of the child. Moreover, we have come to appreciate better the exciting possibilities inherent in the fact that adults are themselves prone to change under the impact of their offspring's challenge. Where child rearing is concerned, in short, we have come of late to recognize new and promising partners, fellow adventurers, junior colleagues of sorts, in our own children!

Not a moment too soon, one might add, for our record in child rearing by more conventional and costly precepts (the child as a *tabula rasa,* deficient, incompetent, and so on) is a very sorry one. As Hans Peter Drietzel says,

> In spite of all the public attention given to problems of socialization, modern society creates a generally unfavorable climate for children; the tolerance of childhood as a developmental stage in its own right and the permissive attitudes toward children are probably more the result of resigned helplessness than of positive acceptance of their different needs and perspectives.[3]

Similarly, the school, as the second major socialization agent, is in no less trouble than the family: "The fact is that the schools serve more as an agent for the socialization into political acquiescence with an unloved system than as an institution which offers optimal opportunities to acquire useful skills and meaningful knowledge."[4] Together both the nuclear family and the conventional primary school are judged by many to provide "a pathological milieu for the children."[5]

A number of reforms explored in this chapter can help promote the steadily building changes now underway and introduce some fresh and bold goals as well. The chapter opens with a challenging call for a new attitude toward childbirth, one that will ensure its being an emotional and psychological gift of life for the parents as well as for the child. Next is a brief account of a related reform, the moral issue of male paternity leave. Immediately thereafter, the pros and cons of the controversial new reform of abortion on request are discussed, the better to underline the critical point that both childbirth and child rearing are best encountered as eagerly sought options rather than unwelcome obligations.

The child-rearing reforms reviewed in this lengthy chapter include the likes of "junk" playgrounds (sometimes known as adventure parks), children's savings accounts, children's book-promotion maneuvers, classroom educational TV matriculation, "survival-learning" adventures, subsidized summer jaunts, educational parks (sometimes known as educational campuses), and the voucher plan. As everywhere else in the volume, the aforegoing is plainly only a small sample of the possible sources of child and adult gains, but it will suffice to make the point that the possibilities are exhilarating and the stakes, in terms of the generations unfolding, as high as they can be.

Childbearing

Childbirth. Controversy about childbirth is widespread, heated, and unlikely to abate soon, as it sets the technocrats against the generalists in a very special way. On one side are the medical specialists, with their commitment to hygiene and the physical safety of the expectant mother and the unborn child. On the other side are the generalists, inside and outside of medicine itself, who insist that hygiene and safety should be supplemented by a comparable concern for the emotional and psychological well-being of *all*—expectant mother, unborn child, expectant father, and attending physician.

A sense of the controversy can be had from a statement made by a mother of six, Mrs. Lolly Hirsch, who in 1973 helped organize the first feminist conference to "make women aware of the dangers of many hospital childbirths, and to talk about alternatives." As she explained it,

> Childbirth can be one of the most wonderful experiences in a woman's life—except when you're drugged out, strapped down, shaved, lying on your back with your feet in the air, for the doctor's convenience, not yours or the baby's. We have the only society where babies have to be born uphill.

Other speakers went on to criticize the use of the drug Scopolamine, the indiscriminate use of forceps, the dehumanizing aspects of the maternity ward, and the rewards of breast feeding. Consistent with the serious qualms about the dangers in the technocrat's dominance was the alarming suggestion made by Dorothy Haire, founder of the International Childbirth Education Association (ICEA), that "modern" obstetrical practices might be responsible for the high incidence of brain damage and mental retardation in children.[6]

In the essay "Childbirth: Progress in Dignity," which appears at the end of this chapter, many of these points are considered by a sympathetic doctor. Indeed, his comments draw on a speech originally given to a Los Angeles chapter meeting of the ICEA.

Male Paternity Leave. Since 1967 a male school teacher in New York City, thirty-one-year-old Gary Ackerman, has been fighting in the courts for "paternity leave"—with all the rights and privileges that the Board of Education routinely grants to female teachers who get pregnant.

It all started shortly after his three-year-old daughter, Lauren, was born. As he recalls, Ackerman began to feel like a left-out "visitor," only his summer vacations offering him really full days with his own child. He began to ponder the need for "a masculine image in the home, as well as a mother." In time he concluded that "in a society which is stressing the importance of family unity—especially in the schools, where there are so many problems because of a lack of family cohesiveness—the Board's denial of my role as a father is ridiculous."

After his application for paternity leave was denied, Ackerman turned to the American Civil Liberties Union. With the help of their lawyers he has won a ruling from the U.S. Equal Opportunity Commission that "there is reasonable cause to believe" that the Board maintains a child-caring policy that "discriminates against male teachers as a class."

Ackerman himself is quick to point out that there is money as well as principle involved. In federal court his attorneys have argued that his civil and constitutional rights have been violated, even as they also point out that the Board's "exclusion of males" policy deprives Ackerman of per diem pay for possible substitute teaching, which would have been open to him were he a woman teacher on four-year maternity leave.

What has been the public's reaction to his case? With a sigh he explains that "some people think it's a trick or a gimmick. But teachers I have known have been unanimously in favor of it." A number of women's liberation groups, he adds, have volunteered support and given favorable publicity to his arguments in their literature. Should he win his court case, he might or might not leave his temporary second career in community newspaper editing and return to his first love, junior high school social studies: "But, I want the right to make that decision."[7] [In late 1973 the Board finally agreed to all of Ackerman's demands!]

Abortion on Request. The best estimates were that every minute, in the early 1970's, two women somewhere in America underwent illegal abortions. Every hour or so, one of them died trying. (In 1968, some 350,000 women were hospitalized after illegal abortions; over 8,000 of them died.[8]) And the botched abortion by quacks who used coat hangers, kitchen knives, castor oil, or gasoline, the single greatest cause of maternal deaths in America and one of our most common forms of illegal activity, remained the practice of desperation across the land as prohibitions remained firm.

Although abortions on request were readily available in Britain, Czechoslovakia, Japan, Russia, and Yugoslavia, with major liberalizing reforms pending in France and West Germany, up until 1972 only four areas in this country left the matter entirely to the doctor and the patient (New York, California, Hawaii, and the District of Columbia). Elsewhere in the United States—and despite the proabortion ruling of the Supreme Court in 1973—the matter of an abortion has been deliberately entangled in medical and legal regulations that effectively hold down the number of legal abortions. In the last year (1967) before liberalized reforms gained enactment in a handful of states, only 8,000 abortions were recorded, though some 1 million additional abortions, or over 99 per cent, were estimated to have occurred in sleazy back-alley and clandestine hotel-room settings that endangered all involved.

Indeed, the very magnitude of the hazardous abortions forced underground by our legal prohibitions was long used by the antiabortion forces to discourage legislators from proabortion reforms. The argument was that the already hard-pressed medical system of a modern state could not possibly sustain the heavy demand for service that might follow any relaxation of prohibitions against abortion.

This has become the first of the major issues in this exceedingly controversial area to receive a full and fair test in the field—and to produce substantial and revealing data. After two years' worth of groundbreaking experience (1970–1972), the unique program in New York State was hailed as "an enormous success," one that demonstrated "conclusively" the safety of abortion on a mass scale:

1. Some 402,059 women had received abortions under the 1970 Act (80 per cent Caucasian; 63 per cent, under twenty-five).
2. Costs were reduced from $500 in the early months of the law to under $200 (with Medicaid support).
3. A maternal mortality rate of 2.9 deaths per 10,000 live births was achieved in 1971, as compared with 5.3 deaths in 1969, the year before the liberalized law was enacted.[9]
4. The first decline (in eighteen years of keeping count) in out-of-wedlock childbirths was recorded in 1971.

Pulling it together a state official concluded that "legalized abortion is feasible on a large scale, it can be provided safely, and widespread access to abortion can indeed generate beneficial social consequences."[10] That this is hardly a unanimously held verdict is underlined by the fact that this very same heralded law had been dramatically repealed by both the House and the Senate of the New York State Legislature earlier in 1972, only to survive by grace of the governor's veto of the repeal measure.

Clearly, then, feasibility—and even ancillary health benefits for the women directly involved—is a secondary matter, at best. Far more critical in the surrounding controversy is the political issue of just who is the appropriate legal guardian of American uteri, the mother or the state. Some of the deeply arousing and highly personal and philosophical considerations involved are suggested in Table 7–1. This table, of course, only hints at the large and seemingly endless number of substantial items the antagonists have been able to draw into the fray at one time or another, though the propositions listed in the table are sometimes regarded as more central and basic than most (other topics include birth defects, mongolism, battered children, mental illness, juvenile delinquency, and guilt and remorse—to cite only a few).

TABLE 7–1. Proabortion and Antiabortion Positions

Proabortion	*Antiabortion*
1. The moral issue of abortion as murder is insoluble, a matter of religious philosophy and religious principle.	1. The moral issue of abortion as murder is incontrovertible and conclusive.
2. Those who believe abortion is murder need not avail themselves of it. But that conviction should not limit the freedom of those not bound by that religious conviction.	2. None should feel free to violate higher moral laws.
3. The decision to abort is a "medical decision" and should be left up to the doctor and the patient.	3. It is not logical to leave such a decision up to the doctor and the patient, both of whom are under extreme pressure.
4. The concern for the unborn child should focus on his "right to survive" and his "right to be wanted" rather than only on his "right to life."	4. There is no higher right than that to life.
5. A fetus is a human life but not a human being. It is not a member of the species *Homo sapiens* and does not have an independent nature capable of sustaining and regulating its own metabolic pattern.	5. Each unborn human infant is a human being. Geneticists have long since firmly established that from the time of implantation there is a new individual with a genetic code differing from that of any other being.
6. The highest moral calling is to minimize injustice and avoid unnecessary suffering—and this, at the very least, entails that where possible the basic needs of every living human being be satisfactorily met.	6. The highest moral imperative is that mankind should unite in its opposition to death. A fetus is a living human being, and induced abortion is homicide.
7. Adoption is a prospective mother's option—to choose or to reject. Abortion is a tenable alternative—and a woman's right.	7. Adoption is a much preferable route. Families are eager to adopt a baby and give it love and care. Better this than murder!

Overall, it seems reasonable to expect more gains than losses for the pro-abortion forces in the months and years ahead:

> Six of 10 adult Americans now favor abortions for reasons other than saving a mother's life. Indeed, half of the group is ready to remove all legal restrictions! (Pro-abortion adults tend to be younger, better educated, and earning higher incomes).[11]
>
> As some 61 per cent of New York State's abortions in 1971 were performed for out-of-state residents there would appear to be a large pent-up demand in non-permissive states (women came from 48 of the 50 states). So long as this demand for abortions, a national phenomena, is blocked in certain states, the resulting travel and maintenance costs to legal "aid zones" will penalize poorer women, and add still another political pressure to the entire matter.[12]
>
> As a large proportion of the women involved are unwed (56 per cent in liberal Great Britain) pro-abortion forces have considerable public concurrence with their insistence that repeal would mean renewed resort to "back-alley butchers" and botched-up operations of inexcusable cost (psychic, physical, and financial).
>
> The law's implementation has ushered in an entirely new and overdue approach to the delivery of health care. Well over half of the abortions are being performed without costly overnight hospitalization—either as outpatient procedures in hospitals or in free-standing clinics.[13]

As if to confirm the proabortion movement there seems to have been a gradual change in public attitudes. As recently as 1963 less than 6 per cent of the public approved of liberalized abortion laws. By the summer of 1972, some 64 per cent (including 56 per cent of the Roman Catholics surveyed) appeared to favor strongly full liberalization of laws that restrict abortions. (Relevant in this connection is the fact that about the same percentage of Catholic women seem to have abortions as do women from other religious groups.[14])

Not surprisingly, therefore, the National Association for the Repeal of Abortion Laws looks forward now to dramatic breakthroughs in the courts, in state legislatures, and in referendums. From 6,000 legal abortions in 1965 the figure went up to over 600,000 in the entire United States in 1972, and major victories thought possible in Connecticut, Illinois, Iowa, and Ohio could help make abortion on request available throughout much of the country by 1976.[15]

For with censorship everywhere relaxing, state governments entering the lottery (gambling) business, and the Gay Liberation movement slowly securing new gains for homosexuals, our nation appears increasingly accepting of a worldwide tendency to relax prohibitions against certain kinds of morally controversial acts. Increasingly we ask: *Must* the state be involved? And with impressive regularity where the so-called morality "crimes" are concerned, we answer "no"!

Except, that is, in the case of the "crime" of abortion. Opposition here remains intense, as the 1972 Election Day defeats of hotly contested proabortion referendums in Michigan and North Dakota make clear. The White House continues to lend its prestige to the opposition ("Unrestricted abortion policies would demean human life," explained President Nixon, when in 1971 he ordered military hospitals to abandon liberalized abortion policies). And the strategy-guiding National Right to Life Committee proves regularly to be one of the toughest political monoliths now operating. Founded in 1968 as a clearinghouse and coordinating arm of antiabortion (or "prolife") movements in all fifty states and their Catholic, orthodox Jewish, and Protestant supporters, the Committee engages in a hard-nosed brand of politics that commands the respect of various nervous legislators everywhere. The Committee, however, is weakened somewhat by its association in the popular mind and media with Catholic Church "politics" and its opposition to abortions even in the special circumstance of rape and incest. Although it has refused to join the Church in opposing the IUD, a contraceptive device, on the grounds that "abortion takes a life, contraception only prevents it," the Committee, as a member explains, "gets clobbered again and again by the charge that this movement is the Catholic Church attempting to foist its ideas on the community."[16]

In the last analysis all of us will probably be called to account as this issue turns up in the electoral process in each of the fifty states. Governor Rockefeller tersely summarized the reform side of the controversy in his 1972 veto message: "I do not believe it right for one group to impose its vision of morality on an entire society. Neither is it just or practical for the state to dictate the innermost personal beliefs and conduct of its citizens."[17] In response, a Catholic male leader of the New York State Right to Life Committee conceded that prohibition of abortion is, in fact, an attempt to impose a standard of morality upon society: "But, isn't that what the Civil War was about, too? Didn't the North impose a standard of morality on the South then, and that issue was slavery; we're talking about murder. Which is worse?"[18]

To which Barbara Rose, a proabortionist journalist, shoots back,

> In the matter of abortion, no man is a peer of a woman whose body is the object under consideration. . . . Those men running around with bottled fetuses are using a pathetic fallacy to cover one obvious fact: they hate and fear women. As for the Church, it has shown itself capable of change in the past when it abolished the Inquisition. It can abolish other vestigial relics of medievalism as well in the interest of human survival.[19]

Marya Mannes, the journalist, lends additional light with her insistence that "for a woman, the decision to stop life is pain enough, and penalty enough. To add to it not only the risk of butchery but the humiliation of subterfuge and the squalor of crime is, I believe, indefensible."[20]

Taking a related tack, but one seldom heard above the battle's roar, Madeline Sims, a British reformer, patiently and narrowly argues that without Britain's 1967 liberalization the situation would have steadily deteriorated: "Emergencies would certainly have increased as criminal abortions and back-street surgery abortions rose . . . as [they are] doing in so many Roman Catholic countries today, where criminal abortion rages in epidemic proportions."[21] Conceding that averting a nasty situation is a negative virtue, Sims gently points out that "the best thing that can be said for democracy, after all, is the things that do *not* happen to you under it"—the negative virtue of *not* being imprisoned without a fair trial, for example. To prevent a long-term deterioration in a situation is *not* trivial.[22]

Consistent with this viewpoint the Supreme Court in 1973 partially rewarded abortion-on-request advocates by ruling that state laws restricting early abortion are unconstitutional. By a vote of 7 to 2, the Court overruled the restrictive laws of forty-six states, holding that "the right of privacy . . . is broad enough to encompass a woman's decision whether or not to terminate her pregnancy."[23] In dismissing the contention that the state has a compelling interest in protecting the embryo from conception on, the Court concluded, "In short, the unborn have never been recognized in the law as persons in the whole sense."[24] The state's interest in potential life begins only at the point of viability, which the Court defined as starting from twenty-four to twenty-eight weeks after conception.

Terence Cardinal Cooke of the New York Roman Catholic Archdiocese found the Supreme Court decision "horrifying" and expressed the hope that "our citizens will do all in their power to reverse this injustice to the rights of the unborn child."[25] Although no official word was published on the subject, comparable dismay probably greeted the later announcement by the Internal Revenue Service that for the first time in its history it would allow tax deductions for abortions (and birth control pills and sterilization operations).

The Cardinal's dismay notwithstanding, the apparent victors insist with Roberta Gratz that their victory will not be complete:

> until dignified and safe abortions are available to all who seek them, poor women as well as those who can afford the current inflated price; until we have defeated the ingenious maneuverings that are already being tried to forestall compliance; until women will no longer be made to feel guilty by condescending doctors; until all state laws pertaining to abortion are wiped off the books, and abortion is no longer treated differently from other medical matters.[26]

Other questions that continue to perplex include the following:

1. To what extent will health codes limit where abortion may be performed after the first twelve weeks—in hospitals only, or in clinics and doctors' offices as well?
2. What will happen to the doctors and nurses across the country who have either been jailed or had their medical licenses revoked for performing abortions?
3. What can be done to increase the use of paramedics and midwives? The Supreme Court has given the states the option of specifying that only doctors may perform abortions, and this option results in persistently high costs.

Although a large part of the legal question may have been resolved by the Court, its 1973 decision leaves us a host of *unresolved* issues of a regulatory, economic, and ideological character. At least a dozen bills were submitted to Congress in 1973 to amend the Constitution to overturn the Court's ruling. And Congress was asked to permit a bare majority of a hospital's board of directors to impose an antiabortion rule on the entire staff of the hospital, regardless of the proabortion orientation of any of them.[27] We seem to face controversy without end.

Child Rearing

Playgrounds. How might we better help our youngsters celebrate their fast-passing youth? So much now seems arrayed against such celebration, from the weekday loss of fathers who go to work to the insidious narcotizing of TV and the awful loneliness of children kept deliberately motionless lest they stray off the block into alien turf or into the clutches of the seeming army of "strangers" the FBI warns us against. Nevertheless, some small gains can be and are being made—even at times by a turning back of the clock. More specifically we have discovered still another way to enhance childhood in that very special province of the young, the playground.

One happy idea imported from Great Britain appears only now to be gaining importance, an idea that turns playgrounds back to the kids and to the junk they love to play and create with. Developed first in Denmark and in England in the 1940's, the adventure or junk playgrounds have become so successful that they have now spread across Europe and have premiered stateside in New York City.

Building and changing, tearing down and creatively rebuilding are at the heart of this kind of playground. It began when adults noticed that wartime children who were left to their own devices would go to play in rubble-filled lots and build things out of the litter day after day, without ever becoming bored. A description of Manhattan's first such venture captures its essence:

> At first, there appears to be nothing but a littered space, with the usual vacant-lot inventory. . . . Then one notices a strange looking structure in one corner of the lot. On closer inspection, it turns out to have "rooms," a kind of front porch, a sort of half-covered terrace, and bit of "furniture"; it is a couple of stories high and is topped by a post, ringed with rubber tires.

The city, prodded by a park-oriented citizens' group, has graded and fenced the lot and pays the rent on it and a related store-front for indoor poor-weather activities.

Play is supervised by adult recreation leaders, whose budget (mostly salaries) of $12,000 to $16,000 annually is raised by the local citizens' group. The park is not without critics, some local mothers maintaining that it is an eyesore and a place where their children could get hurt despite the presence of the recreation leaders. The young builders counter that they prefer to stay off the street and out of trouble and want to be where they can make friends. Above all, not surprisingly, they love the idea that "you can make whatever you want," as well as change your mind and "knock it all down."[28]

Savings Accounts. What if we wanted to encourage habits of rainy-day savings? We might adopt a variation of current Swiss practice. In Switzerland almost 2 million youngsters have their own savings accounts, many of which were started at their birth by their parents or grandparents. These accounts earn 5 per cent interest, whereas adult savers receive a lower rate. To encourage further thrift by youngsters certain key Swiss cities provide parents with savings incentives in the form of an income tax deduction of $120 per child per year for deposits made in junior savings accounts. Not surprisingly, the savings rate in Switzerland approaches 30 per cent of the GNP in contrast to 18 per cent here.[29]

Children's Books. How might we ensure the availability of children's books? Perhaps by the head-on approach recently taken by the Danes. In 1970, they passed a law that requires each municipality to maintain a public library with both children's and adults' departments. In a similar vein, the Swedes tackled the thorny question of how to get more serious critical attention paid to children's literature, both by potential writers and by likely parental users. A 1970 ruling in Swedish universities now requires the inclusion of courses on books for children in every literature curriculum, with stress placed on the history of ideas and how they affect juvenile writing.[30]

Classroom TV. While we continue to putter about, with every little decentralized school jurisdiction going its lone and bumbling way, the more centrally directed schools of various nations abroad turn increasingly to sophisticated TV instructional systems for unique educational aid.

"No other nation," writes Marvin Leiner, an education researcher, "whether economically advanced or underdeveloped, has taken the medium so seriously as has Cuba." A staff of 162 instructors and consultants prepare lessons broadcast four hours each day on every high school subject, with 92 technicians and directors assisting in production. Essentially, TV is used to raise the quality of instruction by exposing children and teachers alike to talented personnel. With almost every secondary school classroom in the country equipped with not one but two TV sets, Leiner concludes, "Cuban viewers may yet become the first people in the world to think of television as a machine wired for culture—rather than commercials."[31]

High School Television Matriculation. Lost sight of in our understandable excitement over the millions going on with their formal education after high school is the perplexing challenge of the larger number yet who fail initially to secure even a high school diploma—and come soon to miss it sorely. A reform technique has been pioneered since 1967 by the West German state of Bavaria—with fairly encouraging results.

Bavarian officials were anxious to help citizens pass a high school equivalency test that opens the door to specialized colleges and academies (nursing, social work, technical work, and so on) and that is necessary for many careers. At an initial cost to the state of nearly $4 million in 1966, they prepared one-hour TV lessons to run six nights a week for three consecutive years on a special state-owned channel. With a dropout rate among the thirty thousand first-year registrants running now at about that expected of evening or correspondence schools, officials view with satisfaction the attainment of the equivalency diploma by over fifteen hundred of the first thirty thousand aspirants.

Viewing, of course, was only a part of the project. Homework went back and forth weekly through the mail, and every three months the TV enrollees met in local discussion groups on a Saturday to explore course subject matter. Observers from the other ten German states and various other European nations hovered over the scene, and the TV films themselves are now being rented and widely used elsewhere.

Could we use this system to reach our own dropouts? Possibly. Many might prefer the comfort of their living-room easy chair to the hard-to-reach classroom of a dismal evening school. And many might be excited by the creative visual possibilities inherent in educational TV. Bavaria's example justifies a trial of the project here, if, that is, we are serious about helping our educational have-nots to help themselves to a better set of life chances.[32]

Survival Learning. How can we gain new personal strength and insight—at a consciously desired and considerable risk to our own safety and sanity? Interested? So were over eighteen thousand young people who are now alumni of thirty-four worldwide schools of the Outward Bound organization.

Established in 1941 at Aberdovey, Wales, the first Outward Bound school was designed to reduce the loss of young British merchant sailors whose ships were sunk by German submarines. Because the older, more experienced sailors managed to survive, it was reasoned that success in meeting severe challenges depended much more on attitude than on mere physical prowess. A series of carefully supervised trials and seemingly hostile situations were evolved, and young apprentice seamen were exposed to these for four weeks. The Outward Bound program was so successful that it has continued and grown larger ever since. It promises its students, who range from businessmen to delinquents, nothing except the satisfaction of confronting two very special entities: fear and one's own very private self.

Still administered from London, the thirty-four far-flung subsidiaries on five continents have considerable autonomy. Each of our five American extensions, in particular, is distinctive, though they all share these features of the Colorado school:

> Each training group, made up of 10 plus two instructors, takes off for an isolated spot, such as Mexico's Baja, for a 10 day or 21 day expedition. Together the men plan a course through the rapids, mountain climb, and rappel down cliffs. Each activity requires teamwork as well as individual effort. The course winds up with each man living alone by his own resources for three days.

The twenty-six-day, $450 expedition for teen-agers has only small variations in the general ordeal. For twenty-three days the fellows and girls scale 14,000-foot mountains, rappel down 120-foot cliffs, run a 20-mile marathon, shoot rapids in a kayak, and finally "solo," an experience that "evokes a reaction ranging from mystical enlightment to sheer terror." Since 1962, with eighteen thousand alumni, Outward Bound has lost only four enrollees.

Adventurous in defining its own mission Outward Bound has expanded considerably beyond its early survival concepts. There are now wilderness expeditions for business executives, with IBM, Martin Marietta Corporation, Ralston Purina, Unilever, Imperial Chemical Industries, and British Petroleum on the client list. There are also urban encounters for teachers in methadone clinics, penitentiaries, and hospitals, and there are specially designed full-semester Outward Bound courses for high school seniors and anthropological investigations for college students.[33] How much further can this British innovation spread? How many more Americans may it soon aid? Well, are *you* interested?

Subsidized Jaunts. Since 1967 Canada has been encouraging tens of thousands of young Canadians to "go on the road" and see their own country, a model we could well emulate in our own undertraveled nation. The government, Prime Minister Pierre Trudeau explains,

> believes that there is a positive and beneficial value in travel by young Canadians. National unity is a product of national understanding and national pride. Never in our history has there been the same opportunity for mobility of young people as now exists. With or without help, young people will be traveling. . . . We should help make their experience more worthwhile.

Some $10 million is spent annually to help finance youth travel, as the Canadians seem convinced that their country will be truly united only if it is run by a generation that knows how the other half lives.

Specifically, the government sponsors five major services to promote young Canadians' seeing Canada:

1. A chain of 96 youth hostels, run at a low $1.2 million, charge 50¢ to $1 a night to young visitors. Those without the fee can stay anyway in return for some simple chores.
2. In another federally sponsored program, staffed almost entirely by students, large numbers of youngsters who have to earn money during the summer are placed in jobs in other parts of the country.
3. Young people who speak only one of the two official languages may apply for placement in a university in a province other than their own for a tuition-free six-week summer language course.
4. The Government also administers the Young Voyageurs program, which has given 5,000 students aged 15 to 17 an opportunity to visit an area of Canada of their choice.
5. Finally, the Government sponsors the travel of various petitioning groups: Among the 15,000 so aided in 1972, for example, were 53 French-speaking Quebequois who visited a group of English-speaking Canadians in Calgary for a mini-cultural exchange.

In all these efforts priority is given to those who do not have enough money to travel, young people, those from remote regions, and groups of Indian people, handicapped people, and senior citizens.

Conversely, we do very little to facilitate internal travel by our youngsters, and no serious attempt has been made to show American youth that there is a lot to do and see in this country. (People overseas regularly complain that they cannot find out much about America from Americans because most have not seen this country!) Canada's example urges us to recognize soon that travel induces maturity, encourages independence, and broadens horizons: "there is a definite far-reaching cultural advantage to bringing up a generation that has seen Kentucky bluegrass and West Virginia strip mines, Dakota badlands and Iowa plains, Oregon forests and Arizona deserts."[34] Perhaps as part of a bicentennial gift from adults to the nation's youth the government, by a change of attitude and a commitment of funds, could begin to provide various opportunities for Americans to see America—an overdue, small-scale reform with big-scale possibilities.

Educational Parks. A new and larger school that permits the consolidation of school resources, an educational park would include a much larger school attendance area to facilitate racial desegregation. In both educational and interpersonal ways (with particular reference to race relations) the educational park would permit substantial improvements in the quality of education for *all* pupils.

Consider, for example, a plan for parks submitted in 1968 by a citizens' committee (of which I was a part) to the Philadelphia Board of Education. The plan called for the conversion between 1968 and 1980 of the city's 284 schools into a consolidated system of twenty educational parks. Each park would have an enrollment of 15,000 youngsters in two senior high schools of 2,000 pupils each, four junior high schools of 1,000 pupils each, and eight primary and nursery schools of 800 pupils each. Each park might also school exceptional or physically handicapped youngsters on the site, and five of the city's twenty parks would each house a 4,000-student two-year junior or community college. The site in each case would encompass some one hundred contiguous acres, or an area of about four by six city blocks. With roads confined to a subsurface level the park would boast contiguous modern buildings and athletic fields in a green, campuslike, landscaped setting.

Educational parks in the Philadelphia plan could have made available for the first time to *all* of the city's 240,000 school pupils the latest and the finest in educational resources. Each of the twenty proposed parks would have science laboratories, multipurpose theaters, natural science centers, remedial reading clinics, swimming pools, tennis courts, and the like. Each might also have an aviary, an arboretum, a British-style "junk playground," a closed-circuit television center, a comprehensive health facility, a counseling center, a main library, a planetarium, a staff training center, and a university-linked research and development center. Beyond even these conventional facilities some more daring thinking suggests that each park could boast such novel and overdue resources as an Israeli-style nursery, a student-run activities center, a parent-run home and school association headquarters, and a number of short- and long-stay dormitories conditionally available to park pupils as young as seven years of age.

Twelve of the twenty necessary sites were pinpointed by the plan's sponsors. All of these sites were located within the city, and each was chosen to promote racial integration by drawing carefully from areas of distinct de facto segregation. Located generally on the borders of black and white population concentrations, nearly all of the parks would have had a 70 to 30 black-white ratio, reflecting the best race ratio that could be secured by 1980 *if* a park system managed to stem an ongoing white exodus from the public school system (in 1968 whites comprised 42 per cent of the city's population and at present departure rates may constitute only a highly geographically concentrated 20 per cent of the Philadelphia school system by 1980).

Although land is as tight in Philadelphia as elsewhere, the twenty sites of one hundred acres each were pinpointed for such feasible, if novel, locations as above a little-used reservoir, in the air rights above a major railroad terminus, in the air rights above a major highway complex, and in the place of run-down blocks of depressed light-industry facilities. By design the plan avoided the dislocation of a single homeowner and the forfeiture of a single dwelling. Also by design the plan provided that no site location would necessitate a bus ride of more than a half-hour's duration for any of the 300,000 youngsters involved. (These three considerations—and the achievement of the best possible race ratio at each site while using the largest number of sites possible within the limits of a half-hour commute—explain why twenty, and not ten or thirty, parks were recommended.)

Not surprisingly, estimating the costs of the twenty-park plan proved the most difficult part of the entire effort. Reliable data on school construction and equipment costs were rare, land and air-right costs were negotiable, and steady inflation in all costs had to be taken into account. With all of these considerations, a price tag of $2 billion was put on the plan by its sponsors. Each park was budgeted at $100 million, it being clearly understood that the financial outlay would be spread over the next twelve years, the first park to be opened in sixteen months' time, the twentieth park not until 1980. In 1968 the city was spending $500 million over a current six-year period (1967–1973) to rebuild many ancient, fire-vulnerable school buildings on the racially segregated sites they occupied and to build some few others that only complemented (and compounded) the city's de facto segregation. Park proponents pointed out that for an expenditure only three times as large—spread out over a period twice as long—the city could secure a brand-new twenty-first-century school system and reverse the tide of school segregation at the same time.

In 1968 the city was (and still is in 1973) under orders from the State Commission on Human Relations to reverse the steady tide toward citywide school segregation, and it was therefore increasingly attentive to the contentions of the park-system advocates. The city's Board of Education commissioned the detailed planning of three specialized prototype parks (a vocational high-school cluster, an academic high-school cluster, and a science-oriented interschool cluster), and formal hearings on the park plan in 1967 later resulted in an unpopular compromise that shelved the twenty-park system in favor of a two-park proposal with very few advocates. To date (in 1973), nothing has come of it all.

Why? Part of the answer involves sponsorship. In Philadelphia the original support for the concept of the educational park came from the education director of the Urban League. In 1967, with the endorsement of the League's Philadelphia Board of Directors, a Citizens' Committee was formed to generate public interest in and support of the park concept. In the early 1970's, however, the Urban League allowed its advocacy to lapse, reflecting the pressure many black interest groups have been under to substitute "quality-now" goals for "integration-now" goals in education. Advocacy was temporarily led in 1969 by the staff of the School Board's own Office of Inter-Group Relations, a revealing and short-lived development.

So much for the particulars of one illustrative park proposal. It cannot be stressed strongly enough that there are as many definitions for educational parks as there are people defining them. The nation's two most advanced parks, those in Acton, Massachusetts, and in Fort Lauderdale, Florida, along with the eighty others in various stages of development, differ in the number of grade levels served, in acreage, in the size of the attendance area from which students are drawn, and in the type of program envisioned. All, however, are similar in their unique ability to combat de facto segregation and to make educational advances available to students regardless of race or social class.

Park advocates everywhere make much of current trends in institutional racism, particularly in the intensification of housing segregation and in the continued resistance of school district officials to federal pressures for school integration. These trends are cited as evidence of the irredeemable shortcomings of the park's major alternative, the neighborhood school plan. Continued support for neighborhood schools is condemned as support for increasing racial isolation.

Park advocates also make much of the inadequacies of compensatory and integration programs that are predicated on the continued existence of neighborhood schools. Evidence from the Coleman Report and elsewhere is alleged to suggest that such programs do *not* substantially remedy the educational harm arising from class-biased and racially segregated schooling. Park advocates believe that their case is also supported by the continued white exodus to suburbia, the current intensification of the educational "head start" provided suburban white youngsters, and the severe erosion of the municipal tax base underlying school support. Of late, the withdrawal of black pressure groups from the overt struggle for school integration has also been considered an important justification for switching to parks.

Finally, park advocates make much of structural trends in educational technology that allegedly favor the park over competitive forms of schooling. The economic facts of life seem to suggest that especially large units like fifteen-thousand-student parks are far more able to use the technology efficiently than are widely scattered and much smaller units in a neighborhood school system. Indeed, as computer technology is sure to have a disturbing effect on any social system into which it is fitted, the potential advantages of being a part of a new system from the very start are perhaps equally great to the educational park concept and to the development of computer technology.

Critics ask: Can the giant parks be kept "human"? Can school pupils be protected against the trend in large bureaucracies toward bureaupathic attitudes and behavior? Park supporters respond by urging that the popularity at present of parent participation in education makes continued promotion of this reform imperative. Substantial rewards are possible in student morale, parent reinforcement of the school's educational mission, and staff responsiveness to student needs otherwise more easily ignored. But how, the critics ask, is parent participation to occur when a park involves ten thousand heterogeneous families from an area of several square miles? Must formalization of parent participation necessarily result in insipid imitations of the old PTA's?

The current increase of impersonality in education makes advances against this bureaupathic development imperative. In the park system substantial rewards can flow from the provision of idle time for joint socializing between students and faculty, the minimization of status barriers to interpersonal relationships across rank and generation "gaps," and the creation of small living or schooling units (as in the Harvard house plan) with which one can personally identify. But how is this to be accomplished when a park involves fifteen thousand pupils from widely disparate backgrounds? Must gigantism in educational institutions necessarily result in insipid imitations of the old counselor-and-adviser system?

Beyond even these primary matters critics and advocates alike ask: Will exposure at the same site to the success models of older generations of students encourage youngsters to view schooling as something they too can succeed at? Will exposure at the same site to the teaching example—and sheer human company—of several hundred other faculty members encourage adult staffers to experiment with educational innovations and to value their chosen careers more highly? Finally, will exposure of all participants to a completely new facility, one entirely free from accumulated grime and negative historic connotations ("P.S. 17 has always been a dumping ground"), encourage all to new educational effort and achievement?[35]

Educational Park Plan of the Philadelphia Committee on Educational Parks: 1968

What Is an Educational Park?

A complex of school facilities which includes all levels of grade organization.

All facilities are located on a single site and serve a population large enough to insure both integration of students and concentration of resources necessary for quality education.

Each park contains individual, administratively and physically identifiable units of elementary and secondary schools. . . .

Will All Children Have to Be "Bussed" to Parks?

NO.

Secondary school children (ages 12 and up) presently walk or take public transportation. The same would be true for a park.

Many younger children living close to a park could walk. The others would have to be provided with transportation.

The cost for this could be reduced by making greater use of State subsidy for transportation.

The "logistics" of extra transportation will, of course, have to be carefully worked-out for a large urban center like Philadelphia.

WHAT HAPPENS TO EXISTING FACILITIES?

Some could become part of a park until all new facilities are built.

Others could be sold—to industry, to the City, to other school systems.

Some could be used for community centers, adult education centers, etc.

WHY EDUCATIONAL PARKS?

The park frees public education of limitations inherent in the present system.

Each park can provide integrated education for all children because of its location and size.

Faculty integration can be achieved or continued and strengthened (this is not to be construed as an implication that faculty integration must await development of parks).

The park removes the stigma of "neighborhood" on a school and eradicates the existence of high status and low status schools based on class or race.

The park provides each school unit with access to specialty teachers, remedial training, psychological counselling and guidance services, coordinated evaluation and unified administrative procedures.

The park offers the possibility of offering modern education of the highest quality for a highly mobile population. It eradicates the present and formerly recurring patterns of overcrowding and under-used schools in a system.

The park offers *equality* of education to all children.

Voucher Plan. If the voucher system, now being experimentally tested in San Jose, California, should become widespread in the late 1970's, it will probably revolutionize the present American educational system—a system that still sees 13 per cent of all children fail to finish eighth grade and 42 per cent fail to complete high school.

The key to educational reform, at least according to psychologist Kenneth Clark, is probably "aggressive competition." It would help if the schools competed by promising to educate better than do alternative sources. A responsive school system, former OEO Director Donald Rumsfeld explained in 1971, must be one in which "poor parents would be able to exercise some opportunity to choose similar to that now enjoyed by wealthier parents who can move to a better public school district or send their children to private schools."[36]

The key to these reforms may be the voucher system, with its concept of consumer sovereignty in the school marketplace. Although the basic idea is proudly traced by conservative enthusiasts back two hundred years to Adam Smith, academics generally credit its modern renown to the British economist E. C. West. In his 1965 book, *Education and the State,* Professor West argued that education should be removed from the direct control of the state and that the poor, as well as the rich, should be able to exercise some measure of control over the education of their children. Almost immediately Americans otherwise as far apart as conservative economist Milton Friedman and liberal educational critic Christopher Jencks—as well as various government types—hailed the idea as exceptionally worthy of field experimentation.

More specifically, the basic voucher plan scheme is that an issuing agency—school board, town, city, state, or federal agency—gives to the parent of a pupil (or to an adult learner himself) a voucher equal to the cost of tuition at any school he chooses. The school, in turn, routes the voucher back to the issuing agency, and the agency reimburses the school for the cost of the pupil's education.

Enthusiasts see three gains over and above those that West stressed:

1. A voucher plan could stimulate the growth of tuition-free "alternative schools."
2. It could provide relief for parents and students who are dissatisfied with their neighborhood public schools but cannot afford any other kind of schooling.
3. And it should help create a wider range of educational choices for students and parents.

Parochial school supporters were quick to press for their inclusion in this exciting range of possibilities, and as of 1973 legal tests are pending that seek to affirm their legal participation. (It is expected that "indirect" aid, such as a voucher construed as a scholarship, can and will be found constitutional by the Supreme Court.)

Especially exciting, by the way, is the extension of the entire idea into the realm of higher education. Typical is a bill proposed for adoption in New York State in 1973:

1. As many as ten thousand high school seniors in New York City would receive vouchers of about $1,800 a year.
2. The only condition on such vouchers is that they must be used at private colleges within the city.

Three substantial gains are foreseen by the bill's sponsors: the plan would bolster financially troubled small private colleges, reduce overcrowding at free public universities, and allow many young adults far greater freedom than ever before in choosing a college.[37]

Conservative economist Milton Friedman insists that the voucher plan system is "entirely feasible." In his view it is simply the principle of the GI educational grants brought down to elementary and secondary schools. The major obstacle to adopting it, Friedman charges, is as removed from child-growth concerns as possible: "it is the vested interest of school teachers and school administrators who fear competition and much prefer the shelter of civil service." The major gainers, Friedman concludes, would be children, families, and an entire category of Americans: "The major gainers would be poor people in the slums. For the first time, they would have effective power as individuals to influence the quality of schooling their children receive."[38] With this kind of backing, it is little wonder that such high-level OEO administrators as conservative Daniel F. Joy III, a former official of Young Americans for Freedom, expect much from the voucher plan.[39]

From the opposite end of the political spectrum, support comes from the followers of Ivan Illich, who urge attention to the first article he proposes for a "bill of rights" for a modern humanist society: "The State shall make no law with respect to the establishment of education." In his provocative book *Deschooling Society,* Illich urges us to replace our schools with "educational networks" that have four ingredients:

1. Libraries, warehouses, laboratories, and rental agencies which can supply any educational tool or object a child—or adult—may want;
2. "Skill exchanges" where persons list their skills and the remuneration they want to serve as models for those who want to learn their skills;
3. Peer-matching agencies where those who wish to learn may find a partner for their inquiry; and
4. Reference services where students may locate "educators-at-large"—elders—who are competent to advise, direct, and criticize the person in pursuit of an education.

To help pay for passage through this educational network Illich would have the government issue each citizen at birth an "edu-credit card." This would entitle each citizen to a sum of money—the same for all persons, rich or poor—to be used whenever and wherever he saw fit for his education.

"The disestablishment of schools will inevitably happen," Illich contends, "and it will happen surprisingly fast." The education voucher, usable at any school or school substitute of a family's choice, could prove an especially efficacious way of disestablishing schools so wretched that many educationists fear no one would stay in them if there were alternatives.[40]

The key supporter of this plan so far, the *only* one to back up rhetoric with money, has been the OEO. Accordingly, the voucher plan may ultimately resemble in practice the details of the nation's first large-scale ($2.2 million) experiment, the 1973 OEO trial given the scheme by thirty-eight hundred pupils in San Jose, California:

1. A voucher was worth $680 for a child in elementary school and $970 for a seventh- or eighth-grade pupil.
2. Families could choose among a wide range of curriculums offered by twenty-two minischools in the public school system.
3. Over 60 per cent of the participating pupils chose nontraditional public schools, for example, a school with a fine arts emphasis that used sheet music to teach mathematics.
4. One half the participating students, or those who qualified for free school lunches under an unrelated federal program (a family with less than $1,000 income per member annually), were classified as "poor" for purposes of the voucher experiment. Their vouchers were made worth one third more than all others in an effort to make these pupils more attractive to school administrators.

Observers are quick to point out that the San Jose experiment was *not* a full voucher system. As parents could not use their OEO vouchers to send their children to private or parochial schools, and as only six of twenty-four eligible public schools chose to participate, the California project did not represent a useful test of a chief criticism—the possibility that a voucher plan would be used by parents to segregate their children at schools where one race predominates. Also, affluent parents were not able to supplement the voucher allocated to each child, as they would be able to under a pure voucher system. Nor could the San Jose schools choose among applicants. Moreover, safeguards were built into the experiment to keep teachers and administrators on the payroll even if their programs proved uncompetitive.[41]

With all of these drawbacks, however, the San Jose field trial seems to have secured two of the major goals of voucher systems, reforms in education and a fresh variety of choices in educational style:

> The experiment got under way when the six staffs organized 22 "mini-schools," most of them innovative, some of them traditional. The mini-schools, each with its own teaching staff and classrooms in one or another of the six school buildings, included:
>
> A futuristic "School 2000," featuring the use of computers and space technology.
>
> A daily-living school that teaches camping, cooking and gardening.
>
> An enrichment program open to any child whose parents think he is gifted, whether or not he is.
>
> Six mini-schools, one in each participating school, stressing the basic 3 Rs.
>
> The basic subjects are taught in all 22 mini-schools, not just the six that stress the 3 Rs. But they are taught in different ways. In School 2000, for example, children are learning math by learning how to use computers. And no matter which mini-school a child attends, he is still tested on the basic subjects to check whether the school is keeping up with state standards.[42]

There were also such related gains as less absenteeism and vandalism, record turnouts at meetings of the parent-teacher associations, and more enthusiasm for school on all sides. Did the children learn more? Results of a detailed evaluation will not be available until the summer of 1974, but as journalist Evan Jenkins explained in May of 1973, "no one in more than a score of interviews suggested that the children were learning less, and many thought that there was marked improvement."[43] And an additional seven schools voted to join the original six in the 1973–1974 school year.

Encouraged in part by the San Jose successes, OEO officials are now testing the voucher plan in New Hampshire—but with a major difference: this time children in private and parochial schools *will* be part of the educational experiment. Possibly as much as $5 million in OEO support is entailed for a two-year (1973–1975) program.

Teachers and civil rights organizations remained vehement in their opposition as late as 1973. The latter cite the "segregation academies" that sprang up in the South several years ago in response to school desegregation orders. An official of the American Federation of Teachers goes further to insist that "the voucher system will mean the death of public education in the United States," and the National Education Association warns that voucher plans "could lead to racial, economic, and social isolation of children."[44] Further objections are that:

1. The voucher plan will turn public schools into "dumping grounds," serving only children rejected by all other schools.
2. The plan will make "hucksterism" the order of the day: private schools will dazzle parents with fads and gimmicks, and parents will be too bewildered to choose schools wisely.
3. Vouchers will encourage the growth of parochial schools at the expense of others.

Supporters insist that the San Jose variations—for example, the bonus for poverty-handicapped youngsters, the OEO prohibitions against racial and class segregation, and so on—meet and override some of these criticisms, though they concede that the maturity of the parents involved remains an uncertain variable.

Still more significant, however, is the growing division in the ranks of supporters between liberal backers of the San Jose model and conservative backers of the New Hampshire model, which avoids all conditions on participation. The San Jose model, designed by Christopher Jencks, and the New Hampshire model, built along the lines of Milton Friedman's suggestions, try the patience and the politics of all involved: "The differences between the Friedman and Jencks proposals," an OEO official explains, "reflect the philosophical primacy which Friedman gives to liberty and Jencks to equality."[45]

All supporters, regardless of their politics, however, remain firm in their insistence that teachers and administrators, as well as children and parents, stand to gain considerably from the voucher plan:

> First, principals will be able to utilize many concepts from specialization. A principal's ability to outline a specific educational program will facilitate the employment of a more homogenous staff. In-service training can be narrowed to focus on the more specialized educational program.
>
> Second, teachers can find schools that are compatible with their own teaching philosophies. Teachers with special skills can select a school where their skills will be utilized.
>
> Third, internal staff conflict can be reduced. Principals and teachers will no longer face the frustration of meeting the needs of all segments of a traditional school population.[46]

No wonder then that a spokesman for one of the teachers' unions concedes that "Vouchers introduce us to a whole new ball game. San Jose is just the top of the first inning."[47]

Will we endorse the voucher plan or soon lose interest? One commentator sees the answer in terms of three related questions:

> What social and political tensions or benefits emerge when parents usurp the educator's role in decision-making?
>
> Does the educational marketplace function as some might predict, i.e., do new programs and options develop? Are the customers satisfied? Does the cost of education change?
>
> Do students learn more, or differently, or worse, than under conventional school patterns?[48]

Data from San Jose, New Hampshire, and other programs will help to answer these questions, but only *our* personal assessment will finally promote or put down a genuine and exceptional alternative to the status quo in American education.

Summary

Plainly much of merit did not find space in this chapter. The discussion of abortion could have been extended, for example, to include the reform of voluntary sterilization procedures (from 260,000 in 1969, the number has soared to over 1,000,000 vasectomy and tubal ligation patients in 1973[49]). And the array of child-rearing reforms could have included the new Children's Defense Fund, formed in 1973 to reform laws dealing with children's rights (as in juvenile justice, educational neglect, the treatment of institutionalized children, and the use of children in medical experiments).[50] Similarly, the discussion of educational reforms might have included the popular idea of year-round schools (the 5 per cent savings achieved by Virginia schools, traced to better use of facilities and so on, has earned national attention and applause[51]).

It will suffice, however, if the chapter's review of new approaches to birth control, childbirth, childhood, adolescence, and formal education whet *your* appetite to learn more about our options in these matters . . . and encourage you to dare to risk more to gain more in all of them.

> . . . The West and Christian culture on one level deeply wants love to win—and having decided (after several sad tries) that love can't, people who still say it will are like ghosts from an old dream.
>
> Love begins with the family and its network of erotic and responsible relationships. A slight alteration of family structure will project a different love-and-property outlook through a whole culture.
>
> GARY SNYDER

FOOTNOTES

1. John S. Miller, "Childbirth: Progress in Dignity," reprinted at the end of this chapter.
2. Jonathan Kozol, "Death at an Early Age," as reprinted in A. David Hill et al., eds., *The Quality of Life* (New York: Holt, 1973), p. 275.
3. Hans Peter Drietzel, "Introduction: Childhood and Socialization," *Childhood and Socialization,* Hans Peter Drietzel, ed. (New York: Macmillan, Inc., 1973), pp. 11–12.
4. Ibid., p. 12.
5. Ibid, p. 9.
6. Lindsay Miller, "Lib Women Look at Having Babies," *New York Post* (June 4, 1973), p. 13.
7. Edmund Newton, "Fights for Father's Rights," *New York Post* (January 18, 1973), p. 33.
8. James MacGregor, "Abortion Counselors," *Wall Street Journal* (June 23, 1969), p. 1.

9. "Community Service Unit Sees a Fight on Abortion Laws in 1973," *New York Times* (November 5, 1972), p. 39.
10. Jerry M. Flint, "Abortion Backers Hopeful of Gains," *New York Times* (October 9, 1972), p. 9.
11. "Six of 10 Adults Approve Abortions," *Philadelphia Inquirer* (March 9, 1972), p. 22.
12. Jane E. Brody, "City's Year-Old Abortion Record Hailed," *New York Times* (June 30, 1971), p. 37. "New York would be happy to relinquish its role as abortion center for the country," explained Dr. Jean Pakter, Head of Maternal Services for the city.
13. Barbara Rose, "The New York Abortion," *New York* (May 29, 1972), p. 73.
14. Helen Smith (Chairman, Illinois Citizens for the Medical Control of Abortion), "The Religious Issue," *Playboy* (April 1972), p. 196.
15. "Antiabortion Forces Demonstrate a Growing Influence in State Legislatures Across the Country," *New York Times* (June 28, 1972), p. 21.
16. For an excellent antiabortion overview, see Denis Cavanagh, "Reforming the Abortion Laws: A Doctor Looks at the Case," *America* (April 18, 1970), pp. 406–411.
17. As quoted by Fred C. Shapiro, " 'Right to Life' Has a Message for New York State Legislators," *New York Times Magazine* (August 20, 1972), p. 43.
18. Ibid., p. 40.
19. Rose, op. cit., p. 73.
20. Marya Mannes, "A Woman Views Abortion," *The Petal Paper* (November 1966), p. 1.
21. Madeline Simms, "The Abortion Act After Three Years," *The Political Quarterly* (July–September 1971), p. 285.
22. Ibid. See also Betty Sarvis and Hyman Rodman, *The Abortion Controversy* (New York: Columbia U.P., 1973).
23. As reported on in Jimmye Kimmey, "How the Abortion Laws Happened," *Ms,* (April 1973), p. 118.
24. Ibid.
25. Ibid.
26. Roberta Gratz, "Abortion Victims: Never Again," *Ms* (April 1973), p. 44.
27. Louis Cassels, "Abortion Question Rages On," *Philadelphia Evening Bulletin* (June 2, 1973), p. 9; Eileen Shanahan, "House Urged Not to Curb Abortions," *New York Times* (May 3, 1973), p. 24.
28. Arvid Bengstton, *Adventure Playgrounds* (New York: Praeger, 1972).
29. Zena Sutherland, "Small Countries, Big Projects," *Saturday Review* (October 24, 1970), p. 66.
30. Ibid.
31. Marvin Leiner, "Cuba's Schools, Ten Years Later," *Saturday Review* (October 17, 1970), p. 61.
32. Gisela Mahlmann, "Educational TV: The Idea of Germany's *Telekolleg," School and Society* (February 1969), pp. 106–107.
33. Fascinating on the gains possible is an essay, "Going Solo," by June Hanson, in *Ms* (April 1973), pp. 71–73, 104.
34. Stephen Kinzer, "Youth in Canada: Drifting Around with the Government's Blessing," *New York Times* (April 22, 1973), pp. XX–1, 7.
35. On educational parks, see Wayne Jennings, "Educational Parks: Tomorrow's Schools," *Audiovisual Instruction* (October 1970), pp. 42–44; Max Wolff, "The Educational Park Concept," *Wilson Library Bulletin* (October 1967), pp. 173–175, 232; Thomas F. Pettigrew, "The Metropolitan Educational Park," *Science Teacher* (December 1969), pp. 23–26.

36. Both Clark and Rumsfeld are quoted in John Coyne, "The Voucher System," *Intellectual Digest* (November 1971), p. 26.
37. M. A. Farber, "Bill Would Have State Pay Tuition of 10,000 Public-College Students at Private Colleges," *New York Times* (March 18, 1973), p. 61.
38. Milton Friedman, "Busing: The Real Issue," *Newsweek* (August 14, 1972), p. 69.
39. As cited in Evan Jenkins, "A School Voucher Experiment Rates an 'A' in Coast District," *New York Times* (May 29, 1973), p. 54.
40. Ivan Illich, "Why We Must Abolish Schooling," *New York Review of Books* (July 2, 1970).
41. "Vouchers Reshape a School District," *New York Times* (September 25, 1972), p. 12.
42. Joan S. Lubin, "California Purchase," *Wall Street Journal* (June 4, 1973), p. 1.
43. Jenkins, op. cit., p. 54.
44. Evan Jenkins, "Voucher System in Schools Gains," *New York Times* (April 20, 1973), p. 11; the NEA is quoted in Lubin, *op. cit.,* p. 1.
45. Quoted in William F. Buckley, Jr., "The Voucher Plan," *New York Post* (May 24, 1973), p. 38.
46. W. E. Patton and R. A. Anderson, "Educational Vouchers for the Community," *Theory into Practice* (February 1972), p. 62.
47. Quoted in James Mecklenburger, "Vouchers at Alum Rock," *Phi Delta Kappan* (September 1972), p. 25.
48. Ibid.
49. Sylvia Porter, "Sterilization 'Boom,'" *New York Post* (May 9, 1973), p. 46.
50. Bill Kovach, "New Unit to Fight for Child Rights," *New York Times* (May 23, 1973), p. 16.
51. Charles L. Blaschle, Letter to the Editor, *Business Week* (June 2, 1973), p. 4.

READING

Childbirth: Progress in Dignity

John S. Miller

The principal function of all living things is reproduction and other forms of creation. So if there are those who have been wondering if, after all these years, it is still necessary and appropriate to talk about childbirth, and to emphasize the dignity of childbirth as if this were all that life is about, be assured. This *is* what life is all about. Reproduction should be the most beautiful, the most mind freaking, the most unforgettable, the most heralded and celebrated and sanctified experience of life.

Is it? If not, what happened? Well, to epitomize a quarter of a million years of the history of man in a few sentences, we perverted and degraded the most glorious of our functions—our sexual function—into something base and evil; and thus, childbirth, the publicly acknowledged result of our sexual function, became shameful, sorrowful, terror-filled, equated with illness and death. And in more recent generations when science took over, it

Reprinted by permission of *Journal of Humanistic Psychology* (Spring 1971).

became mechanized, routinized, or totally ablated from consciousness. And still sorrowful and terror-filled. Have I overstated the case? Of course. Many women have been proud to be pregnant. Childbirth has been celebrated, children honored. But too often the experience of pregnancy has been degraded, and childbirth something worse. Fifty years ago in many subcultures a pregnant woman would not appear in public. Around the house she wore a mother hubbard kind of dress, which of course really announced her condition to all who saw her, but which was designed to hide the visible expression of her sin. The horror of labor offered atonement for her sin, and I suppose the more horrible, the more atonement.

A few people here and there began to recognize this stupendous folly a number of years ago and to start the long weary fight to correct the wrongs of countless generations. They were given impetus from a number of simultaneous revolutions: the intensifying emancipation of women, the sexual revolution, the human rights revolution. And even Science, that Deity we have worshiped so long, began to realize that it didn't have all the answers. Science is by no means dethroned in our culture, but it has had to share its pedestal lately with some new upstarts, like human dignity, emotion, and others.

But if the generation of Grantly Dick-Read provided a few troops and my generation a few more to wage this battle, the present younger generation, the present consumers of obstetric care have come up with a veritable army to wage the battle on all fronts, simultaneously, everywhere. And why? Because these long-haired, barefooted, beaded, freaky hippie kids have seen through all the phony plastic facade of our culture, have pushed it rudely aside, and have said we're going to live our lives joyfully, sensually, excitedly. They are not about to sit in stuffy concert halls and clap prissily at appropriate times and then go back to sleep for the next movement of the symphony. They want their music outside when possible and they want to participate and they want it loud and maybe vulgar, and to react to it with their entire bodies. The clothes they wear—their jewelry, their art, their food and drink—are all expressions of their excitement with living. And it was inevitable that they should see in childbirth a transcendental trip, a trip to outrip all other trips, one in which to be deeply and spiritually and completely involved.

I don't know whether these young people have shown up in your community yet, but when they do, beware, childbirth educators. They are way ahead of us. We thought we had won a victory in some hospitals when we nailed down the husband's right to be in the delivery room. Now they want all their friends in the delivery room. Or better yet, they don't want the delivery room at all but rather to have their babies at home. We fought for years to establish a workable rooming-in plan so mothers could have their babies with them for their waking hours. The kids are saying, "What do you mean twelve hours a day? I don't want that baby taken from me at all." We thought our parents' classes, now in their twenty-fifth year, were pretty good, as we dispensed a modest measure of information. Now we find our patients far ahead of us. They have read a dozen books before they ever come to class, and they ask very sophisticated questions. Several fathers have asked me if I would stand by to assure safety and let them deliver their wives. I have not acquiesced as yet. But this is how the new childbirth is going to be. These kids need us and want us to help them. But they know it can be a good trip and that is what they insist on. If we insist on making it a bad trip, they will bypass us and find someone else to help.

Progress in dignity. I have said that reproduction is our most important function and that childbirth should be the single most beautiful expression of our lives. Now we have the problem of population control. Precisely because it is necessary for families to limit their children to two, we cannot afford to goof. Those two experiences become supremely important. I have had many women in years gone by come to me saying something like, "I have had such lousy experiences in the past, I'd like to have at least one good experience before I quit having children." This isn't possible anymore. We can't botch the first one anymore. It may well be her only child.

Let me digress for a moment. Mr. Hickel in his celebrated memo to Mr. Nixon said, "It is time for this nation to change its priorities from concern over its security to concern over the quality of life." Brave and beautiful words those, and from a quarter where we hadn't really expected to hear them. I don't know whether the nation will hear those words and act upon them but if it doesn't, we all know that in our time our ABM's will stand guard over a country transformed into a vast cemetery, three thousand miles wide. I think there is an analogy in this statement of Mr. Hickel's which could be applied to the modern practice of medicine, especially as it applies to obstetrics, and especially that part of obstetrics which takes place in the hospital.

Security in our obstetrical suites is coming to mean hooking every baby up to a continuous EKG machine, catheterizing scalp veins for frequent pH determinations, continuous epidural anesthesia—making certain of course that proper equipment is at hand for treatment of respiratory arrest or cardiac arrest or whatever other complications may arise. Security is coming to mean a Caesarean section rate of 10 to 12 per cent in many of our hospitals. Compare that to Holland, where their perinatal mortality is better than ours and where only obstetrical complications are cared for in hospitals, yet their Caesarean section rate is about 2 per cent. Security for years has meant separation of mother and baby for twenty-four hours, and now more and more it means transferring babies to infant intensive care units at the slightest suggestion of trouble where all manner of remarkable and esoteric treatments go on. The mother and father are included in this treatment only at the cashier's window, where they are presented with the bills. Security means doing everything humanly possible to discourage breast feeding, so that "we will know" what the baby is getting. Security means making sure the patient has her bill paid by the seventh month.

I don't think Mr. Hickel meant that we should scrap every airplane in our air force. Nor do I mean that we should scrap all of our sophisticated technology. I do suggest that if we are to begin thinking of the quality of life as it applies to obstetrics, nothing will do short of a total revolution of the hospital routines, attitudes, and methods as they apply to over 90 per cent of patients. Is it any wonder that young people by the score are bypassing the hospital altogether, saying in effect that they will take a chance on dying of natural causes rather than subject themselves or their babies to this kind of care?

It is indefensible today for a doctor to allow his patient to reach the end of pregnancy without some degree of prenatal education. It is indefensible today for any hospital people, admitting clerk, maid, orderly, nurse, intern to treat a young couple in labor with anything less than all the friendliness, compassion, respect, patience born of their knowledge that to this particular couple, this particular adventure, labor, child is the most important and meaningful experience of their life. There is no reason today for any woman to be separated from her husband during labor and delivery unless she or he wishes it that way. There is no reason today for a mother and baby to be separated in the hospital unless one or the other is ill. The central nursery for the care of well babies is as obsolete as a Model T—a comment made in substance by Dr. Thaddeus Montgomery twenty-five years ago, and still not heard.

I remember the post-partum wards in a wretched little hospital in Peru which I visited eight years ago. The mothers slept in ancient 30-inch wide steel army cots. And do you know where the babies slept, twenty-four hours a day? In that same bed. The only babies that went to the central nursery were the sick ones, there to die. I remember the wretched clothes the mothers wore, the miserable rags they had for their babies, the unchanged sheets on the beds. But the mothers knew it was breast milk or nothing for their babies. Fortunately, they didn't have to fight the hospital for the right to nurse their babies.

I don't know whether it's possible for hospitals to change enough fast enough to rewin the trust of our young people. If not, we will surely have to proceed with great haste to devise other types of facilities for our mothers to have babies in.

It appears that women never forget their childbirth experiences. This is an incredible fact. How many events in your life can you remember in minute detail? Perhaps a few. Ask any woman to tell you about her labor and delivery and she will tell you the hour and minute of the most seemingly insignificant details. A couple of wretched experiences got Marjorie Karmel[1] pretty indignant, and look what happened. A wretched experience made Lester Hazell[2] pretty indignant and changed the entire direction of her life.

I had an interesting experience in Lexington, Kentucky just a month ago. I was the guest on one of these call-in radio talk shows. Within minutes the conversations got onto the question of fathers in the delivery room as it always seems to. Very early in the hour a call came in from a woman who told us that her only child was born thirty-seven years ago when she was forty years old. This seventy-seven-year-old woman wanted us to know that she still remembered what a potentially frightening experience it was—how in those days it was considered pretty dangerous for a woman to have her first baby at the age of forty, and that she didn't think she would have been able to make it if it had not been for her husband's being there with her every step of the way. The last call of the hour was from a grandfather who told us from a man's point of view how important for him it had been to be with his wife during the difficult delivery of their first child, again many years ago.

I wonder how often we obstetricians, and nurses too, stop to think of just how serious our responsibility is, as we play our roles in an experience that our patient is going to remember that vividly for the rest of her life.

Let us consider then the three principals in the drama of childbirth. The mother has to get top billing. Dignity describes, as no other word does, the attitude of which she is deserving whether she be the Queen of England or the most promiscuous fifteen-year-old in town. Because in childbirth she is co-creator with God, whether she knows it or not. She needs to be nurtured and, insofar as possible, understood, and educated, both in her head and in her body. We must remove from her as many fears and misconceptions as we can. And she doesn't need to have a lot of new fears to take the place of the old ones. Understanding, compassionate support during labor, more than any other single service, and regardless of what kind of labor she has, is the one ingredient which will allow her to leave the labor and delivery area either with a new-found sense of self-respect, self-fulfillment, and pride or, in its absence, with a sense of hurt and bewilderment which nothing will ever completely cure. Above all things we must remember that having a baby is a creative experience that she is privileged to have. It is not for us to do it for her, or take it from her, or in any way diminish her glory.

If a woman truly does not wish to experience the birth and wants an anesthetic, I don't think we need necessarily coax her into a more natural childbirth—although I frequently do and without shame. But if a woman wants the experience of birth and it is taken from her, or if she is rendered mentally or emotionally helpless by the injudicious or thoughtless use of drugs, I consider that an unforgivable crime. She does not come to us to be hurt, or demeaned, or scolded, or shamed, or judged. She is willing to trust us, until experience tells her that her trust is misplaced.

Co-starring with the mother in a role only slightly less important is the father. He has cared for this woman for nine months. He has done the best he could do. He has worked and worried and made his wishes subsidiary to hers. He is profoundly concerned about her welfare, about the quality of the care she is receiving, about her labor and delivery, and about his baby which is to be born. It is his earnest hope that he will not be found wanting as a person, husband, father, that the advent of the baby will be a blessing to his home, an enrichment to his and his wife's lives, and especially to their relationship. At some level of his consciousness he feels these things no matter what kind of a father he is. All too often the treatment he has received in hospitals has been at best mild contempt, at worst flagrantly insulting. This man is again going to pick up the reins of responsibility, now for two people rather than one in just a few hours. He does not need to be told that the time his wife spends in the labor and delivery room are none of his business. At the very least, he is entitled to our respect and to have his dignity remain intact. If we are interested in more than the very least, we might recognize that he too has need for support, reassurance, explanation of how things are, what to expect, and so on; he has a need to be comforted from the pain that he too is feeling. And he has some creature needs that need to be served too.

Needless to say, I don't think this is enough. I believe that a father has the right, no less than his wife, to experience the joy of birth. And that means the moment of birth, not vicariously described by his wife or the doctor at some time later. But the father has more than the right to this experience. He has a very real need for this experience. For only by being witness to the transfiguration of his wife, and sharing with her the emotion of the moment of birth, can he avoid a sense of guilt "over what his wife has gone through" and replace it with rightful pride for the gift he has given her.

And finally, the third principal in the drama, the one who steals the show—the baby. The baby's principal right, of course, is to be born safely, with as few drugs as possible, with as little interference as is consistent with sound obstetrics in his birth. The baby also has a right to dignity. This can be expressed in the way he is delivered, the gentleness and security with which he is held, with reasonable concern for his warmth, for protection from glaring light, protection from unpleasant sounds in the way he is handled by the nurse. And it would seem reasonable that to make the transition from womb life to earth life as gentle as possible would demand that the baby be placed in his mother's arms at the earliest possible moment. There, cradled in her arms against her breast, with her familiar heartbeat again heard reassuringly in his ear, with her nipple for him to take if he wants it, there it seems to me is the only security he will ever again know which can at least partly substitute for the security of the womb. Most of us spend the rest of our lives looking for or longing for that security. Why should we deny it to a baby at the moment of birth?

Mothers and babies are guests in our maternity departments for such a short time—a day or two or three—that it becomes easy for personnel to think that the quality of our hospitality doesn't really matter very much. What's the point in trying to relate very much to a woman who is going home tomorrow? Perhaps we should look at the problem in precisely the opposite way. Because the time is so short, why not try very hard to make those hours very meaningful? Let's make sure that the baby is with its mother for as many of those hours as possible, that we do as much as we can to help our guests get acquainted. Knowing as we do beyond all doubt that breast milk is best, let us do away with bottles of water and nipple shields and formulas and all the little regulations that tend to ensure the failure of breast feeding among all but the most determined of mothers. In short, if we believe there is really anything we can offer a new mother and her baby, let us offer it. If there is not, then we should close our lying-in suites and send all mothers home directly from the delivery room.

Among the supporting cast, nurses are the most important, of course. There are others too numerous to mention—everyone whose path crosses that of the new family. But nurses occupy a unique position, unique because of their dual role—inescapably they are both professionals and women. And as women they are either consumers or potential consumers of obstetrical care as well as deliverers of care. Thus, they find themselves identifying on the womanly level with their patients, and under a certain chronic tension between their role as professional and their role as woman. There are many splendid maternity nurses and they function well in any spot in the department. They are, invariably, nurses who are also sure of themselves and proud of themselves as women. Patients spot them instantly, react to them positively, and never forget them. The dignity they bring to an obstetrical department cannot be exaggerated.

There is also a place in the supporting cast for the doctor. I'm not going to attempt to define that role here. This is not because I think it unimportant—I'm very proud of my specialty. But I have great faith that physicians will always write their own parts in the drama of birth. My only prayer is that they try to remember theirs is a supporting role, not a principal role. If doctors want to be stars, perhaps they should transplant hearts, not deliver babies.

FOOTNOTES

1. Marjorie Karmel (deceased), author of *Thank You Dr. Lamaze* and founder of The American Society for Psychoprophylaxis in Obstetrics (APSO), an organization which has done much to promote humanistic baby-birthing.
2. Lester Hazell, author of *Common Sense Childbirth,* past president of International Childbirth Education Association (ICEA), childbirth educator, a zoologist—until her children were born!

READING

One's views on child rearing, one of the preoccupations of this chapter, are an integral part of one's total personal philosophy. For example, Gloria Steinem, a member of the women's liberation movement, looks forward to a time when the problem of caste, the "most profound and revolutionary of the crises we must face," will succumb in child rearing to a "concerted effort to eliminate all the giant and subtle ways in which we determine human futures according to the isolated physical differences of race or sex."

*Another child-rearing philosophy, that of hippie spokesman Abbie Hoffman, looks forward to a time when "child having and child rearing will be more a part of the play sphere of life than the work sphere. . . . Laying your trip or your hands on the kid (adult chauvinism) will be frowned on by society." Similarly, humanistic writer George B. Leonard expects a glowing tomorrow: "The family of the future will be larger, less narrowly defined. No one will be childless; no one will lack for affection. The outworn roles of 'man' and 'woman' will be discarded. As high-pressure sex becomes less important, all of life will become more erotic. Indeed, as roles and classes and even seperate nations fade in importance, we may see the emergence of a family as wide as all humankind, a family that can weep together, laugh together, and share the common ecstasy of a world in transformation." Conversely, psychologist Bruno Bettleheim contends that "much as reform might be desired, it's not knocking at the door in 1973, and I doubt it will be in the year 2000 either."**

How will it really be? Only you and I, and our children, can finally determine that—and the novel ideas in this essay can help us considerably if we will only "time-trip" with it in an attentive and concerned way.

* The material from Steinem, Hoffman, Leonard, and Bettleheim is from their untitled contributions to a *Newsweek* (March 7, 1973) feature story, "How Will We Raise Our Children in the Year 2000?" pp. 29–33.

A City for Children: The Year 2005

Warner Bloomberg, Jr.

At last we have passed that once compelling benchmark "The Year 2000." Now as we approach the perennial question, "What are our children learning?" we citizens of 2005 obviously must look at what kind of society we have become—or are becoming. It is difficult to know how far back we must look to gain adequate perspective.

New generations still seem to emerge every five or ten years, with respect to innovation in life styles. The United States, and to only a somewhat lesser degree other fully industrialized and urbanized nations, remains changeful, still occasionally turbulent, almost as troubled as a few decades ago. But since this pattern persists, even though we continue to rail as if it were pathological rather than the norm, let us extend our time line and resort to the old notion that a "generation" is about thirty-five years. We can then make comparisons between present communities and those we knew as far back as 1970. What were those of us who were children in the first years of the seventies "taught" by the experiences we had in the cities, where most of us lived?

The first thing every child learned, especially in the United States, was that children weren't really wanted. We learned this fact not from what anyone said, for almost all adults asserted exactly the opposite. Indeed, children were told over and again that the whole community was oriented to their nurture and well-being. Only their experiences and intuitions could inform them how false was this assertion, and the incongruity between what they were told and what they sensed may have had something to do with the increasing proportion of angry urban youth whose growing numbers in the 1970's helped motivate many of the changes enjoyed by children in this first decade of the twenty-first century.

For example, a majority of the 1970's "kids" emerged each day into an environment that was in the most rudimentary ways inhospitable, if not downright unsafe. One of the community's first imperatives impressed upon every toddler who might rush out into the street or cross without looking both ways was that top priority went to the automobile. If a child were hit by a car, people assumed in almost every case that the fault was the child's "carelessness" (in not remembering to care about the prior rights of the great, rushing, wheeled monsters and their drivers). No wonder most children in the United States, almost without regard to differences in class, ethnicity, race, religion, or whatever, grew up yearning to possess an automobile, with becoming a driver almost the *sine qua non* of adulthood. They didn't even have to know that adults in the cities in which they lived spent more money for parking than for parks, or that state and federal budgets allocated far more to constructing expressways than to building schools. Statistics are not needed by children to make obvious the self-evident.

Reprinted from *Childhood Education* (January 1972) by permission of Warner Bloomberg, Jr., and the Association for Childhood Education International, 3615 Wisconsin Avenue, N.W., Washington, D.C.

A second big lesson we children of the early 1970's learned, as soon as old enough to go about our neighborhoods, was that ornamental flowers, grass and shrubs, and something more abstract called "private property," all took precedence over the well-being of children. In most residential areas, land available between houses or apartments and the streets was "off limits" for children, except for the sidewalks. Such land was used mainly to grow "lawns," an activity to which most adults attached substantial symbolic value, rationalized by claims of aesthetic pleasure. These frivolous if not ridiculous residues of rural imagery were supplemented by an even more nonsensical rhetoric of civic virtue, as if extirpating crabgrass and dandelion had anything to do with solving community problems. A youngster who ran across lawns or picked other people's flowers was therefore seen as irresponsible, destructive, and unappreciative of "beauty"—a term obviously applying more to trim bushes than to happy children.

Creating basic elements of a much more amenable physical space for children right in our own neighborhoods was, as we now know, rather simple once this country actually gave a high priority to child well-being. By the late 1980's most of our major cities had passed "residential environment acts." As a result essential arterials for transneighborhood traffic have been fenced off and bridged with overpasses, and the rest of the streets crisscrossed with constructed "bumps" that make it almost impossible for drivers to exceed five to seven miles an hour. Bicycle lanes through the "bumps" have helped further the shift of adults to that mode of transportation, which does much to diminish, though not quite destroy, the automobile as a major symbol of adulthood (as well as providing substantial benefits in terms of physical health and reduction of air and noise pollution). For the first time in over half a century, most city streets have become safe for children.

Equally important has been the designation of all land between residences and streets, except for a few feet in front of each house, as part of neighborhood communal property. Funded and supervised by neighborhood corporations, "block clubs" now have something real to do, and amazingly innovative uses of the space have provided children with an urban out-of-doors full of opportunities and amenities. Every street except the arterials is now integrated into what becomes in effect a minipark accessible to the youngest children. Now children know they really are valued by the community, and most have less reason to perpetrate the mischief and petty vandalism that had grown so steadily with the increasingly hostile, rejecting character of the urban environment. Predictably, we also have room for a variety of neighborhood amenities for adults as well. Now, in the twenty-first century, we understand how infantile was our compulsive fascination for the automobile, how corrosive our valuing of property above human well-being, how destructive of a sense of community our exaggerated privatism. And we understand there could never be enough psychotherapists to undo the damaging "lessons" taught by the city to the children of the early 1970's.

An appallingly large minority of those children and youth had "learning experiences" even more destructive of their self-worth, their sense of being part of a humane community, their motivation for constructive and creative activity. Those of us born into impoverished families were informed by the mass media about the "high standard of living" from which we were excluded and at the same time were given to understand by almost every authoritative message we encountered, including those voiced by the schools, that our deprivation reflected the defects of our parents, not of the society. Those who came to believe the official dicta could not help but denigrate their "failure" parents, with serious psychological consequences for themselves; while children who sustained love for those who sought so unsuccessfully to provide for their material well-being could hardly identify with communities that shamed their whole family in so many ways, obvious and subtle. And nonwhite children endured the oppression of institutionalized racism, which proved almost as unyielding through most of the seventies as it had been in the sixties. Again the schools accepted and reflected the values and practices of the larger community, for the most part renouncing racial segregation only when forced to by court edict and having to be practically bludgeoned into providing even token expressions of cultural pluralism in their curricula. Interestingly, an increasing minority of more affluent children and youth identified with their deprived and oppressed peers during the late sixties and early seventies. Their concern and episodic anger provided one dimension of the restlessness and volatility that waxed and waned and waxed again among the emerging generations of our cities.

But the pathology of the urban order in the United States of the seventies was most evident in the truly tragic experiences of a startling number of urban children.

We did not decide until much nearer the end of the century that children were not the private property of parents (to be used or misused as the latter desired) and had a right to protection by the community. We therefore do not have accurate data on child abuse prior to the late eighties. Estimates are that probably more than thirty thousand were badly battered each year in the preceding decade and probably a quarter of a million annually needed protective services, which they seldom got. And the use of police power against "runaways," whose numbers rose so rapidly during this period, highlighted the fact that about a fourth of the children incarcerated as "juvenile delinquents" were "guilty" of actions that could not possibly be described as "crimes" had the accused been but a few years older: truancy, sexual activity, pregnancy, being designated as "incorrigible" by teachers or "ungovernable" by parents—in short, having rather severe versions of the problems that attended "growing up" in what sometimes seemed an antichild society.

Perhaps the most revealing indicator of the reality, as against the rhetoric, of the United States thirty-five years ago was the degradation of children and youth by hunger in rural areas and by heroin in great metropolitan centers. The revelation of serious malnutrition among some children in impoverished areas of the South and Southwest logically would have brought forth, in the most affluent nation on earth, immediate massive corrective action. Even modest proposals were further diminished, however, for the sake of political vested interests. And equal tolerance was granted the proliferation in our cities of heroin and other death drugs, even among very young teen-agers.

The appearance of thirteen- and fourteen-year-old junkies (and, inevitably, muggers and prostitutes) produced more in the way of sensational news stories than substantial new social policies.

Although the total number of children grossly damaged by either malnutrition or drugs was quite small relative to the total, it was a critical indicator of the character of the community "normal" children sensed in so many ways. *What we understand now is that a community wishing to teach its children to value life must itself value the life of each of them.* And that value must be expressed not just in its pieties and everyday rhetoric but overtly through the policies and practices of all its institutions.

By the year 2000 we had at least made a good start in this direction. Nurturing the new generation is now the responsibility of the whole community and one of the city's highest priorities. In every neighborhood, school, and recreational facility youthful paraprofessionals serve as ombudsmen, responding to any indication that a child is troubled. Easily identifiable by their bright emblems, they are every child's access point to the multiplicity of services now provided directly to anyone who evidences need, without requiring an intermediate contact with "related" adults.

Since our concern in this review has been to deal with what children are "taught" by the community, schools have been mentioned only in passing. We should note that in 1970, at the very time when the courts were once again forcing needed change on career educators by requiring respect within school buildings for the constitutional rights of children and youth, the use of drugs to control so-called behavior problems was gaining in popularity. Perhaps 300,000 pupils were already being required or pressured to take stimulants, amphetamines, tranquilizers, and antidepressants while in school, with exactly the same purposes and results involved in voluntary drug abuse by youth in the larger community: suppression of symptoms arising from problems people preferred to evade rather than to try in meaningful ways to solve. The drugged pupil population zoomed to approximately 2 million by 1975 and was over 5 million by 1980, when the situation became the focal point of another round of volatile protests by high school students and subsequent legal intervention by external agencies. Once again the schools were caught aiding and abetting the larger community in teaching by its practices the very opposite of what was preached in its pieties.

Finally, one of the most fundamental changes, and one that met with greatest resistance, has been to rid both children and adults of the notion that all people who procreate must forever after be willing and able to nurture adequately the new individuals they have brought into being and that all children must both love and live with their original parents, no matter what. Older children and youth of the seventies began the dissolution of that frequently destructive myth by running away from home in increasing numbers, and in urban centers they established an informal (and often tragically inadequate) network of places to "crash." By leaving them largely to their own devices—and to the danger of predatory adults as well—the community of that day reinforced what the young people had already come to know: that neither love nor nurture was unconditionally available.

Today, the provision of the 1970's for a handful of "foster homes," with their susceptibility to inadequacy and occasional exploitation, has given way to the institution of the "alternative family" in which children may live and be nurtured, whether briefly, for many years, or permanently. "Second families," like second marriages, have demonstrated high degrees of success. These "new families" are available not only to children who have lost their parents but in cases where for any reason the children and their original parents would benefit by separation. Alternative families include, of course, both the old nuclear family and the multiple and communal families that began to appear in the early seventies.

In this way, as in the others previously noted, we accept and act upon the dictum that the whole older generation is collectively responsible for the well-being of the new. From communities with such an orientation our children are learning values, feelings, and motivations that may enable them to construct an even more humane society of which we still dream. Indeed, we have already discovered that a community really attempting to nurture its offspring is, in the end, better for everyone. Quite different from the seventies!

READING

From the conservative point of view there is much that can and should be done immediately to overhaul our educational system. In the controversial issues of tracking, scheduling, grading, and so on the conservative rails against counterproductive measures likely to produce only "illiterates with a degree." A series of conservative reforms, on the other hand, would allegedly make possible a new generation of "rational, well-educated human beings prepared to face the demands of life."

Now the liberal educator might champion instead a system that helps mold a new generation of socially concerned citizens prepared to shoulder more of the burdens of life. Radicals, on the other hand, might want a new generation eager to overturn the arbitrary institutions of life, and visionaries might favor an open-ended educational system that enables learners to explore themselves and the worlds "inside" as well as out. This dizzying (and often immobilizing) array of objectives notwithstanding, this essay makes plain the particular contribution the conservatives make to this vital dialogue.

High School Reform: A Plea for a Viable Program

Hal Schuster

In the field of education, conservatives manage to bend over backwards to support programs that in any other area of life they would approach with scorn. This contradiction is symptomatic of a deeper problem which underlies

Reprinted by permission of *New Guard* (September 1972), 1221 Massachusetts Ave., N.W., Washington, D.C. 20005.

popular thinking on the public schools. Schools have taken on a mystical quality that makes it *verboten* to oppose any of their policies. Any change is viewed with apprehension by conservative parents. This feeling of necessity in preserving the status quo arose out of the riots in our colleges. The incidents have driven parents into a state of insecurity in which they attempt to preserve a school structure which is familiar to them, the same one they went to school under twenty or thirty years ago. By doing so they play right into the hands of the professional revolutionaries. They leave their children with legitimate gripes and with no one to turn to. The New Left is quite willing to lend an ear in exchange for a new power base.

Fearful parents have created a self-fulfilling prophecy. As long as they blindly oppose change they force their children into the hands of those self-same destroyers whom they fear. The only way to break this cycle is by presenting and supporting a program of rational change *as conservatives*. However, in doing so, we shouldn't fall into the trap of supporting change for the sake of change. I will proceed to outline a rough sketch of the type of programs which we should support.

A mutation of merit ranking, tracking, has been tried in many schools with little success. In the form in which it was tried it had many tragic flaws. Briefly, what was done was to test students and then place them at a certain level in all their classes. Each level was composed of students who had scored similarly on all their tests.

The oversimplicity of the system resulted in several unforeseen results. The system created a school structure in which every student was expected to have exactly the same level of ability in each of his classes and to keep exactly that level of ability. No test of general knowledge can be comprehensive enough to place all students at their level of ability in each of their subjects. Furthermore, the test wasn't administered frequently enough. As a result of these two flaws the system was abandoned.

If these flaws are remedied by administering a battery of tests to frequently register student ability in each subject separately, the system could be re-adopted with gratifying results.

It is imperative that merit ranking return because students are individuals and don't learn the same amount in the same time. The present system of education doesn't allow for these differences but attempts to educate all students as a faceless mass.

Modular scheduling allows a student to take subjects which he normally couldn't due to time limitation. In most high schools and junior highs, a normal day is broken into six or seven one-hour periods. Modular scheduling divides the school day into modules of fifteen minutes each. A course could consist of as many modules as a school's administrators saw fit. Courses wouldn't have to be of the same length. This would allow students to fit more courses into their schedules or to take longer courses. Students would have the opportunity to learn more material. Modular scheduling would involve scheduling problems; however, these have already been worked out in several experimental schools.

One facet of the school system which conservatives shouldn't abandon is the grading system. It shouldn't be abandoned for the very reason its opponents would cite for abandoning it: it is an incentive to competition. Phrases such as "learning, not competition" are meaningless. At a good school in order to get good grades and compete it is necessary to learn the material. At the same time conservatives shouldn't operate under the illusion that grading is perfect. It isn't. Grades don't distinguish between a student who earns an "A" in higher calculus and one who earns it in business math. Nor does the grading system communicate what a student has learned and what he hasn't. In a subject such as English, which is composed of such diverse components as grammar, spelling, writing, and literature, it is possible for a student to master literature and writing and still get a barely passing grade. The reports sent home with a student's grades should contain information on how well a student did in each area of the subject and on the difficulty of the subject. Finally, no grade should be based on nonobjective criteria such as class participation or interest level. If this is allowed, the grade will measure how well the teacher likes the student rather than how much the student knows.

Students who graduate from high school and can barely read or write are living testimony to the failure of our schools. All schools should return to a policy of putting primary emphasis on basic skills. But these skills should be regarded as tools and not as an end in themselves. The only reason to teach reading is so students can read. The only reason to teach writing is so students can communicate. Once these skills are learned the student's real education can begin. The purpose of education should be to teach students to think. The ability to think is the chief weapon of survival of a human being. Once people cease thinking not only will civilization collapse but man will be subjected to the whims of any beast with bigger teeth or claws. School is the place in which the young learn what mankind has already learned during its existence on the earth. If the members of the next generation fail to learn the wisdom of the past, they must relearn it for themselves and repeat all of the errors mankind has suffered through. Before graduating from high school students should have a thorough knowledge of history and should have read a sprinkling of the works of the masters along with contemporary writings. A basic knowledge of science and of business should also have been learned. Discussion groups and student book reviews should have been used to encourage a better understanding of subject material and to facilitate the student's ability to communicate, not with a brick or club but through civilized discussion. A look at today's institutions of higher learning will illustrate the degree to which our school system has failed to do this. Finally, debating should be made a part of all English classes. Debating is necessary to the teaching of rationally organized thought. Elementary skills must be taught and then built upon.

The ultimate goal which all conservatives should work toward is the voucher system. The voucher system would permit the birth of private competition with the public school system and prevent the extinction of parochial schools. This system issues a voucher which can be exchanged for tuition at the school of the student's and/or parents' choice. Presently, the only students who can attend private or church schools are those who can afford to pay two tuitions, one through taxes to public schools and one through tuition to the private. The voucher system would end this and allow any student to attend.

Many public servants are becoming concerned with the quality of inner-city schools. Some feel that the answer is to bus students out of the inner city, while others feel that the answer is to pump more money in. As the first solution loses supporters the second gains them. If the schools were starving and unable to hire decent teachers or equipment, pumping money in would make sense, but this isn't the case. Studies have shown that while some areas which spend virtually nothing on education have good schools, others which put a fortune into education have bad ones. The answer to the crisis in education is neither to bus the students out nor to pump money in but to improve methods of teaching. Mere money, in and of itself, can't teach. Students' being bussed from bad to good schools isn't the answer. First of all, where will the students in the good schools go, to the bad ones? The only real solution to the problem is better teaching in all schools.

Most students who graduate from high school are prepared for nothing except college. After they go to college for four years they are prepared for nothing. A large percentage of college graduates are out of work. An even larger percentage are doing work for which their college courses didn't prepare them. High school must prepare students for what comes after, work. Most students are not suited for college. Flooding our institutions of higher learning with students who are unfit destroys their basic purpose. College isn't for everyone, only the gifted. High school must prepare the students for work which doesn't require a college diploma. Some of these occupations pay better than those which require a college degree. Even the college-bound can use a job skill while going through college. Although students must be educated in order to better enjoy their leisure time they must be able to earn a living to have the leisure time. High schools must begin a program of vocational and business courses in earnest. For too long we've ignored the noncollege student. It is time this snobbery ended and a more realistic program began.

It should be obvious by this time that a conservative program for education reform does exist. If this program is applied properly, we can lure back those students who have been enchanted by the siren call of the radical left. We will also win ourselves schools that produce rational, well-educated human beings prepared to face the demands of life, not merely illiterates with a degree.

CHAPTER 8

Producing: Workplace Reforms

Work can be a chance to innovate, fraternize, and serve. Its tools and patterns can be filled with transcendent symbolism. It can be a fulfilling expression of the personality.

THEODORE ROSZAK

. . . everyone seems to ignore what is perhaps the primary significance of the blue-collar trap: that the environmental abuse from which the worker now suffers most keenly, and in which he must participate in order to live, may soon affect us all. . . . If laborers are on the front line of a great surrender process, how far behind is the rest of society?

KENNETH LASSON

According to an enthusiastic former industrialist, Senator Charles Percy, the United States "is on the brink of a major breakthrough in the effort to change our ideas about work . . . 'quality of work' is an idea whose time has come!"

Senator Percy placed much of the blame for workplace dissatisfaction on "an entrenched, authoritarian industrial system that has taken decades and decades to build. . . . There is a strong feeling," he has asserted, "that managerial and labor institutions have sometimes grown too rigid. Too often they have become blind to the broader needs of our society." And these needs, in turn, are being shaped by new forces now changing every American institution, from marriage and the family to schools and churches:

> Outside the plant gate or office door is the new American: a future-oriented, demanding, expectant, educated, freedom-loving individual. Inside that gate or door this interesting, creative, inventive American is required to conform to a past-oriented . . . hierarchical, class-based, freedom-fearing social system.

The American worker, this former corporation executive concludes, "has stubbornly remained virtually the last redoubt of yesteryear's values."[1]

Accordingly, it was not surprising to learn in 1973 from a new government task force that an "increasingly intolerable situation" is being created by the employment of millions of Americans, white-collar as well as blue-collar workers, in meaningless work. A controversial HEW report, *Work in America,* drew a profile of an increasingly educated and near-affluent nation, where the legacy of Ford's assembly line and stopwatch "speed-ups" often:

1. Leaves the worker with a narrow, routinized task.
2. Has recent high school and college graduates end up in jobs that make little use of their training.
3. Has skills rapidly become obsolete.
4. Nurtures the desire for a whole range of psychological satisfactions at least as important to many workers as monetary rewards.

Boring, dehumanized work, the HEW consultants concluded, is producing "blues" of staggering proportion—throughout the entire labor force.[2]

Some of what is at issue is tersely suggested by the following complaint and insight of a young woman worker: "I think what all of us are looking for is a calling, not just a job. Most of us, like the assembly line worker, have jobs that are too small for our spirit. Jobs are just not big enough for people." The most pertinent of all questions, suggests journalist Studs Terkel, is asked *sotto voce:* "What is there to show? Does my job have any real meaning?"[3]

Fortunately, a combination of complementary pressures (including the job satisfaction expectations of 22 million young adults in the 85-million-member labor force, the productivity pressure from overseas competition, and so on) now urges a major breakthrough in this anachronistic situation. Already a number of leading companies, including Corning Glass, Olivetti, Volvo, Saab, TRW, Sears, Avis, Chrysler, GM, GE, General Foods, Chase Manhattan Bank, and others, are engaged in experiments that suggest that there are techniques already available to help solve certain of the problems of worker dissatisfaction.

Why *should* work be humanized? For one thing, because men are coming to expect more from work than ever before. The quality of the job is as important as and, after the attainment of a certain level of income and security, even more important than increases in wages:

> Although there are personality differences, workers in general want to avoid jobs that are monotonous, repetitive, over-controlled, and isolated from interaction with others.
>
> In contrast, they seek jobs that require activeness—planning and judgment—autonomy on the job, variety, and that are demanding enough to stimulate learning.
>
> Beyond these psychological factors, workers are also concerned with the dignity associated with the job and with opportunities for career development.
>
> They are also increasingly concerned that the work be "meaningful," that it involve clearly useful tasks and sufficient skill to be worthy of respect.[4]

In combination these attributes of a job are thought to help stimulate the development of a mature, productive individual who is in keen and constructive touch with himself, his work, and his fellows.

A second reason to seek to humanize work is the budget-sheet, hard-headed goal of cost reduction. When the demand for self-enlarging work meets little or no response, the price, strictly in terms of lowered productivity and excessive absenteeism, accident rates, and sabotage, is much too high to pay (especially as international competition puts a new premium on increases in productivity and quality).

Finally, it is argued that work should be humanized because it undeniably influences the human development of each worker and the character of our society. Indeed, unless work improves, the values of our democratic society are increasingly jeopardized. For workers frustrated in their jobs, confined all day to tasks that have little variety, challenge, autonomy, or dignity, are generally also "alienated." They may suffer a decline in physical and mental health, family stability, and community participation, along with increases in aggression, delinquency, and drug and alcohol addiction. Many tend to think that government makes little difference in their lives, are susceptible to political demagoguery, are unlikely to vote, or, when they do vote, vote emotionally rather than rationally.

To be sure, some of this is old hat; the alienation of the worker from society, for example, has long been a favorite explanation of many political analysts for labor's shift toward conservatism. But what has often been missed, and is now increasingly back in focus, is the idea that a large part of the cure for alienation may lie in changing the very nature of work itself. Or as one excited researcher, Michael Maccoby, explains,

> Workers with job tasks allowing for greater variety, autonomy, and responsibility are more likely to be men who take an activist orientation toward their lives, who feel they themselves have something to say in affecting their personal lives and fate, and who also feel their voice means something in the political process of society.

Although few are ready to declare categorically that it is boring jobs that cause alienated attitudes, Maccoby and many others urge long-range experiments to find out if making jobs more satisfying can revitalize the political and social attitudes of the labor force.[5]

In this chapter attention is paid to five workplace reform challenges: flexitime work scheduling, job enrichment, profit sharing, workers' codetermination, and the government as catalyst. Even as you weigh these matters you might also ponder the import here of an aphorism from Albert Camus with which the 1973 HEW task force on work in America chose to conclude: "Without work all life goes rotten. But when work is soulless, life stifles and dies."

Flexitime Work

At present over 30 per cent of the industrial labor force in Switzerland, nearly 10 per cent of Germany's work force, and sizable groups of employees in France, Holland, Japan, and Scandinavia are on flexitime, although just a few years ago the reform was considered pie-in-the-sky nonsense that nobody wanted to hear about.

Although the overseas experts in the subject list over a hundred variations, all of the flexitime plans have in common the feature of allowing workers largely to set their own hours. A simple but dramatic system of innovative work-hour allocation, flexitime earns plaudits from everyone: employees, who appreciate the freedom, and employers, who want the productivity increases that follow on the reform's adoption.

More specifically, the company involved (flexitime especially appeals to banks, insurance companies, and food, cosmetics, and equipment manufacturers) extends the workday to 7 A.M. until 7 P.M. and designates a "core" number of hours, such as from 10 A.M. to 4 P.M. During the core hours all employees are obligated to be at their work locations. The balance of the work time, however, can be made up at either the beginning or the end of the core time.

Typical of the problems encountered, and solved, are the following:

> The assembly line coordination problem at the Swiss Omega Watch factory was solved by building up a "buffer stock" at each point along the line. Omega officials report that production has dropped slightly, but quality has improved substantially enough to produce a net gain.
>
> The problem of how to apply flexi-time to a Swiss foundry, where teams of men operate large furnaces was solved by specifying that each team must "float" as a group. Team members agree on the next day's starting time before leaving work each day.

Not surprisingly the well-satisfied director of the Swiss Employers Association proclaims that flexitime is "in tune with modern society and will therefore continue to spread."[6]

Why bother? For one thing, the core hours satisfy the need to interact with other organizations, and the optional time provides a reasonable part of the day free from telephone interruption in which routine paperwork can be handled. For another, this reform enables employees to avoid rush-hour commuting schedules and the undesired company of one another. Above all, however, the notion of core and flexible hours substantially expands the realm of personal discretion. Although possibly small potatoes in the larger scheme of things, flexitime remains a substantial gain in real-world nitty-gritty—as contrasted to sanctimonious moralizing—for the appreciative men and women involved.

Is America ready for flexitime? Many Europeans do not think so and point derisively to our preoccupation with compressing the work week into four ten-hour days. Some allege that we have bred a money-grubbing work force interested only in getting work out of the way—by compressing the work week, if necessary—rather than in enjoying the more relaxed approach to work inherent in flexitime. These critics see our four-day experiments as deriving from the idea of work as a chore without prospects of enrichment. They voice fears of the impact of the ten-hour day on family life and on the health and safety of the workers themselves.

However ready we may or may not be for flexitime (called "gliding working time" by the Germans), we are even more challenged by the remarkable labor policies of the Ohmi Transport Company, a Japanese concern that caused the most discussion of all at a 1972 conference on work scheduling of 150 labor experts from twenty-two nations. Ohmi takes into account the "lunar cycle" of every male employee, or those few days every month when, according to some physiologists, a man functions below par in a manner comparable to that of a woman during her menstrual period. Ohmi will not assign a man to a hazardous job during this period, thus protecting temporarily depressed workers from industrial dangers. Claiming a 30 per cent drop in its accident rate since the initiation of the lunar cycle program, Ohmi is now helping other Japanese companies institute this reform.[7]

An American delegate to the 1972 international conference summed it all up: "The more you work with changed work schedules, the more you realize that each case is different. The only real trend that is clear today is the move to break away from the five-day, forty-hour mold."[8]

Humanizing Experiments

The enriched job, as viewed by industrial psychologist Edward Glaser, has four major attributes:

1. The presence of some actual decision-making power in small groups of workers.
2. Feedback regarding progress from baseline.
3. Open three-way communication, up, down, and lateral.
4. The presence of small-group economic incentives for increases in productivity.[9]

Still another industrial psychologist, Frederick Herzberg, although agreeing with Glaser, suggests another dimension: "An enriched job is a complete piece of work. That is, it is a piece of work that has an identifiable beginning and end for the person who is doing the job."[10] On the other hand, it is well to remember the caution of the HEW *Work in America* task force: "Single remedies (e.g., 'job enrichment,' 'job rotation,' 'management by objectives') abound for the ills of work. Such efforts have failed because there is no single source of job dissatisfaction."[11]

However that may be, job enrichment, the leading humanizing effort today (at least in terms of industry and media attention), is a reform to reckon with in American industry. Although it has been the subject of fleeting faddish concern in almost every decade since our post-World War II economic recovery, job enrichment may have today more of a following—and more detractors—than ever before.

What does it mean in practice? The relevant experiments at the Chrysler auto plants, for example, are explained by their director in these terms. "We've got to get our people back into this thing, get them involved. Ten men in Detroit can't run Chrysler Corp. We've got to stop bossing and start managing. We can't run the plants on fear any more."[12] Specific reforms include the following:

1. Workers in two small-parts departments at a Detroit plant currently work without a foreman. At another Detroit plant, workers and a foreman designed a new engine line and then took it through its "launch," or initial break-in, without higher supervision. Both experiments are regarded by Chrysler as "smashing successes."
2. A strife-ridden plant employing twenty-seven hundred workers has been regrouped into three independent units to create the environment of three small plants rather than one huge, impersonal outfit. Along with improved efficiency, there are thought to be substantial gains in worker-manager communications and plant morale.

3. In an effort to involve production employees in the entire production process, workers in one Detroit parts plant were asked to reevaluate the entire manufacturing operation. One department was rearranged thereafter, eliminating seven jobs; the seven men were reassigned to jobs on which they were needed elsewhere in the plant.

Chrysler's annual turnover rate fell from a crisis level of 47 per cent in 1969 to 17 per cent in 1973, and the absenteeism rate has dropped from 1969's 7.8 per cent to 5.6 per cent. Supporters also think the humanizing effort buoys the image of Chrysler's cars among buyers.

A number of other American innovations merit passing attention:

1. At a California mountaineering sports equipment company the seamstresses are now asked to sew their own personal labels into their work. Each employee is a minority stockholder and is paid at piecework rates (none average less than $10,000 per annum). So free and trusting is the atmosphere that in an industry in which quality rejects sometimes run to 50 per cent, there are no inspectors.
2. A well-publicized new General Foods plant operates without supervisors, a personnel manager, or a maintenance or quality control department. Instead, self-governing teams of workers take care of everything by themselves. What is more, the men are paid on the basis of the number of different jobs they can do, rather than on the basis of the particular work they are doing at any one time. As a result, the young worker continues to have something to gain and somewhere to grow as he becomes older.
3. Donnelly Mirrors, which makes automobile mirrors, not only has divided its work force into teams with decision-making powers but also shares productivity gains and guarantees that its workers will not be unemployed because of technology.

Vastly unimpressed with the aforegoing, a Detroit labor writer insists that the phrase "job enrichment" still only "conjures up visions of production bosses braying about teamwork and asking . . . hourly workers to give the company one more ounce of sweat."[13]

Abroad, the picture is very much the same. Employers initiate, labor only reacts, and cynics hurl brickbats—save for this one critical difference: hundreds of thousands are involved, and jobs are tackled that are considered resistant to enrichment in America:

> Britain's Imperial Chemical Industries includes 55,000 workers in 75 plants in a five-year old plan aimed at removing restrictive work practices and enhancing self-esteem through greater responsibility at work. In many cases, men program their own work day and check the quality of their own work. Time clocks have been abolished, and workers take tea and lunch breaks according to their individual work schedules. Productivity has gone up about 11 per cent, wage increases have been as much as 22 per cent.[14]

Saab auto company takes ads in American magazines that explain:

Bored people build bad cars. That's why we're doing away with the assembly line.

Working on an assembly line is monotonous. And boring. And after a while, some people begin not to care about their jobs anymore. So the quality of the product often suffers.

That's why, at Saab, we're replacing the assembly line with assembly teams. Groups of just three or four people who are responsible for a particular assembly process from start to finish.

Each team makes its own decisions about who does what and when. And each team member can even do the entire assembly singlehandedly. The result: people are more involved. They care more. So there's less absenteeism, less turnover. And we have more experienced people on the job.

We're building our new 2-liter engines this way. And the doors to our Saab 99. And we're planning to use this same system to build other parts of our car as well.

It's a slower, more costly system, but we realize that the best machines and materials in the world don't mean a thing, if the person building the car doesn't care.[15]

As another example:

Volvo, Sweden's largest car manufacturer, will open two new plants in 1974 without mechanized assembly lines. Instead, teams of 15 to 25 men will be responsible for assembling major sections of each car. The team members will agree among themselves on who does which job and how often different tasks are rotated among the group. They will choose a leader to represent them at team planning sessions with foremen and supervisors. When on the job, they will work at their own speed.

At Volvo's Göteborg plant, workers change jobs every four hours to relieve the monotony. Small groups, composed of machine operators, work analysts, supervisors, planning engineers, and designers have been formed to identify and deal with current problems. These groups now tackle previously specialist functions such as quality control and equipment maintenance.

Scoffers in this country insist that such overseas innovations are rarely easy to adapt. Volvo, they note derisively, will employ only six hundred workers at its key plant and turn out only 30,000 cars a year—whereas the Lorain, Ohio plant of Ford Motor Company alone produces over 300,000 cars annually.[16]

Indeed, ambivalence at best, antagonism most commonly, and admiration only rarely probably characterize the stance of American industrial relations academics, industrialists, and labor leaders.

Typical is the view among certain professors that the worker is "soiled" on arrival at the hiring gate and should be helped in the outside world rather than "manipulated" in the factory. Conservatives of this persuasion insist that job enrichment (like improvements in health care, treatment for drug abuse, and so on) is being vastly oversold, that it is really *not* a very promising "cure for alcoholism, absenteeism, and the whole gamut of society ills, including the growing incidence of hangnails and warts."[17]

Work does not cause the various social problems that employees bring with them. And there is no substantial evidence to support the claim that boring, routine, and unchallenging jobs actually cause crime, discontent, and other social ills. Not surprisingly then, enrichment techniques such as job rotation and enlargement have allegedly been partial or complete "failures" in two thirds of the companies that have tried them. Purdue Professor Jim Windle explains,

> Someone is going to have to show me that employers can replace, through tinkering with jobs, the missing link—that is, self-respect—the one thing that can cure the "nobody-gives-a-damn" syndrome. Any long-lasting effect of motivational techniques is highly doubtful without self-respect. Self-respect is an individual problem, not an industrial one.[18]

If self-respect were restored, not only would a majority of employees enjoy their jobs, work hard, and find their work rewarding, but the few noisy others, the malcontents, would be best worked on outside the workplace—where they were damaged—than in any frillish and fraudulent job-enrichment prank.

Impressed with this line of reasoning many hard-headed executives find it very difficult to accept the contrary social science assumptions on which most of the humanizing experiments are based:

1. That workers want to be challenged, that people want to grow psychologically.
2. That pay, good benefits, and working conditions, although important, are not as crucial in motivating people as the challenge of the job itself.
3. That if you make certain changes in the environment, the behavior of people will change in the desired direction.

Suspicion of these assumptions, including especially the optimistic view of human nature, holds many executives tightly in its grip.

A conservative business adviser is probably not alone in wondering if catering to "a vocal minority of dissatisfied young workers" might not be counterproductive:

> To the extent that the new "permissiveness" in the plants, tolerated at least in part to placate the militants and some of the young, contributes to the distraction of highly productive workers, or even to their early retirement . . . the net effect could be bad.[19]

Similarly, a GM vice president scoffs:

> There may be some differences in the new work force. But in my opinion, the work ethnic is far from dead.[20]

And the head of the GM Assembly Division explains:

> The workers may complain about monotony, but years spent in the factories lead me to believe they like to do their jobs automatically. If you interject new things, you spoil the rhythm of the job and the work gets fouled up.[21]

This view, in turn, links to a warning offered by the chairman of the GM Corporation himself:

> All these efforts involve extra costs which must inevitably be reflected in the price of the product—that is, the price the consumer must pay.[22]

No wonder, then, that American business has chosen thus far to involve only about 3,000 workers in humanistic experiments out of our labor force of 86 million.[23]

Organized labor is comparably unsympathetic. Attitudes range from skepticism through suspicion to condemnation, with enthusiasm conspicuously absent. Typical are the following sentiments:

> Nobody has ever come up to me and asked the union to help enrich his job. . . . If you asked me how to humanize the plants, I couldn't tell you how to do it (UAW officer Douglas Fraser, 1972).[24]

> If you want to enrich the job, enrich the paycheck. The better the wage, the greater the job satisfaction. There is no better cure for the "blue-collar blues" (Machinist Union officer W. W. Winpininger, 1972).

> In my union we will never let our members be used as guinea pigs in a speedup designed as a job enrichment program.
> The cutter wasn't unhappy about his job until we told him he's unhappy (ILGWU officer Joseph Schwartz).[25]

> Substituting the sociologist's questionnaire for the stopwatch is likely to be no gain for the workers. Job enrichment programs have cut jobs just as effectively as automation and stopwatches. And the rewards of productivity are not always equitably shared (labor historian Thomas Brooks, writing in the *AFL-CIO Federationist,* October, 1972).

Labor is especially incensed over the inclination of companies to begin their job enrichment experiments without consulting the unions involved—and the UAW bitterly condemns the Chrysler, GM, and Ford projects for this high-handed, officious, and union-baiting oversight.

Perhaps the labor response is best captured in the overall UAW stance: "Since it is not feasible to do much on the assembly line to improve jobs without making American cars unable to compete with imports, they should try to get the next best thing: more time off."[26] In striking contrast is the response of a union of chemical workers in Great Britain, confronted like the UAW by a fait accompli in a company-dictated experimental work project. They have told management that the next logical steps are to develop a new system for promoting men from the shop floor, to provide more operation and financial information about the company, and to bring workers onto the company's board of directors.

At present, then, it would seem as if the codetermination impetus is far behind on points. Revealing in this context is the alleged record of the otherwise very liberal Auto Workers Union:

> The UAW—like nearly all large American labor unions—works for little more than a larger share of American abundance. It makes no effort to win

> what the union leadership so enthusiastically speaks of, the progressive achievements of European labor: the placing of workers on boards of directors or the establishment of worker councils to allow workers to have important voices in production and management. The idea of worker participation in management or worker democracy is as foreign to UAW as it is to General Motors.[27]

Yet festering and unreached in the workplace itself is a growing sense of the inadequacy of old-line approaches. A member of the revolutionary Congress of [auto plant] Black Workers angrily explains:

> Woodcock is a model man, compared to Meany. But that doesn't mean anything in terms of real problems people run into in the shops. These fuckers, man, they got a nice position on the war, nice position on civil liberties, blah, blah, blah. It ain't got a goddamned thing to do with the conditions that's kicking the ass out of the motherfucker out there in Department 78, Department 25. On the question of conditions, the company ain't done a motherfucking thing about it, and the union don't do nothing.[28]

Whether "doing something" includes moving into *and* beyond the humanization of work to a share in its direction is a question reopened by this man's rage, however much others who are more easily satisfied might prefer to avoid that Pandora's box.

Meanwhile, back at the *Wall Street Journal,* an ace labor reporter gleefully predicts that worker beneficiaries of enrichment experiments will soon question the need for paying union dues or signing a union-organizing petition. It seems inevitable to the journalist that "the clashing objectives of union leaders and job enrichment advocates herald an intensifying battle for the hearts of the nation's workers, both organized and unorganized." It remains possible, however, that the worker himself may emerge "with the best of both worlds—a redesigned job from management and more money and job security from his union."[29]

To which proponents of the humanization of work might retort, "Inadequate!" For the *Wall Street Journal* writer entirely misses the point! The goal here is not to get "things" from others but to help create a climate inside of which one can enlarge and enjoy oneself, at work as well as away from it. The goal is increased autonomy, a significant voice in determining our own lives. Until this is better understood by the "old men" on top, corporation heads, union leaders, and labor journalists alike, the rift between them and the many discontented millions in the labor force will widen and will tax and threaten us all.

Profit Sharing

If workers are to share in the responsibility of increasing productivity it is only reasonable, argue some workplace reformers, that they share as well in the profit of their special effort. Job enrichment experiments without profit sharing, these reformers insist, are basically exploitive—and should be rejected by the workers. Participation in profits is necessary if the workers are not to conclude that enrichment projects merely work them harder with no special gain to themselves. Indeed, experience suggests that short-term productivity gains from humanizing efforts dissipate quickly without the related reward of profit sharing.

Why, then, is there no special clamor for the immediate and wide-scale incorporation of profit sharing into American industrial practice? In large part because nearly fifty years of experimentation, from the Scanlan plan of the 1930's through the celebrated Kaiser plan of the present, have made plain a demanding set of objectives that must be met if this reform is to succeed:

1. Profit-sharing payments must be clearly in addition to adequate base pay and fringe benefits.
2. Profit sharing must be tied to the "profitability" of the worker or his small group and not to the "profitability" of the entire firm.
3. Payments must be sensitive to small-group productivity, requiring, among other things, a redefinition of productivity to account for indirect costs such as turnover, absenteeism, and so on.
4. Payments must be immediate and based on productivity. (Ideally, the distribution of profits should follow closely the period of productivity.)
5. The plans must be contractual. (Arrangements that can be arbitrarily rescinded are seen as paternalistic and, therefore, unsuitable to the current and future labor force.)

HEW consultants size up profit sharing as follows:

> Both human goals (autonomy and interdependence) as well as economic goals (increased productivity) can be achieved through the sharing by workers in both the responsibilities of production *and* the profits earned through production. Most workers will willingly assume responsibility for a wider range of decisions (and by so doing increase productivity and profits) *if* they are also allowed to share in the results.[30] (Italics added.)

Worker's Codetermination

Popular abroad for over a hundred years, this reform calls for self-determination and a "bill of rights" for the workingman at his place of work. Few other potential political changes at work challenge social inequality under capitalism as keenly as does this one.

What is at stake is a vision of extending democracy to the workplace as part of a more sweeping effort to secure a self-governed and self-managed America. As John Case argues, "an enterprise in which workers collectively determine what they produce, how they produce it, and how to distribute the income they earn can better realize human values than a capitalist enterprise."[31]

Perhaps, though, the turmoil likely to accompany the steady securement of the following "rights" will probably be considerable:

1. Workers should have the right to create their own plant safety committee, with the power to inspect, and to order any safety reforms whatsoever.
2. Workers should have full access to all job evaluation and time-motion study reports; this includes the right to veto any evaluation report and

to refuse to abide by its conclusions if significant errors, inconsistencies, or prejudices in the evaluation can be shown.

3. Workers should have the veto right to oversee all hiring, transfer, promotion-demotion, recall and work assignments.
4. Workers should have the veto right to oversee all setups of production lines and the determination of production line rates.
5. Workers should have the right to elect or veto the appointment of all foremen.
6. Workers should have the right to determine all issues relating to discipline by a two-thirds majority vote of all workers in the particular work unit.
7. Workers should have access to all reports determinative of work schedules, shifts, vacations, overtime, inventory shutdowns, and so forth; along with the right to veto the implementation of any management decision relating to such.
8. Workers, by a two-thirds majority decision, should have the right to strike to insure the prompt resolution of grievances by management, including the right to resort to sitdown strikes.
9. Workers should have the right to review and to veto, if necessary, all decisions relating to plant shutdowns, relocations, layoffs, and so forth.
10. Workers should have the right, eventually, to veto decisions concerned with prices and investment.[32]

Many advocates realistically see the success of this plan as plainly a long-term two-stage process, the first focused narrowly on restraining and limiting management. Only years or decades thereafter, possibly in a period of economic collapse when management's right to make decisions unilaterally has been seriously questioned, might American workers attempt to assume authority to make decisions directly.

Why bother to press for codetermination? A number of reasons appear in the material already discussed, but one merits special attention: writing of the twenty-five-year-old West German experiment Eberhard Mueller notes a subtle and yet profound learning gain:

> Employers and workers began to share in a common thought process. The workers realized, as they did not always before, that the economy is not a cow that can be foddered in heaven and milked on earth. For the employers a cultivation of good relations with the worker representatives became increasingly a prerequisite for their own professional position. Thus both sides are coerced into making cooperative decisions, and, at the same time, both benefit from a gradual learning process.[33]

The emphasis that codetermination places upon human capabilities is hailed as one of its most promising aspects. For it becomes a countervailing force to the excessive power otherwise commonly placed in technical-economic capabilities. Codetermination, in short, to judge at least from twenty-five years of democratic German experience, contributes substantially to the humanizing of an industrialized society.

American labor unions currently show little interest in this reform, leaving to their Israeli, Yugoslav, and Scandinavian counterparts the distinction of pioneering in this field. However, at least one student of this reform, Marcus Raskin, believes that the narrow American preoccupation with wages, hours, and working conditions might give way soon to a broader and more political position—if the unions are "pressured" from within and without. A four-part program of union reform aimed at the corporate structure would include:

1. Securement of the power to see that all workers who desire to can learn different jobs, including white-collar and managerial tasks.
2. Enlargement of a substantial decision-making role for workers in the choice, quantity, quality, and price of manufactured goods.
3. The development of skills, and the management of investment funds, so that the unions themselves can begin to operate their own plants under worker management.
4. The establishment of independent worker-schools where workers will study, assess, and practice applying techniques of gaining control over work processes.

All of this, of course, requires that unions *first* question their twentieth-century stand against worker participation and control in favor of narrow dinner-pail demands.[34]

Does codetermination, then, have much of a chance today—or soon—in America?

There is no gainsaying the considerable depths of the average American's suspicion of this plan—the predictable shying away from programs directed at changing from within, a corollary of the fear of leftist ideology. Far more popular are efforts to solve relevant problems by benignly adding something (more leisure, higher pay, safer work conditions, and so on). In this way, and not through the calm-shattering political campaign that codetermination would entail, many believe we can miraculously escape the consequences of a fundamental conflict of interest between profitmakers and worker welfare. Perhaps . . . and then again, possibly not.

Government as Catalyst

If anything substantial is soon to be gained in the reform of working conditions, the federal government may have to spark and sponsor it, not only for humanitarian or political reasons but also for hard-headed tax-saving reasons as well. The failure to encourage management and labor to redesign work adds to the tax burden of us all through increased social costs:

> For example, to ignore the trade-off potential between increasing the satisfaction of work and paying ever-more and ever-higher medical bills is to choose spending over investing. More significantly, it may also be the equivalent of persisting in a "no-win" policy concerning the health of Americans.
>
> . . . .
>
> That jobs can be made more satisfying and that this will lead to healthier and more productive workers and citizens is no longer in doubt. What re-

> mains is to find a way to overcome the reluctance of employers and unions to act.[35]

Government, in short, has a legitimate role to play as a catalyst where the half-hearted parties and their lackadaisical efforts to redesign jobs are concerned.

But how? The Scandinavian experience provides a model worth emulating. In Norway, for example, the government, the labor unions, and the employers jointly sponsor the Norwegian National Participation Council, a full-time professional aid to job humanization experiments throughout the country. The three political parties have also formed a parliamentary commission to work with labor and management at every level, from law making to plant particulars, to encourage the redesigning of jobs. Similar efforts in Sweden have helped create the climate that explains the celebrated Saab and Volvo reforms.

The Scandinavian experience, an HEW task force suggests, might be adapted to our system through the formation of a public corporation with the following kinds of functions:

1. To compile and certify a roster of qualified consultants to assist employers with technical problems in altering work.
2. To provide a resource to which management and labor can turn for advice and assistance.
3. To provide an environment in which researchers from various disciplines who are working on job redesign can meet with employers, unions, and workers to pool their experience and findings.

In connection with workplace reforms, the $20-million Research and Technical Assistance Bill proposed by Senators Edward Kennedy and Jacob Javits would attempt to identify the causes and dimensions of worker alienation and to test some methods for making jobs more satisfying. (One of the most far-reaching of the bill's measures would have the government take job satisfaction into account in letting contracts for government work.) HEW consultants, although sympathetic to the call for new laws, stress that much can be immediately accomplished by the transfer of existing research, training, and demonstration money from other fields to job enrichment concerns.[36]

Overall, the reform call is for government leadership in helping us become an experimenting society, for the problem of dissatisfying work can be solved only by an experimental approach, such as the design and trial of a pilot plant. The options for government action to help in the humanization of work are considerable. Spurred by an aroused public the legislators *can* do much to ensure that work increasingly bears out the Talmudic saying, "Great is work, for it honors the workingman."

Summary

Here, as elsewhere throughout the volume, we are challenged by questions as provocative as many of the suggested answers.

Not the least of these questions involves the choice we must soon make between experiments in the humanization of work design or employee codetermination. The first, whether in the form of flexitime, profit sharing, or the like, essentially serves the cause of a rehabilitated and reinvigorated capitalistic order. The second, whether in the form of worker councils, worker representation on corporate boards of directors, or the like, serves the cause of redefining power, prerogatives, and privilege and would probably move this country further along toward our own American version of egalitarian socialism.

It now seems necessary that we go beyond the narrow goal of maximizing profit to other job considerations that are more consonant with the newly recognized social responsibilities of big business. A high regard for good workmanship, the will to achieve, and the need for challenge are all deeply rooted in each of us—however unfulfilled they may be in our work.

A vision offered by Gerald Piel in 1961 is germane and encouraging:

> The liberation of people from tasks unworthy of human capacity should free that capacity for a host of activities now neglected in our civilization: teaching and learning, fundamental scientific investigation, the performing arts and the graphic arts, letters, the crafts, politics, and social service.
>
> Characteristically these activities involve the interaction of people with people rather than with things. They are admittedly not productive activities; nor are they profitable in the strict sense. But they are highly rewarding to the individuals involved and add greatly to the wealth of the nation.[37]

Either we must soon elevate work to a point where it is as attractive as the remarkably neglected activities that Piel cites, or we must redesign our social order to liberate ourselves from labor that fails to honor us. Or so some contend . . . and you?

FOOTNOTES

1. Charles H. Percy, "Work Days Don't Have to Be Dull," *Philadelphia Inquirer* (April 20, 1973), p. 11-A.
2. *Work in America: Report of a Special Task Force to the Secretary of Health, Education, and Welfare,* James O'Toole, Chairman (Cambridge, Mass.: MIT Press, 1973), *passim.*
3. Studs Terkel, "The Daily Bread Isn't Enough," *Philadelphia Evening Bulletin* (September 3, 1972), p. 6.
4. "Boredom Spells Trouble," *Life* (September 1, 1972), p. 38.
5. I draw here on a speech by Michael Maccoby, "Principles of Humanizing Work," given at the 1971 Meeting of the American Association for the Advancement of Science.
6. "Europe Likes Flexi-time Work," *Business Week* (October 7, 1972), pp. 80–82. See also the employer-union debate on the 4–40 work week in *Manpower* (January 1972), pp. 14–19.
7. "Europe Likes Flexi-time Work," *Business Week,* op. cit.
8. Ibid.
9. Nancy and Michael Creedman, "Angst, the Curse of the Working Class," *Human Behavior* (November–December, 1972), p. 8.
10. Quoted in David A. Whitsett, "The Well-Designed Job," *The Personnel Administrator* (September–October 1972), p. 17.
11. *Work in America,* op. cit., p. 114.

12. Lawrence G. O'Donnell and W. Mossberg, "A Day's Work," *Wall Street Journal* (December 8, 1972), p. 1.
13. William Serrin, "Inside a Major Strike: Woodcock's UAW vs. General Motors," *The Washington Monthly* (August 1972), p. 25.
14. "ICI Breaks Its Bottlenecks," *Business Week* (September 9, 1972), p. 119.
15. Saab advertisement, *Business Week* (March 26, 1973), p. 106.
16. *Life* (September 1, 1972), op. cit., p. 36.
17. Quoted in "NGAD Syndrome," *Behavior Today* (January 8, 1973), p. 2.
18. Ibid.
19. Frank E. Armbruster, "A Vocal Minority of Dissatisfied Workers," *New York Times* (February 12, 1973), p. 27.
20. Laurence G. O'Donnell, "A Day's Work," *Wall Street Journal* (December 6, 1972), p. 23.
21. James Toms, "Auto Assembly Line Falls in Disrepute as Workers Seek 'Meaningful' Jobs," *Philadelphia Inquirer* (October 26, 1972), p. 24.
22. Agis Salpukas, "Jobs Rotated to Fight Boredom," *New York Times* (February 4, 1973), p. 1.
23. Agis Salpukas, "Can a Worker Find Happiness in a Dull Job?" *New York Times* (December 24, 1972), p. F-3.
24. Philip Shabecoff, "Percy Says U.S. Is on 'Brink of a Major Breakthrough' in Attempt to Change Ideas on Work," *New York Times* (March 27, 1973), p. 32.
25. "Keeping Workers Happy on the Job," *U.S. News & World Report* (January 29, 1973), p. 68. This is the source of the two quotations immediately above it, as well.
26. Agis Salpukas, "U.A.W. Is Avoiding Economic Goals," *New York Times* (February 18, 1973), p. 41.
27. "Inside a Major Strike: Woodcock's UAW vs. General Motors," *The Washington Monthly,* op. cit., p. 25.
28. Ibid., p. 23.
29. Bryon Calame, *Wall Street Journal,* p. 1.
30. Drawn from *Work in America,* op. cit., pp. 105–112.
31. John Case, "Worker's Control: Toward a North American Movement," *Workers' Control,* Gerry Hunius et al., eds. (New York: Random, 1973), p. 443.
32. Jack Rasmus, "Another Way to Work," *Social Policy* (November–December 1972 and January–February 1973), p. 110.
33. Eberhard Mueller, "Humanizing Industrial Society," *Worldview* (April 1973), p. 40.
34. Marcus G. Raskin, *Being and Doing* (New York: Random, 1971), pp. 103, 105.
35. *Work in America,* op. cit., p. 112.
36. Ibid.
37. Gerald Piel, *Consumers of Abundance* (New York: Fund for the Republic, 1961), p. 14.

READING

Here is a high-quality double-barreled selection, with a potential of considerable value. To begin with the author opens up the sensitive subject of just what college students can do in an earnest reform alliance with "hard-hat" blue-collarites, and his unusual plan for cooperation is as promising as it is hard-headed and overdue. On top of this the author introduces the little-discussed subject of workplace pollution—noise, dust, chemicals, radiation, heat stress, and fumes—which, as a microcosm of the pollution everywhere, is more intense and harder to escape from. Little understood and seldom measured, workplace pollution "inflicts far more damage to health than does the admittedly serious pollution which descends upon an entire community."

Any group of American workers today experiences some work-related health and safety hazard, and one in every twenty workers comes down with an occupational disease or illness annually (more die of work-related injuries each year than of car accidents!). Count in noise exposure, and you get a ratio of one out of every four workers hurt in some way by an environmental insult in the workplace. Not surprisingly, then, health and safety hazards ranked as the number two complaint of all American workers in a 1971 scale of nineteen sources of worker discontent. (Industry plans a 26 per cent increase in spending in 1973 over 1972 in health and safety reforms, largely to comply with the 1970 Occupational Safety and Health Act, which Business Week *believes "may be the most spectacular issue since the pollution problem hit the front page."*[1]*)*

Edith Van Horn, a UAW staffer, describes the day-to-day struggles of a union representative with health and safety issues: "At least 80 per cent of my grievances were directly related to the health and safety of my women like the fight for gloves, for protective clothing, doors on the toilets, protection from fumes and excessive heat (for fans), protection from excessive drafts (for canvas shields), from hours standing on concrete floors (for platforms), short-term confinement on jobs like the solder pots (so they wouldn't be sentenced for long periods on excessively hazardous jobs), accessible water fountains, better food on the lunch wagons, the right to eat or drink coffee on the job, plant hospital neglect and care, speedup hazards, danger from moving lines, a place to hang their coats, space for their pocketbooks and personal belongings (the fight for drawers with locks), for toilet paper that wasn't like sandpaper and for soap that wasn't like scouring powder. These and many more are some examples of the basic fight to be treated like human beings and not like machines." As workers become increasingly conscious of their environmental rights the struggle intensifies . . . and may become bitter.

In a remarkable book by UAW journalist Franklin Wallick, The American Worker: An Endangered Species, *from which the following reading and all of these quotations are drawn, a number of promising reforms are championed, not the least of which takes the form of a "Workers' Bill of Health Rights," an instrument that both capsulizes what is missing* and *what must soon be won:*

1. *The Right to Protection from Job Hazards.*
2. *The Right to Work Without Fear.*
3. *The Right to Medical Information.*
4. *The Right to Information About All Potential Job Hazards.*
5. *The Right to Have Known or Fixed Dangers Clearly Described by the Employer.*
6. *The Right to Have Variable Dangers Measured Regularly.*
7. *The Right to Discover and Preserve a Record of Job Hazards.*
8. *The Right to Corroboration of Information and Enforcement of Standards.*

9. *The Right to be Protected and to Protect Himself.*
10. *The Right to Limit Hazardous Work Exposures to Working Hours.*
11. *The Right to Recover for Damages Resulting from Violation of Standards.*
12. *The Right to Recover the Full Value of Health Damaged by Employer Failures.*
13. *The Right to Recover for Hidden or Delayed Injuries to Health.*
14. *The Right to Recover an Adequate Level of Workmen's Compensation for all Job-Related Health Impairments.*
15. *Every Worker Has the Right to Receive Health and Life Insurance Equivalent to the True and Complete Value of His Life to Him and to His Family, From His Employer at a Rate Equivalent to That Which Federal Employees Receive.*
16. *Every Worker Has the Right to Bargain for Stricter Standards Than Those Established or Provided by Law.*

Wallick adds that the list is only a beginning and a general outline, as each work situation offers challenges of its own.

Wallick remains optimistic about the chances of securing reforms: "With the passage of the new job safety and health laws, with a quickened attitude of environmental vigilance, and with a better educated generation of young workers—we shall see a more aggressive attack on the health hazards of the workplace. There once was a vigorous occupational health movement in the United States, but it fell by the wayside as people put blind faith in the ability of science to master all problems. Now we are entering a period of environmental concern and skepticism which extends to the places where people work. A summons to act has been put upon union leaders, young workers, scientists and environmentalists, enlightened employers, and government. The dimensions of this attack on job hazards are far flung—they are as vast as the working world. Success is attainable. The day will come, according to UAW's Paul Wagner, when workers will care as much about the air they breathe at work as they care about the speed of the production line." Perhaps. And more likely still if you and I decide to "give a damn" and lend a hand!

Wallick recruits for a handsome "army," one anyone could be proud to join: "a band of true believers who sense a new time, who walk with a new beat as the ones who will make the new law, even go beyond the law, if need be, in demanding workplace environmental excellence. They will be workers—union officials some, many union stewards and staffers and rank-and-file members. They will be employers who care, who realize that the workplace environment can enhance unit output and provide humane employment. They will be government officials who catch the new tempo of workplace concern, and will take the law and run with it. They will be public officials, who realize that job safety and health is an issue whose time has come. And they will be scientists, who will relate the world of the test tube with the world of the person in our delicately-balanced environment of work with its hidden technological hazards." With the well-being of 80 million working Americans at stake (57 million, or three out of four civilian workers in 4.1 million workplaces, now covered by the enormously promising Occupational Safety and

Health Act of 1970), Wallick's invitation to "make a contribution" merits every possible consideration on our part . . . and then some.[2]

FOOTNOTES

1. The $3.2 billion expenditure is discussed in *Business Week* (May 26, 1973), p. 27. See also Sylvia Porter, "Health and Welfare," *New York Post* (June 4, 1973), p. 28.
2. For an account of the first joint effort by unionists and environmentalists on behalf of job safety, see *Business Week* (May 26, 1973), p. 63.

Toward a Worker-Student Alliance

Franklin Wallick

There are few notions which contain more wishful thinking than the perennial notion that workers and students can rise up in an alliance that will remake the world. During the past decade there have been numerous false starts, sometimes from the union side, mostly from the student side. The most recent wave stems from student unrest. Some students have faddishly assumed since workers and students are bothered equally by big, faceless institutions, they can work and fight together for some vague and romantic kind of liberation.

The issue of occupational health and safety is, however, a natural issue which we believe can ultimately link students and workers into an effective alliance. Some halting beginnings in this direction have been made, others are underway, and the prospects for more worker-student togetherness on this issue are excellent—provided a few ground rules are understood. Union members, even in the most progressive, democratic unions deeply resent young people who come to save them from their ignorance. Students, for their part, have a difficult time fathoming the union clubbishness which tends to be suspicious of outsiders who go "slumming" around union halls.

While both of my parents were union leaders—my father an officer of a printer's union and my mother an officer of a teacher's union—the fact that I went to college for a few years was enough to create barriers between me and union officials who either looked upon me as a threat or an interloper. What I had going for me was some technical competence in writing and the ability to use the media for the union. More recently my interest in occupational health and workmen's compensation has broken down still more barriers. I mention this because many students with starry-eyed ideas about labor make their overtures to unions with no real skills in mind and are, in fact, often trying to use the union to promote some narrow and preconceived ideological doctrine.

There are very good reasons why unions tend to be hostile toward students and intellectuals who try to "save" them. Workers band together in unions for practical reasons to protect themselves from hostile employers and any-

Reprinted with permission from *The American Worker: An Endangered Species* by Franklin Wallick (New York: Ballantine Books, 1972), pp. 140–148; 184–186.

body else who seeks to use them, and that must include "student slummers." Some unions with a strong conservative bias are probably beyond student reach—they may have a few house lawyers who will feed them ideas, but they will undoubtedly remain hostile toward the most friendly overture.

Unions for their part have been overly protective of their turf and have too often turned aside young people with genuine skills and a willingness to crank the mimeograph machines and stuff the envelopes.

Occupational safety and health offer some unique possibilities for worker-student cooperation. We have noted how complicated the law is. Obviously law students and young lawyers with an interest in the worker's side of the law will find new union doors opening. Unions will increasingly be seeking help in setting up and running training programs. They will seek out technical personnel—safety engineers and industrial hygienists who are in very short supply. Unions will need people who can translate the mass of technical information into ordinary talk in booklets, pamphlets, and data sheets. The opportunities for the enlightened engineer are unlimited. Architects, machine tool designers, and economists will have a ready market as the issue of occupational health and safety comes into its own.

Mere competence and willingness to be of service to unions is not enough. I have seen many unhappy situations where bright, willing people have been rudely rebuffed by union people. And I have seen some successful link-ups. There are no surefire rules which can guarantee success, but there are some obvious things to avoid. One thing which unions resent the most is "elitism." It is an attitude that "here we are the bright, enlightened product of college, and how lucky you are that we are here to help you." I can remember a young man who came to my office in Washington right out of college looking for a job. The night before he had decided that he was going to offer his services to a union and he had come to tell me that he was available, but I had better hurry because he might get a better offer from management. This lad was quite pleasant about it all, but he was thoroughly arrogant in his attitude that his college diploma gave him some automatic entry into labor's hallowed ranks. While this was an extreme situation, it all too easily typified the attitude of many students who can't understand why the great working class is not begging to be saved by them.

Let me cite an example of a different kind. During the summer of 1971, the Alliance for Labor Action (ALA) set up an occupational health project which contained about ten young students with various levels of competence and interests. One of these was Mary Win O'Brien, who had worked with the Nader Task Force on Occupational Health and Safety during 1970 and spent the summer of 1971 monitoring the law. She spent all summer working up legal comments on the various interpretations appearing in *The Federal Register*. She worked harmoniously with the UAW Legal and Social Security Departments, and much of her work was picked up and used in wholesale lots. She is eager to continue her work even though no union has hired her yet; with her developing skills, I'll wager that Mary Win will be in the forefront of the occupational health and safety movement for as long as she desires.

Some of the worst "elitists" manage to con a few unions and rip off some of their time and money. What the "elitists" lack is an appreciation of the native intelligence and finesse of a lot of union leaders who may lack sophisticated polish but have a keen sense of timing, mood, and what is possible. Unions are political institutions and must be understood in that context; a union leader stays a leader because of his political ability to feel his membership's pulse and translate their wants into contracts and programs.

Unions looking for ways to handle job safety and health problems should consider the help of willing students, some of them not trained specifically, who will work with the dedication which moved through the old CIO during the organizing days of the thirties. Students can be useful in making health surveys, in locating experts in the community, in researching scientific information about particular problems, in keeping after government officials, in preparing complaints, in taking highly technical language and reducing it to ordinary talk. These are but a few of the chores which young people and environmentalists can and should try to do.

There is the danger that workers will be discouraged by rising expectations. A group of students who make inquiries about job safety and health, make promises, and then fail to deliver—can do much harm.

It will take the most careful, diplomatic moves by students and unions to make an alliance work. But it can work. It will not be an alliance of multitudes with mass meetings and fiery resolutions—although that could come—but it will be rather the quiet, plugging work of sincere young people who are willing to do the unspectacular and are willing to make good on what they promise. To turn that kind of help away would be rank foolishness by any union.

One of the best books describing how unions respond to the friendly outsider is Harold Wilensky's *Intellectuals in Labor Unions*. It is full of anecdotal material and provides the person without union experience with a framework for understanding unions' behavior. Hostility toward intellectuals in unions has quieted down considerably from the New Deal and post-World War II eras. There are a number of reasons. First, collective bargaining today involves many highly technical factors like pensions, health insurance, and contracts; in this situation unions welcome aboard a person who can "read the fine print." Secondly, a lot of union officials who came up from the ranks won their battle stars in an epic strike, and once were hostile to "any kid with a glib college manner," probably now have children or grandchildren of their own who went to college and talk that way, too. Finally, a younger breed of union officials is coming along with more education and with an appreciation for books, law, and science.

As a union bureaucrat for twenty years, I have learned as much from my fellow union members as I have been able to impart. I am always amazed at the wealth of information and experience which is percolating in union ranks. I have seen many college graduates in PTA or political party ward-meetings go absolutely berserk from ignorance about parliamentary procedure. But I have never seen a union meeting not adhering closely to *Roberts' Rules of Order*. I am sure this does not happen universally, but the democratic skills by which most union meetings are handled is in stark contrast to the parliamentary fumbling better-educated types engage in.

With rare exceptions, any young person with a yearning for unionism who works at a job and will go to the union meeting, will find an open door where problems can be thrashed out, where grievances can be aired, where solutions can be found. None of this happens automatically or instantaneously. Acceptance has to be won, often painfully.

I talked recently with some students who were bitterly opposed to the UAW, its leadership, and felt that this union was a big fake put over on the working class. The UAW is far from perfect, it suffers from bigness and tired blood—but it is basically an open union, with the constitutional machinery whereby any member has an opportunity to be heard and stand or fall on the merits of a stated issue. It is fashionable among some self-styled revolutionists to denounce all union leadership as corrupt and unresponsive, but I have little sympathy for those who are unwilling to use the machinery which is theirs, as it is anybody else's.

Occupational safety and health is uniquely qualified to bring students and workers together, because it requires people of technical competence. One of the most useful accomplishments of the ALA's 1970 summer project was preparation of a "how to use the law" booklet prepared by a Georgetown Law School student, Miles Kaufman. A manual on how to fight occupational noise was prepared. A guide to locating dangerous chemicals and how to combat them was another product of the summer project. And a tactical study showing how different unions had dealt with different occupational health problems was still another. Each of these booklets and studies required contact between students and workers, including union officials. They are but samples of a broader, more sustained program which will inevitably grow in the future.

When we talk here of a student-worker alliance, we are not talking of a mass movement. This is a selective phenomenon. A group of students, with both skills and a willingness to listen instead of preach, can usefully work with unions and their members to improve working conditions. This work will not consist of mounting the barricades, firing off personal manifestos at plant gates, or wisecracking about the ingratitude of union leaders. Some of the best, most devastating descriptions of bad working conditions appear in radical publications. But what is lacking by these young radicals is a political skill inside the union to combat the problem once it has been identified and publicized.

An effective young intellectual working in occupational health is Dr. David Wegman of Boston. He has a group of students trained to assist unions in getting at the roots of their in-plant health problems. Wegman has a natural talent which union people need and want. Not every doctor, however well-intentioned, could open the doors and do the follow-up as skillfully as Dave Wegman. Many occupational health traditionalists, including doctors, have lost their welcome because they have retreated into a shell of professionalism and have been unwilling to put their skill and training at the service of working people.

Another success story is that of a young political scientist, Dan Berman of Washington University in St. Louis. Berman picked up an interest in occupational health, did intensive study, tried many times to get unions interested in what he was doing, and nearly became discouraged and quit trying. He was part of the ALA's 1970 summer project and worked with the Teamsters Union in St. Louis, where he helped coordinate a local union program which will be discussed elsewhere in this book. Berman's story is a tribute to persistency, to waiting until the time was ripe to make a move, and then to offer a service to a group of workers looking for help.

Another project, The Scientists Committee on Occupational Health, is basically a student/intellectual enterprise, but instead of polemics about the evils of capitalism SCOH is offering a professional service which any union can use.

There is another facet to the student-worker alliance idea which is worth exploring. This is the very apparent fact that young workers today are unlike any generation of workers we have ever seen. They are more restless, smarter, much more antiauthoritarian, and possess a life style which has counterparts to the behavior pattern of modern college students. If you visit the huge Lordstown, Ohio plant of General Motors, which makes the compact, Vega, you will be struck by the many beards, long hair, and mod life-style of the workers. This plant hired new and younger workers from the current crop; and thus the membership of that union is representative of this new breed of workers who closely resemble college students.

The studies of this new breed by Robert Shrank of the Ford Foundation tell what makes them tick. "The new worker," writes Shrank, "says, 'We're glad Philip Murray was a great man but what are you doing about the misery of the assembly line I am now working on?' The new work force is concerned with the quality of the 'now' not with the past and not even much about the future. His interest in pension and insurance may be far less than it was in my generation. Management will kick and scream that the organization of the workplace and its effects on the community are exclusively their concern. Some old-line unionists will agree with them. I submit that they are both wrong." Says Shrank, "The young worker is rightly insisting that we try to make life at the workplace more challenging, less degrading, more meaningful."

All of the studies about young people agree they are a smarter breed, more impatient about bad working conditions, and less willing to take any authoritarian guff from either unions or management. But to assume, as some young radicals do, that the American worker is itching to overthrow the system by bombing, by general strikes, or by a union headquarters sit-in is the most arrogant nonsense.

Real abiding change will come in working conditions, but it will not happen all at once. Workers want practical answers, not pie-in-the-sky rhetoric. It will come from persistent and intelligent attacks on working-condition abuses which can be identified and dealt with by whatever skills and engineering knowledge we have. This, in my judgment, presents an enormous challenge to young students and intellectuals who may look at the sleeping giant in modern unionism and wonder when and if it will awaken. The challenge will not come from pontificating; it will come from people who can make a useful contribution, a contribution which may not at first seem glamorous, but a contribution which will surely help wear down the opposition.

So the student-worker alliance we are talking about here is built around young people who bring their skills and competence to help solve working conditions which increasingly loom at the prime issue in the day-to-day life of work people. Students who can enlist scientists, economists, engineers, architects, and physicians to help workers grapple with the workplace environment will find ready takers among the unions, even those unions which have heretofore been suspicious of meddling by young well-wishers.

A Job Safety and Health Quiz

1. The government safety limit for carbon monoxide is four times weaker for factory workers than it is for people on the outside. ______True ______False
2. The Nixon Administration asked for $1 per citizen to run the Occupational Safety and Health Act of 1970 during the upcoming year. ______True ______False
3. The American Conference of Governmental Industrial Hygienists is an official U.S. government agency. ______True ______False
4. If mercury drops on the floor where you work you can breathe in dangerous levels of mercury which are harmful to health. ______True ______False
5. According to Assistant Secretary of Labor Guenther, most of the complaints made by workers so far are for health hazards on the job. ______True ______False
6. Federal government studies show that dangerous levels of noise at the workplace affect the following number of workers in the United States: ______10 million ______15 million ______20 million ______25 million
7. Workers under the new Occupational Safety and Health Act of 1970 have the following rights. True or False.
   a. ______ Right to shut down an unsafe machine.
   b. ______ Right to go to court to halt an imminent danger to health and safety.
   c. ______ Right to safety standards which will not impair health or shorten life as a result of work exposure during working life.
   d. ______ Right to sue Secretary of Labor if he fails to protect your health by some act of negligence.
8. A Chicago survey of worker health hazards showed that among 1 million workers the following percentage of workers faced "serious and urgent" hazards.
   ______5 per cent ______15 per cent ______30 per cent ______45 per cent
9. When noise levels go beyond 80 decibels (the sound of a ringing alarm clock) scientific studies show that a certain percentage of workers will lose their sense of hearing. ______True ______False
10. The official government standard for noise is no more than 90 decibels (you have to shout to be heard six inches away) during an eight-hour period.
    ______True ______False

11. A private citizen can sue a company for negligence but a worker working for that same company cannot sue; he can only collect workmen's compensation.
    ______True ______False
12. A U.S. Department of Labor study on working conditions among all workers showed "health and safety hazards" to be the fifth highest source of job discontent on a scale of nineteen sources of worker discontent.
    ______True ______False

The Correct Answers

1. False—it is five times weaker for workers.
2. False—Nixon Administration asked for 25¢ per citizen.
3. False—ACGIH is not an official government agency despite the sound of the name.
4. True—mercury vapors can be picked up at dangerous levels from drops on the floor.
5. True—most complaints are health complaints.
6. Twenty million workers work at more than 80 decibels, which is enough to expose people to loss of hearing and other dangers of noise.
7. a. False—no right to shut down unsafe machines without formal complaint—some state laws do permit inspectors to shut down unsafe machines; this section of federal law was lost in Congress.
   b. True—if Secretary of Labor fails to act on an imminent danger complaint, a worker has the right to sue the Secretary to get an explanation and a hearing on the merits of the complaint.
   c. True—workers have right to health standards which do not impair health or shorten life.
   d. True—law gives worker right to sue Secretary of Labor if Secretary has failed to act and injury to worker results.
8. Forty-five per cent in Chicago worker survey faced "serious and urgent" health hazards.
9. True—anything above 80 decibels will mean loss of hearing for some people.
10. True—government noise standard is 90 decibels during eight-hour period.
11. True—you can sue a company for negligence as a citizen but not as a worker.
12. False—"health and safety hazards" are the second highest source of worker discontent in U.S. Department of Labor study.

READING

I regularly ask students to prepare scenarios of possible futures, so that we may explore alternative responses to social perils and social gains before *the fact. In this essay a graduate student, back on campus taking advanced studies as part of a distinguished career in government service, tackles the critical questions of how our future may unfold if certain present environmental challenges go unmet . . . and of what special toll this neglect may take of the nation's blue-collarites. His grim prognostications are a suitable note on which to close, as there is still time to remedy many of the hazards he spotlights . . . if the quality of our mutual caring is as sound and compelling as our mutual survival would seem to require.*

A Scenario of Blue-Cholera Concern

Raymond Smith

Economic Surprise. The nation's balance-of-trade problems continue to intensify over the next decade with major impacts on our dreams of affluence. Associated with this problem is the growing shortage of energy and the increasing importation of gas and oil. There is further recognition that we cannot compete internationally in consumer goods except where we have a considerable research and development edge.

We recognize that our energy problems can be best satisfied through gasification of coal. Coal gasification, however, will require approximately a tripling of our production of coal. Food becomes one of our most viable export products. The government mounts searches for our best young brains and completely subsidizes their education in full recognition of the importance of ideas and research and development to our continuing prosperity.

As our industrial plants close down because of lack of international markets, the government begins a concerted and successful effort to shift industrial workers into the growing and processing of food and into the mining, processing, and gasification of coal. Various types of subsidies are used to make this geographic and technological shift of the labor force successful because of our urgent need of labor in these areas.

Deurbanization of our major urbanized population begins at a rate far greater than the rate over the last thirty years of migration from rural to urban areas. Communities in the coal mining and agricultural areas are revitalized. We accept and meet the challenge for New Town types of communities in these revitalized areas.

The suburbs find that their health is tied to the health of the core city. They actively support the core city's efforts to obtain the necessary funds for redevelopment and their joint pressures are successful. The depopulated portions of the inner city now provide considerable opportunity for leveling and redirection of use into intown community parks, New Towns in the inner city, and research parks in the inner city.

The blue-collarite is devastated. His neighborhoods are destroyed in the outward migration. Most efforts to maintain the expanded family through joint migration fail. He is forced once again to learn skills, such as farming, that were perhaps known to his father and grandfather. In a decade, however, he will find his condition somewhat reversed for the good.

The new agricultural and mining communities have a variety of needs for manual skills, including construction skills. In many instances, the blue-collarite is the right man in the right place with his ability to repair and utilize equipment. Increasingly in these new communities, he provides various types of services as a small entrepreneur.

In the old cities, those who remain find their children's schools improved because of the impact of suburbanites now returning to the revitalized inner city. They find diversified community life, if not the Sennett survival type of community. Their children find increased employment opportunities, at least at the technician levels of the new research and development effort, and broader opportunities to enter and complete college and move into professional jobs. I cannot predict whether or not these better-educated children of the blue-collarite will suffer from cultural shock as they move from the culture of their youth into that of their new life.

Social Surprise. The increasing population of well-educated older people and a less materialistic and more idealistic youth combine to form a new liberal political front. Both groups reject ownership of automobiles as they recognize the full impact of the cost on their desire to enjoy their relative affluence in diversified ways. With the continuing lack of adequate mass transit, both groups are drawn increasingly to center-city areas for housing.

The added pressures for inner-city housing primarily fall on the neighborhoods of the blue-collarites and the racial minorities. Economic and social tension increases between the new arrivals and the existing inhabitants of the areas. The blue-collarites and the racial minorities endeavor to react through the political system, and, lacking power and an understanding of how to use the system, they fail. This failure further intensifies their existing irritation with the bureaucracy. The new liberal front also becomes irritated with the bureaucracy but more typically because of its remoteness than its centralization and slow response. The groups, in a loose alliance, tear down the existing bureaucracy and force its replacement by administrative decentralization.

The present inner-city inhabitants are spun further outward under the pressure of migration of the young and the old into the city. As suburbia feels the pressure of population loss to the center-city areas, it increasingly lets down its bars to low-income housing, and diversification of population becomes widespread. Substantial portions of the inner city return once again to a substantial mixture of types and classes.

Some fringe benefits occur for both the blue-collarites and the racial minorities in the suburbs and the inner city through better schools and broader social contacts. Both find increasing opportunities for employment in service trades, but overall neither their life style nor their economic security is substantially changed. Those families unable to adjust to the more diversified neighborhoods receive repeated cultural shocks, first from their neighbors and then from their children.

Political Surprise. After initial success, and regardless of initial intent, the Nixon block-grant and revenue-sharing programs are perverted to political ends. The programs become an effort to destroy the last vestiges of strength in the Democratic Party—that is, the major Democratic urban areas and states—through insufficient and inequitable funding. Although at first Democratic mayors and governors are criticized and in some instances toppled from power in elections, the people increasingly realize that the blame for local shortages of funds for social programs or increases in taxes lies in Washington.

By the third year, urban riots and an understanding of the political causes has aroused the "silent majority." The heads of defeated Republicans roll in the streets at election time along with the water putting out the fires from the urban area riots. Both the Republican Administration and the Democratic Congress overreact in both words and funding. Although the civil unrest is quieted by the flood of federal dollars, inner-city and suburban populations react politically against the state governments and the federal government, whom they feel have been responsible for the whole mess regardless of party. The new day of the city-state dawns as the state legislature provides means for regionalization. A new uneasy alliance is forged between suburbia and the core of the city in total planning under one central government; however, those powers that can be decentralized are decentralized as a price of this alliance.

With a better share of federal dollars and what was formerly state power, the new city-state sets about the job of planning and renovation. Construction trades flourish as we tear down and build up. The education system is improved generally because of the more equitable distribution of dollars across the whole urban area.

This surprise would provide marginal impact on the blue-collarite. He might have increased choice in where he lives in the urban area. He might have better opportunities for education. But fundamentally his social and economic stresses would remain substantially the same.

Cataclysmic Surprise. A shipment of monkeys for use in medical research falls from a truck at Kennedy airport in New York; the case splits and twenty monkeys spread through the terminal, having considerable contact with people before recapture. Three of the monkeys are noted to be ill, and they die within thirty-six hours of the escape.

Forty-eight hours after the initial escape, a severe illness is reported in over two hundred of the people who were in the terminal. Within four days the number of cases quintuples and the first deaths occur. The illness is diagnosed as viral and previously unknown in man. It is unresponsive to available treatments. Although the warning now goes out, it is too late, for passengers have spread to all major portions of the United States and, in fact, the world. Within six months, approximately 30 per cent of the world's population is dead, and the disease has run its course. (A similar situation actually occurred in London several years ago. Some monkeys, although they did not escape, were found to be diseased with a virus, communicable to man, for which there was no effective cure. Similarly, several years ago medical researchers in an East Coast laboratory were accidentally infected with a new disease virus brought to this country for testing from Ghana. Fortunately, the virus was contained.)

Obviously, consumption patterns, service patterns, and government patterns are completely disrupted by the destruction of life; but unlike war, the disease epidemic has left the country's physical plant intact. The core of the city and suburbia have now been depopulated to a substantial degree. The opportunities for regrouping and rehabilitation—in both the physical and the social sense—are clearly there.

I have now supplied four surprises and three endings. (Give me an ending to this one. I'll offer the hint that the ending depends on the manner in which we endeavor to maintain economic viability and on whether or not we succeed in the effort.)

CHAPTER 9

Producing: Personnel Reforms

His weariness is that of the gladiator after the combat; his work was the whitewashing of a corner in a state official's office.

FRANZ KAFKA

. . . nonviolent guerrilla warfare: start dismantling our organizations where we're serving them, leaving only the parts where they're serving us. It will take millions of such subversives to make much difference.

ROBERT TOWNSEND

How does one stay alive and vital in bureaucratic work? Is it possible to avoid the fate of the tragically flawed "organization man" of the 1950's and the unattractive model of the amoral and purposeless "dodo" of the 1960's? Or, as reformer Nicholas Johnson asks, "how do you stay free as a member of a large, bureaucratized institution? How do you avoid the depersonalization of patterned jobs, of work you don't care about, of a life-style leading nowhere except to an early death of mind and spirit, if not body?"[1]

Much can be learned from the cheery iconoclasm of executive Robert Townsend, whose total rejection of our present fate ("we've become a nation of office boys . . . we're but mortals trained to serve immortal institutions") has him urge "nonviolent guerrilla warfare" on us all ("start dismantling our organizations where we're serving them, leaving only the parts where they're serving us").

Dedicated to helping us spot the idiocies now built into the system, Townsend offers the following advice:

> Anyone who has an assistant-to should be fined a hundred dollars a day until he eliminates the position;
>
> Try calling yourself up at the office, and see what indignities you've built into your own organizational defenses;
>
> Require the chief executive to use every form in the company before it is installed;
>
> If you're the boss and your people fight you openly when you think you're wrong—that's healthy. If your men fight each other openly in your presence for what they believe in—that's healthy. But keep all the conflict eyeball to eyeball;
>
> All decisions should be made as low as possible in the organization; and
>
> There is a time for engagement and a time for withdrawal. A time to walk around the job. A time to just laugh at it.

Along with dozens of other nuggets of this sort Townsend urges the establishment of a sort of vice president in charge of antibureaucratization: "He must have a loud voice, no fear, and a passionate hatred for institutions and their practices. In addition to his regular duties, it's his job to wander around the company looking for new forms, new staff departments, and new reports. Whenever he finds one that smells like institutionalization, he screams 'Horse-shit' at the top of his lungs. And keeps shouting until the new whatever-it-is is killed."[2]

Consistent with this general orientation I am concerned in this chapter with four exciting and promising, if often taxing and frequently risky aids to personal integrity and vitality in corporate employ. The first of these, a plan for a democratic workplace, sets the tone for all that follows. The second reform comes at the problem from the opposite angle and examines the thorny matter of whistle blowing, or the options we have to protect our own integrity—and the well-being of the public—when it is necessary. The third reform is a form of underground employee press, a constructive variation on whistle blowing. Finally, I will discuss creative and progressive personnel work. The chapter's summary explores some of the considerable progress still to be made in this matter of life *after* corporate employ.

The Democratic Workplace

Reformers as widely disparate as Peter Drucker on the moderate right and Michael Harrington on the socialist left urge that as a matter of public policy wherever a group of people have a continuing relationship with a bureaucracy, they should help fix its rules. Drucker, for example, calls for the development of a kind of law called "organizational law" that would presumably help "make organizations perform" and "safeguard the individual's freedom."[3] Harrington urges enactment of a national bureaucratic relations act similar to the National Labor Relations Act (the Wagner Act) of the 1930's:

> In the long run, which happens fairly quickly in this century, the problem of bureaucrat and citizen will be seen as just as important for the common good of the country as the clash of management and labor in the Thirties. When that moment does come, a national policy establishing legal rights for those who challenge impersonal authority might well accomplish as vast an increase in individual freedom as that achieved and maintained by the trade-unionists.[4]

Critics of the ideas of both gentlemen have made much of the lack of specificity in their proposals, sidestepping in this way any direct confrontation with the issue of citizen rights for employees.

All the more valuable, therefore, is a comparable—and somewhat more systematic—proposal advanced by Marcus Raskin, Washington Director of the Institute for Policy Studies.

To begin with, employees would elect representatives from their number to serve in a local worker-community assembly (neighbors of the workplace would also elect representatives). This new assembly would then try to help its members comprehend the effect of the goods that the employee members make—as well as decide questions about hours, wages, and the administrative conditions of the workplace. The authority of the assembly would go still further, however, to encompass decisions about the investment of corporate profits in social endeavors. Similarly, employees would have the unprecedented right to choose their own foremen and supervisory officers. Overall, then, the local assembly would concern itself with all of the problems of the workplace, its relationship to the city, its effect on the environment, its investment policies, and the social value of the very product itself.

Representatives of the local worker-community assembly would elect delegates to an executive parliament for each nationwide corporation involved. At the same time elections inside the corporations would help determine who the next company president will be. The head of General Motors, for example, would stand for office every four years. He and his advisers would operate the corporation within the limits set by the assemblies at company locations and by the executive parliament. Broad guidelines, however, would draw all such corporations together; for example, after paying taxes and reinvestment, the democraticized companies would invest in "rebuilding, health, sabbatical, education, social-entrepreneurial, and artist activities."

Does the plan have a chance? Only if the new, young middle class welcomes its opportunity for participation and the older middle class elects to value self-governing above profits—or so Raskin concludes. He quickly adds that much hinges on a public assessment of its own right to control industrial enterprise so that human values and environmental quality are not persistently undermined.

Redrafting the "social contract" at the workplace (and taking into consideration the people living close by) to include responsibility and participation in and some measure of control over corporate matters is an extraordinary proposition. The obstacles are substantial and range far beyond the lone issue of middle-class response that preoccupies its (middle-class) author (What of the labor movement, for example? Is it absorbed, replaced, or supplemented?). Nevertheless, for lending additional clarity to the call for the democratization of the workplace we owe Raskin our considerable appreciation.[5]

In 1969 twelve federal employees issued an exciting call to arms that lends additional depth and reality to this issue.

Publishing in a reform-oriented journal popular with their colleagues, *The Washington Monthly*, the twelve began by laying out and then dissociating themselves from all the pieces of conventional "wisdom" and practice that explain why a government bureaucracy reflects the conditions in all of our society; for example, our being taught that we have little right or opportunity to participate in decisions affecting our work and our lives.

As a consequence of a large number of such factors, federal employees tend to become alienated from their colleagues, their work, and themselves: "Rules are volumes thick and work is carried out in an atmosphere of pettiness. Employees are seldom allowed to participate in formulating agency policy decisions; they are merely expected to carry out the orders of their supervisors." Challenged to knuckle under or get out, the twelve reformers declare their rejection of that choice and "assert instead that we have an obligation and a responsibility to stay and seek changes in those agencies that are failing to contribute to the well-being of all Americans."

Accordingly, the twelve urge everyone to begin working toward the creation of a genuine "participatory democracy," both within our federal agencies and within our society at large. Rejecting job enrichment and human relations efforts as necessary but inadequate ("we do not simply want a less inhumane bureaucracy"), the twelve offer the following suggestions:

1. Employees should have a voice in the basic policy formulation of their agency and in decisions affecting the programs they administer and conditions under which they work!
2. Privileges of class and status should be eliminated whenever they create barriers among workers! Carpeting and couches, for example, should be equally distributed or abolished when not directly related to the work. Rigid work hours, docking employees for lateness, and other highly arbitrary regulations must also be eliminated. People should be permitted to do their work in any manner, so long as they perform their assignments.
3. The hierarchy within the Federal Bureaucracy must be reduced to a minimum! Positions should reflect the quality and amount of work done, rather than those which are allotted through seniority or political maneuvering. A supervisor's authority should stem from his leadership and expertise, and from his employee's democratic acceptance of his policies. Programs developed in this way would be far easier to follow than those which are arbitrarily handed down. Salary levels should also be correspondingly simplified with perhaps no more than five or six levels, the lowest amply sufficient to meet today's living needs.
4. Limits to Government service should be set! This would not mean that employees would automatically be fired after three or four years, but that they would be encouraged to try other phases of public service or return to the public sector. The Peace Corps' "five year flush," which ensures a regular personnel turnover and the introduction of new ideas, might be such a precedent.
5. All invasions into personal affairs must be prohibited! Government should reflect the mobility and interests of today's youth, as well as a concept of public service which spans a wide range of activities. In order to further facilitate this approach, full rights of free speech, association, and political participation must be guaranteed every Government worker. Employees' life-styles, as reflected in their appearance and sexual behavior, should not be the determinant of their work performance.
6. Workers should be allowed to refuse to perform work which is contrary to their consciences or their sense of justice! They should be allowed to appeal to another authority and criticize their superiors, without having those actions held against them, and they should be free to leave their agency without fear of future reprisal.

In closing their unusual and earnest manifesto, the twelve "inside" reformers pointedly ask, "Are you willing to make a commitment for a more humane government?"[6]

Whistle Blowing

Until recently, as Ralph Nader has explained, all hopes for change in corporate behavior focused on external pressures on the organization, such as regulation, competition, litigation, and exposure to public opinion. At present, however, new attention is being paid to the reform possibilities that inhere in whistle blowing—the protest of an employee who, believing that the public interest overrides the interest of the organization he serves, publicly blows the whistle if the organization is involved in corrupt, illegal, fraudulent, or harmful activity.

The key question, Nader points out, involves an employee's resolving that his allegiance to society, to the public well-being, *must* supersede allegiance to the organization's policies and then acting to inform outsiders or legal authorities. At issue is whether or not one reports:

1. The vast waste of government funds by private contractors;
2. The connection between companies and campaign contributions;
3. A pattern of discrimination by age, race, or sex in a labor union or company;
4. Mishandling the operation of a workers' pension fund;
5. Willful deception in advertising a worthless or harmful product;
6. The sale of putrid or adulterated meats chemically camouflaged in supermarkets;
7. The use of government power for private, corporate, or industry gain;
8. The knowing nonenforcement of laws being seriously violated, such as pesticide laws;
9. Rank corruption in an agency or company; or
10. The suppression of serious occupational disease data.[7]

Thousands of employees are probably privy to such information and, heavily burdened with this knowledge, nonetheless remain silent.

Blue-collarites, for example, know an enormous amount about abuses, which they encounter, endorse, observe, or try to avoid every day:

> For example, workers know that there is virtually no difference between different brands of gasolines of the same octane level. They know generally which factories dump what pollutants into waterways and that there is more pollution under cover of darkness. They know how car manufacturers fudge inspection on the line. They know how government inspectors tip off coal mines of their impending arrival or how their coworkers smoke in prohibited areas. They know which meat and poultry inspectors are on the take or which fail to exercise their duties. They know how taxi meters and automobile odometers are rigged by design or manipulated to cheat the rider or driver. They know of violations of work safety laws.[8]

Similarly, white-collarites know much about which they say—and do—little:

> For example, the twenty-year collusion by the domestic automobile companies against development and marketing of exhaust control systems is a tragedy, among other things, for engineers who, minion-like, programmed the technical artifices of the industry's defiance.[9]

Employees, Nader contends, *must* be permitted to cultivate their *own* form of allegiance to the rest of us—and to exercise it—without having their careers or employment opportunities destroyed.

Responsibility, of course, flows in several directions, and one who is considering raising a hue and cry is advised to consider the following:

1. Is his knowledge of the matter complete and accurate?
2. How far can he go *inside* the organization with his concern or objection?
3. Will he be violating any laws or ethical duties by *not* contacting external parties?
4. What is it that he expects to achieve by whistle blowing in the particular situation?

Although Nader and his associates offer a series of possible strategies to help, they stress that the decision to act and the answers to these questions are unique for every situation and every individual.

What is not unique, however, is the present-day lack, across the board, of reasonable protections of the rights of employees regardless of the policies of their employers. A number of reforms are necessary if we are to nurture and profit from an ethic of whistle blowing. Every corporation, for example, should have a "bill of rights" for its employees and a system of internal appeals to guarantee these rights. As a condition of employment, workers at every level in the corporate hierarchy should have the right to express their reservations about the company's activities and policies, and their views should be accorded a fair hearing. They should also have the right to "go public," and the corporation should expect them to do so when internal channels of communication are exhausted and the problem remains uncorrected.

Unions and professional societies should strengthen—or adopt—ethical practices codes. They should put real powers of implementation into their codes and require observance of these codes not only by members but also by organizations that employ their members. Similarly, government employees should be guaranteed the right as a last resort to bring agency dereliction to public attention. And they should have the right to go to court to protect themselves from harassment and discharge for doing their duty.

All areas of the law touching upon the employee-employer relationship should be amended to include provisions protecting employees who cooperate with authorities. And more publicity should be given to the Clearinghouse for Professional Responsibility (P.O. Box 486, Washington, D.C. 20044), a group dedicated to helping those who are considering blowing the whistle.

As well, "going public" requires a broad enabling environment if it is to be effective. The courts, professional and citizen groups, the media, and the Congress must commit themselves, as additional links, to secure objectives beyond the mere exposure of abuses. Only the provision of potential backup support will really make possible a reversal of the passive and acquiescent role of employees without whom the betrayal of the public trust could not be carried out.

Senator William Proxmire, for one, is introducing legislation to create a safety net for federal employees threatened with loss of their jobs without just cause: "A man ought not to be punished for committing truth before a congressional committee."[10] Law Professor Arthur S. Miller, for another, is impressed with what can be accomplished even without new legislation:

> The Supreme Court can make the constitution's due process principle applicable to corporations and labor unions. This would ensure employees a constitutional right to be treated fairly.
>
> On a less lofty judicial plane, courts could allow for damage suits for "spite findings," much as the law traditionally has given protection against "spite fences" erected by feuding neighbors.[11]

Miller concludes that:

> if a society is to be built on the human scale, if we are not all to be immersed forever as nameless and faceless cogs in public and private bureaucracies, then we had better get on with the job, create some law protecting the whistle blower in proper instances, and also give hard, sustained thought to the type of society we want.[12]

Critics, when not arguing that the present laws are adequate or muttering about "squealers" and "finks," are quick to insist that whistle blowing means increasing costs and reducing profits. To which Townsend retorts, "the answer is clear: whistle blowing may save the free enterprise system—but if our system in fact depends on unpunished lying, stealing, and murder, then who wants to save it?"[13] To the cynical contention that few employees really care one way or another, Townsend replies,

> People from coast to coast are sick of the nauseating phoniness, triviality, and waste of big organizations. Give them a chance to work for a company which fires the paid liars, deals openly, tells the truth—in short, a company they can be proud of—and maybe you've started to save the free enterprise system.[14]

Collaboration between employees and employers to create a supportive climate for whistle blowing is a (faint?) possibility. Nader himself concludes that "the challenge for both the individual and the organization is to develop personal and institutional responses to accommodate [projob citizenship] principles."[15]

Why bother with this Pandora's box? In part because whistle blowing could lead to internal organizational reforms that would enhance employees' respect for their work. Many workers might grow as laborers and as people if protected in the right and the opportunity to apply their sense of justice on the job. A second reason is that lives are at stake. Whistle blowing on defective Corvairs, GM school buses, Firestone tires, and Colt arms for Vietnam came only after the tragic accidental loss of many precious lives. Third, whistle blowing heals. Silence in the face of abuses takes a hellish toll on individuals who in remaining silent subvert their own consciences. Whistle blowing, in Ralph Nader's judgment, can and has "illuminated the dark corners of our society, saved lives, prevented injuries and disease, stopped corruption, economic waste, and material exploitation. Conversely, the absence of such professional and individual responsibility has perpetuated these conditions."[16]

Beyond even these reasons, however, is the awesome contention that the willingness and ability of insiders to blow the whistle may be the last line of defense we have against organizational totalitarianism. As giant organizations relentlessly push deeper and deeper into our lives—through pollution, poverty, income erosion, and invasion of privacy—more and more of our rights and interests are threatened. The potential tyranny of organizations *must* be prevented from silencing a man's conscience, and only the on-the-job citizenship of employees and the creative insecurity of organizations can ensure renewed self-esteem and organizations that are responsible to society as a whole.

The application of ethics to work by men and women who make the conscientious and difficult choice not to become "organization men" is what is finally required—the extraordinary act of choosing personal conscience over institutional lawlessness.

Power to the People's Press!

A variation on whistle blowing that merits attention and replication is the underground company newspaper, a simple and effective means for employees to make their feelings known. Under such titles as *Quest, The Advocate,* and *The Stranded Oiler,* these clandestine, anonymously edited minipapers take bosses to task for everything from not providing enough parking space to tolerating office racism and supporting the Vietnam war.

The oldest of the in-house protest papers probably is *The Advocate,* published since 1968 by its GS-12-level, thirty-one-year-old founder, Madeleine Golde, for her HEW co-workers. Over five thousand copies are hand-delivered to HEW workers in the District of Columbia, and others are mailed around the country. A typical biting article began, "There exists in the Social & Rehabilitation Service a small but extremely powerful group of individuals who most SRS employees have come to either fear or hate." The Department of Housing and Urban Development has an intermittent newspaper of its own, *Quest,* one of whose aims is to "make faceless bureaucrats accountable." In 1971, it announced awards for key HUD executives, including then Secretary George Romney, who got the "Three Monkeys Award" for "seeing, hearing, and speaking no evil about racism in the department." Similarly, 140 public employees in the Los Angeles City Planning Office irritated many with their *Outhouse News* publication of the results of an employee poll rating their bosses as administrators and as planners.

One of the most strident underground company publications is *The Stranded Oiler,* a more-or-less monthly newsletter averaging six pages that has been published since 1970 for employees of the Standard Oil Company of California in San Francisco. About one thousand copies, priced (in 1971) at 10¢ each, are sold from boxes outside company buildings and by volunteer news vendors, some of them ex-employees. The *Oiler*'s publisher, who says he is a professional member of middle management in his thirties, explains that he runs the paper "to show the employees of Socal that they can have a mind of their own—and to show the company the same thing." (For example, in the September 1971 issue the *Oiler* accused Otto Miller, Socal's board chairman, of telling stockholders that there were two environmental experts on Socal's board, when one of the experts had allegedly left the board a month earlier and the other was a vice president, not a director).

Perhaps the biggest underground company paper is the *AT & T Express,* which is circulated free of charge among twenty thousand employees of the Bell System's Pacific Telephone & Telegraph Company and Western Electric Company. A typical *Express* story dealing with the status of women employees asked why their base pay was lower than that of men in the company and why there were no top women officers in the union. Similarly, *The Met Lifer,* an irregular underground project of employees at the San Francisco office of Metropolitan Life Insurance Company, lampooned Metropolitan for "treating sex as a health risk" by turning down the insurance application of a twenty-six-year-old single man who had admitted having had sexual relations. It also slyly insinuated that a Presidential commission report on inefficiencies at the Pentagon, prepared under the direction of then Metropolitan Chairman Gilbert Fitzhugh, was actually an appraisal of his own company.

As of 1971, when *Business Week* published the foregoing information on employee newspapers, the relevant corporate powers were insistent that no retaliatory measures were under consideration. However that may be, the engaging combination of inside knowledge and embarrassing disclosures possible in the underground press suggests a long and constructive future for this zesty variation on the always risky whistle-blowing theme.[17]

In a fascinating variation on this theme, by the way, a company newspaper actually ventured into muckraking exposé journalism. National attention was paid in 1972 to *The Western Voice of Motorola,* the house organ of the Phoenix branch of the Motorola Corporation, when it broke a major story on the high cost of local hospitalization. A by-lined story by Motorola's vice president for human relations accused particular hospitals in the area of inflating medical costs through waste, incompetence, and foolishness. Issue after issue of the company paper blasted alleged instances of flagrant mismanagement and consumer abuse. Negotiations thereafter between the company and the hospitals resulted in substantial reductions in the cost of medical services to Motorola employees . . . and to the entire community as well. A model of a *new* use of corporate "clout," the Motorola example calls out for emulation.[18]

Still another variation worthy of emulation is available in the recent "liberation" of Swedish house organs by employers newly interested in the potential rewards of honest cross-communication:

> Torsten Svensson, a Swedish trade union leader, wrote an article not too long ago attacking the management of a large Swedish company, AGA, for laying off 100 engineers. The article appeared in the company's employee publication, AGA-Klipp.
>
> At about the same time, Molekylen, the employee monthly of Astra Pharmaceutical Co., the biggest such company in Scandinavia, printed a front-page story on a plant accident. It quoted an injured worker: "It's obvious the accident was Astra's fault. They told me the job was not dangerous."
>
> At the State Power Board, a running debate is under way between board chairman Erik Grafstroem and employees who disagree with his opinions.

> Grafstroem's column in the employee monthly tackles topics ranging from the U.S. role in Indochina to Tolkien's novels. Employees who see things differently get equal space to say so.

Part of a management campaign to solve problems of worker discontent akin to those in this country, the Swedish innovation in employee publications is a three-year-old project of the Swedish Employers Federation. Convinced that two-way communication increases the satisfaction of workers with their jobs, the Federation gives an annual prize for the liveliest publication (the 1973 contest focused on problems of the workplace and employee attitudes toward the company).

Perhaps the last word should go to a "convert" in management's ranks who strikes a note of openness and maturity that represents the best aspects of the message of this entire chapter:

> The advantages of an open press outweigh the disadvantages," says Lars Fredholm, personnel manager of the giant Kockums shipyard in Malmoe. "We have learned it's a lot better that criticism about the company come out in the open and up for discussion then that people go around grumbling and discontented. Nothing stops workers or the union from saying what they think, but nothing stops me from coming back with a reply."[19]

Personal Aid—Progressive Variety

Despite years of dedicated effort by personnel specialists, many employees remain fearful or hesistant about seeking aid from bureaucratic representatives of the employer. Executive Robert Townsend explains that "the trouble with personnel experts is that they use gimmicks borrowed from manufacturing: inventories, replacement charts, recruiting, selecting, indoctrinating and training machinery, job rotation, and appraisal programs. And this manufacturing of men is about as effective as Dr. Frankenstein was." Accordingly, Townsend advises that corporations "fire the whole personnel department."[20]

An alternative is an exciting variation with apparently profound implications now being pioneered by the Utah Copper Division of Kennecott Copper Corporation. Called INSIGHT, an acronym for the phone number dialed by Kennecott employees who want help, the project has a staff of three social welfare professionals available day and night to assist eight thousand employees and their dependents.

INSIGHT advances the art of corporate social aid in five valuable ways. First, it avoids the "kiss-of-death" stigma that accompanies such labels as "alcoholism program" and so on. Second, it draws no line concerning aid possibilities and goes into very personal issues other companies have long shied nervously away from:

> In doing his job, Jones [the Director] has arranged the transfer of an employee embroiled in a wife-swapping arrangement with a fellow worker. He has reassured an eight-year-old who was convinced, on insufficient evidence, that her father was seeing a girlfriend. He engineered the assignment of a heroin addict to the night late shift to enable him to receive

> methadone at a Salt Lake City clinic each morning. His secretary has unblushingly submitted other women's urine samples for pregnancy tests. Jones has answered 15 suicide calls, and has sat up all night with several of the would-be suicides. He has dealt with homosexuality, racial discrimination, tangled insurance claims, and even organ transplants.

Third, it zealously protects the anonymity of its employee clientele. Fourth, it eschews orthodoxy in response and makes full use of all relevant aid sources—on a custom-tailored basis. Finally, INSIGHT dares to help fill "gaps" even outside the plant gates ("Unable to reach an Indian worker afflicted with alcoholism because of the culture barrier, Jones helped organize a Salt Lake City alcoholism recovery center run by Indians. Discovering that south Salt Lake City had no mental health clinic available for INSIGHT referrals, Jones not only established one but arranged for its financing by a community action group").

Budgeted at $30,000, the four-person project has already helped twenty-three hundred employees or dependents since its July 1970 initiation. Popular with Kennecott's nineteen unions, INSIGHT is credited with a 44 per cent drop in absenteeism, among other valued gains. Perhaps most revealing is the recent announcement by the Pacific Telephone and Telegraph Company that its evaluation of Kennecott's project (now expanded to a New Mexico site, as well) has led it to begin an INSIGHT program for its twenty-one thousand employees at its San Francisco main facilities.[21]

Much is at stake here—creativity in identifying problems and the ways to solve them; employee protection; and flexibility and dynamism in approach, as well as hard-nosed economy in operations and incontrovertible results. It remains to be seen how many corporations will find the courage to leave well-ploughed (if underproductive) personnel department pathways for this exciting new direction in corporate social well-being.

Summary

Perhaps all of the reforms discussed in this chapter could be cautiously drawn together under the label "self-government." Most of our corporations (including "second cousins" like universities and labor unions) are currently despotisms, more or less benevolent depending on the tolerance of their "absentee" or acquiescing "ruling class" (comparable in irresponsibility to absentee slum landlords and absentee stockholders, or those who ignore value-laden proxy fights). From virtually all such corporations, and judged at least by social critic W. H. Ferry, "emanates a heavy whiff of the medieval barony, with the hierarchy of vassalage well-marked and understood."

Ferry urges the modern corporation to open itself to new experiments in genuine self-rule:

> It is no good to say that the constituents of a corporation have not the capacity, since these constituents demonstrably have the capacity, as citizens, to govern the most powerful of nations. It is no good to say that the constituents are not interested, for indeed they are, since the corporation is where they spend the bulk of their waking hours, where they invest their

> sweat and their hopes, where they experience pleasure or lassitude, justice or injustice, achievement or ennui.
>
> It is no good to say that self-government will not work, for it has seldom been tried. Even in the small-scale experiments in this direction success has more often been the result than failure. I am aware of the declaration by economists and political scientists that corporations must be undemocratic. This is because, they say, the quest for efficiency cannot be carried on except by decisions at the top based on total information about markets, processes, and costs. These arguments are old and respectable, and I challenge them. No one knows whether they are true because no one has tried to find out. In any event, the assertion that men can collectively make the judgments for a nation but not for a smaller political entity is a travesty of logic, to say nothing of a slur on the democratic doctrine.

The main reason for self-government, Ferry contends, is that men are entitled to a voice in the affairs that touch them daily and intimately.

There is even a little bit of evidence, he adds later, that self-government might prove efficient. When employees have been allowed to set their own conditions of work, they have not ordinarily come up with a counsel of anarchy. Production and standards have been met and a good time had by all:

> The having of a good time by all is not an incidental consideration. It is near the heart of the case. Aside from the privileged few, there are not many who find joy, self-expression, or freedom in their offices and factories. A man is not free unless he is free to do his best, and this is a condition seldom encountered. Business and industry are not organized with this thought in mind. R. H. Tawney said: "Since even quite common men have souls, no increase of material wealth will compensate them for arrangements which insult their self-respect and impair their freedom."

If life at work, Ferry concludes, "cannot be made enjoyable, let it at least be interesting. This is a legitimate aim of democratic participation."[22]

Interesting? What sorts of things might that include in a corporation characterized by self-government? Would you believe a quality of organization that makes it quite natural for a colleague to write to the corporate president "a top-secret epistle" beginning along these lines:

> Dear Jefe de Oro: With regard to your latest pronunciamento, if you say so, it will be my hourly concern to make it so. But before I sally forth in service of this your latest cause, I must tell you with deep affection and respect that you're full of shit again . . . etc., etc.[23]

Or, an organizational climate compatible with the notion of adding a poet to the corporate staff? The editor of a poetry journal recently put the matter quite directly to the editors of the *Wall Street Journal:*

> Have you ever considered the good some poets could do in the boardrooms of American business? You mention approvingly that poets have gifts for expressing passion, emotion and imagination. Did it ever dawn on American business that those qualities, applied to their activities, might yield very

tangible results—the kinds that can be cost-benefit analyzed in the modes so dear to the hearts of people who believe that what can't be measured doesn't exist?

At the moment, American corporations are spending millions of dollars to read the public pulse, check the public's motivations, discover new life styles (it's called "market research"), figure out what it means to be a citizen in a democracy (called "community relations" or "urban affairs"), when all those could have been done for them at a tiny fraction of the cost if they would have employed a really competent radar scanner: a poet.

Corporations spend foolish millions to find out that people are often bored, lonely, alienated and want to live in a lot of varied ways—and then after they've spent millions to discover that, they don't know what to do with the information once they've got it. I respectfully suggest to your business readers that the poet may have useful function not only on space trips, but in the boardroom as well.

When modern corporate boards of directors were forced to deal with minorities and women, the door to humanity was forced open a small crack. They ought to open it further and have poets as members; that way they could get a reading on the whole human race.

William Packard
Editor
The New York Quarterly[24]

Overall, then, what we are after is an organizational climate that is created around people and our need to grow in our work. Management specialist Douglas McGregor recommends an "agricultural" approach: provide the climate and proper nourishment, and let the people grow themselves.[25]

FOOTNOTES

1. Nicholas Johnson, *Test Pattern for Living* (New York: Bantam, 1972), p. 121.
2. Robert Townsend, *Up the Organization: How to Stop the Corporation from Stifling People and Strangling Profits* (Greenwich, Conn.: Fawcett, 1970), pp. 67–68.
3. Peter Drucker, *The Age of Discontinuity* (London: Heinemann, 1969), pp. 248–260.
4. Michael Harrington, *Toward a Democratic Left* (New York: Macmillan, Inc., 1968), pp. 147–150.
5. Marcus G. Raskin, *Being and Doing* (New York: Random, 1971), pp. 328–330.
6. Mike Ambrose et al., "The Condition of the Federal Employee and How to Change It," *The Washington Monthly* (June 1969), pp. 53–59.
7. Ralph Nader et al., *Whistle-Blowing* (New York: Bantam, 1972), p. 5.
8. Kenneth Lasson, *The Workers* (New York: Bantam, 1973), p. 4.
9. Nader et al., op. cit., p. 4.
10. Ibid., p. 15.
11. Ibid., p. 31.
12. Ibid., p. 33.
13. Ibid., p. 24.
14. Ibid. See also Townsend, op. cit.
15. Nader et al., op. cit., p. 243.
16. Ibid., p. 7.

17. "Underground Papers Needle the Bosses," *Business Week* (October 9, 1971), pp. 86, 88.
18. "Motorola Blocks Health Cost Rise," *New York Times* (January 28, 1973), p. 59. See also Nicholas von Hoffman, "In the Pink of Health (and in the Black) in Phoenix," *Washington Post* (October 6, 1972), p. C-1.
19. "Letting Workers Let Off Steam," *Business World* (April 28, 1973), p. 112.
20. Townsend, op. cit., p. 126.
21. "He Cures Kennecott's People Problems," *Business Week* (April 15, 1972), p. 32. See also Jack Gordon, "'Do Gooder' in Action," *New York Times* (May 2, 1971), p. E-6.
22. W. H. Ferry, "The Corporation for Good as Well as Gain," *The Center Magazine* (November, 1972), pp. 28–36.
23. Townsend, op. cit., p. 68.
24. Letter to Editor, *Wall Street Journal* (January 23, 1973), p. 18.
25. Douglas McGregor, *The Human Side of Enterprise* (New York: McGraw-Hill, 1960).

READING

This is a moving and encouraging account of how a group of "do-gooders" recently met a heart-wrenching, hard-nosed challenge to "do good" while making changes in their own ranks. I include it here not only for its description of some unique efforts to help humanize the workplace but also for its sensitive and imaginative response to an organizational commonplace, the need both to stay current and to be concerned about the personnel threatened by change. With adult frankness and common sense, the Detroit Industrial Mission has applied to its own reorganization the principles it exists to promote in other organizations.

Christman, Hinsberg, Russell, Terry Leave Detroit Industrial Mission

George Colman

Jesse Christman, Tom Hinsberg, Michele Russell, Bob Terry—these persons, their concerns, and their activities are DIM for many. The Mission is not the abstraction, "an agency committed to social justice." The Mission is

Michele interpreting the politics of bussing to Detroit Edison managers.
Jesse exploring the dynamics of racism with construction workers.
Tom, at Chrysler, helping foremen design more satifying jobs.

Reprinted from *Life and Work* (Vol. 14, No. 1) with permission of the Detroit Industrial Mission.

Bob and the president of Borg & Beck examining alternative affirmative action policies and debating the merits of a color-conscious versus a color-blind policy on hiring and promoting.

These four have shared in the shaping and the leadership of DIM and they are all leaving. They and the five who will continue with the Mission (Jim Campbell, George Colman, Phil Doster, Bill Sumner, and Doug White) agree that we are now in the most important and potentially most creative transition period in our sixteen-year history.

Michele Russell left the staff of DIM on November 1, 1972, in order to give more time to political organizing. Tom Hinsberg has resigned effective January 1, 1973, in order to give full attention to his work as Director of the Archdiocese Commission for World Justice and Peace. The only good thing that can be said about their departure is that they will continue as consultants to the Mission, providing leadership on certain projects as frequently as their schedules permit. A fuller recognition of our indebtedness to them will come at a later time because we want to focus primary attention here on the reasons for the departure of Jesse Christman and Bob Terry, who will leave the Mission as of January 1, 1973.

We have long recognized that we needed more black men and women on the staff to increase our effectiveness as advocated on social justice. When Michele, the only black person and the only woman on a staff of eight, announced her resignation in August 1972, our concern with the racial and sexual composition of the staff of DIM was intensified. As a result of a careful reexamination of our needs, the entire staff agreed that the number of white males had to be reduced and the number of blacks and women had to be increased. To that end, Jesse and Bob will leave DIM. The reasons for that decision begin with the purpose and character of DIM's work.

DIM's Purpose

From its beginning in 1956, DIM has been concerned with the issues that make and break life for men and women in their vocational settings. *The basic question for us is, "How can the policies of large corporations be changed so that the human good of those who must work in them and those who are affected by them is not denied but served?"* That is the issue pressed by the black community and by women in their demands for an end to exploitation and for equal opportunity to work and to earn. It is similarly the challenge of all workers, black and white, male and female, blue collar and white collar, who want to express their creativity and exercise their human powers on the job as well as off it, who want to influence their working conditions and their working relationships, who do not want to be reduced to obedient, unreflective robots coming alive only after "work."

These challenges are not going to diminish; they well up from deep national and international currents. Nor should they diminish, for they testify to real grievances and represent people's claim to freedom and fulfillment. "Equal employment opportunity," "affirmative action," and "job enrichment" are pedestrian, rather unexciting terms which point, nonetheless, to the exhilarating fact that human beings do fight against the reduction of their lives and do affirm their rich, largely unexplored, unrealized potential to create new communities committed to life enhancement.

DIM's experience in Chrysler, Hudsons, Procter & Gamble, Borg & Beck, Blue Cross, Detroit Edison, and National Cash Register is clear: corporations can respond creatively to these challenges. Corporations can develop and implement policies which reduce racism and sexism, policies which do increase workers' creativity and satisfaction, policies which do serve rather than deny human good.

For example, after an extended DIM workshop on equal employment opportunity, the managers of one company committed themselves to the creation and implementation of an affirmative action policy, elected their own representatives to a new management committee, and charged them with the responsibility to make affirmative action a reality in the corporation. In this way those who regularly hire and promote workers became primary advocates of an aggressive equal opportunity policy.

The president of another manufacturing company in Detroit recognized that in ten years the majority of his work force would be black and that he must take action now to change the all-white complexion and character of his management personnel. A conscious policy of increasing the percentage of black managers has now been adopted and training programs are being developed with DIM to help whites understand the importance and implications of that action.

"They sit around waiting for orders, they don't take initiative, and they don't work together well." A company officer was talking about white managers in his corporation and was exploring options for dealing with the problem. DIM was interested because we believe all workers, including managers, should have more power to influence their job environment, more responsibility to make decisions in the areas of their competence, more control over their work. Motivation is related to power. The former rises with the latter. Drudge jobs create drudges. DIM's current intensive work with several corporations, normally catalogued as "organizational development" or as "job enrichment," is our attempt to expand the range of human freedom, power, and responsibility inside large bureaucratic organizations.

DIM Staff Needs in Light of Our Work

"Affirmative action" to ensure equal employment opportunity is a positive response to the pressure from blacks and from women to end institutional racism and sexism; "job enrichment" to expand individual power and responsibility is a creative response to the "new work force" of all ages which opposes oppressive working conditions. DIM is committed to both as part of our response to the basic question, "How can the policies of large corporations be changed so that the human good of those who must work in them and those who are affected by them is not denied but served?"

To do this work, DIM's staff must be composed of men and women, blacks and whites. There are eight staff positions. With Michele's resignation the staff was made up of seven white men. We all agreed that composition had to be changed because blacks and women are needed to shape DIM's analysis, objectives, and programs. We do not need blacks and women simply to do what we have been doing; their perspective and initiative is needed to help shape a Mission which is more sensitive and responsive to racism and sexism in its own structure and culture as well as in the institutions with which we work.

These desired staff alterations could be achieved three ways:

1. *Expand the staff.* We rejected this option because the money is simply not available for such a move. Last year we conducted a special fund-raising drive to add more black staff and we were unsuccessful.
2. *Fill vacancies created by the resignations of white male staff.* Over the past few years the number of white male staff has been increasing, not decreasing, and no resignations were expected in the years just ahead. We concluded that this was not a real option.
3. *Reduce the white male staff from seven to five immediately, so that with Michele's resignation there would be three vacancies to be filled by blacks and women.* This was our choice and is understood as a first step, leaving to the new staff the decision as to further staff realignment.

We recognized that the decision we had to make would be particularly painful for two reasons. First, all seven men are valued, highly skilled activists, and each has made a unique contribution to the Mission. Second, our relationships are extremely close and involve friendships which, for some, span twenty-two years. Yet it was clear that we, not someone else, should make the decision. We knew our strengths and weaknesses best and believed we could engage one another in all aspects of necessary discussions with the required candor.

The process upon which we then unanimously agreed and implemented was this:

1. Each of the seven white males wrote a self-evaluation of his perspective as well as his strengths and weaknesses in these areas:
   a. Politics-values:
   Relationship between empowerment of blacks and women and your self-interest.
   Relationship between your politics and values and your work at DIM.
   b. Intellectual resources:
   Knowledge in areas of concern to the Mission.
   Capacity for intellectual work.
   c. Change skills:
   Interest and capacity for work in teams with women and blacks; in large industrial organizations with top managers and with rank and file.
   Analysis of project completed in past year.
   d. Organizational maintenance: proposal writing, fund raising, staff collaboration.
   e. Contacts in variety of public and private institutions and organizations.
   f. Personal style: patterns of personal behavior which contribute and detract from effectiveness as social justice advocate.

g. Self-development: relationship between major personal goals in year ahead and work at DIM.

2. A staff team composed of Doug White, because of his role as executive director, Michele Russell, because of her insights as a black woman into staff behavior and staff needs, and a third staff member selected by each man reviewed the self-evaluation and drafted a team evaluation. Doug White was evaluated by a team composed of Michele plus two staff members selected by the staff as a whole.
3. Each person's self-evaluation and team evaluation was then circulated to the entire staff, which met to discuss both, correcting, clarifying, and enlarging on points so that as accurate a description as possible of each man was formed.
4. We requested Dr. James Crowfoot, a member of our Board and the faculty of the University of Michigan, to serve as a consultant to us in this process and found his contribution to be invaluable.
5. The advice and counsel of the Board's Operating Committee and the black Board members was sought and obtained.

Though seven men were evaluated, the entire staff, including Michele Russell and Tom Hinsberg, participated in the process of review and decision. Throughout, we focused on the mix needed to work most effectively in the context of a new staff. The choice was not simply between individuals measured against one another but between combinations of individuals, each of whom brought certain needed strengths.

The staff needs a mix of administrators, organizational developers, trainers, designers, planners, thinkers, writers, and activists. We were therefore not choosing the five best racism seminar leaders or the five most advanced trainers on the staff; we were choosing a mixture, a blend of the skills needed in our present and future work. From the beginning of the process we were clear with one another that no individual inferiority or insufficiency was implied if we were not selected. On the contrary, we recognized that each man brought unusual strengths; that selections would involve hairline differentials; that no man brought all the skills needed; and that we were selecting a team, not five unrelated individuals.

It became clear as we proceeded that this process introduced two additional calculations. Each of us examined our desire to continue with DIM and compared the Mission as a work environment with other opportunities we could imagine. Our relative desire to stay and the opportunities for relocation were therefore considered seriously by each man as he related to the decision about the best mix of personnel for the future. It is clear that these considerations were involved in the final decision.

That final decision came after long days of careful and strenuous deliberation: Campbell, Colman, Doster, Sumner, and White would remain; Christman and Terry would leave.

Those remaining experience a profound sense of personal loss in the departure of two close friends and colleagues. Bob and Jesse experience the pain of separation and uncertainty and the confidence that their skills and commitments are needed and will be used in some as yet undefined situation. Full salaries are guaranteed through June 1973 so that an eight-month period of relocation is provided.

Looking back, we all affirm the necessity of this decision and the process used to reach it. Though we experienced more distress than anticipated, we believe that this is the price of taking responsibility for our own future rather than placing our lives in others' hands. We believe the process was a good one and commend its intentions as well as its procedures to others wrestling with the same issue. Church agencies, social-change groups, and business and industry experience the same external and internal pressure to make affirmative action a reality in their systems. We are prepared to discuss our experience more fully with those who are seriously considering making similar moves themselves.

The five of us remaining on the staff now look expectantly to the addition of three more—probably a black man, a black woman, and a white woman—as early in 1973 as possible.

We share a common commitment to a new, more just social order which will oppose racism, sexism, and alienating work. All of us are confident that the new DIM will be a stronger, surer advocate of those purposes because of the increased number of blacks and women on the staff. As our white male consciousness has been expanded and sharpened by the black movement and by women's claim to freedom, so we are certain that the corporate consciousness of the Mission will be enriched and empowered by the presence and perspective of blacks and women on the staff.

The years immediately ahead are as important as any have been in the life of the Mission; and we expect the pace of our change to accelerate, for we understand we are part of a broader movement which works to set men and women free. All of us, those leaving and those remaining, believe that the decisions described here represent a first critical step toward the creation of a new DIM better equipped to participate in that press toward freedom and fulfillment.

CHAPTER 10

Producing: Corporate Social Responsibility

What people must see is that ecologically sane, socially responsible living is *good* living; that simplicity, thrift, and reciprocity make for an existence that is free and more self-respecting.

THEODORE ROSZAK

Democracy in the long run is not viable unless its citizens recognize that there is a right way to remedy a wrong and a wrong way to secure a right.

SIDNEY HOOK

The "big question" currently disturbing the majority of political and social scientists in America, wrote critic Melville J. Ulmer in 1971, is "how to bring the corporate giants under effective democratic governmental control so that their activities may be directed toward the public interest. Or, stated another way, how to shape the policies of big business and keep it from shaping us?"[1] The question continues to perplex and answers effectively elude us. Indeed, our anxiety about controlling the behavior of our corporate juggernauts dates back at least two hundred years, to when their activities began on a serious scale. Although the tactics of big business have changed during this period, the malefactions that give us alarm have remained fairly constant: "price fixing, market division, consumer deception, exploitation of natural resources, political maneuvering for subsidies, and related giveaways, imperialistic knavery, and an irrepressible tendency to homogenize and degrade existing cultural levels."[2]

Several potential aids to corporate social responsibility are reviewed in this chapter, always with an eye toward both their previous track record and their susceptibility to subversion by the corporate giants they are supposed to help keep honest. The first, social service leave, is a glowing example of the best kind of social invention that business has recently come up with, and the second, the use of investor clout, is a promising if currently impoverished aid to the conscience of the corporation. Efforts at costing out corporate good deeds, the third reform considered, have far to go but may yet pay off handsomely for the reform cause. Corporate-crime deterrents are weighed next, along with the case for the restrictive chartering of corporations by the federal government, rather than the present, more permissive chartering by the states. Finally, attention is paid to the case that socialists make for a gradual switch from private to public forms of corporate structure. This challenge to nationalize America's "free enterprise" system closes our review of the reforms we must weigh *now*—lest giant corporations play checkers with our lives at the peril of our souls.

What does "corporate social responsibility" really amount to? A helpful guide is available in the delineation *Esquire* makes in awarding CSR advertising awards in four categories:

1. Improving society or making life more comfortable, meaningful and safe for the general public. This includes antipollution programs, social action, minority training, research and development programs designed for the benefit of the public, etc.
2. Helping the consumer to improve his own quality of life. This includes advertising which tells how to avoid diseases and accidents, how to make better use of increased leisure time or retirement, and in general how to live a better life.
3. Product advertising which best presents the benefits to the consumer of products with provable values. These may include nonpolluting features, nutrition, safety, education, etc.
4. Advertising of services which offer the consumer greater protection including readily understandable warranties backed up by service, reduction of electrical hazards, insurance policies which clearly define the benefits and limitations, clearly displayed and defined explanations of the side effects of pharmaceuticals, etc.

Esquire goes on to complain that

> the trouble is, not too many people know of business' growing responsiveness. Individually, corporations have been taking steps to clean up the environment, to promote minority job training, to improve their communities, and to produce better products and services. But for the most part, they've been doing it quietly—too quietly.[3]

An index of corporate response to social responsibility, by the way, is available in the fact that whereas only thirty of one hundred companies sampled by *Business Week* in 1970 made any mention of "concern for corporate social responsibility" in their annual reports, the figure had risen to sixty-four by 1972. Attention is paid to pollution control, minority hiring practices, and general corporate citizenship.[4] Scovill Manufacturing Company, for one, included a new "Social Action Report" in the form of a balance sheet in its 1972 annual report. Under the employment opportunities section, for example, Scovill cited as an asset an increase in minority employment from 6 per cent in 1963 to 19 per cent in 1972. Balancing this in the liabilities column is the statement that the company needs "more upgrading of minority employees into higher labor grade jobs."[5]

An example of the kinds of new roles corporations are assuming is suggested by the following April 1973 advertisement:

THE BORED OF EDUCATION NEED HELP

And Citibank has help to offer. In the past few years we've been learning a lot about why a student tunes out in high school. And we've learned it right on the premises—in the schools themselves.

It all started with the Economic Development Council—a group of leading New York corporations trying to help with some of the city's problems. Like education.

Citibank is an original member of the Council's Education Task Force. It assigned personnel from its own training division the full-time job of going back to high school. Only *this* time around not as students, but as on-the-spot consultants—looking and listening for ways to help.

And they *found* ways to help: ways to help open new lines of communication by involving parents, teachers, students—even business; ways to help teachers get a fresh perspective on their materials, themselves and their students by using some of our own management techniques. And they have applied learning methods we've used at the bank for the needs of secondary education.

We hope the things we're learning can play a part in helping solve education problems throughout the city.

If your organization would be interested in exploring ways to help improve education in New York, call EDC at 684-2300, Ext. 28, or us at 559-0917.

After all, better education will make a stronger, more productive citizen. And we at Citibank feel that's the kind of citizen New York needs more of.

NEW YORK:
WE'RE ALL IN IT TOGETHER[6]

Similarly, much can be learned from the vignettes reprinted here from a *Saturday Review* supplement on corporate responsibility:

In the opinion of many observers, *Levi Strauss,* the jeans manufacturer, ranks as the most socially progressive company in the nation. Its longtime social commitment is reflected in the fact that minorities make up one-third of its U.S. employee force and—even more impressive—10 per cent of its officials and managers and 15 per cent of its professionals. Levi's board of directors includes both a black and a woman. When Alabama's impoverished Greene County elected an all-black slate of office-holders, Levi looked at the county's economic needs and opened a plant there.

Standard Oil of Indiana used its muscle to accomplish what the federal government could not—integration in the ranks of the Chicago construction trades. In putting up its new skyscraper headquarters building on the city's lakefront, Indiana Standard insisted that minority employment goals be used in the selection of the construction work force. This resulted in construction crews with a minority representation of about one-third.

Last year, when Senator Frank E. Moss (D.–Utah) asked the top 300 companies on the *Fortune* 500 list to provide him with information on their consumer protection programs, he heard from *Maytag,* even though this appliance maker does not rank in that group. This was a typical response from a company that has pioneered in consumer service. Maytag broke with industry practice by not introducing new appliance models every year. It changes a model only when real improvements are possible. Its advertising has emphasized quality performance for more than ten years. Every Maytag product on a dealer floor has a comprehensive information tag. Warranties were rewritten in 1969 to make them easier to understand. In every major U.S. city the company has a "Red Carpet Service," under which a dealer is required to provide service within 24 hours after a customer calls.

Organized in 1965, the *Mutual Real Estate Investment Trust* functions along the lines of other real estate trusts, which have become favorite tax-shelter devices. However, M-REIT has never wavered from an uncommon policy: it buys apartment developments that are all-white—and then integrates them. That's its raison d'etre, and it has worked, both financially and socially. M-REIT's portfolio now carries 15 properties in 8 states. The book value of its property has more than doubled in the past five years to surpass $25 million. Of the $10.5 million that as been invested by shareholders, $1.5 million has been returned to them in cash distributions.[7]

Many other corporations, of course, could be cited.

Progress comes rapidly—and unevenly—with reform demands accelerating all the time. For example, the annual report of the largest commercial bank in the nation, the Bank of America, a target of social protests since 1969, captures the scene quite neatly with its changes—and the reactions to them:

In 1964, when the B. of A. was first challenged, CORE demanded the disclosure of personnel records to show the extent of minority employment. The bank refused, stating that it would never release this information to a nongovernmental agency. In 1973 the Bank of America not only released this information, it published it in detail in its annual report, covering both minority and female personnel. It was the fullest disclosure of its kind ever made in a corporate annual report. In addition, the 1972 annual report broke new ground by publishing a list of the 50 largest holdings in the bank's trust department. That was the first time this information has appeared in such detail in a bank's annual report. These actions did little to mollify the protesters of 1973. They would have been revelations to the protesters of 1964.[8]

In this same vein, it should be noted that corporate *anticipation* of problems, a major goal of reformers, has also made some encouraging strides. The 3M Company, for example, has a new staff of thirty-eight whose major assignment is to predict pollution problems and search for solutions. The 3M department annually prepares a five-year forecast on environmental matters for each of 3M's thirty divisions, complete with budget recommendations covering anticipated environmental problems and an estimated cost of their solution.[9]

Public reaction to all of these developments varies widely and includes a firm sort of realistic expectations. Typical is this "Letter to the Editor," commenting on a lofty and general statement of intent by a leading business spokesman:

To the Editor:

Congratulations to David Rockefeller for his "Essential Quest for the Middle Way" (Op-Ed March 23). As reinforcement may I suggest a few specifics toward what he calls "integrating its (capitalism's) economic and social functions," "social accountability," "making social responsibility an integral fact of corporate planning."

1. Close tax loopholes.
2. Stop fighting legislation for industrial safety, food and drug inspection, and against pollution.
3. Stop breaking the safety laws that already exist.
4. Stop poisoning food and distributing drugs.
5. Stop committing "white-collar" crimes.
6. Stop using payola to persuade legislators.
7. Stop destroying free enterprise by conglomeration and administered prices.

HENRY ZOLAN[10]
New York City

In a show of another sort of corporate responsibility, a two-hundred-unit food chain in Philadelphia pays a unique marketing firm to preread and screen pocketbooks that might otherwise be sold to child purchasers through the chain's book racks. The two business organizations rely on the judgment of paid housewife-readers to ban pocketbooks that employ "so-called four-letter words relating to sex . . . descriptions of violence . . . open advocacy of the overthrow of the government."[11] Bans, for example, were put on *Love Story, The Godfather,* and *Portnoy's Complaint,* best sellers readily available elsewhere, of course. Should the seller-as-censor idea catch on, however, the public would be called upon to consider whether their rights were being infringed on.

Reform Focus

Three particular tools in the matter of corporate responsibility merit special scrutiny, as each is prominent in the movement and, naturally, has both detractors and enthusiasts.

Social Service Leave. Social service leave is a new aid to corporate vitality and social responsibility that has already engendered considerable enthusiasm in and outside of business. The Xerox Corporation, a pioneer in this area, after screening two hundred applications from employees with more than three years' service in 1972, chose twenty-one for year-long full-salary grants. The eighteen men and three women designed welfare tasks for themselves that included developing a literacy program in Arkansas, helping Palestinian refugees, assisting elderly people, advising minority groups on business matters, and assisting low-income families in buying their own homes. Convinced that such employees returned from these experiences better trained and profoundly motivated, Xerox has since renewed the project—and urges other corporations to institute similar programs.

Similarly, since 1971 the IBM Corporation has detached a group of one hundred top professionals who have volunteered to teach in colleges with predominantly minority enrollments. IBM pays the full salaries of these people while they are on leave and in 1973 helped place twenty-five volunteers in black colleges, as well as schools serving American Indians, Mexican Americans, and residents of Appalachia.[12]

A friendly critic notes, however, that even if other enlightened business firms were to provide pools of employee talent on the same basis, the total would still be too small. The need is so great that an annual cadre of several hundred white-collarites and executives-on-loan would be absorbed without sufficient impact. Accordingly, it is suggested that the top five hundred corporations also undertake a variation on social service sabbaticals whereby they underwrite the services for state government of one senior executive per year in each state in which they have a significant facility. (If the average number of such locations for each corporation were fifteen states, some seventy-five hundred people a year would be available to state government. The sponsoring corporation, of course, would pick up the difference in salary between corporate and state paychecks.)

Why bother? The sponsor of the reform, himself a state official, contends that:

> first-hand knowledge of the working of state government is indispensable to corporate effectiveness in truly serving our citizens. . . . By making the state a laboratory for corporate executives, we not only provide skilled public servants, but we begin to bridge the knowledge and experience gap that presently exists between corporations and the states in which they do business. After a year in state government, these executives would return to their jobs not only with a new dimension of experience but with a new ease and familiarity with the legislature, the state house, and the bureaucracy whose influence on their corporate growth and profitability can be so vital. The executive and legislative branches of state government would in turn have a far better understanding of the role and nature of business.

The concept of a partnership between public and private sectors is no longer a "pious platitude," the reformer concludes. "It must become a working reality."[13]

Do-Good Funds and Raise-Hell Investors. Another approach involves combining publicity with outrage in financial ventures variously called do-good funds, conscience funds, corporate responsibility funds, or social concern funds. The four such ventures recognized by the Securities and Exchange Commission explain to potential investors that they are committed to using the prototype of the mutual fund on behalf of social change in America. Specifically, the four new funds invest in the stocks of only those companies they judge socially responsible and superior in certain areas.

Pax World Fund, Inc., for example, declines to invest in any companies that accept military contracts. The other three corporate responsibility funds stay away from polluters and look for firms with good records in civil rights, consumer, and safety areas. Typical is the effort made for the Dreyfus Third World Fund by David Bronheim, who heads their research effort, to measure social responsibility:

> Having determined that pollution control, equal opportunity, and product purity and safety would be the fund's areas of concern, Bronheim concluded that it would be meaningless to attempt to rank all of the 3,000 or so publicly traded companies. Instead, he decided to compare companies only with others in the same industry.
>
> The fund's researchers spent last spring and summer developing their procedures for eliciting and analyzing information about corporate behavior. To measure a firm's impact on the ecology, for example, they devised a system that separates an industry into its various production stages—extraction, manufacturing, transportation, etc. Bronheim's staff interviews company executives to discover their firm's performance in each of these operations. Researchers also look at information on company activities found in government documents such as the request corporations submit to obtain federal permits to discharge waste into waterways. The analysts then grade a company—usually on a scale ranging from one to twelve—on its performance in each phase of production.[14]

Those companies that are approved go on an eligible list from which a portfolio manager selects stocks for actual purchase, the theory being that someday dozens of such funds will deny millions of critical investment dollars to companies that are irresponsibly damaging the ecology, discriminating in hiring, violating consumer trust with faulty products, or profiteering in military matters.

Not surprisingly, outside financial pressure on behalf of social responsibility has a very poor record to date. The four new mutual funds have all had considerable trouble attracting investors and gaining enough assets to use as leverage for social change. Nevertheless, action of sorts has been undertaken. First Spectrum, for example, with a hundred shareholders and $250,000 in investments, bought Bohack shares and prepared and distributed to its shareholders a leaflet urging them to patronize the grocery chain—after the supermarket signed an agreement with Operation Breadbasket to hire and promote more blacks. One official of the Fund, however, concedes that it will have to grow to the $50-million or $100-million size before corporations will really pay attention to its attempts to force social changes.

Another limitation is suggested by the sharp criticism of Philip Moore, a corporate reformer who urges the more direct route of stockholder ballot challenges. "It's a head-in-the-sand approach just to build a clean portfolio," he explains, and adds, "You've got to go to the companies and raise the issue with them." With the collaboration of representatives of major religious denominations, foundations, universities, and the Project on Corporate Responsibility, Moore relies on proxy proposals and questions from the floor at the annual meeting to explore corporate investment in South Africa, minority hiring and upgrading, the broadening of the membership of boards of directors, and the disclosure of military contract business, political contributions, and lobbying activities.

In response to Moore's sort of criticism one fund manager snaps back, "Our aim is to be an effective force—not a pain in the ass." And another points to the failure of Moore's own recent efforts to rally stockholder support:

> At Ford, for example, only one per cent of the stock was voted in 1972 in favor of a Project on Corporate Responsibility proposal for minority representation on the Ford board. Only 1.6 per cent voted for a proposal calling for more specific Ford disclosure on minority hiring, air pollution control and safety devices, and spending in those areas. At the General Motors Corporation meeting a proposal for more information on the company's controversial role in South Africa received only 2.34 per cent of the stockholder vote, with other parallel proposals getting even less.[15]

To which the activists rejoin that winning isn't everything. Even though proxy proposals dealing with social responsibility draw only nominal support, they are still considered an effective tool for getting a vital message across. "Proxy proposals," insists a staffer of the Project for Corporate Responsibility, "have an enormous educational value for shareholders and the public. They keep pressure on, and there has been a lot of reexamination by management because of them."[16] As an example, the recent proxy-fight pressure on GM produced enough publicity so that it placed a black on its board and established a corporate council on social policy. Getting the last word, however, critics sarcastically suggest that token responses by management, substantial corporate public relations and political expenditures, and the sheer resources and staying power of the large corporations will nullify and ultimately render ineffective such reformist efforts.

At the same time, it can be said for the less direct corporate-responsibility-fund approach that the final verdict is still not in. Indeed, new developments come to light with impressive regularity:

> The Field Foundation in New York has submitted three proposals to Pittston Co. One requests that Pittston make periodic reports on how it is compensating victims of a West Virginia flash flood early last year, caused by the collapse of a dam owned by Pittston's Buffalo Mining Co. A second proposal would create a public policy committee to work on mine safety and ecology measures. The third asks the company to report the proceedings of each annual meeting to all shareholders. When representatives of the Field Foundation asked for a flood-victim accounting from Pittston at last year's meeting, it marked one of the first forays of a foundation into the social responsibility fray. And Field still is the only foundation challenging a company whose shares it holds.
>
> Harvard University President Derek Bok wrote some 100 universities, foundations, and other institutional investors, asking if they would be interested in setting up a research group to gather facts on corporate-responsibility proxy contests. The response led to the formation of Investor Responsibility Research, Inc. The 50 institutions that support IRRI include universities,

> foundations, banks, mutual insurance companies. So far, the Washington-based group has issued reports on South African investment and equal employment opportunity for its subscriber list. When the proxy season is over, IRRI will launch a series on such topics as strip mining, nuclear power safety, and employment for women. The reports analyze the issues, without attempting to side with one group or another.[17]

It is true, nevertheless, that the pressure-in-investment approach may require *millions* of like-minded, socially concerned investors before it has the impact enthusiasts desire . . . and hard-nosed critics never expect to see.

According to Milton Moskowitz,[18] two possibilities remain open. The first is that eventually the social responsibility funds will dramatically outgain the mutual funds that invest in socially irresponsible corporations and will, as a result, naturally attract more investors.

A *Socially Responsible Firms*	*B* *Socially Irresponsible Firms*
CNA Financial	American Brands
Cummins Engine	American Can
First Pennsylvania	American Home Products
Johnson Products	Bethlehem Steel
Levi Strauss	Colgate-Palmolive
Lowe's Companies	E. I. duPont
McGraw-Hill	Farah Manufacturing
Quaker Oats	Federal Mogul
Rouse Company	Great Atlantic and Pacific
Standard Oil (Indiana)	Kraft Co
Syntex	Standard Oil of California
Weyerhaeuser	Texaco
Whirlpool	U.S. Steel
Xerox	

Or, with or without this happy development (Moskowitz "harbors the suspicion that a socially-insensitive management will eventually make enough mistakes to play havoc with the bottom line"), change may still come from the campus: college students may begin to put pressure on campus endowment managers to look at "what" as well as "how" a company is doing—with startling results.

Costing Out Corporate Good Deeds. Finally, new efforts at costing out the corporate social conscience are being hailed as a coming answer to hard-boiled critics of employee "coddling."

One such technique, human resources accounting, was designed by its developer, Rensis Likert, to help corporations assign dollar estimates in answer to such questions as:

1. Do a company's employees think they have a say in how they do their jobs?

2. To what extent do its employees think they have a say in how they do their jobs?
3. Has a company's decision-making process improved or gotten worse?
4. Are its performance goals higher now than a year ago?

Dr. Likert contends that in measuring the value of its assets, a corporation should place a monetary value on its personnel. Answers to the questions posed help put such a dollar value on changes in a company's personnel climate.

These variable factors, Likert contends, have a significant relationship to a company's productivity and financial performance. The practice of ignoring them in the annual report is extremely counterproductive:

> To illustrate his latest twist in human resources accounting, Likert cites the case of a chemical plant with severe cost problems. The management fired 200 of its 600 employees and saved $250,000 a year in direct labor costs without an immediate loss in output. Likert had conducted employee attitude surveys in the plant before the cutback. When Likert surveyed attitudes after the cuts occurred, he found conditions even worse than before. "The excessive manpower in those departments was a symptom of poor management," Likert recalls. "The top officials simply treated the symptoms while the basic problems got worse—poor communication, distrust of management, and high absenteeism."
>
> Tapping the Institute of Social Research data bank, Likert estimated the value of the plant's human resource organization had decreased by $1-million because of wildcat strikes, equipment sabotage, and quality product deterioration. Likert contends this was a clear case of achieving short-run improvements by methods that reduced productive capability.

Much more to his liking are pioneering moves such as that of an Ohio shoe company that lists training and development costs as an investment rather than an expense. Ever the optimist, Likert explains that "there will be an awful lot of people we won't convince. But remember that cost accounting took more than five years to gain acceptance."[19]

A second promising technique is the corporate social audit, a very primitive effort by corporations to measure their performance in areas of social responsibility or at least to assess the true costs of such activities. Specialists in the matter recommend a four-step social audit:

> First, the company would make an inventory of its activities that have a social impact; then it would explain the circumstances that led up to these activities; next there would be an informal evaluation of those programs that are most relevant, perhaps by an outside expert; and finally, the company would assess the ways in which these social programs mesh with the objects both of the firm itself and of society.

Special stress is placed on the notion of intelligibility of results, lest the social audit merely replace mystery with meaningless numerical wizardry.

Resistance comes especially from the lower echelons of the large and lively companies that are experimenting with the tool:

> The process and outcome of the audit might take up their time and disturb regular operations; expose deep political and philosophic differences within the firm; usurp prerogatives (who has the right to see personnel files?); create anxiety that new standards of evaluation are suddenly being applied; stimulate debate over tough issues like who should see the data; and reveal findings that may prove embarrassing if exposed to the public either deliberately or unintentionally. . . . In some decentralized companies it seems to smack of "headquarters" meddling and kibitzing.

Despite such objections, interest remains high as more and more companies try to "measure the immeasurable," that is, the impact of social programs in terms of costs, benefits, performance, and even profits. (One company is already evaluating its executives on social performance as well as on financial results. Executives do not get bonuses unless they are performing up to standard on such things as minority hiring).[20]

A provocative variation on the corporate social audit takes the form of a never-ending survey of public wishes concerning desirable corporation activities, a so-called social audit proposed by a well-known motivational researcher. "What business needs is a price list for action," Dr. Burleigh B. Gardner explains. He urges the development of a scientific survey, probably by regions, to feed back to management sponsors up-to-date news about changing public priorities in social needs. His version of a "social audit," although leaving management free to do as it will, can help the responsive corporation "know what kind of social credit—what kind of value judgement—you use in looking at alternate courses of action. . . . [For] when you talk about social responsibility, it's a moving target."[21]

Are human resources accounting and the internal social audit real and permanent? Or are they flash-in-the-pan, incidental PR gimmickry? Only as you and I, the corporate employees or the concerned outsiders, cast our vote—emphatically—will the issue soon be resolved . . . with far more than the "souls" of inanimate corporations being at stake.

Voluntarism or Nationalization?

In many important ways this puzzle of how to make the corporation healthy "for women and children and other living things" boils down to a question of confidence and conviction. Either you believe that the corporation can and will reform by itself, whatever the motivation (to stay ahead of the law, to check public interest in harsher laws, and so on), or you do not. If you are of this latter persuasion you confront the dilemma of constructive alternatives to "free enterprise," three of which—criminal penalties, the federal chartering of private corporations, and the nationalization of formerly private corporations—are explored here.

Criminal Penalties. If we would nurture corporate social responsibility perhaps we must pay new attention to corporate crime, a concept so long neglected that you cannot find it defined in legal dictionaries, listed in statistical reports on crime, or even mentioned in the criminal index to the laws of the United States.

Corporation theft means excessive price increases, shoddy products, shortcuts on health and safety requirements, or the diversion of funds from the public purse. For many businesses, penalties for violations of the law, whether of the tax code, the safety laws pertaining to employees or customers, building codes, or pollution laws, are simply another cost of "doing business." Typical is the $1-million fine paid by Chevron Oil Company in 1972 for violation of offshore antipollution laws:

> The financial statement of Standard Oil of California, Chevron's parent, shows that the fine was about .03 per cent of the company's gross income (about the same as a $10 traffic ticket for a person making $25,000 a year). The attorney's fees for defending the case are tax deductible, maybe even the fine itself.

The whole affair, understandably, was a bit sticky for the public relations of both oil companies, but the memory of it has faded, and Chevron executives "are not likely to be spurned for future jobs because of their criminal connections."

How much does corporate crime cost us? An official at the Department of Justice estimates that the cost to taxpayers for reported and unreported violations of the federal corporate regulatory statutes is $10 billion to $20 billion a year. The Internal Revenue Service contends that about $1.2 billion in taxes is unreported under the corporate income tax laws. And Senator Philip A. Hart has estimated, as a result of investigation by his Judiciary Subcommittee on Antitrust and Monopoly, that the cost to the consumer of faulty goods, monopolistic practices, and other criminal corporate acts is between $174 billion and $231 billion annually.

What can be done? Possible reforms would compel a corporation to pay the prosecution's legal costs when companies seek to overwhelm federal or state prosecutors with frivolous and costly legal tactics. Corporate repeaters could also be required to report all criminal indictments in their annual shareholders' reports, in filings with the SEC, and perhaps even in certain advertisements. Congress could impose criminal penalties—jail sentences, probation, and other restraints—on corporate officials who direct the corporation's policy in acts that violate the law. Attorney Sarah Carey, author of these ideas, goes on to suggest that it might be helpful as well to increase penalties for repeaters by imposing super fines for major violations or by barring a person from any corporate office if his management decisions have led to more than one conviction for a corporate crime.

Finally, perhaps the "death penalty" should be applied to corporate-crime regulars. If a company is found guilty of certain crimes or is certified as a repeater, then it would be required to sell its assets and have its charter revoked. Congress has already built in the death penalty for certain foundations, lawyer Carey reminds us; it and the states could do the same for criminal corporations. Alternatively, the death penalty could be applied to managers and boards of directors by requiring the stockholders to fire them and find law-abiding replacements.[22]

Federal Chartering of Corporations. There is a growing school of thought that insists that even the controls suggested by Sarah Carey will not suffice, that a far more radical effort is required to compel corporations to "do good":

> The basic drift of corporate policy is fixed by the joint interest of management and the stockholders in increasing earnings per share and raising the market value of the company's outstanding stock. These objectives are a central component of the ethos of the corporate community; they are the primary criteria for evaluating management performance; and their adequate fulfillment remains a necessity for obtaining full approval of the management by owners and lenders. Substantial and permanent change, and even major reform, in corporate behavior and in patterns of corporate expansion is therefore extremely unlikely to occur without an attack that strikes at the underlying structure of control and incentives. This will require a major political movement—one that does not now exist and that may or may not be helped into being by the present schemes for encouraging or forcing "corporate responsibility."[23]

What form this political movement might constructively take remains an open—and very contentious—question.

Support exists, however, for an idea as old as James Madison's advocacy of it in 1787, a reform that entails the *federal* rather than the state chartering of giant corporations, to achieve strengthened corporate accountability. To control national power, it is argued, requires at least national authority ("General Motors, with ninety times Delaware's general revenues, could buy Delaware—if Du Pont were willing to sell it"). In other federal systems—German, Mexican, Brazilian—firms that do business between the states or provinces must be formed under federal law, and we could follow suit if we are serious about redirecting our corporations.

In what direction? What is needed, contends sponsor Ralph Nader, is not a corporate "bill of rights" but a corporate "bill of obligations." It might include such provisions as these:

1. Greatly enlarged disclosure requirements, forcing corporations to divulge facts and figures with regard to antipollution expenditures, racial distribution of employees, and so on.
2. Public representatives on boards of directors, chosen to represent various constituencies such as suppliers, customers, workers, or simply the public at large.
3. Stiffer penalties for violation of laws that protect the consumer or the environment, with penalties that include the suspension of irresponsible executives.
4. The required appointment of corporate officials charged with responsibility for assuring the compliance of their companies with existing legislation.
5. Cumulative voting of shares, so that small share owners, who now can cast no more than one vote for or against *each* director, may concentrate all their voting power for or against one director.

6. Full availability of corporate income tax returns for public inspection.
7. Imposition of involuntary "social bankruptcy" for corporations that have failed consistently to abide by existing legislation.
8. Protection of the rights of corporate employees against corporate retaliation for public testimony with regard to acts of the corporation.

Especially at issue is the ability of a federal corporate charter to "constitutionalize" the corporation. The Fourth Amendment, for example, if finally applied to life inside the organization, would prohibit a company from searching an employee's private belongings at work (a not uncommon practice in these days of corporate antidrug hysteria) without a search warrant.

Hovering over all of these provisions, Nader explains, would be graduated penalties for violation of the federal charter. Unlike the meaningless penalties imposed by the states, federal penalties could run from small absolute fines to fines as a percentage of sales; from management reorganization to executive suspensions; from public trusteeship to the dissolution of the charter.[24]

Does the charter campaign have a ghost of a chance? Possibly, if we take into account the fact that 77 per cent of a 1973 Harris Poll said they wanted the federal government to take a hard line toward business.[25] A 60 per cent majority of Americans surveyed by Opinion Research Corporation in 1973 expressed "low" approval of business, leading that polling company to warn its business clients that "if, by word and deed, business cannot dispel public mistrust, further government intervention is certain."[26]

Economist Robert L. Heilbroner is optimistic, but with revealing reservations:

> It seems highly probable that we will move toward a considerably stricter legal framework for corporate behavior within the next decade, particularly if the accumulation of social problems turns us, at the polls, in the direction of a New Deal.
>
> What is perhaps a more sobering question is the difference that such laws could make. The absorption of the regulatory agencies by the corporate sector gives us good reason to regard the lasting effects of these changes as considerably less than their initial impact. . . . The stiffer penalties, the personal liability, the Federal law of incorporation will weed out the more outrageous cases of wrongdoing but will leave the normal run of corporate life much undisturbed, although no doubt somewhat more circumspect.[27]

To which Nader rejoins,

> it would be defeatist and irresponsible to urge no more federal reform measures because some have failed. . . . a new federal agency is a necessary but not a sufficient remedy. If it is badly organized with weak powers and no citizen access and participation, it will be ineffective. The form is crucial, and so are the powers. But most crucial of all is the effort—one required by the current state of corporate inaccountability.[28]

Nationalization. Exactly *what* form "the effort" should take remains an open question, of course, and some reformers are persuaded that only if we "go the distance" will we secure Nader's goals, escape Heilbroner's "sand-traps," and really assure ourselves a *full* measure of corporate social responsibility. The prescription of these reformers is the nationalization of American industry, soon and in earnest. As they reason, we have no choice but to insist on a governmental take-over of our private corporations:

> Essentially because . . . private ownership, under the dynamic conditions of capitalism, constitutes a direct barrier to the widest possible self-direction of man. A society in which less than 2 per cent of all family units own some 80 per cent of its corporate assets is, from the standpoint of a philosophy that seeks the widest possible individual autonomy, as anachronistic and indefensible as the societies of feudalism or antiquity, where tiny fractions of the population enjoyed the privileges of their social orders.[29]

This advocacy by socialists of public ownership, albeit rife with immense problems of administration and bureaucracy, is plainly worth our open-minded and thoughtful assessment.

What is proposed is not a sudden, wholesale take-over by the state but a steady, long-term process progressively abolishing private decisions in favor of a democratic direction of enterprise. It is argued, for example, that:

1. The right to locate or relocate a plant in a given area can no longer be conceded to be a private matter, for regional planning requires that the geography of employment be publicly determined.
2. The right to set profit goals can no longer be conceded to be a private matter, for government cannot trust to the good conscience of the corporation.

What is proposed is a gradual "buying into" corporate control on behalf of the government (the people).

American socialists are sensitive, of course, to the question "Why bother?"—as the socialist parties of Western Europe have recently abandoned their once-sacrosanct insistence upon social ownership and now dismiss the classic case for nationalization as irrelevant. Instead, they put their trust in the rational, plan-oriented, professional managers who have recently taken over from anachronistic "robber-baron" capitalists. These new-style executives are judged to be smart enough to identify their best interests with observing the broad priorities of the European socialist states. At the same time, the government claims prerogatives sufficient to promote the kind of full-employment policies that yield a growing fund for social welfare spending.

This projected "honeymoon" of calculating private enterprise managers and a bountiful and tolerant socialist government leaves Michael Harrington and other American socialists unconvinced. They distrust the European socialist notion of the state's programming a market economy with social goals, and they cite two particular explanations of their preference for the older model of public control over management:

> First . . . the recent experience of the Continental social democrats confirms the tendency of the corporations to try to dominate, rather than obey, the government that is supposed to be controlling them.
>
> And second, it is now possible to have a relatively painless transition to social ownership.[30]

This latter point—or our new-found ability to nationalize in a very practical, unapocalyptic way—cannot be overestimated in an explanation of why American socialists persist in their advocacy of nationalization.

Just how might a state take-over of private industry be achieved—relatively painlessly? The mechanics of this reform are intriguing. Structural changes under consideration include:

1. Abolishing the voting rights of all speculative, short-term shareholders; this would make it clear that many of the transactions on the stock market are nothing but a socially-approved form of gambling—and an enormous waste of resources and energy in a parasitic operation without real economic function.
2. Instituting the right of the Government to act as if it were the majority stockholder in all major industries, but without taking legal title; when private egotism leads to antisocial behavior, the Government would see to a change.
3. Adopting a confiscatory tax on the stock holdings of the rich, as through prohibitions on large inheritances.
4. Establishing a government investment bank as the recipient of the stock paid as a death duty, and also of the savings of the workers.
5. Controlling profits through selective price and wage controls in an inflationary period; requiring big companies to open up their books and justify any increase in process before an independent board; and using a vigorous tax policy.[31]

None of these changes alonc means enough. They come into their own, it is argued, only as interrelated parts of a gradually unfolding, and therefore politically tenable, comprehensive policy aimed at steadily reducing the rights of private property in the means of production.

Will it work, this reform of nationalization? American socialists contend that we have a sparkling model in the Tennessee Valley Authority of what a public corporation (one of several nationalization possibilities) can accomplish. Like a private corporation the TVA is able to accumulate capital for future investment out of present income. It is therefore free of the constraints of the money market, and like the corporate "big boys" (GM, GE, the *Fortune* 500, etc.) it enjoys an unlimited capacity for future growth. Unlike them, however, the TVA is directly under the broad supervision of the federal government. Far more efficient than its private competitors, the TVA galls many American conservatives who disdain its crisp demonstration of the considerable merits of a governmentally chartered and socially concerned enterprise.

It is the proud TVA, then, rather than our anarchic Postal Service, that American socialists insist we consider as a model of the public corporation. They also disparage the degeneration of principles represented by the Port of New York Authority, a second-rate public corporation, for its ill-advised independence from effective democratic control has apparently allowed it to misuse its resources for increasing pollution, for snubbing local political wishes, and other antisocial behavior.

John Kenneth Galbraith, a leading liberal economist, parts with the socialist blueprint at precisely this point. He warns that if the socialist state tries to exercise too close a control over a TVA, PNYA, or Postal Service type of organization, it almost guarantees waste and incompetence. But if it grants the right to independent action, these public corporations will find it hard not to follow their own plans rather than those of outside political authorities.[32]

Harrington and others soberly concede the very real risks involved (inefficiency, dullness, poor service, and so on). They accompany this concession, however, with a fervid insistence that such risks are preferable to the alternative of leaving the corporate state in its present irresponsible form:

> There are, in short, no "perfect" solutions to these enormous problems, and any intelligent person can foresee difficulties in any proposal. Nevertheless, the public corporation with both the right to internal financing and the responsibility to democratically elected representatives of the people is, with all the problems admitted, a right step in the best direction.[33]

Perhaps. Though as keen a critic of corporate irresponsibility as economist Robert Heilbroner gently but firmly demurs,

> I feel that as a general prescription for assuring a high level of responsible performance, nationalization is not a cure-all. . . . nationalized corporations also pollute the environment, abuse authority, create impenetrable bureaucracies, exploit workers, defy public opinion, and generally misbehave.[34]

Although conceding this point, socialists might insist that more *potential* well-being inheres in the public than in the private form of corporate structure . . . this being finally a proposition for *you* to decide. Keep carefully in mind, as you weigh the case, Heilbroner's closing admonition: "The cause of reform, not to mention that of constructive revolution, is too important to be nurtured on anything but the truth."[35]

Summary

If we are to have corporations worth their salt, accomplishments like these will be necessary:

> In 1968, only one major corporation had a black man or woman on its board of directors. By 1971, the figure was 25, and rising.
>
> Since 1968, corporations have doubled the portion of their bank deposits they assign to minority-owned financial institutions.
>
> Special hiring programs, spurred by the National Alliance of Businessmen, have brought millions of minority workers into the labor force.
>
> Plant relocation is being used on behalf of social change: Quaker Oats, for example, told the city of Danville, Illinois, that it would be favorably disposed to putting a pet foods plant there if the town passed a fair housing ordinance; the town did—and got its plant. IBM has exerted similar leverage in Lexington, Kentucky, and in other places where it has large facilities.
>
> In hot water, along with many other companies, because of its presence in South Africa, the Polaroid Corporation instituted a program to increase the

> opportunities open to blacks in South Africa and then invited other U.S. corporations to join it in this experiment. The invitation came in a full-page advertisement which Polaroid placed in newspapers across the country. The ad served notice to the South African government that Polaroid can continue to do business there only by fighting the apartheid system which rigidly segregates whites from blacks. It was the first time that a U.S. Corporation publicly pledged its opposition to the political policy of a foreign government.[36]

These examples are taken by Milton Moskowitz, a specialist in corporate involvement, to demonstrate that "social responsibility is compatible with profitability, and moreover, that responsible corporate behavior is simply good business."[37]

At the same time, however, this same author adds:

> Two dozen distinguished black citizens did not suddenly become qualified for board of director seats in 1971. Instead, corporations realized that their future was inextricably entwined with the future of the entire society, and they removed some of their blinders. There are, unfortunately, a great many blinders left.[38]

Similarly, in the related matter of the *internal* world of the organization (as the previous chapter made clear) the blinders are numerous and comparably costly.

Nevertheless, conservative economist Milton Friedman is very impatient with today's advocacy of corporate social responsibility, a "fundamental subversive doctrine" in a free society. In such a society:

> there is one and only one social responsibility of business—to use its resources and engage in activities designed to increase its profits so long as it stays within the rules of the game, which is to say, engages in open and free competition without deception and fraud.[39]

To advocate any other version of corporate social responsibility, says Daniel Sisson, is to "preach pure and unadulturated socialism. Businessmen who talk this way are unwitting puppets of the intellectual forces that have been undermining the basis of a free society these past decades."[40]

At the same time a new book of scholarly musings on our American future includes these expectations:

> A general invasion of public policy arenas will accompany the growth of neocorporatism as business firms provide more and more of the services once reserved to government.
>
> The increasing spread of computers will enhance the manipulative powers of the establishment.
>
> The emphasis on liberty is likely to change from "negative" liberty to "positive" liberty.
>
> We will have to supplant the Protestant Ethic with a less exploitative view of nature; a post industrial ethic will be required.[41]

Corporate social responsibility, anyone?

We are sharply challenged, then, to earn soon an exemplary kind of corporate maturity, with both internal self-government and external social responsibility, from the American business system. For as economist Robert L. Heilbroner points out, we have dilemmas we haven't yet begun to acknowledge, much less resolve:

> Ahead lies a series of much more difficult problems, many of them not even on the agenda of the reformers, much less the corporations. There is the problem of the tedium of much work, both in the factory and in the office. There is the problem of the corporate role in promoting or selecting technological change itself. To these challenges, more complex and more subversive by far than those to which the current reforms are addressed, there are as yet no proposals for corporate responsibility. But their time will come, once the present problems begin to yield to the efforts that are now being mounted against them.[42]

We must also add to the agenda the extraordinary challenge in control posed by the global corporation or multinational enterprise. For in the opinion of some specialists, when we in the United States encourage, assist, and support our global corporations, insisting that what they do is the basis for universal progress, we defeat the efforts of other countries seeking to improve their conditions of life, and we invite retaliation: "Allowing the multinationals (like ITT) to seek their own best interests, without regard to who must bear the burden, is to accept domination by the mechanical mind of the capital accumulators."[43]

Our agenda, then, is impressive, even somewhat overwhelming—what with reformers expecting more from American business institutions than ever before in our history:

> the new demand is . . . a demand that business and businessmen make concern for society central to the conduct of business itself. It is a demand that the quality of life become the business of business. The traditional approach asks: How can we arrange the making of cars (or of shoes) so as not to impinge on social values and beliefs, on individuals and their freedom, and on the good society altogether? The new demand is for business to make social values and beliefs, create freedom for the individual, and altogether produce the good society.[44]

Specifically, this chapter asks us to pay attention to democratizing the workplace, promoting corporate social responsibility, facilitating whistle blowing, aiding a free press, and weighing the case for more voluntarism against a switch over to intense federal control or even nationalization. Add to this the three social problems listed by Heilbroner and the serious matter of reining in "runaway" multinationals, and the urge to roll up one's sleeves and "dig in" is very strong indeed.

It is as well, accordingly, to close with a constructive reminder from Robert Townsend, lest our eagerness carry us too quickly beyond our craft: "If you don't do it excellently, don't do it at all. Because if it's not excellent it won't be profitable or fun, and if you're not in business for fun or profit, what the hell are you doing here?"[45]

FOOTNOTES

1. Melville J. Ulmer, "The Corporate Snare," *New Republic* (September 18, 1971), p. 13.
2. Ibid.
3. Advertisement, *New York Times* (March 6, 1973), p. 39.
4. "The Annual Report Becomes a Confession," *Business Week* (April 21, 1973), p. 44.
5. Ibid., p. 46.
6. Advertisement published by First National City Bank in the *New York Times* (April 25, 1973), p. 12.
7. "Kudos for Conscience," *Saturday Review* (April 1973), p. 60.
8. Milton Moskowitz, "The Greening of the Bank of America," *Saturday Review* (April 1973), p. 57.
9. Douglas W. Gray, "The New Environmental Executives," *New York Times* (March 18, 1973), p. F-14.
10. *New York Times* (April 14, 1973), p. 33.
11. Trudy Prokop, "Screening Service Guides Chain on Selling Books," *The Philadelphia Inquirer* (September 30, 1972), p. 14.
12. "Kudos for Conscience," *Saturday Review*, op. cit., p. 60.
13. Dan W. Lufkin, "Exchange Students," *New York Times* (August 5, 1972), p. 25.
14. Harvey Shapiro, "Wall Street's New 'Social Responsibility' Funds," *Saturday Review* (August 26, 1972), p. 45.
15. Les Gapay, "Mutual Funds and Social Conscience," *The Progressive* (March 1973), pp. 40–43.
16. Ibid.
17. "Activists Step Up Their Annual Attacks," *Business Week* (March 31, 1973), p. 76.
18. Milton Moskowitz, "Why 'Good Guy' Funds Have Flopped," *New York Times* (February 11, 1973), p. F-15.
19. "A New Twist to 'People Accounting,'" *Business Week* (October 21, 1972), p. 68.
20. "The First Attempts at a Corporate 'Social Audit,'" *Business Week* (September 23, 1973), pp. 88–92.
21. Martin J. Siroka, "Business 'Must Respond to Social Action,'" *Philadelphia Inquirer* (September 15, 1972), p. 26.
22. Sarah Carey, "America's Respectable Crime Problems," *The Washington Monthly* (April 1971), pp. 44–54.
23. Edward Herman, "Greening of the Board of Directors?" *Social Policy* (November–December 1972 and January–February 1973), p. 63.
24. Ralph Nader and Mark Green, "The Case for Federal Charters," *The Nation* (February 5, 1973), pp. 173–175. See also Ralph Nader, "Chartering Corporations," *The New Republic* (March 11, 1972), p. 9.
25. Louis Harris, "Tougher Regulation of Business Backed," *Philadelphia Inquirer* (February 5, 1973), p. 2-C.
26. "America's Growing Antibusiness Mood," *Business Week* (June 17, 1972), p. 103.
27. Robert L. Heilbroner et al., *In the Name of Profit* (New York: Warner Paperbacks, 1973), p. 220.
28. Nader and Green, op. cit., p. 176.
29. Robert L. Heilbroner, "Roots of the Socialist Dilemma," *Dissent* (Summer 1972), p. 466.
30. Michael Harrington, *Socialism* (New York: Saturday Review Press, 1970), pp. 296–297.

31. Ibid., p. 305.
32. John Kenneth Galbraith, *The New Industrial State* (Boston: Houghton, 1967). See also J. K. Galbraith, *American Capitalism* (New York: Houghton, 1966).
33. Harrington, op. cit., p. 303.
34. Heilbroner, *In the Name of Profit,* op. cit., p. 212.
35. Ibid., p. 224.
36. Milton Moskowitz, "Conscientious Corporations: A Record," *Sloan Management Review* (Fall 1971), pp. 27–28.
37. Ibid., p. 29.
38. Ibid.
39. Milton Friedman, "The Social Responsibility of Business Is to Increase Its Profits," *New York Times Magazine* (September 13, 1970), p. 33.
40. Daniel Sisson, "Social Futures Relating to Health Care Delivery," *Center Report* (February 1973), pp. 14–15.
41. Daniel Bell, *The Coming of Post-Industrial Society* (New York: Basic, 1973).
42. Heilbroner, *In the Name of Profit,* op. cit., p. 221.
43. V. Lewis Bassie, "The Multinational Computer," *The Nation* (February 5, 1973), p. 173.
44. Peter Drucker, ed., *Preparing Tomorrow's Business Leaders Today* (Englewood Cliffs, N.J.: Prentice-Hall, 1969), p. 77.
45. Townsend, op. cit., p. 40.

READING

Cooperatives

Arthur B. Shostak

As American an idea as apple pie, the cooperative has been with us since Benjamin Franklin founded a mutual-assistance fire-fighting association in 1736. Today, well over 38 million Americans belong to old-line cooperatives, as in farming and housing, and several million more belong to rudimentary co-ops—consumer cooperative buying clubs, campus food stores, poor people's co-ops, and the various communes. Indeed, the recent revival of public interest in a possibility long dismissed as vaguely related to Populism and the New Deal is a critical development where the reversion of capitalism is concerned. Many see new hope for "welfare capitalism" in an idea that combines both the essential elements of democracy and the most productive aspects of the profit system.

The classic cooperative, a business enterprise owned and controlled by the people who use it, has three distinctive principles: democratic control; limited returns on invested capital; and operation on a cost-of-doing-business basis. Its main purpose is to generate savings for its members rather than profits for investors (see Table 1).

In finances, the big difference between a cooperative and a conventional corporation is not how much money is made but how much is kept. The politics of cooperatives also contrasts with that of big business: personal rights take precedence over property rights, with each member getting a single vote, regardless of how many shares he holds.

TABLE 1.

Features Compared	Corporation: Investor-Oriented	Corporation: Cooperative
1. Who uses the services?	Generally nonowner customers.	Chiefly the owner-patrons.
2. Who owns the business?	The stockholders.	The member-patrons.
3. Who votes?	Common stockholders.	The member-patrons.
4. How is voting done?	By shares of common stock.	Usually one-member, one-vote.
5. Who determines policies?	Common stockholders and directors.	Member-patrons and directors.
6. Are returns on ownership capital limited?	No.	Yes, to 8 per cent or less.
7. Who gets the operating proceeds?	The stockholders in proportion to stock held.	The patrons on a patronage basis.

Source: Adapted from Farmer Cooperative Service, *Cooperatives in Agribusiness* (Washington, D.C.: Government Printing Office, 1972), p. 6.

More significant, however, than their superiority in distributing wealth and power is the ability of cooperatives to dare things that their investors champion, even if these are financially hazardous, and to infuse everything they do with "heart." Typical of the risky ventures that only ideologically guided cooperatives attempt are these:

1. The Book Co-op at the University of Wisconsin sells political works and avant-garde literature not handled by regular distributors.
2. At the University of Illinois the Earthworks General Store sells leather goods and handmade crafts that are not available in commercial stores.
3. At the University of Minnesota, four hundred natural food supporters have formed the Ecology Co-op, which sells only organically grown food, much of it flown in from California. Despite the costs involved, the store manages to sell most of its food at less than retail prices.

The key to survival—and the essence of the cooperative spirit—is the volunteer labor offered the co-op by the enthusiasts among its members. An Illinois co-op member explains, "For the first time, for some people, there is an awareness of the dynamics of cooperative effort. They may feel a little more love for their neighbor who unloaded the truck and weighed out their order for the week."[1]

Comparably unusual is the network of possible beneficiaries. The Berkeley Co-op, for example, has donated some of its profits to a local child-care center and to the Berkeley Free Clinic. The Defense Boutique, a cooperative clothing store at Kent State, donated profits to a legal defense fund for students arrested in the 1970 tragedy. Boston and Philadelphia campus cooperatives are regularly patronized by low-income people in the nearby communities, and a food co-op near the University of Minnesota's campus in

TABLE 2. Cooperative Ranks: 1972

Type	*Number*	*Membership*
Credit	24,000	22,000,000
Electric	1,000	6,700,000
Farm	7,700	6,400,000
Consumer	900	1,000,000
Student	800	800,000
Telephone	235	650,000
Housing	900	500,000
Memorial	105	325,000
Health	5	250,000
Nursery	1,440	45,000
Fishing	80	9,500

Source: Richard J. Margolis, "Coming Together the Cooperative Way," *The New Leader* (April 17, 1972), p. 7.

Minneapolis delivers food to the homes of older customers who are unable to get out.

No wonder, then, that an admirer suggests that the role of cooperatives is to "restore a measure of free will, to light up for citizens a few possibilities concealed in the long, mechanistic night."[2] Or, as President John F. Kennedy once explained, "United, there is little we cannot do in a host of new cooperative ventures."[3]

Do these alternatives to "plastic capitalism" have much of a future, or will they flounder and recede, as happened before in the 1930's? By and large, cooperatives remain weak, marginal, and in the eyes of many Main Street types somehow far-out. Nevertheless, as journalist Richard J. Margolis points out: "Wherever the system grows too burdensome, wherever it breeds alienation or powerlessness or poverty, there one finds cooperatives." After six months of studying cooperatives in 1972, Margolis concluded on an optimistic note:

> one gets the feeling at times that if cooperatives lose many of the battles, they may nevertheless be winning the war. . . . No one can doubt in these troubled times that the cooperative idea is once again capturing the imagination of many Americans, particularly among young people. . . . Thanks to a century of painful progress, cooperatism's base today is broader and stronger than ever before.

Nevertheless, Margolis believes substantial new progress may require at least three interrelated developments:

1. The establishment of cooperative banks capable of providing low-interest loans to new co-ops.
2. The opening of a consumer cooperative service in Washington—possibly within the Department of Commerce.
3. In general, the establishment of cooperatism as an explicit goal on our national agenda.[4]

All of this requires a mass-based political movement to revivify the cooperative ideal and offer Americans a genuine alternative to state-corporatism. For all practical purposes, that struggle is just beginning.

FOOTNOTES

1. "Students Learn to Save by Using Co-ops," *New York Times* (March 23, 1971), p. 24.
2. Richard J. Margolis, "Coming Together the Cooperative Way," *The New Leader* (April 17, 1972), p. 7.
3. Ibid., p. 32.
4. Ibid., p. 33.

CHAPTER 11

Prosumerism: Power to the Consumer!

. . . the very persistence of the corporation gives to the search for responsibility a deeper significance than the remedy of the abuses of the movement. The creation of a responsive and reasonable corporation becomes an indispensable step in the creation of a responsive and responsible state—perhaps the central social problem of our age.

ROBERT L. HEILBRONER

Each member of the public is saying, "Treat us as real. Regard us as human. Talk to us as you would to any friend. Don't insult our intelligence, or make snide emotional appeals to our social snobbery or our sexual vanity or our lurking sense of inferiority."

ROBERT S. WHEELER

Prosumerism is a new word coined to mean business support for one of the major social reform movements of our time, the consumer revolution. For to the charge that consumerism is antibusiness, many knowledgeable parties contend instead with David R. Inerfield that it is actually far more against "mediocrity and failure . . . . a revolt against the faceless and often parasitic bureaucracy in which government has been the leader. Business is the nearest and handiest victim."[1] This tie-up of consumerism with the desire for excellence in all things Inerfield, who is a probusiness *and* proconsumer spokesman, concludes, "could be a very effective blessing in disguise for American business."[2]

Perhaps. Still, it is true that much of the consumer's movement has origins in the resentment hinted at in some data given by Ralph Nader:

> Senator Philip Hart has estimated that of the $780 billion spent by consumers in 1969, about $200 billion purchased *nothing* of value. By nothing of value he meant just that: over $45 billion was drained away by monopolistic pricing, for example, and over $6 billion by oil import quotas which drive up the prices of fuel oil and gasoline. His estimate, and it is only a preliminary one, shows how crucial is the need to evaluate how corporate and government wealth is being used—or misused—for individual and social purposes.[3]

For another thing, there are the garden-variety complaints acknowledged by as conservative a source as the Morgan Guaranty Trust Company of New York:

All too common, unhappily, are such things as auto repairs that are high in price but worthless in value; warranties and guarantees that proffer in bold print but take away in fine print; computers that bill falsely; letters of complaint which are studiously ignored; and store clerks who are surly, uninformed, and quite unhelpful.

In addition to such complaints there is a more worrisome and deep-going source of discontent; the feeling that technology sometimes has been applied to consumer products without adequate understanding of the ultimate danger to users.

Examples cited by government agencies include cosmetics which each year injure an estimated 60,000 people seriously enough to require medical attention and poorly designed kitchen ranges that are held responsible for one out of three of all clothing fires that cause personal injury.[4]

"It is no longer merely a question of a better buy for the individual," the bank concludes of this new phenomenon it tags "collective consumerism." Rather, consistent with an educated public's changing concept of the social responsibilities of business, it has become "what is the best for all consumers. . . . And consumer protests can be ignored only at the price of deepening economic and social strain."[5]

What are some of the specific concerns of "collective consumerism"? What might *we* want to reform? Well, where would you like to begin?

In 1973, the Food and Drug Administration had 212 inspectors to examine the nation's 60,000 food plants.[6]

The occupational Safety and Health Administration has 400 inspectors to keep an eye on 4 million business establishments.[7]

Of the nearly 8,000 practicing lawyers in Washington, only about 50 represent the public in such things as consumer matters on a full-time basis.[8]

Nearly half of the nation's population today drinks water that does not meet the present, low federal standards.[9]

We were consuming five pounds of food additives per person in 1971, according to the American Chemical Association. By 1980, chemists expect an increase to six pounds per person.[10]

In the Fall of 1972, columnist Jack Anderson contended that a device that would cut the homeowners' gas bills by 20 to 30 per cent has been kept off the market by the American Gas Association. The fuel saver, known as Vent-o-matic, is an automatic damper, which can be attached in the flue of a gas furnace. It has been approved by the Canadian Gas Association, which tested the device and found it safe.[11]

20,000,000 Americans annually suffer from safety-hazard accidents connected to household objects. Some 110,000 are permanently disabled, and 30,000 die.[12]

The cost in 1973 of nearly identical term life insurance policies varied as much as 140 per cent in the United States.[13]

The list, of course, could be extended, but the point is clear: a long agenda of proconsumer reforms stretches out before us!

There is reason to believe that the public feels "something must be done," to judge at least from a typical 1973 survey of American opinion: 77 per cent wanted more product laws for health and safety (up from 70 per cent in 1967), and 21 per cent felt they had been "cheated or deceived recently on a purchase of a service or product," particularly on groceries, meats, autos, and appliances.[14] The pollsters, a business service group, advised their corporate clients—on the strength of this and much corroborative trend data—that "consumerism will continue to force companies to deliver what the public legitimately expects of them."[15] In some considerable part business has been responsive, with self-mandated reforms heralded by business spokesmen now including the following:

> More and more food packages are carrying nutritional information as an integral part of their labeling.
>
> Buyers of a leading make of TV sets automatically receive calls from company headquarters asking if they're satisfied with their purchases. And fast action if they aren't.
>
> A major automobile manufacturer has formed a whole new division designed to make servicing cars as important as selling them.[16]

> Among individual firms, Whirlpool handles customer complaints by a toll-free "cool line." Telephones are manned by people with technical backgrounds; recommendations are followed up by calls from repairmen stationed throughout the country. A similar approach to complaints is used by many types of businesses from insurance companies to auto producers.
>
> Federal Department Stores and Maytag are experimenting with "teltags" which explain not only what to do with an appliance but what not to do.[17]

The list, of course, could go on for pages, but the point of impressive proconsumer moves by certain progressive corporations is clear.

Government help has also been considerable, and although generally taking the form of new laws or regulatory agency regulations, it can extend in more creative directions as well. Typical is this account by Dorothy Brown of a proconsumer reform maneuver by Virginia Knauer, the President's Special Advisor for Consumer Affairs in 1973:

> Her latest victory—an open-window policy on bacon packaging so the shopper can see how much fat he's buying—revealed a more subtle way of twisting industry's arm.
>
> "When we approached the bacon industry they said, 'The state of technology is such that we can't change our packaging,' " Mrs. Knauer explained. "But we're sneaky here," she added, grinning. "We love these end runs."
>
> "We went to the packaging industry and asked if they could design a packages costing no more than the current ones. They came up with seven different varieties. Then we had another meeting with the bacon people. We announced, 'Gentlemen, the technology of the packaging industry has suddenly improved. Which of you will be the first to give us open packaging of bacon?' "[18]

Far more conventional, at least in earning public recognition, is the following sort of gain:

> Sweeping changes in food labelling announced by the FDA in 1973 are hailed as helping to "make nutrition education relevant." One of the many proposals involved "would tell the consumer how many shrimp are in a seafood cocktail, or the amount of cherries in a cherry pie. This also encourages comparison shopping and eventually may upgrade the whole food industry."[19]
>
> A buying guide that rates the costs of the 50 largest insurance companies in America has been published by consumer-oriented Pennsylvania Insurance Commissioner Herbert S. Denenberg. He estimates that $100-million could be saved by the public annually if comparative shopping and a stronger element of competition were injected into the term insurance marketplace.[20]

Again, the examples are many, but the point of constructive responsiveness by certain agents of government is clear.

Resentment against a sort of know-it-all attitude that is associated with government "interference" in the marketplace prompted one bold critic to challenge the very premise that there are too many accidents, too much fraud, and not enough information. How does one decide, the critic asks, on the right amount of fraud and the correct amount of information? To which question a college student friend of consumerism, Karen Stein, quietly responds:

> The answer is a very simple one—any avoidable accident, any knowing fraud is too much. Any child burned and maimed because of flammable clothing, any infant born malformed because of thalidomide or another inadequately tested drug is too many.[21]

This response helps explain the deep emotional hold that this particular crusade has on its followers. It goes *beyond* a revolt against mediocrity and failure to issues as basic as life and death!

Consumerism, however, especially as an exercise in old-fashioned, grass roots militancy, has generated more effective citizen action across the nation than most other causes in recent years:

> Volunteers from consumer protection groups, armed with a list of almost 1,000 banned toys, regularly search in the nation's 500,000 or more toy retail outfits for hazardous playthings that have escaped the FDA recalls.[22]
>
> *Ad hoc* housewife boycotts of meat purchases in Winter and Spring of 1973 gained millions of consumer supporters, helped direct remedial scrutiny to the food price "chain," and helped generate increased pressure to keep alive federal wage and price controls.[23]
>
> A buying guide that rates about 50 local drug stores as being good, average, poor, or erratic in terms of their prices was published in April, 1973, by the Connecticut Citizen Research Group, an arm of the Ralph Nader-affiliated Connecticut Citizen Action Group.[24]

This chapter is particularly concerned with the issue of citizen participation, especially in relation to six or so reforms of special promise.

The first of the chapter's preoccupations, the case for reform in auto repairs, is a crisp example of overdue change in a strife-marked area of fraud and impotence. The second, law care for the middle class, explores an innovation (forty years old in Germany!) that would strengthen our hand in law actions against consumer fraud. And the third reform, the use of the government's power to censor advertising in our behalf, assesses a weapon whose peril to its user (as well as to its targets) commands respect and extremely cautious employ. Finally, the chapter's summary section discusses at some length the considerable distance we have to go before we can trust to our marketplace for business exchanges that honor us all.

Auto Repairs: A Case Study

Crippling personal impotence—and how to replace it with a strategic and dynamic sense of growing personal power—goes to the very heart of *every* reform discussed in this book. We are especially challenged in our dealings with *things*. They still threaten to climb into the saddle and ride us, a specter that some caustic commentators prematurely declare an already established fact. In truth the peril is great but the outcome unclear. As we evolve steadily into our postindustrial, service economy phase of societal development, the peril intensifies, for the service phase encourages an insidious reliance on gadgets and their repairman-partners. Daily we come to know less and less about the more and more things we greedily gather about us. Our dependency on bewildering gadgets and beguiling servicemen grows—even as our self-reliance and self-esteem shrink.

Basically the challenge is fourfold. We can learn how to purchase or home-produce more selectively. We can learn how to diagnose problems and repair our own gadgets. We can help legislate an interrelated and sophisticated system of consumer aids. And we can explore going without, a visionary notion only slightly more far-reaching than the other three. Taken separately or together these reform directions hold out promise of relief from and possibly even the reversal of our apparent tendencies toward "gadget-ishness," a state far more painful and unlovely than even that atrocious word itself.

In our fight against marketplace exploitation we require new allies, and we finally seem about to get them in an area in which we are notoriously weak—auto repairs. Because we can apply much of what we learn about the auto repair field to other consumer plights, let's take a good look at it.

Thanks to several reforms we may be about to make some substantial gains against a serious problem, our collective vulnerability to fraud in auto repairmanship. It apparently is not without cause that we regularly rank "auto repairmen" and "used car dealers" at the bottom of lists of the people we feel we can trust: after four years of study a Senate committee now warns that perhaps 33 per cent, or $10 million of our $30 billion annual repair bill may be fraudulent (charges for unnecessary or inferior work).

All the more encouraging therefore is a new governmental reform that may finally take the guesswork out of car maintenance and repair. Some $50 million was appropriated in 1972 for states to set up by 1975 experimental vehicle inspection stations. As a result, the car owner will no longer have to rely solely on mechanics in private garages, who are often poorly trained and are also under pressure from their employers to replace parts. Instead, the car owner can use the machinery and the expert advice available in the experimental inspection stations to learn what is wrong—and later to check on how well it has been repaired.

Some thirty-eight states have had such stations, but before the new federal law, standards in the states were generally disappointing: brakes were not tested at high speed, and inspectors checked the steering by rocking the front wheels back and forth and the shock absorbers by pushing down on the fenders. Under the new Department of Transportation plan, sophisticated test equipment, costing possibly as much as $500,000 per center, would provide an early warning to the car owner about defects and evidence for recalls. A long-range goal envisions highly automated, computer-equipped inspection stations where a car owner could get within minutes, for $10 to $15, a card that would tell him the condition of most of the major parts of his car.

Not the least of the likely gains is one reported by the head of the Missouri Auto Club, which has operated a diagnostic center for the past five years. The center helps "create a feeling of trust between the motorists, automotive manufacturers, and repair facilities."[25]

A similar reform effort, and one likely to promote trust in still another way, focuses on the auto mechanic himself. In the fall of 1972 the College Boards, the Law Boards, and other nationally standardized tests were joined by comprehensive tests for mechanics, a series of four eighty-question examinations designed to certify qualified automobile mechanics (men with two or more years of shop experience). About 30,000 of the nation's 800,000 mechanics were expected to sign up for the $40 set of tests given in 150 cities. Sponsored by the new National Institute for Automotive Service Excellence (NIASE), a private group funded with $300,000 from the four American automobile manufacturers, the tests would enable dealers to promote the certification of their successful mechanics, thereby giving you and me as motorists a new standard by which to judge the caliber of those doing repairs.

The first round of tests in November and December of 1972 produced some startling statistics:

1. Only 13,512 mechanics of the 30,000 hoped for actually took the tests.
2. Although 65 per cent passed in at least one of the five skill areas they could sign up for, only 17 per cent passed all five tests.

Consumer advocates seized on the failure rate of 35 per cent of the participating mechanics to criticize the auto repair industry roundly. But the managers of the certificate program were not dissuaded from their impression that this is "the greatest thing that ever happened to repairmen and their customers." The quality of automobile repair is "the leading cause of consumer complaint in this country," the president of NIASE explains, "and this is a mammoth first step toward solving it."[26]

While praising this voluntary certification program, Senator Vance Hartke (D.-Ind.) has pledged to continue to work for the federal licensing of auto mechanics. The NIASE insists, however, that its voluntary standards will be higher than any mandatory plan the government might establish. Confident that its test fees will soon enable it to be self-supporting, the Institute plans to spend $1 million by 1975 to encourage and earn public respect for its upgrading effort.[27]

A third and final reform focuses still elsewhere and is concerned not with the bewildered driver or the trust-seeking mechanic but with the crusty self-help agent himself, the weekend mechanic. Encouraging is the fact that a group of former General Motors executives and a university professor of mechanical engineering have joined forces recently to bring to America an overdue reform pioneered abroad in Sweden and England, the do-it-yourself auto repair shop.

Two such shops in Detroit are doing so well that nationwide franchised shops are expected to open up far and wide. Each shop will provide space, equipment, tools, and charts and diagrams, along with expert advice. Designed to help you do your own light repair—tune-ups, oil changes, grease jobs, shock absorber installations, repair of exhaust systems, brake work, and minor maintenance—the shops charge about $14 for space rent for one and one-half hours, use of engine diagnostic equipment, and exhaust emission analysis.

Savings can be considerable—an average eight-cylinder auto tune-up can cost under $23, as compared to regular repair shop bills of $40 to $100. Savings aside, the big attraction appears to be the availability of expensive specialized tools and equipment. Many car owners, the record now bears out, would like to do their *own* work—if only they had a suitable place and the right tools and equipment at their disposal—without having to invest a lot of money.

Along with the well-publicized oversubscribed course in mechanical repairs instituted in 1970 at Goucher College, the popular auto repair course at Bennington College, and the invaluable home repair mechanics column in *Ms,* the Detroit U-Tune shops serve a need we all feel for mastery over things, for liberation from reliance on (unreliable) repairmen.[28] Interested? Call to reserve a stall . . . and finally make that car *really* your own.

Legal Insurance: "Lawcare" for the Little Man

Although the average middle-class consumer has to make his way through a marketplace hazardous with defective goods, faulty services, and deceptive ersatz warranties, he can rarely exact legal retribution. The Mafia, to be sure, has its *consiglieri,* and corporations have floors full of lawyers who are at their beck and call, but the middle-class American has no such clout. Rather, it is estimated that some thirty thousand matters a day go unattended by lawyers because people of moderate means cannot afford average legal fees.

The problem of making the law more available to the average citizen is finally beginning to receive reform attention, as we watch grow a steadily developing new industry in legal insurance, comparable to the crop of health insurance programs in the medical field. For premiums ranging from 50¢ a month to over $100 a year, a variety of plans are appearing that promise to pay an individual's legal costs—nearly all of them or at the least certain specified costs. Estimates of the total number of such plans nationwide vary from three thousand to five thousand.[29]

Once again, we follow in the wake of others. Germany, for example, has had legal insurance for over forty years. And we progress slowly: only one state, New Jersey, is seriously considering a statewide insurance plan. The prospects, however, are considerably brightened by the fact that the American Bar Association, the nation's high arbiter of legal matters, is solidly behind the idea. The ABA points out that this potential source of new business could help make lawyers forget the $1 billion in fees they are expected to lose with the coming of no-fault auto insurance.

The ABA has recently joined forces with certain labor organizations to back experiments with the "open panel" prepayment concept. As with Blue Cross, a participant simply contracts for legal services from participating attorneys and the plan pays all or part of the fee. Under a Shreveport, Louisiana plan, construction union members are discouraged from frivolous appeals to the law; members must pay the first $10 of any fee, as well as the first $25 for any case. In addition, only $190 of court expenses and trial preparation costs are covered. Under a Los Angeles plan, school union members would agree voluntarily to a $3-per-month deduction from their salaries that would entitle them to two hours of legal consultation, the right to have a simple document drawn, and a guaranteed law fee on all other services. A divorce, for example, would cost only about $200. Under a local plan negotiated by the Amalgamated Clothing Workers the employers pay a modest fringe benefit that provides about 50¢ per month per member for purchases of legal services, the unionist still paying some of the cost. When such programs are linked to a discounted fee schedule, the consumer plainly benefits, but critics urge safeguards lest the user feel himself becoming a second-class client.

Observers expect that major insurance companies will soon begin to offer prepaid legal service coverage. One plan promises that for $5 a month individual subscribers will have the right to legal counsel in a variety of situations ranging from misdemeanor traffic violations to bankruptcies and civil trials. (Families would pay less than $15 a month for the same service.) Subscribers are also entitled to an additional eight hours of attorney's consultation on a variety of problems, such as real estate purchases or simple debt management. Overuse is discouraged by a $2 registration fee for each office visit. Conferences being held nationally on the subject are well attended by representatives of the insurance industry, and breakthroughs may be imminent.

Proponents of the prepaid concept contend that a democratized legal process will enable more of us to hold business and government as accountable to the law as we are. Prepaid law-access can mean new citizen strength to use the law against defective products and hidden interest rates. And citizen activists, secure in the knowledge that astronomical law fees are no longer an Achilles' heel, can challenge government action as never before. To ensure, however, that the reform stays "pure" and doesn't degenerate into a device to inflate legal fees, a coalition of labor unions and consumer groups has formed the National Consumer Center, a nonprofit organization devoted to promoting and studying group legal services. "The ultimate question," explains Curtis Berger of Columbia Law School, "is whether the consumer or the professional is going to be running things."[30]

Overall, however, Sheldon L. Greene, a progressive lawyer friendly to the prepaid "Lawcare" notion, concludes that "the willingness of the organized bar to adapt . . . could provide much of the stimulus and resilience needed to see this society into its third century."[31]

Television

Children's TV. How does our children's television stack up against that of the rest of the industrial world? Not very well, to judge at least from the first comparative study (1971) of children's programming in sixteen industrialized Western nations. At that time America was the only such nation that did not have network programs for children on weekday afternoons. We were alone in allowing more commercials on children's programs than on adult evening TV. We permitted twice as much time (sixteen minutes an hour) for commercials on children's programs as did any other industrial nation. And we joined only five of the sixteen in allowing any commercials whatsoever on such TV fare; eleven other nations barred all huckstering from this particular brand of television.

Learning from 1971 overseas practices, a reform group called Action for Children's Television has since been urging substantial upgrading in American TV practices: their 1972 petition to the FCC recommends a minimum of fourteen hours of children's programming a week on all TV stations. It could be divided into at least two hours a day and aimed at the six to nine and the ten to twelve as well as the preschool age brackets. At least 50 per cent of such programming should be more than pure entertainment, and commercials should interrupt no more often than twice an hour, if at all.

Asked to comment on the network plans to provide more informational "specials" for children, a spokesman for ACT impatiently explained, "We will still only be catching up with the rest of the world, and there will be no real change as long as there are no weekday afternoon network programs and as long as 16 minutes per hour of advertising are permitted."[32] ACT has since won a victory of sorts with a pledge that it has secured from three major drug companies. The commercial sponsors have agreed to end their $4-million worth of vitamin advertising on children's TV programs. Expressing pleasure with the voluntary corporate decisions (the FCC had been weighing a ban), ACT immediately followed up the victory with a plea for a total FCC ban on *all* commercials on children's TV programs.[33]

At stake is ACT's contention that commercial television does not produce programs for children, only children for the advertisers. They are enraged by the admission of a copywriter that "When you're advertising to kids on Saturday morning you're convincing them. You're turning them into little salesmen."[34] ACT spares no effort to see to it that the FCC acknowledges the following expert testimony, in this case from a nutrition educator who wants children protected from TV food commercials:

> No food on children's television is crisply fresh like an apple or a salad; nothing on children's television is tart or spicy or meaty. Everything is fun, sweet, sparkly, gay, colorful, thick and chocolaty, magically or crunchily delicious. The appeal is repeatedly a sweet one. It's either a chocolaty mouthful or, in the words of one particularly revolting commercial, a "frootful snootful."[35]

ACT connects such dangerous nonsense to a wide range of indirect costs. As Joan Ganz Cooney, a specialist in children's television, explained at a 1972 ACT symposium, these "range from our children's bad teeth to a warped value system and the possible psychic damage that is done to hundreds of thousands of our youngsters who are urged to buy and to own what their parents cannot possibly afford to get them."[36]

Trying to sell children anything, ACT supporters insist, is dead wrong: "It is like shooting fish in a barrel. It is grotesquely unfair. The target audience is, after all, illiterate, uneducated, unemployed, and hopelessly dependent on welfare from others."[37] If, "in our fantastically wealthy country," Cooney goes on, "this means less commercial TV programming for our children, then so be it."[38] But there *are* alternatives:

1. Perhaps each of the three commercial networks could rotate broadcasting children's cartoons on Saturday mornings.
2. Perhaps fewer but better programs would be a blessing.
3. Perhaps institutional advertising could substitute for product ads, as with the mention of corporate sponsors at the end of *Sesame Street* and *Electric Company*.

Overall, ACT insists that children be removed from TV as an "electric shill," from this distortion of the free enterprise system. Children's programming, a pro-ACT specialist concludes, must be liberated from the profit center of broadcasting. And, off to one side, FCC Commissioner Nicholas Johnson wonders aloud, "Would programing be different if it were designed for children, rather than for products?"[39] More emphatically, he concludes, "Children's programming on commercial broadcasting stations should be cleansed of attention-getting violence and hucksterism aimed at making children superacquisitive consumers."[40]

Opponents argue that most people approve of and like what children are offered and pay no attention to the "hard-sell" commercials. The specter of government control is raised as the price for the use of tax dollars rather than ad revenues to sponsor children's TV. Typical is this contention of a South Carolina TV station spokesman:

> The vast majority do not object to commercials or host selling. Intelligent parents are aware that it is certainly more appetizing to have advertisers paying for free television in contrast to tax-supported Government-controlled TV.[41]

A more radical type of criticism insists that ACT does not go nearly far enough. In Tom Geohegan's words,

> If ACT had its way, TV would be a house divided, half public interest and half free market: BBC for the kids in the afternoon, "Hee-Haw" for parents at night. Perhaps from the corporate jungle of commercial TV a little child shall lead them—but I suspect children's TV will suffer so long as us grown-ups put up with *our* TV.[42]

Agreeing that the question of how to assure constructive sponsorship, whether public or private, is a knotty one and conceding that proquality reforms in TV must go beyond children's fare, ACT insists all the more that the real question is "Can we afford not to begin?"

In the final reckoning, the issue goes deeper than the mere bid for children's money. Hard-sell TV commercials, especially when they hawk shlock or even dangerous merchandise, twist a child's perception of the adult world in a very hazardous way. Robert Lewis Shayon asks,

> When a TV ad tells a child that a racing car goes "1,500 miles per hour (in scale)," and the child later learns the truth, does he merely shrug it off as a game, as harmless blandishment, or does he begin to develop the slow, poisonous cynicism that eventually can rob him of that which is more precious than his money—his confidence in the worth of his country's future?[43]

What with the average child's viewing 15,000 hours of TV before kindergarten, witnessing 18,000 deaths (murders and suicides, by and large, almost always violent) by his fourteenth birthday, and wrestling with 350,000 commercials by his eighteenth birthday, the note of urgency in ACT pronouncements is grimly understandable:

> A.C.T. PURPOSE
>
> A.C.T. aims to persuade TV networks, stations, advertisers that children are special human beings, and not simply miniature consumers.
>
> A.C.T. aims to encourage and support good entertaining programming for children of all ages.
>
> A.C.T. aims to eliminate commercialism from children's programs and to require a reasonable amount of programming each week designed for children of different ages.
>
> A.C.T. aims to substitute a new system of financial support for children's programs by commercial underwriting and public service funding, in the belief that this system would look to the benefits to children rather than the profits to the advertisers.[44]

Viewer Education. A fascinating rebuttal from an ad executive contends that neither a total ban on ads nor a substantiation doctrine will really do the job. The first ignores all the ads that children can watch during adult viewing time; the second cannot deal scientifically with the attractions of a toy, the sound of a record, or the lure of a cool drink.

Instead, the answer may rest with applied education. Ad executive Robert B. Choate urges development of a new TV series for children that would school them in the critical perception of commercials: "Perhaps 26 three-to-five minute mini-programs should be aimed at the young viewer during his show times to alert him to be a prudent purchaser rather than a burned skeptic." The content for such a series might include:

1. Ancient rules that protected children from overzealous salesmen.
2. The techniques that make certain advertisements such powerful communicators.
3. The use of motivational research and competitor put-downs.
4. The use of testimonials, heroes, just slightly older sex and maturity symbols, and pseudoscientific analysis.

Arguing that "if they are to be affected by it, they have a right to interpret it," Mr. Choate insists that these and other production techniques "should become everyday knowledge to the nation's advertisees much as bike safety, molester avoidance, poison dangers, and traffic safety are taught to the young from the day they can walk."

How might this new series of educational minishows be financed? A 1 per cent tithe per year on all advertisers to the two-to-eleven-year-old crowd should help. Why might advertisers contribute? Because they have nothing to fear, insists Mr. Choate, Chairman of the Council on Children, Media, and Merchandising: "Advertising agencies that feel secure in their ethics must now join the consumer activists who fear for the gullible child. What could be more American than describing the tools of the trade of America's most visible $4-billion industry?"

To which some critics might add, "Amen," but go on to insist that more is to be gained by combining *all* three reforms—bans on commercials during children's time, substantiation trials for all commercials aimed at children, and public exposure of ad gimmickry—than by reliance on any one of them alone. Provided, of course, that the proposed TV "course" on advertising itself is put to a substantiation test and is shorn of the puffery and self-serving PR pap that Mr. Choate quietly includes in his recommended syllabus ("Why advertising in our economy? The way an ad is conceived, written, story boarded, produced, sold, and aired").[45]

In the last analysis, one is left wondering if a little learning might not be an inadequate (dangerous?) thing. A mini-series of "Be-on-your-guard!" telecasts may be capable of only mini-results, whereas the hazard apparent here (the seduction of the innocents) appears to be a maxi-threat to the mental and moral well-being of us all.

Summary

An index of how far we have to go is available in an account of legislation that was *still* being sought in 1973 in New York City to help protect consumers and promote their interests:

A requirement that druggists post prescription prices publicly.

A rule that automobile, TV, and appliance repairmen be licensed.

A prohibition of "harassment of debtors by a collection agency."

A requirement that people who sell insurance state in detail precisely what coverage the buyer is getting.

A bonding and licensing for travel agencies.

A rule that mail order houses must ship goods within four weeks.

Extension of the three-day "cooling off" period—which allows buyers to decide if they do not want to accept something they have agreed to buy—to include places other than the seller's place of business.

Legalization of class actions and class recovery in consumer cases. Under this, a single lawsuit could recover damages for all consumers who suffer in a case of fraud.

A requirement that all drugs be labeled as to the last date on which they can be used before they lose potency or become dangerous.[46]

This list, of course, only skims the surface, as the quality of a marketplace safe for "women and children and other living things" is a large concern and not a petty and small-minded notion.

Some of this concern is hinted at in a reform prescription from the indefatigable Ralph Nader:

> Computers should be made directly available to the citizen and should be accessible both at shopping centers and by telephone. Such a cheap and simple source of information, which would give advice on the quality of products and of government and private services, could do much to squeeze the waste and deception out of the economy and give value to the dollar.[47]

To help move us along toward a future of such extraordinary sophistication Nader urges on us an immediate expansion in our role as data gatherers, analysts, and publicists. Writing in 1971, Nader struck a note still timely today:

> Even the data on pollution must be fought for if it is to be extracted from corporations by government agencies and individuals bringing law suits. The task of the consumer movement now is to gather and analyze and disseminate this type of information by demanding it from the three branches of government and by mounting private actions by consumer groups to publicize it. Such information is the currency of economic democracy, the first tool for changing the perception of citizens and society itself.[48]

Fortunately, citizen activists across the nation seem to have gotten the message, and buying guides, pollution exposés, price-protest picketing, and the like are increasingly common.

What remains, then, are an extraordinary amount of hard work for citizen consumer advocates and a host of demanding decisions for resolution by all of us. For example, the House of Representatives was asked in 1973 to pass legislation making advertising expenses no longer tax deductible for the cigarette industry. The sponsors of this unprecedented bill argued that "the harmful and deadly effects of the product which cigarette manufacturers market should prevent these industrialists from enjoying this otherwise universal privilege." Supporters further explained,

> Of course there will be an uproar if this legislation seems likely to pass. Alcohol is harmful too, and lobbyists for the liquor interests as well as those of the cigarette industry will rave and roar about do-gooders and health nuts. But isn't it better to brave such onslaughts than to make ourselves ridiculous by issuing official reports on the perils of cigarette smoking, while cunningly contriving messages in its favor?[49]

Note that cigarette companies will remain free to advertise if they wish, but at their *own* expense. Either their advertising will diminish or the industry's profits will drop, or the cost of cigarettes will rise to still higher and possibly prohibitive levels. But all of this hinges on *your* willingness to support selective-punitive or proconsumer tax advocacy. Your vote . . . ?

Similarly, Senator Gaylord Nelson (D.-Wis.) has introduced legislation to limit the patent protection of drug makers. He cites a recent case in which an American firm was selling the same tranquilizers to our armed forces for

$32.62 a thousand and to the Canadian military for $2.60 a thousand. Patent protections in such a case amount to an "oppression of the public," the Senator insists. His bill would permit the Federal Trade Commission to require that a drug become available for manufacture by other firms at a reasonable royalty rate if the drug is selling at five times what it costs the company to make it or if sales have been more than $1 million for three years. Drug industry spokesmen snap back angrily with their insistence that any limit on patent rights "would almost surely cause further depression in innovation in the drug industry."[50] Your vote . . . ?

Conversely, you are also challenged to find and take a position in the matter of sharply *curtailing* public protection through the use of public means.

Certain proconsumer reformers, for example, urge us to free ourselves from unthinking belief in the problem-solving capabilities of government. They insist that as consumers of public services and private goods we may actually be harmed, indeed nearly smothered, by all the government agencies set up to protect us. Indeed, it is argued that well-meaning people who promote regulation by government often help bring about the exact opposite of their original intentions.

A crowning example of how government regulation can work against consumers is the story of the great quality and price gulf between air commuting in California and air commuting on the eastern seaboard. As Caspar Weinberger points out,

> Pacific Southwest Airlines, operating within California and hence not federally regulated, is able to fly passengers from San Francisco to Los Angeles fully as safely, fully as fast, far more comfortably, and with added services, at about half the price charged for the shorter flights from Washington to New York on federally regulated Eastern Air Lines.
>
> Furthermore, the forces of competition being still alive, regulated United and Western airlines have had to lower their California commuter rates because of P.S.A. No such forces of nonregulated competition prevail along the Atlantic seaboard, because the numerous state boundaries turn a flight of any distance into an interstate, federally regulated operation.[51]

Many such cases are cited in support of a recommendation for deregulation. The Federal Communications Commission, for example, is urged to give up government licensing and rationing of channels and air space and to rely on free, "impersonal" market mechanisms to allot station franchises. This would get the FCC out of commercial licensing and, incidentally, out of its incipient brushes with censorship, a potential threat in any licensing operation.

The time has come, these reformers conclude, to consider a virtually untried alternative: substituting private-sector remedies for ever-increasing and frequently disappointing reliance on the public sector. Central to this promarketplace reform is consumer education, which reinforces consumer sovereignty, the best regulator of all.

None of these suggestions, advocates insist, are meant to render government weak and ineffectual. Rather, they grow out of an honest "recognition of the efficacy of the market, of the inherent incompatibility between economics and politics, of the built-in shortcomings of government intervention." Indeed, government is to be strengthened in the form of a reinvigorated judicial system that can better absorb and perform the contract-adjudication and consumer-protection functions now handled so badly by so many hapless regulatory agencies.[52]

"Balderdash!" thunder the procontrol advocates in angry retort. They insist that the *only* course is one that entails more and not less federal regulation. For example, Senator Abraham A. Ribicoff (D.-Conn.) insists that we have nowhere enough protection at present for the voiceless consumer:

> In August, 1972, the Federal Power Commission established an optional pricing rule for new supplies of natural gas which may result in higher gas prices to consumers. When the FPC was considering this rule, who spoke for consumers?
>
> In February, 1973, with the price of beef at record high levels, the Department of Agriculture advised turkey farmers to reduce production in the latter half of 1973 to assure "reasonable prices." When the department was considering this recommendation, who spoke for consumers?[53]

Senator Ribicoff and his associates continue to urge passage of legislation that would establish a consumer protection agency to assure the "little man" proper representation in government. (A supporter, Pennsylvania Insurance Commissioner Herbert Denenberg, contends that special interest groups "already have a herd of wolves and foxes in the federal henhouse. The consumer is entitled to a fox or two snapping on his behalf."[54])

And your vote?

FOOTNOTES

1. David R. Inerfield, "Letter to the Financial Editor," *New York Times* (December 10, 1972), p. F-11.
2. Ibid.
3. Ralph Nader, "A Citizen's Guide to the American Economy," *New York Review of Books* (September 2, 1971), p. 18.
4. "New Consumerism: Potential Help, Harm," *The Morgan Guaranty Survey*, as reprinted in the *Philadelphia Evening Bulletin* (November 8, 1972), p. 21.
5. Ibid.
6. Robert Sherrill, *New York Times Book Review* (March 4, 1973), p. 3.
7. Ibid.
8. Ibid.
9. Ralph Nader, "What Do You Drink?" *New Republic* (April 8, 1972), p. 8.
10. Ralph Nader, as quoted in Dorothy Brown, "Nader Calls Virginia Knauer Powerless," *Philadelphia Evening Bulletin* (October 4, 1972), p. 42.
11. Jack Anderson, "Washington Merry-Go-Round," *Philadelphia Evening Bulletin* (October 20, 1972), p. 68.
12. Stanley Klein, "A Product-Injury Surveillance System," *Saturday Review* (September 23, 1972), p. 67.
13. Judy L. Mann, "Term Life Insurance Costs Vary Widely, Survey Shows," *Washington Post* (December 27, 1972), p. C-1.
14. "America's Growing Antibusiness Mood," *Business Week* (June 17, 1972), pp. 102, 103.
15. Ibid.

16. *Good Housekeeping* advertisement, *New York Times* (September 21, 1972), p. 84.
17. *The Morgan Guaranty Survey,* op. cit., p. 21.
18. Dorothy Brown, "You Think You've Got Headaches?" *Discovery* (October 22, 1972), p. 12.
19. Richard D. Lyons, "FDA Proposes Sweeping Change in Food Labelling," *New York Times* (January 18, 1973), p. 30. The quotation is from Dr. Charles C. Edwards, Commissioner of Food and Drugs.
20. Mann, op. cit., p. C-1.
21. Karen Stein, Letter to the Financial Editor, *New York Times* (December 10, 1972), p. F-11.
22. Miles Cunningham, "Consumer Units Search Stores for Banned Toys," *Philadelphia Evening Bulletin* (October 28, 1972), p. 3.
23. "The Beef Boycott," *The Nation* (April 2, 1973), p. 420. See also Paul L. Montgomery, "Consumers Hold Rallies at Shops on Eve of Boycott," *New York Times* (April 1, 1973), p. 1.
24. "Pharmacists Sue to Bar Sale Guide," *New York Times* (April 1, 1973), p. 37.
25. Agis Salpukas, "Supervised Inspection Centers for Autos Proposed," *New York Times* (July 23, 1972), p. 24-S.
26. John D. Morris, "Auto Mechanics Being Certified," *New York Times* (March 19, 1973), p. 19.
27. "A Series of Tests for Mechanics Will Certify Them as Qualified," *New York Times* (July 30, 1972), p. S-22.
28. James H. Dyzert, "Drive Right In and Fix It Yourself," *Parade* (April 16, 1972), p. 18.
29. Thomas De Boggio, "Legal Insurance," *Saturday Review* (September 23, 1972), p. 45.
30. Quoted in Tom Goldstein, "Breaking New Ground," *Wall Street Journal* (October 6, 1972), p. 30.
31. Sheldon L. Greene, "Is 'Lawcare' Next?" *The Nation* (December 11, 1972), p. 593.
32. George Gent, "Survey Faults Children's TV in U.S.," *New York Times* (July 2, 1971), p. 61. See also Evelyn Sarson, *Action for Children's Television* (New York: Avon, 1971).
33. "Drug Firms Halt Children's TV Ads," *New York Times* (July 21, 1972), p. 51.
34. Christopher S. Wren, "How to Find the Live Ones on Children's TV," *Saturday Review* (September 16, 1972), p. 59.
35. Ibid. See also R. A. Blake, "Children's TV: Ethics and Economics," *America* (October 21, 1972), pp. 308–311.
36. Joan Ganz Cooney, "Isn't It Time We Put the Children First?" *New York Times* (December 3, 1972), p. 17-D.
37. Ibid.
38. Ibid.
39. Blake, op. cit., pp. 308–311.
40. Nicholas Johnson, "An Open Letter: Planks for the Platforms," *New Republic* (July 15, 1972), p. 21.
41. "Consumers Union Asks F.C.C. to Ban Ads on Children's TV," *New York Times* (January 10, 1973), p. 67.
42. Tom Geoghegan, "Batman in the Heavenly City," *New Republic* (November 4, 1972), p. 24.
43. Robert Lewis Shayon, "Caveat Pre-emptor," *Saturday Review* (January 9, 1971), p. 37.
44. Richard L. Tobin, "Murder on Television and the Fourteen-Year-Old," *Saturday Review* (January 8, 1972), p. 39.
45. Robert B. Choate, "Fair Play for Young Viewers," *New York Times* (September

17, 1972), pp. 3, 15. See also Letters to the Financial Editor, "Sales Pitch for Youngsters," *New York Times* (January 28, 1973), p. 4-F.
46. "City Consumer Unit Plans to Introduce 26 Bills in Albany," *New York Times* (December 3, 1972), p. 74.
47. Ralph Nader, "A Citizen's Guide to the American Economy," *New York Review of Books* (September 2, 1971), p. 18.
48. Ibid.
49. "Continuing Cigarette Problem," *The Nation* (April 2, 1973), p. 422.
50. "Drug Costs $32.62 Here, Only $2.60 in Canada," *Philadelphia Inquirer* (September 30, 1972), p. 1.
51. Casper W. Weinberger, "With Friends Like the Regulatory Agencies, Consumers Don't Need Enemies," *Fortune* (June 1972), p. 177.
52. Mary Bennett Peterson, *The Regulated Consumer* (New York: Nash, 1972), p. 37.
53. Quoted in "Denenberg Supports Panel to Speak for the Consumer," *Philadelphia Evening Bulletin* (March 21, 1973), p. 5.
54. Ibid.

READING

How can we stay in touch with one another when our struggles as consumer activists are similar and the lessons each of us learn are of potential aid to all of us? How can we keep in mind the critical notion that it is "the system," and not especially ourselves, that needs substantial overhaul? And how can we innovate with impact and consolidate our efforts across hundreds of miles? Clues to the answers to all of these questions are offered in this encouraging account of an unusual effort by teen-agers to help one another—and indirectly, all of us as well—in a fashion we could, many of us, profitably emulate.

Dear Student Information Center: Help!

John Mathews

Every day a half dozen or so letters are delivered to a Spartan office two steep flights above Ikaros-Airborne Hot Pizza, the popular carryout in Washington, D.C.'s Georgetown section of historic homes and teen rock-music emporiums. The letters are written by high school students from virtually everywhere, USA, who somehow have heard of the High School Student Information Center, a unique consultant service created by high school students to help other high school students reform their schools.

The daily batch of letters amounts to an uninterrupted litany of the anguish, frustration, loneliness, and uncertainty faced by the relative handful of scattered and isolated students who want to change their high schools but don't know how to do it and aren't sure what they want as alternatives. A typical early stage of student disaffection, born of frustration, was expressed in a recent letter to the High School Student Information Center by the freshman editor of the *Peaceful Co-Existence,* an unauthorized student newspaper in Irvington, New Jersey. He wrote:

> The major problem at my high school is the idiotic student council. You can't run for it if you are not going to be a junior the following September (this just for the lower offices), or a senior (you must be one by Sept. to run for president), and you can't be "subversive" according to the administration. . . . Some students suggested holding elections in the fall; this would include the enthusiasm of the incoming freshmen and it would eliminate the apathy of the outgoing seniors. Mr. ______, our principal, said, "Well, we'll take it into consideration." That was in September; it's now June.

A senior from Lansing, Michigan, well beyond dealing with unresponsive principals, was operating at a higher level of discontent:

> I'd like to radicalize the high schools. Something simple, right??? Well . . . let me tell you about it: The schools are divided between "straights" and "freaks." The straights do dope, ball a lot, have sexist and money-oriented goals. Most of them resent their folks and school, but don't like to show it. Most "freaks" are identical to straights, except they look freakier and make their dope and sex resentments a lot more open. The "straights" will end up just like their conservative parents. "Freaks" will be as bad or worse. . . . I see the problems and I've got the resources (helpful people, freak newspaper, lots of fears and resentments to play on). But, I'm not sure what to do or how to do it. All I want to do is get kids to see the alternatives so they'll get off their death trips. Can you help me out?

What the handful of young people at the High School Student Information Center try to do in response to such pleas for help is to "act as a personal support to people criticizing the system," says Mary Wilson, the group's untitled but clearly evident leader, who has been the driving force in establishing the center and keeping it going. "We try to reassure them that they're not the only people doing this and that the system is the problem, not them. You know," she adds, "it can help break down the isolation."

Mary and her colleagues—Pat Wilson (her sister), Steve Spector, Peter Grunwald, Susanna Lowy, Erik Phillips, and Greg Guy—are all in their late teens and recently out of high school, except for Susanna, a high school senior in an affluent Virginia suburb. Together they have served as a morale-boosting squad and an organizational resource during the last two years for hundreds of high school students. One of their main activities has been firing off personalized letters of advice to student "organizers"—the term they prefer—in a constant effort to establish a network of activist students in other schools and student organizations. They also place each newly formed organizer on the mailing list for their occasional newsletter, which is usually crammed with information about the latest hair-length and dress-code court rulings, the tactics of the opposition (for example, a National School Public Relations Association booklet citing one defense measure against student unrest is to "lock all restroom doors"), and the latest small gains in the struggle, such as more students on local school boards.

And, more important, the Student Information Center sends off packets the staff has written on subjects such as student rights, grading, curriculum (entitled, "Look What They Done to My Brain, Ma"), the draft, birth control programs, and school board elections. One of these pamphlets, a manual on high school organizing called "Sowing the Seed," deserves to become a minor classic when the chronicle of the liberalization of American high schools is compiled. Several thousand copies of "Seed" have been distributed in the past two years—not only to students but to school administrators, teachers, and counselors, who probably think it prudent to know what the enemy is up to.

In its twenty-five mimeographed pages "Seed" spells out in detail the techniques and tactics of high school organizing. The merits of long-term organizing through use of underground newspapers or the establishment of new student service organizations, for example, are compared with those of short-term campaigns organized around ad hoc issues such as "dress and hair codes, student rights, open campus, getting specific teachers fired, getting new courses, cafeteria food, discipline procedures."

The "Seed" section on tactics weighs the pros and cons of "taking over a student council." Control of a council, "Seed" counsels, means legitimacy, a source of funds, a room for an office, access to such school equipment as the all-precious mimeograph machine, and the unquestioned right to hold meetings. But on the debit side:

> 1) You couldn't win the election, 2) the administration would sabotage the election, 3) even if you won officer positions, the representative assembly would not cooperate with you, 4) philosophically you don't agree with the concept of student councils . . . 5) you view it as total cooptation.

As for the crucial area of negotiating, the "Seed" manual suggests that "when you go to negotiate, have a fairly long list of demands so that you have some to compromise on. . . . Don't threaten or harass administrators too much. They cannot negotiate with you if it looks like they're breaking under your demands." And finally,

> Never underestimate your opponents. They may be very skilled at using bullshit platitudes and evading issues. Keep them on the subject. Get your opponent's position in writing. Ask him to write out and sign any promise that he makes. Otherwise, he may deny ever having said what he did. . . . Use negotiating to get across to him/her what will happen if he does not come through on your demands. People act quickly when they are truly threatened.

The "Seed" manual also deals with money-raising activities for student activists, mentioning as one potential source the private foundations, which the High School Student Information Center itself has tapped with great success. "Foundations are nonprofit corporations set up by people who have a lot of money that they don't want to pay taxes on," the manual says somewhat ungraciously. It notes further that foundations "are especially afraid, except for a few rare ones, of giving money to high school age people because of our lack of experience and because of new and stricter tax laws."

But Mary Wilson and her associates have managed to overcome the fears of foundations to the tune of about $65,000 in the last two years. The largest grants have been $20,000 from the Stern Fund in Washington, which kept the center alive for its initial two years; $10,000 from the JDR III Fund to initiate a new media project; $20,000 from the Drug Abuse Council, a national organization involved in drug abuse education; several thousands from sources variously described as "Peter's uncle" and "a nice rich lady"; plus $7,000 from church groups to support the center's activities at the White House Conference on Youth, held in April 1971.

According to Mary Wilson, eighteen, the center's wide-eyed and exuberant co-founder and director, the center now has enough funds for about a year of activity, including salaries of about $220 a month for full-time workers. But, in her matter-of-fact manner, Mary adds, "I don't know whether we want to continue indefinitely. Maybe someone else should take over." Her doubts arise partly from a candid appraisal of the effectiveness of the center, partly from concern about turning twenty and losing credibility as an advocate of high school students, partly from personal skepticism about the long-range prospects for meaningful educational change.

Mary's view comes from a unique perspective on schooling. She has grown up in a family of seven children; her mother is a former teacher, and her father, Dr. Dustin W. Wilson, has followed the classic professional progression from teacher to principal to superintendent, then to a position in the U.S. Office of Education's Bureau of Education Personnel Development, where he is in charge of programs for the training of administrators for urban schools. "I've always been a type of critic of schools," he says, "and we have always tried to be honest with the children about schools, impressing on them that we are more concerned that they learn something than that they get grades."

Her father's peripatetic career brought Mary to three different high schools in three years: Dover High School, where Dr. Wilson was superintendent of the Delaware capital's public schools; prestigious Newton (Massachusetts) High School, when Dr. Wilson was a Whitehead Fellow at Harvard; and, finally, Walt Whitman High School in Bethesda, Maryland, a high-income suburb of Washington. At Whitman Mary succumbed to the typical syndrome of disaffection, exhibiting, as a former counselor put it, "a tendency to act as if she knew better than adults, telling teachers how to manage their classes."

As a fifteen-year-old junior in September 1969, Mary took advantage of a liberalizing trend at Whitman High School to begin her own work-study program, which allowed her and other students to attend classes part time and find part-time jobs in the afternoons. With her collaborators, Mary got in touch with Toby Moffett, who had been brought to the U.S. Office of Education by its late commissioner James Allen to head a division on students and youth. Moffett referred Mary to an HEW task force on youth, which began an informal, unfunded student information center. Mary recalls that the center did rather distasteful things, such as compiling newspaper clips on student unrest.

At the time Mary and the handful of other students were hopeful that they would get an information center established on a firmer basis within HEW; but after Moffett quit, blasting the Nixon Administration's attitude toward young people, and Allen resigned under pressure after denouncing the invasion of Cambodia, HEW made clear that potentially troublesome students were not wanted in their midst. Thus, Mary and her friends "went public" late in July of 1970. "In trying to work through the system," Mary was reported as saying in a news article at the time, "the members of the Student Information Center ran up against the massive bureaucratic inertia present even in the most 'liberal' of the government agencies, HEW. The disappointment we felt, especially in the light of recent statements by administration officials stressing the need for communication and cooperation with responsible activist youth, is acute." Mary then turned her considerable energies toward finding private-foundation funds to support the creation of a new student information center outside of government. In the process she failed that year to complete all the requirements for a high school diploma. She has not bothered since to get the credential and is somewhat proud of being officially a dropout.

With high school and two years' experience in running the information center behind her, Mary and her friends have developed into what amounts to a new generation of pragmatic, nondoctrinaire activists. Mary rejects as antiquated the tactics of the slightly older radicals of the 1960's, which she and other high school activists once espoused. "We went through a period of protest, saying, 'We demand you don't oppress us,' but we found out the power structure would not stop," she says. Generally, high school activists in the last half-dozen years have found easy acceptance of their demands for an end to dress codes and hair restrictions, for new liberalized curricula, for black studies. But, Mary adds rather ruefully, "There just hasn't been any really successful high school organizing, because the same student-teacher relationships continue." What high school activists have to learn, Mary continues, is that "you aren't done when you get rid of the dress code. Once you've organized against something, you have to begin organizing *for* something. The problem right now," she says, "is people really don't know what they want."

In recent months Mary and her young colleagues have been going through the complex process of moving from a posture of protest to one of program and of trying to spell out what they want in the way of reformed high school education. Mary gets into somewhat heated arguments with older radicals—people in their twenties—about such issues as free high schools. Some of them, she feels, have "taken on radicalism as a profession." In fact, the Student Information Center has taken a strong position against free schools. "People who go to free schools," Mary says,

> are people who don't want to go to school but still think they have to. Free schools are nothing but another track of the existing educational system, which is proven by the fact that a lot of high schools now have what they call free schools. I think free schools are basically elitist. What is needed is free education for all the people, not a change in education for a few people. The work has to be done in public schools, because that's where most of the people are, most of the people being screwed by the system.

Recently Mary has been putting together her concept of what a public high school should be as the ultimate objective of reform. Ironically, HEW, which rejected Mary and her friends and their budding information center two years ago, is now paying the center $500 each for papers on a model high school, student rights, institutional change, and civic education. In an ideal high school, Mary says, there would be no compulsory attendance, no tracking, no age limits for enrollment, and no standard grades, although teachers should be able to work out systems of mutual evaluation with their students.

"In substance," she adds, "individuals would decide what's important for them to learn for their survival. Teachers would serve as resources, and students would make the major decisions as to who is hired and who is fired." The ultimate high school would exist in a decentralized system, Mary suggests, where the central office would be an "administrative facilitator." As administrative lines now exist, she says,

> It all comes down from superintendent to administrator to principal to teacher to student. This has to be turned around so programs and policies come from below to the top. The important thing is not that kids make administrative decisions but that they be able to say a program must be implemented and that administrators respect their requests. They have to provide choices for people, real choices in the system.

As the High School Student Information Center continues into its third year, Mary Wilson candidly observes, "We certainly haven't changed secondary education in the country, but we have helped a lot of students battling the system. We've certainly had a belief in the power of information. We have assumed all along that students can use the support of a central organization." When it comes to determining how many toppled dress and hair codes or how many new curricula the center has inspired, Mary readily acknowledges that there are no hard data.

During this school year the information center has taken on several new projects, including journalism workshops in four states to develop more critical student newspapers, a media project aimed at producing radio and slide tapes on high school organizing, and an ambitious high school organizing drive in Maryland.

Using many of its existing student contacts, the center has identified ten student groups across the nation capable of carrying on local surveys of youth attitudes toward drug-education programs. The local groups are receiving direct grants of up to $2,500 apiece from the Drug Abuse Council. Pat Wilson says the center will evaluate, monitor, and assist the local groups in getting their investigations underway, then later hold a conference to assemble their findings. She hopes the project will give adult planners some sense of what young people think are the most acceptable and effective approaches to drug education.

Perhaps the center's most promising new attempt at bringing about changes in high schools is its work in nearby Maryland. At the state level and in up to ten counties, student researchers, aided by the center, will examine school board and administration policies and practices that directly affect students. Reports with recommendations for changes will then be made public and be presented to superintendents and school boards at the state and local levels.

"Students will then be better able to focus on issues around which to organize," says Peter Grunwald.

To Mary, Peter, Pat, and the other young people at the High School Student Information Center, the Maryland project seems to be a last major effort before they lose the credibility of their teens and pass into their twenties and other concerns. "The center or something like it will continue, even without us," says Mary, "because the business of changing high schools has barely begun."

CHAPTER 12

Penalties and Justice: Crime and Confinement

Thou rascal beadle, hold thy bloody hand!
Why dost thou lash that whore? Strip thine own back;
Thou hotly lust'st to use her in that kind
For which thou whip'st her.

WILLIAM SHAKESPEARE

. . . if we are to reduce crime, what is needed is a willingness on the part of every citizen to give of himself; his time, his energy, and his imagination.

NATIONAL ADVISORY COMMISSION ON
CRIMINAL JUSTICE STANDARDS AND GOALS,
1973 Report

What is the crime picture like today in America? Gallup data suggest that as many as one in three urbanites and one in five suburbanites was mugged, robbed, or suffered property loss as a crime victim in 1972![1] Not surprisingly, then, urbanites regularly identify crime to be their city's worst problem:

> Your chances of becoming the victim of a serious crime have more than doubled since 1964: In 1964, there was one serious crime for every 69 persons; in 1971, one for every 34.[2]
>
> Research in 1967 suggests that 58 per cent of white urban males, and 90 per cent of nonwhite urban males, will be arrested at some time during their lives.[3]
>
> A person who has been arrested once tends to accumulate additional arrests during his lifetime, the average for a white man being seven, for a black man, 12.5.[4]

Not surprisingly, then, Gallup also finds that in 1972 nearly half the population of this country were afraid to walk alone at night in their own neighborhood, and one person in six did not feel safe at night even in his own home.[5]

Our population grew by about 13 per cent in the last decade, but our crime rate increased 144 per cent.[6] Unfortunately, our crime/punish/rehabilitation system grew nowhere as fast. The Eisenhower Crime Study Commission in 1967, for example, developed a discouraging, if illuminating, set of interrelated suppositions. Of one hundred major indexed crimes, as reported by Norval Morris: "50 are reported to the police, 12 people are arrested, 6 of the 12 are convicted of anything, not necessarily of the offense reported; 1.5 go to prison or jail."[7] Similarly, for a young man weighing a criminal career the chances are perhaps only one in ten that he will get caught. Even if arrested he will probably remain free for nine months or longer before going to trial, and his appeal may take two years to be decided. If finally imprisoned, he is likely to serve an average sentence of only twelve months at the Youth Correction Center.[8]

Public misconceptions are legion, with few laymen aware of the following:

> A black man's risk of being victimized in a violent crime is five times greater than for a white man. A black woman runs a risk seven times greater than any white woman. Male or female, blacks are about ten times as likely as whites to suffer criminal homicide.[9]
>
> Routinely, blacks get higher bail, stiffer penalties, harsher prison treatment, and fewer paroles . . . albeit research demonstrates criminal behavior is not the prerogative of certain cultural or ethnic groups.[10]
>
> Nine out of ten criminal homicides involve a victim and an offender of the same race.[11]
>
> Poor people and people living in poor neighborhoods are far more likely to be victims of burglaries and robberies than those in more affluent areas.[12]
>
> Young males—between 16 and 24—are more likely to be victims of assaults than other people.[13]
>
> Upwards of 25 per cent of all New Yorkers violate the laws against the numbers racket daily; one in four also bets on sporting events using bookies 60 per cent of the time.[14]
>
> Fifteen-year olds commit more offenses than any other single age groups, juvenile or adult.[15]

Ignorance of, or indifference to, these data goes far to explain the racism, the anti-youth hostility, and the anti-indigent sentiments of the public at large, attitudes that further undermine the always difficult mission of the nation's justice system.

What might we do to "set it all right"? Conservatives might find themselves especially drawn to a provocative set of reforms recommended in 1973 by Robert Daley, a police department administrator:

> Bold resort to "selective enforcement" policies enable a police department to decide on its own not to enforce gambling laws, sabbath ordinances, and other "nuisance" laws no longer popular with the general public.
>
> Trials should take place within a week, before the witnesses have forgotten or disappeared. After conviction, allow one appeal, also within a week, at which point the convicted criminal goes to jail for the duration of any other appeals.
>
> Let the Health Department cope with the prostitutes by fining them on the

spot, when detected on the streets: "At the sight of a health inspector they will sprint for the doorways. We admit we can't obliterate prostitution, right? We just want to control it, right?"

Make heroin legal: "Qualified buyers could purchase it at cost at the corner drugstore, with minimum practicable controls. Black leaders would call this genocide. We can't afford to listen to them, for they may be wrong. Doubtless when Prohibition ended certain men called this genocide too. How would the Irish race resist its fatal attraction for the bottle? Still, many of the Irish resist manfully, even today."

The jails must be changed. Also, felons must come out with a job waiting, and with some money. This isn't coddling criminals. The alternative is that each convict hits a fellow citizen on the head within an hour, in order to get money to eat, which is what is happening now.

This professional law-enforcer, dismayed by the lack of will for change he detects in the public, applauds the few men around willing to "take a few giant steps on their own. . . . The alternative is our current treadmill backward into the past."[16]

Harsher enforcement continues, then, to have considerable public and governmental support. Some long to return to the crisp efficiency of the "third degree" and station-house "accidents." George Alexander reports:

"In the old days, when a cop was a cop," one policeman says in frustration and exasperation, "there was a direct way of dealing with muggers. You'd get that bastard into the station house, take your nightstick and break his arm. It's very hard being a mugger with only one arm."[17]

Many more hard liners, however, put their trust in covert brutality in the line of duty. Robert McKiernan, the president of New York's Patrolmen's Benevolent Association, for example, angrily writes:

One revolutionary with a large hole blown through him would have been a marvelous deterrent to the next nut who thinks it's a good idea to shoot at cops.

Our civilian controllers make it quite plain that they do not trust us to do the job. They fret about the possibility of innocent people being injured in the battle. They mutter darkly about police states.

Garbage. I say New York City's policemen are among her finest citizens.

We can do the job. We wish the people who run this city wanted us to do it.[18]

However, the harsh approach is as ineffectual as it is divisionary. It turns attention away from level-headed reforms and encourages us to suppose that restrictions on civil liberties (especially of the poor and the blacks) will ensure our safety. Still further postponed is the mental and financial effort we must make if we are really to reduce crime.

Another reform orientation likely to appeal to conservatives, and to many old-line liberals as well, has been publicized by former death-row inmate Edgar Smith. What is needed, he insists, is to go far beyond our first reflex solution of harsh crime control, a solution he casually characterizes as "the standard one":

> Hire more police, give them better training, get more of them out on foot patrol, pour in Federal funding for bigger guns, faster cars and louder radios, give the cops greater powers by repealing the Fourth, Fifth, Sixth, and Fourteenth Amendments, and then build bigger jails to hold the increased number of criminals the more efficient police would arrest.

Such reforms, although certain to "bring smiles of satisfaction to the law-enforcement community—almost any cop on the street would say I was on the right track—would fail to solve the problem." Indeed, Smith believes that such solutions merely reach the symptoms of the disease and not its roots.

Instead, what is needed, he insists, is a whole new attitude toward all crimes:

> We have got to stop accepting crime. We have got to stop making excuses for those who commit crimes on behalf of causes with which we are sympathetic. We have got to stop countenancing selective obedience to the law. We can no longer afford selective outrage toward crime.
>
> Muggers, armed robbers, and car thieves do not work in a vacuum; they work in the atmosphere we create when we excuse some crimes; when we excuse draft evasion or the theft of Government documents because we think the war in Vietnam is wrong; when we laugh over the dinner table about how we cheated on our income taxes, excusing it on the basis that "everyone does it"; when we turn our backs on the breaking of drug laws because we don't think smoking a little grass ever hurt anyone; when we shrug our shoulders at price-fixing by a huge corporation because "that's the old business game," and we don't see how it directly affects us; even when we do something as seemingly insignificant as stealing a handful of paper clips from the office and excuse it because "they" can afford it.

We have reinforced the feeling that the law has become a sometime thing. We *can* bring crime under control, Smith concludes, but only if we stop tolerating it, stop believing there is nothing we can do about it, and "stop locking ourselves in at night and turning the streets over to those who believe we no longer care what they do."[19]

Some additional flavor of what Smith is referring to is conveyed by the many anomalies that abound in this area as in few other areas of social concern. For example:

> Tools for car thieves are sold openly. Ads in the supply catalogues of locksmiths offer such bargains as a $4 Slim-Jim car opener, "the best tool for opening cars with the new no-vent window." Also available for a mere $25 is a set of 150 manufacturers' keys to the ignition and door, trunk and glove compartment on the newest car models.
>
> The 1969 Tax Reform Act allows citizens to deduct all illegal payments, bribes, or kickbacks paid in the ordinary cost of doing business: Think about the payoffs you make to carpenters, plumbers, electricians, doormen and building superintendents to keep your office running; the kickbacks to purchasing agents of your best customer; the "tips" to truck drivers and dispatchers to make sure that the truck with your shipment on it is kept moving; the payola to deejays to get your record played; the liquor you gave to your cus-

tomer's employee to put your order under his boss' pen. They are all deductible if they are ordinary and necessary business expenses.[20]

When $350,000 worth of stolen jewels were recovered for the Brooklyn shrine of Regina Pacis, major credit went to Don Carlo Gambino, alleged Mafia boss of bosses, a parishioner at St. Rosalia's, the shrine's mother church. An irate *Village Voice* challenged the pastor to stand up in church the following Sunday and say to Don Carlo—"The jewels are not important. What is important is that you and your mob stop selling dope to our children!" As for the police role in the affair, the *Voice* found it running counter to an alleged all-out war on organized crime: "Can you fight a war against your partner?"[21]

Other examples are readily available, but the point should be painfully clear by now. We may be living with a crime record—and a failure of justice—that we have earned, all of us, through our indulgence and complicity in "crime" of one sort or another.

Here as elsewhere, then, in the challenge of crime and punishment reforms, perspective is all important! Howard Moody makes the point quite forcefully:

In other words, our society is responsible in part for crime by the brutality of a predatory economic system, by the paucity of its provision for those who grow up in morally impossible conditions, by the harshness with which it throws out on the streets all those who are less talented and less successful, by the loneliness with which it meets those who are least adapted to its requirements. In these ways we all share in the web of guilt for which one person finally receives the punishment.[22]

To attack *these* dehumanizing disorders in our collective life requires attacking the source, rather than the symptom: "It is not the 'bleedinghearts' but the terrible over-simplifiers who believe the symptom *is* the disease, whose prescriptions have no effect in fighting crime."[23] In this same vein, the 1967 Presidential Commission on Law Enforcement and Administration of Justice said that "the most significant action that can be taken against crime is action designed to eliminate slums and ghettos, to improve education, to provide jobs, to make sure that every American is given the opportunities and the freedoms that will enable him to assume his responsibilities."[24]

Some of the difference here between the conservative and the liberal positions are made clearer in Table 12–1.

In choosing the specific reform areas to focus on in this chapter, I have sought topics that were timely, controversial, and especially illuminating where the conservative-liberal-radical-visionary spectrum of opinion is concerned. In the first such area, gun control, America is alone in allowing as much freedom —and suffering as much grief—as it does. The second, prostitution, is comparably marked by immobilizing cross-pressures, as well as hypocritical police gesturing and real-life anguish. The third, reform of the criminal code, leaves us far behind our overseas friends in every regard, and in the fourth, aid to crime victims, we can boast only a dozen or so of the fifty states as "pioneers" in a practice decades old in New Zealand, Great Britain, and elsewhere. Finally, in the matter of capital punishment we find a complex and controversial issue that some take as the fundamental measure of a nation's humanity.

TABLE 12–1.

	Conservative Position	*Liberal Position*
Root Cause of Crime?	Failure of society to be consistent and firm in response to crime.	Failure of society to provide all with hope and skill for social mobility rise.
Victim?	Average law-abiding citizen; ethos of the American civilization.	Victim of crime and offender alike; self-perspective and self-esteem of us all.
Reforms?	Enlarged police force!	More foot policemen in long-term neighborhood placement.
	Elimination of civil liberties, coddling of offenders.	Protection of civil liberties of offender and crime-target alike.
	Money and leeway for law enforcement.	Money and leeway for social renewal of crime-producing neighborhoods.
Internal Controversy?	Support for increased use of probation, legalization of marijuana, and rehabilitation focus in prison?	Support for mandatory drug treatment? Support for use of the death penalty?

Gun Control. Among the major countries of the world there is none except the United States that does not require the registration of firearms (Americans own 30 million handguns, or one for every other household, and about 100 million shotguns and rifles; Senator Edward Kennedy suggests that "American households comprise the largest and most deadly civilian arsenal in the history of mankind"[25]). Among the major countries there is also none in which more people are killed with guns than in the United States (in the twentieth century alone, nearly 900,000 Americans have died of gun wounds in this country—more than the 647,000 who have perished in all of our wars[26]). In no other country of the world do so many people kill and maim each other—and themselves—with firearms.

Accordingly, reformers like Senator Edward Kennedy seek to introduce an element of control through a system similar to the one now used for licensing automobiles: licensing of all gun owners and registration of all guns. Senator Philip Hart urges a total ban on the private possession of any handgun. When brought to a Senate vote in the fall of 1972, the Kennedy reform was defeated 78 to 11, the Hart Bill, 83 to 7.

Why? As journalist Robert Roth explains, the controversy is between two camps:

> In one camp are those who believe that guns are good, that only people are bad. They see the gun as a symbol of manhood, of patriotism, of sportsmanship, of self-reliance, of determination to defend the home, the family and

> all that is best in American life. They believe that anyone who wants a gun should be allowed to have it. They would avoid accidents by training people in the proper use and care of firearms. They would combat wrongful use by imposing drastic penalties on gun-wielding criminals.
>
> On the other side are those who regard the gun as a dangerous survival of a frontier tradition which has no place in modern, civilized society. They believe that ownership and possession of guns should be restricted to those of sound mind and good record, that long guns should be in the hands of bona fide sportsmen only and that short guns, revolvers and pistols should be withheld from all except law enforcement officers and those who can demonstrate they need them for specific security purposes. They want the ownership of every gun of every kind registered, just as the ownership of every automobile is registered.
>
> There is almost no give on either side, each being utterly convinced of the rightness of its own position and suspicious of the motivation of the other. The pro-gun people suspect that many of those on the other side are communists. The anti-gunners suspect that their opposites are Fascists at heart.[27]

Progress in resolving these differences has been miniscule and erratic, at best.

The case against gun control rests largely on both a constitutional point and a practical argument. The Second Amendment, gun lobbyists point out, promises that "the right of the people to keep and bear arms shall not be infringed." What they fail to add, however, is that this refers specifically to the need to keep up "a well-regulated militia." A related argument, that registration and licensing amount to an unwanted abridgement of our liberties, has a certain theoretical validity. But, Ronald Kriss, a procontrol writer, retorts, "so does the argument that traffic lights restrict our freedom. In other words, some rules are necessary in an organized society."[28]

Anticontrol people, however, are likely at this point to say, in a low whisper, that "there's a move to disarm this country, as it happened in Germany and Hungary, and we know who's behind it." However that may be, it is the National Rifle Association that is behind this historically *unsupported* plot line: the NRA gospel has it that the Nazis used firearm registration lists to disarm the citizens of the nations they invaded and that the Communists abolished shooting clubs in Hungary well before the 1956 uprising.[29]

On the other hand, the *practical* case against controls revolves about the argument that registration and licensing would inconvenience all of us law-abiding types without really keeping guns from criminals. There are laws already on the books to help in this matter, perhaps twenty thousand local, state, and federal regulations. But their very unevenness and ineffectiveness leaves no one satisfied: criminals disregard them and gun hobbyists complain bitterly about their burdensomeness. Typical is the complaint of Warren Page, president of the National Shooting Sports Foundation:

> You take a man who lives in Massachusetts and wants to go to a hunt in Michigan or a pistol competition in Quantico, Va., where national championships are held. His situation is very ambiguous. He has to drive through seven or eight states. He couldn't possibly be licensed in all those states and he is technically violating the law each time he carries those guns into a new juris-

> diction. He's not engaged in any criminal activity but he gets tangled in a legal mess that 14 Jewish lawyers couldn't straighten out.

Page would like to see reciprocal recognition of state gun permits, even though state licensing procedures vary. But he is adamant against any further handgun control law on any level.[30]

As Kriss hastens to point out, however, "we take out licenses without undue complaint when we want to get married or own a pet. And dogs and marriages, in most cases, don't kill people."[31] What is more, control laws *can* make things more difficult for the gun-seeking hoodlum, who now simply goes out and buys the hand weapon he wants.

A related argument plaintively asks about those who keep pistols or rifles around for self-protection, to which Kriss's response is:

> First of all, the odds are that the gun-toting householder is more apt to get shot than the intruder, who is likely to be more practiced at using a weapon.
>
> More importantly, a loaded gun is an accident waiting to happen—to a child who happens to discover it, to a newspaper boy mistaken for a burglar, to a husband or wife in the midst of a heated argument.[32]

In fact, in about 70 per cent of all killings by gun the victim knows the assailant; and gun owners are so careless with their weapons that children under nineteen are the victims in half of all accidental killings.[33] The point, procontrol people insist, is that in our highly urbanized society stringent controls are not merely advisable but an absolute necessity.

The 1968 Federal Gun Control Act, once heralded as the answer to every citizen need, is now widely considered a recording device rather than any kind of effective control. A moderately good means of checking gun ownership *after* somebody gets shot, the law, for all its ability to register all gun purchasers, remains, as Paul Good says, "a prime demonstration of the Federal law's inability to prevent the criminally unhinged from wrapping their mitts around a deadly weapon."[34]

Not surprisingly, the National Rifle Association, the bête noire of gun controllists, has long advocated doing nothing. Except, that is, for banning the sale of the "Saturday night special," the gun everybody loves to hate. Even in this regard, however, the 1968 federal ban does not seem to resolve anything. As Good puts it:

> There is so much cut-rate hardware available through clandestine sales that murder-minded bargain hunters will still find what they want. Or free-enterprise laws of supply and demand will encourage the "specialists" to send a few dollars more and come up to quality. Besides, motives on all sides are suspect when it comes to legislating the "special" out of gun stores. Shooters fear it's the opening round in a barrage of antigun agitation. Controllers see groups like the N.R.A. throwing the "special" to the public like a bone to an angry dog, hoping it will go away.[35]

Certain law reforms, however, *are* endorsed by no-control spokesmen like John Snyder:

> The misuse of firearms in crime could be detered by mandatory minimum penalties for the use of firearms during the commission of felonies.
>
> Possession of firearms by certain categories of persons such as convicted felons, fugitives from justice, adjudicated mental incompetents, and habitual drunkards and users of certain narcotics, could be prohibited.[36]

These proposals, if adopted, would attack the crime problem, it is claimed, without restricting the right of law-abiding American citizens to keep and bear arms.

From this perspective, then, Snyder gives us two basic approaches:

> The one is utopian and statist and would blanket the entire population with restrictions on gun ownership in an attempt to get after a problem caused by a small minority. This approach is also ineffective.
>
> The other is democratic. It rests on faith in the people. It does not evidence fear of people possessing firearms as does the statist approach.[37]

It is preposterous, the noncontrol people conclude, to argue that our right to bear arms should be weakened or destroyed by the state in an effort to reduce crime. Typical of the hard-nosed sentiments of the holders of these views are those expressed by this irate protester against a liberal magazine's procontrol editorial:

1. Crime would undoubtedly become far more rampant if the criminal could be assured of an unarmed victim. The one thing a robber fears most is a victim who unexpectedly defends himself with a gun.
2. If the "average" householder chooses to be a helpless rabbit, that shouldn't affect the rights of the rest of us to protect ourselves if and when necessary.
3. A large percentage of honest citizens would refuse to turn in their handguns. It is doubtful if one hoodlum in a thousand would do so. I certainly won't turn mine in. I respect any law that is fit to be respected, but such idiocy as you propose hardly comes under that heading. . . . We are very likely heading into some difficult times of social unrest, and I don't plan on being a victim of the first gang of ruffians to come along.
4. Have you considered the cost of compensating owners of all those millions of handguns? Obviously you have not. You put the number at 30,000,000. I would guess it to be twice that. They are selling fast at about $100.00 apiece now, some at nearly twice that figure.[38]

Similarly, a twenty-eight-year-old IBM technician who owns eleven pistols, and shoots twice a week in a commercial pistol range, patiently explains:

> I feel, sir, that handgun legislation is totally inept at curbing crime like the Wallace shooting. There were 8,224 homicides attributable to handguns last year. Divide that into the number of handguns in the country and it comes out to 34 thousandths of one per cent. To me, calling for the confiscation of handguns jibes with the overreaction to hijackers. Now they're getting to the point where every swinging dip of a bird with long hair getting on a plane has to be patted down. That won't stop hijacking, and taking our guns away won't stop crime.[39]

Clearly, neither gentleman is going to be easily persuaded—or coerced—in any direction save that of broad Second Amendment rights.

For their part, control advocates look longingly abroad and point to overseas nations where gun control legislation seems to get the job done. In all of England and Wales, for example, with a combined population of 50 million, there were only twenty-nine gun homicides in 1970:

> In one week alone, New York City has more gun killings than all of England in a whole year.
>
> If "guns don't kill, but people do," why aren't more people killed in England, where practically nobody owns a gun, and even police have to make a special request to take one on an assignment?[40]

Similarly, in Japan, with fully half our population, fewer than thirty people are murdered with guns every year (our figure is closer to ten thousand).[41]

Anticontrol people strike back with the argument of noncomparability. Warren Page, the prominent sportsman quoted from earlier, explains:

> An Anglo-Saxon might steal a million, but a Negro is likely to commit a violent crime. And that's why there's no point in comparing high American murder rates with a country like England, which denies handguns to its citizens and enjoys low rates. It isn't the unfair British gun laws that are responsible but the homogeneous makeup of a citizenry that doesn't have our ethnic problems.[42]

When not arguing this line, certain anticontrol people draw on seemingly favorable overseas examples. Switzerland is commonly used as an example, as its 600,000 citizen-soldiers (of a population of 6.2 million) keep an army rifle and twenty-four rounds of ammunition at home. Yet the number of shooting deaths is so low that the police do not bother to keep statistics. On the other hand, anyone who seeks to buy or carry other types of weapons—including knives—finds that he has to get the same sort of permits that gun fanciers oppose in America.[43]

When all the arguments have settled, the fact remains that ours is the only industrialized nation on earth that permits gun sales as freely as we do. Two-and-a-half million handguns, hardly sporting weapons, are being manufactured or imported annually, and sales have *increased* since the Gun Control Act of 1968 took effect.[44] In 1971, 51 per cent of all murder victims were killed by handguns and another 14 per cent by rifles or shotguns (firearms have been responsible for more than 95 per cent of all police killings, or a total of 466, in the past decade).[45]

No less a "radical" outfit than the business community's Committee for Economic Development has recently urged the imposition of major criminal sanctions against the private possession of handguns: "The federal and state governments should be the sole owners of such weapons and should issue them on a temporary basis to authorized persons under carefully drawn regulations."[46] The choice between some such control measure and the powerful campaign now underway to repeal the already-weakened 1968 Gun Control Act is a critical and revealing one. On the one side are the anticontrol lobbyists, awesome practitioners of the art of ballot-box clout. On the other side is the hard-to-coalesce sentiment represented in the fact that since 1959 Gallup polls have reported two thirds of the American public in favor of strong gun control laws.[47]

Perhaps the last word can go to a British criminal who recently explained to a reporter the "gentlemen's agreement" in that country between non-gun-carrying policemen and criminals:

> "We don't want any of the American business, do we?" he said. "We don't want any of this 'Stop, it's the law, we'll shoot!' stuff. That's the real danger. Some bloke running down an alley, they shout twice, he's dead. Maybe he's got a hot radio on him. Maybe he's nicked 20 quid. But is a life worth 20 quid?"[48]

Prostitution as Crime. If the data from Masters and Johnson can be relied on, nearly 80 per cent of all American men have broken the law at one time or another through having sexual relations with a prostitute. This so-called crime, marked by sexist hypocrisy (the "Johns" or customers go unpunished) and political hypocrisy ("crackdowns" precede public elections), provides a sorry and discouraging tale.

Two students of the subject, academician Pamela Roby and writer Virginia Kerr, contend that the laws are far more destructive than the profession itself. For one thing, the laws harm rather than help persons who practice prostitution:

> The court processing and bail required of women arrested for prostitution are the two major non-psychological factors tying these women to pimps. Given no money, no counseling, no alternative jobs, prostitutes have no choice but to return to their pimps, who pay the bail, and the streets.[49]

For another thing, the laws, by permanently labeling persons convicted of prostitution as "criminals," make it nearly impossible for them to obtain legitimate jobs and leave the streets.

On both these grounds it is recommended that the laws be eliminated. Such a move would have the additional benefit of eliminating an important source of police graft, of freeing police resources for other more substantial work, and of relieving the overcrowding in courts and women's prisons. Finally, by repealing archaic prostitution laws, Roby and Kerr argue, we would be repealing policies that constitute state interference in purely private affairs that do not affect public order or public safety.

At the same time, no letup is recommended in the prosecution for crimes sometimes committed by prostitutes. Streetwalkers who annoy men through their advances or men who annoy women by harassing them on the street should be liable to arrest as "public nuisances." And prostitutes or pimps who rob and beat patrons should be charged with these crimes, rather than with prostitution. With streetwalking eliminated from the criminal code by these reforms (as in Storey County, Nevada today), it is recommended next that bordellos be licensed, inspected, and kept to high standards of safety and health.

When questioned early in 1973 about the possible gains and costs of legalization, a seventeen-year-old, $50,000-a-year call girl with $118,000 in the bank voiced strong opposition:

> Why should I give half my money to the government? We don't have pensions. . . . A woman has to make her money before she's 20 and then quit. I hate to see an older woman working—I hate to see a 25-year old woman working. By the time she's 25, she can't take 10 or 15 guys a night, and when you're working conventions and things, that's what it's all about. That's where the money is. The money. That's the whole thing, money.
>
> Wouldn't you make $50,000 a year tax-free if you could? Well, wouldn't you? Wouldn't you?[50]

Conversely, however, a twenty-six-year-old massage parlor prostitute, who sometimes earns $400 for a thirty-hour week, proved to be for legalization:

> Most VD in this country isn't coming from prostitutes, but what there is, legalization would clean up. But the main thing is that the government is spending our money hauling off prostitutes. It's a total waste of money and time. But if they *are* going to continue to try and enforce this nonsense, then the johns should be busted too.
>
> A cop who wants to work busting prostitutes isn't a cop. He's just a guy looking for an easy job.

"It's really not sex," she later explained. "You just turn yourself off. It's like being on stage and doing a love scene. I'm sure with quite a few wives it's the same thing."[51]

Support of sorts for legalization also comes a back-handed way from America's best-known pimp, "Silky," the star of Susan Hall's best-seller biography, *Gentleman of Leisure*. At twenty-six, Silky manages six prostitutes in Manhattan and may gross $200,000 annually. Without a single arrest in his record, he explains that he isn't particularly concerned about the city's latest cleanup campaign:

> "It's just a hassle," he says. "All it means is that the girls have to get up a little earlier and maybe work a little overtime." It also means, according to Silky, that Times Sq. is more of a prostitute center than ever: "When things are hot, that's where you go. You know that there's just so many people that the cops can manage to bust, and if there's a lot of you, you sort of thicken the odds."

One thing does concern him, however. He fears that legalization of prostitution might be the wave of the future in this country. "Legalization," he warns, "would be terrible for pimps. It would destroy us. Right down the line."[52]

Roby and Kerr, however, stress that their reforms are meant to be *short-term* goals. Although they represent overdue changes needed to rationalize and humanize society's treatment of prostitutes, they do *not* carry us anywhere near far enough. Prostitution is a concomitant of a backward social order that nurtures sexism, racism, and social class inequality; we must move against all of these if we are finally to rid ourselves of any of them! We'll close with the similar counsel of a "fallen sister," the twenty-six-year-old masseuse quoted earlier:

"I would like to see prostitution become completely unnecessary," she says. "I'd like to see prostitution put out of business—not by the cops, not by the politicians, not by the moralists—but because women fulfill themselves and men, sexually and emotionally."[53]

Reform of the Criminal Code. Few reforms in this book reach as deeply into our culture and as far in terms of the sheer numbers of people involved as the proposed removal of morals law from the criminal code. At issue is a move to cut back the "overreach" of the criminal law, to reduce legal sanctions on human activities (abortion, sexual behavior, and so on) that need not be regarded as criminal. Law professor Norval Morris puts it bluntly:

> An adult has the right to go to hell in his own way, as far as the criminal law is concerned, and the way that I choose is no business of the Attorney General, or of the federal government, or of any state, provided, in the process, I do not injure others directly.[54]

Presidential commissions, police administrators, and certain progressive political figures, including President Nixon, urge us all to recognize that the overreach of the criminal law is both "its leading defect and a major obstacle to the creation of a reasonably efficient and humane criminal-justice system."[55]

This reform idea, then, whose time appears to have come, holds that our notion of what constitutes criminality needs redefinition: offenses that do not damage the person or property of others, for which there is no victim and no complainant, should as far as possible be taken out of the system of criminal justice:

> Though we speak of victimless crimes, we are speaking more exactly of crimes in which the victimization is remote or uncertain and where no one *identifies* himself as a victim. In such situations should we not let stand the judgement of the one who commits these acts that the rewards to him outweigh the costs? Those who would limit human freedom should bear a heavy burden of proof that theirs is a necessary course.
>
> Within these bounds, the function of criminal law is to protect the citizen's person and property, to preserve governmental processes and to prevent exploitation or corruption of the young and helpless. It is improper, impolitic and socially harmful for the law to act the moral busybody, to intervene in or attempt to govern the private conduct of the citizen.[56]

This proposed reform of the criminal code, which is called *decriminalization,* would remove from the scope of the criminal law people for whom that law can do nothing and who are now the principal burden upon it. Half of all arrests at present are for crimes without direct victims, crimes that bring no complainant to the station house and no call to the police switchboard—but do snare 4 million arrested drunks, addicts, loiterers, vagrants, prostitutes, and gamblers[57]).

The argument, then, has three main points. First, the most important responsibility of our criminal law system is to protect our persons and property. Second, this primary responsibility is less well served when the criminal law concerns itself with the enforcement of morals—especially as it degenerates into selective enforcement by the police. According to Norval Morris,

> Per hundred thousand—as a rate—for every white man arrested for gambling last year, almost 25 blacks were arrested. Does anyone really think that that measures the differential incidence of gambling? . . . We do not object to the vices. We object to certain people pursuing certain vices in certain ways, but never ourselves.[58]

Finally, a cost-benefit analysis of the moralistic provisions of the criminal law demonstrates how ill-advised they are.

Our costly experience with Prohibition is such a good example that unless we have completely lost our historical sense, we must conclude that the enforcement of morals through the criminal law only breeds crime. Or as Morris tersely insists, "these criminal sanctions are futile, . . . the suffering from present strictures is vast, . . . the only behavior affected is man's capacity for hypocrisy, . . . the best protections against moral decay lie outside the criminal law."[59]

The support for this reform is as available from conservatives as from citizens with liberal or visionary leanings. Typical is the hard-nosed contention of William F. Rickenbacher, an investment advisory editor writing in William F. Buckley, Jr.'s conservative *National Review:*

> The economics of corruption is rooted in the most cherished delusion of the state, that it can Save Us From Ourselves. Legislators, who have always and everywhere been men of unspeakable purity and innocence, understand perhaps better than you and I how sinful sin can be; so they make it a crime. When the law says no and the market says yes, here comes the cop with his hand out. The cop offers a useful service: not enforcing the law, so that the market for sin can function. For this he receives a fee. The money is paid because the law makes sin highly profitable by restricting the supply without restricting the demand. If New York had enough sidewalk hostesses to satisfy the demand, they wouldn't be getting fifty bucks a trick. If, say, prostitution were perfectly legal, there would be no law for the cop not to enforce for a fee. Adieu, corruption.

Thus, Rickenbacher concludes, we have laws to stamp out sin: "In the name of virtue, they should be repealed."[60]

How might decriminalization be made palatable to those who oppose it? Possibly by the well-publicized reallocation of the savings in lower police costs to the provision of concrete and visible protection against the most feared crimes—robbery, burglary, purse snatching, rape, and mugging. Also relevant would be increases in the operational efficiency of existing agencies, especially the police, that might effect a *general* lessening of crime.

Will we gain these reforms in our lifetime? Perhaps. And then again, perhaps not, with critics insisting that those who propose to strike victimless crimes from the books are possibly morally suspect themselves and are certainly dangerously permissive. It is also true that where there is a social problem (such as alcoholism, prostitution, vagrancy, or drug addiction), we cannot solve the problem by removing it from the scope of our criminal law.

Although we gain in abandoning a wasteful, demoralizing, and counterproductive response, the basic problem remains. Narcotics addicts need medical and vocational aid, as do alcoholics and certain compulsive gamblers and self-abnegating sex professionals. Should the "overreach" effort to control things that the system cannot reach soon win reform, we will have won an empty victory if related social reforms are not *also* secured.

But this is to get ahead of the issue, which is ably and responsibly set out in further detail in the reading at the end of this chapter.

Aid to Victims. "If we are to gain sympathy for the offender we must first demonstrate still greater concern for the victim," reason many concerned reformers. Accordingly, a reform that is relatively new here (though not abroad) is concerned with the financial plight of the crime victim, his dependents, or anyone injured coming to the defense of a victim. Based on favorable experience with many similar measures abroad, a bill enacted by Congress in 1972 appropriated $5 million to be paid to victims of federal crimes and $10 million to encourage states to enact their own programs to reach the victims of nonfederal offenses. The federal act compensates victims for medical and burial expenses, for loss of earnings and support, for therapeutic costs, and for child-care expenses enabling one parent to work, but not for property losses. Senator Mike Mansfield, chief sponsor of the act, explained that the victims of crime had too long been the "forgotten persons in the United States."[61]

A similar law passed in 1971 in New Jersey could serve as a model for the forty-one states that have yet to move in this direction. The bill provides that the victim of a violent crime in the state may be compensated up to $10,000 to cover their medical bills or a loss of income incurred as a direct result of the crime. In addition, claims may be filed by the victims of kidnapping, assault, rape, and lewd or obscene acts, as well as by the dependents of a victim of murder or manslaughter. In 1970, 380 applications were made (there were approximately 20,000 violent crimes), and 40 awards were finally approved at a total cost to the state (compensation claims plus administrative expenses) of about $200,000.

New York State, with a comparable program dating back to 1967, paid 1,609 claims from 1966 through 1972, a figure representing less than 5 per cent of the potential claimants during any year (there were 143,214 "eligible" crimes in the state in 1972 alone). With the average claim being settled for $1,930, the state paid out about $3 million during the first five years of victim compensation aid. Similarly, Maryland paid out about $1 million in its first two years under a similar plan, far below the estimates of up to $10 million that were made before the program started.[62]

Nevertheless, skeptics insist that only public ignorance of the availability of compensation explains the low state costs to date. They fear that such programs could turn out to be outrageously expensive, especially as federal legislation provides up to $50,000 in reimbursement for medical and burial expenses, loss of earnings, child care, and the like. Much additional research is needed to explore the open-ended cost challenge in this otherwise noncontroversial, humane reform.

Proponents, on the other hand, look admiringly abroad to programs far more generous and inclusive than our own. England, for example, which in 1964 developed one of the first modern programs to compensate crime victims, makes awards for pain and suffering (our plans cover only physical injuries requiring medical treatment). Moreover, applicants in England do not have to prove severe financial need as they do here, and there is no financial limit on awards (loss-of-income awards in New York State, for example, are limited to $100 a week up to a total of $15,000). Whether we will soon follow suit is unclear—and probably unlikely, though a comprehensive bill is regularly introduced into the Congressional law-making process to reimburse states for up to 75 per cent of their crime compensation costs. *That* would make a difference.[63]

At stake is nothing less than returning to a concept as old as the Babylonians and rejecting a more recent and far less humane perspective. Ancient Babylonian codes specified that the government should replace the lost goods of a robbery victim if the thief escaped with them. Over the centuries, however, the concept faded and was replaced by a theory that crime was an offense against society and not the individual. Victims were rendered powerless by this crime-against-society perspective and were left with a less than useless recourse: they could file civil suits against criminals, but few criminals had any resources worth demanding. We can now change all of this for the better, if we have the courage to realign ourselves with the ancient Babylonian approach.

Death—as a Penalty. In the matter of criminal sanctions, there is always a serious threat of reversal of reforms narrowly secured. Hostile, fearful, and/or ideological critics persist in crusades to restore "backbone" to our schedule of penalties.

Typical in this regard is the uncertain situation of the death penalty, which has cost over five hundred American lives in the last forty years (twenty-five since 1964). In June of 1972 the Supreme Court ruled ambiguously against capital punishment on the somewhat narrow grounds of "arbitrariness" (a capital sentence is now unconstitutional in cases in which the jury or the court has discretion to impose a lesser penalty—the death penalty is not in itself necessarily cruel or unusual, but to impose it arbitrarily and capriciously is impermissible).

"Arbitrariness," the Court found, was evident in the type of crime being singled out for punishment by death (interracial rape led the list by far) and in the character of the offenders (405 of the 455 men we have executed for rape in the forty years we have kept records were black).[64] The record showed that we execute only social pariahs, a small minority of rapists and murderers too poor, too unpopular, or too unlike the white majority of the population to be sentenced to imprisonment. Although it exists on the statute books, since 1960 capital punishment has been used almost not at all (there have been no executions since June of 1967) and then only selectively—hence the insistence by the Court that its application hereafter be "mandatory" for offenses so specified in state law (typically for a "laundry list" of ten capital crimes, among them being multiple murders; killing for hire; murdering a policeman, fireman, or prison guard; assassinating a public official; or killing in the course of robbery, rape, or skyjacking).

Several court rulings in key cases in 1972 spared 612 men and women under sentence of death, a judgment that Justice Stewart found "so wantonly and so freakishly imposed" that the system could not stand before the constitutional challenge. (No man, by the way, has ever been sentenced to death for the rape of a black woman.[65])

Immediate opposition to the Supreme Court ruling was considerable and included that of President Richard Nixon, who urged retention of the death penalty for murders in kidnapping cases and its new extension to cases of murders in air piracy. Others have since urged its retention for murders for pay and murders in the commission of a major crime. Some critics insist a life sentence is less merciful, as well as far less of a deterrent and far more dehumanizing. Some suspect a soft-hearted, muddle-headed scheme afoot to ban the life sentence next, then ban the thirty-year sentence, and so on down to zero. Citizens of this persuasion took encouragement from the fact that the Court's decision left the way open for reinstating the death sentence, provided a state imposed it uniformly. Accordingly, in 1973, thirteen states reinstituted capital punishment, and another sixteen states will weigh the matter in 1974 legislative sessions.[66] Significant here is a November 1972 Gallup Poll that found public support for capital punishment at its highest level in the past twenty years.[67]

A number of people now urge that the entire matter be democratically put to the public in the form of a referendum. They are confident that the majority of citizens would rather keep the death penalty for certain crimes, although imposed through more logical and unprejudiced procedures than now exist. A 1972 referendum in California, for example, gave the penalty majority support, with voters deciding to overrule their own Supreme Court and restore capital punishment in the most populous state in the union. Columnist Tom Wicker raised some disturbing questions in this connection:

> It is not just that California's action may lead other state legislatures, citing public opinion in the most populous state as their justification, into a flurry of mandatory death sentence laws. If Congress and the legislatures, always sensitive barometers of public opinion, begin limiting the power of the courts to review the validity of legislative acts, they could destroy or badly impair the courts' important function of protecting unpopular principles, unpowerful people and unconforming activities from rampant majoritarianism.

Wicker also condemned the death penalty itself as "inappropriate and outrageous."[68]

A very few citizens urge a total redirection of concern. They say that we should prepare "a master plan to revise the entire penal system which has been obsolete for at least 50 years. Therein lies our problem, not the death penalty."[69] And there are also those who urge Congress to weigh, and presumably to pass, an act outlawing the death sentence on the grounds that it constitutes cruel and unusual punishment and therefore violates the Eighth Amendment:

What is capital punishment, asked Camus, but the most premeditated of murders? It is the "ultimate penalty," incomparably the harshest known to our law, and invoked in a manner imposing the most terrible mental suffering, which can lead to insanity or suicide. An argument is made that since the death penalty was common enough when the Eighth Amendment was adopted it is therefore not unconstitutional. But the countering argument is that the conscience of a nation evolves, that standards of decency change, and that what was once regarded as not being cruel or unusual may be so regarded today. On issues of this sort, Congress has too often passed the buck to the courts; now Congress should exhibit some reciprocity, as well as courage and decency, and relieve the courts from further embarrassment.[70]

A bill to this effect, introduced into Congress in 1971 by Senator Phillip Hart (D.-Mich.), failed of passage—although its supporters characterized it then, and now, as an "act of mercy."

Agitation to remove the death penalty from our punishment options focuses on basic constitutional reasons that supporters like Sol Rubin insist are easy for anyone to follow:

One is the most obvious one of cruelty. I will not take the space to repeat the gruesome descriptions of what happened in executions by gas, by electricity, or by other ways. That they are gruesome, witnesses to them have testified, and by any meaning of the word "cruel," they are cruel. But the Supreme Court has upheld every means of execution, and shows no inclination even to examine the question of cruelty.

One other constitutional argument against the death penalty, a simple one, should doom it. It inevitably deprives any person who has been executed of due process of law. When the condemned man is executed, any errors in the proceedings are placed beyond the reach of later decisions.[71]

Taking heart from the 1973 Supreme Court ruling, those who oppose the death penalty insist that we have achieved a "historic turn in our country toward humaneness and rationality in the administration of justice."[72]

Critics call attention, however, to a reverse tendency elsewhere: only four countries have joined the ranks of the abolitionists in the past twenty-five years. A recent UN survey of sixty-nine leading nations found that 75 per cent still use the death penalty, with hijacking and drug trafficking newly added to the list of punishable offenses.[73] Ban supporters retort that very few are actually sentenced to death abroad and that even fewer are finally executed. In Canada, for example, the Federal Cabinet has commuted all death sentences since the early 1960's, as has also been true in Australia since 1967, though the death penalty remains on the books in both countries.

Ironically, however, supporters of the death penalty are discouraged by their own state-by-state securement of mandatory death sentences. The mandatory approach, they concede, is so rigid that it can encourage a jury to bring in a conviction on reduced charges or even to free a guilty man rather than condemn him to certain death. They are also set back by the April 1973 vote of the British Parliament that saw the "hanging" lobby lose badly in its effort to reverse a 1969 Parliament decision to abolish the death penalty permanently (polls had shown that up to 80 per cent of the British were in favor of restoring the death penalty, at least for some offenses).[74]

The conclusive verdict on this question is still far from in, and the jury stays out pondering the ancient question of the right of the state to take a life and the ultimate effect on a civilization of a heavy-hearted affirmation of that right.

Summary: Reform Prospects. Few issues divide us as sharply as does the issue of crime and punishment. Sociologist Robert Martinson warns that the difficulties of arriving at a long-run perspective capable of producing substantial change in criminal justice systems should not be underestimated:

> A focus on abortion, marijuana, etc., may alienate the middle-American and labor element; a focus on law enforcement stirs liberal fears of a police state; a focus on crime prevention reminds many of the confusion and failures of the war on poverty; a focus on radical reform of criminal justice disquiets those who still maintain faith in the myth of correctional treatment; a focus on "justice for the offender" enrages police and correctional officers' unions and wins no votes among the victimized.[75]

Nevertheless, there *are* reasons to believe that far-reaching progress is more attainable now than ever before in recent history.

Much of merit has already been done that could be adopted more widely across the country. For example:

> While similar restrictions continue across the states Illinois in 1972 repealed archaic and arbitrary licensing laws that bar ex-felons from such jobs as barbers, beauty culture operators, funeral directors, water-well pump installers, livestock and swine dealers, and blood-bank operators.[76]

> The U.S. Manpower Administration is providing bonded coverage to job-applicants who might be regarded as untrustworthy. Administered by state employment service agencies, the program covered 3,600 persons by the end of 1971 (as against 150,000 releases annually) with a default total of only 56—less than 2 per cent in five years.[77]

> An inexpensive, non-cancellable, easy-to-get burglary and robbery insurance policy for high crime areas, established by the Federal Government in 1971 and available in ten states and the District of Columbia, continues to go virtually ignored by millions of eligible urbanites. One official explains that "the biggest problem we have is that the average person still doesn't know about Federal insurance."[78]

> Massachusetts has abolished its system of reform schools for juveniles. It has replaced them with a progressive network of 100 halfway houses, group shelters, foster homes, forestry work, special counseling services, and community action programs. Dr. Jerome Miller, "architect" of the reforms, wants to move the state "away from punitive institutions to child care models. We want to be advocates for children, not jailers. We want to help them right in their own communities." He points to a new recidivism rate of under 20 per

cent, or about a third of the old reform-school rate, as evidence that the modern approach is working.[79]

Pretrial diversion, a new reform alternative to trial and punishment, selects good prospects for voluntary rehabilitation and in effect, puts them on probation before they go to trial. If they successfully complete their probation, they are spared the ordeal of a prison term and the stigma of a prison record. To date, 70 per cent of the "clients" in the dozen or so such programs in operation have had the charges against them dropped.[80]

These, of course, are offered as only a small sample of all the reforms that could be cited.

Especially valuable in the new reforms underway is the creative spark that distinguishes the best of them. For example, resourceful judges with a rehabilitative orientation are setting a new standard in sentencing:

Found guilty of exhibiting obscene movies, and sentenced to two years in jail, a defendant was permitted instead to contribute 100 hours of service to a charity of his choice and establish a $2,000 trust fund to be used to purchase educational films for area schools.

Found guilty of abandoning a refrigerator in which a three-year-old boy suffocated, a woman was sentenced to two years' probation with the proviso that her criminal record would be cleared if she found and reported at least ten illegally abandoned iceboxes. Within a month the woman, who has two sons, had fulfilled the judge's order.

Found guilty of disorderly conduct and resisting arrest a 20-year-old man was given a choice of a year in jail or a year teaching illiterate prisoners to read and write.[81]

Regardless of the merit of any particular sentence, the idea of responsible alternatives to jail sentences is worth continued exploration.

A wide array of European reforms also merit careful American scrutiny:

France enables its gendarmes to fine traffic violators on the spot, and collect the receipted fine as well.

Western European nations emphasize merit rather than politics in all matters connected to their judges. Accordingly, no English judge, for example, has been removed for corruption or anything else since 1700.

British policemen are opposed to carrying guns. "If forced to carry them, a lot would resign," explains the union head. "No one wants to be associated with the first policeman who draws a gun and kills an innocent member of the public."[82]

When confronting a crowd of potentially violent demonstrators, the unarmed police of Britain link arms and close up against the demonstrators face-to-face. There are no plastic shields or protective gear or truncheons, no weapons, and no tear gas. They are expected to show tolerance and even humor, if possible, and above all to avoid behavior which would be provocative or incite the militants in a crowd to real violence.[83]

Again, other examples could be cited in impressive profusion, but the point is clear: we could—and should—be importing much in the way of lessons and examples in superior justice-system strategies from abroad.

How much further, then, do we have to go? A partial answer is available in the fact that the 1973 Report of the National Advisory Commission on Criminal Justice Standards and Goals contains thirty-eight hundred pages and promulgates 290 standards, for example:

1. Take probation out of the courts and move it into the correctional sphere.
2. Abandon the use of parole boards as official institutions and institute them only as advisory committees.
3. Relate prison industry more closely to the larger society.
4. Divert and deinstitutionalize by means of community treatment.
5. Establish a five-year moratorium on new prison construction and seek to destroy large existing mega-institutions.
6. Establish a unified national system of corrections.

Relevant as well is the Report's stress on the part each of *us* might play in a nationwide effort against crime:

> Provide or help find jobs and personal counseling for underprivileged children and former convicts.
>
> Organize to improve street lighting or form a neighborhood crime-reporting committee.
>
> Volunteer as a probation officer for local courts.

And it is exactly this personalizing of the crime challenge that may finally enable us to achieve substantial gains in an area that may otherwise become the national disgrace.[84]

In sum, we are challenged, each of us, to gain and propagate the following sort of insight:

> When you look at the system we've got for preventing and controlling crime, it looks like a system to *perpetuate* crime. But every time you speak of these matters, the law and order evangelist says, "See there, you only care about the criminal, not about the victim." Nonsense, we are all victims of criminals guaranteed and provided by a "punishment system" that does not reduce crime but promotes it.[85]

In the last analysis, then, we must help America move beyond a system that promotes the worst that is inherent in all of us—and our social order—toward the one envisioned by Arthur I. Waskow:

> A decent redistribution of power and income so as to put out the hidden fire of burning envy that now flares up in crimes of property—both burglary by the poor and embezzlement by the affluent. And a decent sense of community that can support, reintegrate, and truly rehabilitate those who suddenly become filled with fury or despair, and that can face them not as objects—"criminals"—but as people who have committed illegal acts, as have almost all of us.[86]

FOOTNOTES

1. "Poll Finds Crime Exceeds Reports," *New York Times* (January 14, 1973), p. 17. Note that the total number of reported serious crimes dropped in 1972 for the first time in 17 years, *New York Times* (August 9, 1973), p. 16.
2. Philip Meyer, "1 in 34: Your Chance of Being a Crime Victim," *Philadelphia Inquirer* (August 29, 1972), p. 2.
3. Aryeh Neier, "Have You Ever Been Arrested?" *New York Times Magazine* (April 15, 1973), p. 16. Drawn from the 1967 Report of the President's Commission on Law Enforcement.
4. Ibid.
5. James R. Dickenson, "If You Pay, Crime Won't," *National Observer* (January 27, 1973), p. 1.
6. Ibid.
7. Quoted in *The Center Magazine* (May–June 1971), p. 10.
8. Carl Rauh, as quoted in *The Center Magazine* (May–June 1971), p. 11.
9. Barry Cunningham, "Muggers and Victims," *New York Post* (April 23, 1973), p. 31. Based on 1967 Report of the President's Crime Commission.
10. Howard Moody, "Are You 'Soft' on Crime?" *Village Voice* (April 12, 1973), p. 7.
11. Franklin E. Zimring, "Some Facts About Homicide," *The Nation* (March 6, 1972), p. 303.
12. Bill Kovach, "Study Finds Crime Rates Far Higher Than Reports," *New York Times* (April 27, 1973), p. 44.
13. Ibid.
14. David Burnham, "Legal 'Numbers' Urged for State to Reduce Crime," *New York Times* (November 26, 1972), p. 1.
15. Kovach, op. cit., p. 44.
16. Robert Daley, "Get the Cops, Courts, and Jails Out of the Public-Morals Business," *New York Times Magazine* (September 24, 1972), pp. 14, 91–92.
17. George Alexander, "The Pause in the Day's Occupation Known as the Mugging Hour," *New York* (April 26, 1971), p. 32.
18. Robert M. McKiernan, "Police Shotguns: 'Devastating to the Animals,'" *New York Times* (February 7, 1973), p. 35.
19. Edgar Smith, "Stop Countenancing Selective Obedience to Law," *New York Times Magazine* (September 24, 1972), p. 93.
20. "Mr. Bumble," "Writing Off Your Bribes," *New York* (April 12, 1971), p. 65.
21. Mary P. Nichols, "Runnin' Scared," *Village Voice* (January 18, 1973), p. 3.
22. Moody, op. cit., p. 7.
23. Ibid.
24. Quoted in Jack Greenberg, "Make Sure Every American Is Given the Opportunities," *New York Times Magazine* (September 24, 1972), p. 98.
25. Edward M. Kennedy, "First in Guns, Last in Controls," *New York Times* (August 24, 1972), p. 41.
26. Ronald P. Kriss, "Gun Control: A Missed Target," *Saturday Review* (August 26, 1972), p. 26.
27. Robert Roth, "Plugging the Muzzles of 'Saturday Night Specials,'" *Philadelphia Evening Bulletin* (August 20, 1972), p. V-Fl.
28. Kriss, op. cit., p. 26.
29. Marylin Bender, "The Gun Business on the Defensive," *New York Times* (March 4, 1973), pp. 1–3.
30. Quoted in Paul Good, "Blam! Blam! Blam! Not Gun Nuts, but Pistol Enthusiasts," *New York Times Magazine* (September 17, 1972), p. 41.
31. Kriss, op. cit., p. 26.
32. Ibid.

33. Kennedy, op. cit., p. 41.
34. Good, op. cit., p. 34.
35. Ibid., p. 36.
36. John M. Snyder, "An Aspect of Freedom: The Right to Bear Arms," *New Guard* (Summer 1971), p. 12.
37. Ibid.
38. William Lynch, Letter to the Editor, *New Republic* (March 31, 1973), p. 33.
39. Good, op. cit., p. 29.
40. Sydney J. Harris, "People Without Guns Have a Low Murder Rate," *Philadelphia Evening Bulletin* (April 4, 1973), p. 23-A.
41. Smith Hemptone, "Gun Talks Again; Will Congress Listen?" *Philadelphia Inquirer* (February 7, 1973), p. 11-A.
42. Good, op. cit., p. 46.
43. "In Switzerland, Many Have Guns but Few Get Shot," *Wall Street Journal* (June 6, 1972), p. 1.
44. Bender, op. cit.
45. "Law and Order Four Years Later," *New Republic* (September 23, 1972), p. 6.
46. Committee for Economic Development, press release, June 29, 1972 (477 Madison Ave., N.Y., 10022), p. 1.
47. Kennedy, op. cit.
48. Alvin Shuster, "Gun Battle in London Stirs Controversy," *New York Times* (January 3, 1973), p. 16.
49. Pamela Roby and Virginia Kerr, "Prostitution and What to Do About It," unpublished and undated mimeographed essay.
50. Lindsy Van Gelder and Larry Kleinman, "Prostitution in New York," *New York Post* (February 15, 1973), p. 47.
51. Ibid.
52. Ibid.
53. Ibid.
54. Quoted in *The Center Magazine* (May–June 1971), p. 12.
55. Norval Morris, "The Law Is a Busybody," *New York Times Magazine* (April 1, 1973), p. 11.
56. Ibid.
57. Ibid.
58. Morris, *The Center Magazine,* op. cit., p. 14.
59. Morris, *New York Times Magazine,* op. cit., p. 11.
60. William F. Rickenbacher, "The Law Forbidding Sin," *National Review* (January 21, 1972), p. 46.
61. "Senate Bill Would Aid Victims of Crime," *New York Times* (September 19, 1972), p. 53.
62. Editorial, "Aiding Crime Victims," *Philadelphia Inquirer* (September 22, 1972), p. 28. See also Ronald V. Teunis, "Cahill OKs Bill to Help Pay Crime Victims," *Philadelphia Evening Bulletin* (October 5, 1971), p. 1; Fred P. Graham, "Plan to Pay Crime Victims Gains Among Democrats," *New York Times* (December 1, 1971), p. 52.
63. Ralph Blumenthal, "State Program to Aid Crime Victims Reaches Only a Few of Those Eligible," *New York Times* (March 15, 1973), p. 45.
64. Francis T. P. Plimpton et al., "Death Penalty Ban: The Anatomy of a Victory," *New York Times* (July 3, 1972), p. 28.
65. Ibid.
66. "Death Penalty Has Been Restored by 13 States," *New York Times* (May 10, 1973), p. 18.

67. "57% in Poll Back a Death Penalty," *New York Times* (November 23, 1972), p. 18.
68. Tom Wicker, "Death Again in California," *New York Times* (November 27, 1972), p. E-11.
69. Plimpton, op. cit., p. 28.
70. "Death Penalty Reform," *The Nation* (June 21, 1971), p. 773.
71. Sol Rubin, "The Burger Court and the Penal System," *The Nation* (June 21, 1971), p. 797.
72. "Death Penalty Reforms," p. 773.
73. Kathleen Teltsch, "U.N. Says 100 Nations Use Execution," *New York Times* (March 25, 1973), p. 6.
74. Alvin Shuster, "Britain: Defeat for the Death Penalty," *New York Times* (April 15, 1973), p. 8-E.
75. Robert Martinson, "The Meaning of Attica," *New Republic* (April 15, 1972), p. 19.
76. Sid Ross and Herbert Kupferberg, "Would You Hire an Ex-Convict?" *Parade* (November 12, 1972), p. 18.
77. Ibid.
78. Grace Lichtenstein, "U.S. Burglar Insurance Is Overlooked Bargain," *New York Times* (October 29, 1972), p. 56.
79. Sid Ross and Herbert Kupferberg, "Shut Down Reform Schools?" *Parade* (September 17, 1972), p. 5.
80. "Judges Seeking Alternatives to Jail," *New York Times* (January 7, 1973), p. 75.
81. Ibid.
82. Felix Kessler, "The Gun," *Wall Street Journal* (June 6, 1972), p. 1.
83. Don Cook, "British Police Face Down Crowds Without Guns or Recriminations," *Philadelphia Inquirer* (April 24, 1972), p. 1.
84. Dickenson, op. cit., p. 1.
85. Moody, op. cit., p. 8.
86. Arthur I. Waskow, ". . . I Am Not Free," *Saturday Review* (January 8, 1972), p. 20.

READING

Crimes Without Victims

Alexander B. Smith and Harriet Pollack

Few people would dispute that crime probably heads today's list of troubles besetting our urban population. City-dwellers are afraid of being mugged, robbed, raped, or murdered. In addition, they are disgusted: by the blatant soliciting from prostitutes; by gay bars; by seedy pornography shops; by openly sold heroin and marijuana; and by crooked cops. The response on the part of our law enforcement agencies has been to attempt better surveillance of high crime areas in order to protect people against assault and robbery,

 Professors Smith and Pollack are also the authors of *Crime and Justice in a Mass Society* (Corte Madera: Rinehart Press, 1972).

and to mount campaigns to clean up the downtown neighborhoods where pimps, female and male prostitutes, bookies, pornographers, et al. assemble.

Whatever the merits and feasibility of increased police patrols to handle street crime, there is at least no doubt that citizens need to be protected against thieves and murderers. There is a real question, however, whether campaigns against gamblers, prostitutes, and dope pushers are not actually counterproductive in terms of producing a decent, stable society.

Despite the attractiveness of the notion of a "clean" Times Square or Loop as morally pure as the more genteel sections of New York City or Chicago, are there hidden social costs to such cleanups that society may not care to pay? Is there some relationship between the use of the criminal justice system to police our morals and its failure to protect our persons? Is how to handle prostitutes and pornographers the problem, or is it the larger question of whether morals offenses should be considered as crimes? Will a fresh look at the penal code be more fruitful in the long run than arguing over whether displaced prostitutes or pornographers will be likely to go to the suburbs if hounded out of the inner cities?

Conceptually, our penal code prohibits two kinds of acts: those that are *malum in se* (evil in themselves) and those that are *malum prohibitum* (evil because prohibited). *Malum in se* acts (murder, rape, arson, assault) are true crimes in the sense that no society can tolerate such conduct and survive. But a large part of our penal code is concerned with acts that are not universally considered evil but that we, at this moment in time, for a variety of reasons, have labeled as sufficiently undesirable to be punished by the criminal justice system. In New York State, for example, gambling is prohibited by law, and the police, courts, and jails are expected to deal with numbers runners, bookies, and the like. At the same time, the state itself not only permits gambling at the race tracks and runs a lottery based on the outcome of the horse races but has set up OTB, a corporation for handling off-track bets, from which the state expects to derive revenue. Nevada, among other states, licenses and taxes casinos and similar gambling establishments. Clearly, nothing in gambling per se is inconsistent with a viable society; yet the resources of our criminal justice system are diverted to the enforcement of antigambling laws.

Our attitudes toward drug use are equally inconsistent. We forbid the use of marijuana and heroin; yet we tolerate the limited use of amphetamines and barbiturates, and we encourage, through ubiquitous advertising, the indiscriminate sale of pills for every conceivable purpose, physiological and psychological. Hundreds of sections of the criminal law are concerned with acts that are criminal mainly because society at large says they are: homosexual activity between consenting adults, prostitution, gambling, possession of obscene and pornographic materials, to name a few. The enforcement of these laws takes the lion's share of our criminal justice resources. For every murderer arrested and prosecuted, literally dozens of gamblers, prostitutes, dope pushers, and derelicts crowd our courts' dockets. If we took the numbers runners, the kids smoking pot, and the winos out of the criminal justice system, we would substantially reduce the burden on the courts and the police. If we permitted the sale of heroin on a controlled prescription basis (as the British do, and as we do with other dangerous drugs), we would probably eliminate well over half of the cases going through our criminal courts. Myths to the contrary, there is no scientific evidence that the use of heroin, in and of itself, causes criminal conduct. By cutting off all legal access to heroin, however, we have driven the price so high that experienced observers estimate that more than half the crimes in New York City are committed by addicts seeking drugs or the money for drugs. The greater part of the social evil incident to the use of heroin, thus, comes not from its use but from the laws that make it impossible to obtain the drug legally. This is not to say, of course, that the use of heroin is not harmful to the addict. It is only that our penal code has extended that harm from the user himself to those who are victimized by his crime. In short, the net effect of our drug laws is highly counterproductive in that they create more antisocial conduct than they prevent.

Morals laws that do not reflect contemporary mores or that cannot be enforced should be removed from the penal code through legislative action, because, at best, they undermine respect for the law and, at worst, as in the case of our drug laws, they exacerbate a tragic situation. Admittedly, such a deliberate legislative policy would fly in the face of all historical American experience. As Morris Ernst once remarked, Americans do not repeal morals legislation; they simply allow such laws to fall into desuetude. Sunday blue laws are a classic example of this process. The New York State Sunday Closing Law currently on the books has in the past been read to forbid movie, stage, and radio performances on Sunday. Of course, this interpretation is archaic at present; the courts have simply stopped interpreting this law in so restrictive a manner. The police also have become so unconcerned with enforcing it that they ignore violations. In 1970, the New York City police commissioner, recognizing that no one any longer cared about the Sunday Closing Law, announced that his men would not even attempt to enforce it. Such forthrightness on the part of an administrative official is unusual; most laws go unenforced by default rather than by deliberate policy.

More important, despite the commissioner's candor and despite the inutility of this law, the legislature has not bothered to repeal it. The reasons are obvious: any such attempt would lead to an outcry by small but militant minority groups who would convert a simple act of legislative housekeeping into a debate over morality. No legislator wants to be cast in the role of the defender of immorality, even in the case of a custom widely accepted and practiced by a good part of his constituency. It is much easier, and politically more sensible, simply to sweep the issue under the rug by ignoring it.

Unfortunately, we can no longer afford the luxury of waiting for administrative action (or inaction) to catch up with public morality. Possibly because we live in an era that has seen great changes in public mores in a relatively short time, we have too many laws that the police are attempting to enforce and the courts to handle that large segments of the public simply will not obey. Gambling laws are an obvious example, as are those forbidding prostitution, homosexual acts between adults, and possession of pornographic materials. The most troublesome morals laws, however, are those forbidding the possession and sale of marijuana, heroin, LSD, and other similar drugs.

There is something very frightening to most people in advocating repeal of morals laws. It is as though, by advocating repeal, the conduct that heretofore has been forbidden is being endorsed. Nothing could be further from the truth. In repealing morals laws, the legislature is not proposing that people become immoral; it is simply declaring that the criminal sanction will no longer be used to enforce a particular mode of conduct. Most human conduct, after all, is regulated by nonlegal institutions: the home, the school, the church, the family, the peer group. Most husbands work hard and support their wives and children because they respond to cultural demands, not because they could be put in jail for nonsupport if they failed to do so. The unpalatable truth is that passing a law does not mean that it will be obeyed or that it can be enforced. Conversely, the repeal of a law does not necessarily mean an increase in undesirable conduct.

Prohibition is probably the most clear-cut example of the effect of enacting and then repealing a morals law. The Eighteenth Amendment had virtually no effect in reducing per capita alcohol consumption in this country, and its repeal did not increase either the amount of drinking or the problems of alcoholism. The only effect the Eighteenth Amendment had was to create a flourishing bootlegging industry, and it was this spin-off—the rise in serious crime due to an unenforceable law—that constituted one of the principal reasons for repeal.

We are in a similar position today. Our gambling and drug laws particularly have created a situation in which an enormous organized crime industry thrives on satisfying a consumer demand that cannot be met legitimately. Worse yet, the effort to cope with the crime wave resulting from our unenforceable drug and gambling laws is destroying our criminal justice system and rendering it incapable of dealing with criminals who violate laws that might, under better circumstances, be reasonably enforceable.

While the chances for legislative modification of morals laws are still poor, there are signs that public opinion is beginning to recognize the need for change, especially in the areas of gambling and consensual adult sex practices. Proposed repeal of drug laws (even those relating to marijuana) has aroused far more anxiety, and there are still virtually no prominent public figures willing to openly advocate the legalization of heroin. There is probably some risk in repealing the ban on heroin. Many policemen, among others, believe that if the ban were lifted, a substantial number of people (especially youngsters), eager to try forbidden fruit, would be hooked into an addiction that would last the rest of their lives. Removing heroin from the penal code does not, however, mean permitting its sale in every candy store. As with many other pharmaceuticals, distribution could be regulated by prescription. But more than that, almost everyone familiar with the drug scene (especially the police) agrees that the present law has not deterred anyone who doesn't want to be deterred. It is easy to get heroin in New York City today, despite the law and the entire criminal justice system arrayed in support of the law. Apparently, those who are not using heroin are abstaining voluntarily, in which case repeal carries minimal risks.

Not only are morals laws frequently counterproductive in terms of their causing more crime than they prevent, but their enforcement is particularly dangerous to civil liberties since crimes resulting from their violation have no victims. The prostitute's client has not been forcibly seduced; the housewife who bets a quarter on the numbers has not been robbed; the dope user has harmed only himself. Because there are no victims available to testify for the state, the burden of producing enough evidence for the prosecution rests entirely on the police. It is this need for evidence to make morals offense violations "stick" that traditionally has produced the greatest number of civil liberties violations by the police. Prostitutes, for example, are frequently victims of entrapment by plainclothesmen. If their customers will not testify, who besides the plainclothesmen can? And what better way of establishing a case than by offering an obviously willing girl a little "encouragement"? Official police records indicate that an incredible number of gamblers and drug pushers "drop" gambling slips and narcotics at the mere approach of a policeman. This so-called dropsie evidence is frequently a euphemism for an illegal search. The amount of dropsie evidence has increased markedly since 1961, when the Supreme Court in *Mapp v. Ohio* banned the use of overtly, illegally seized evidence in state courts.

Such violations of civil liberties occur not because the police prefer to act illegally but because it is difficult to build a legitimate case where there is no real victim. At the Supreme Court level, it is noteworthy that most of the decisions censuring police conduct deal with state and local enforcement procedures rather than federal ones. This is not because FBI agents are inherently more civil libertarian or cognizant of legalities than local policemen. It is because they deal with different kinds of wrongdoings. In such crimes as kidnaping, bank robbery, or counterfeiting, there are real victims, and federal agents can build their cases in an ethical, professional manner: obtaining statements from victims, interviewing eyewitnesses, obtaining fingerprints, weapons, contraband, etc. Local police, in dealing with pimps, numbers runners, and dope pushers, are not afforded this luxury. They must make a case the best way they can, and frequently this involves illegal snooping, searching, and arrests.

The enforcement of morals laws not only involves the police in violations of civil liberties but is the source of most of the corruption within police departments. All police departments are plagued with a small number of rogues who join forces with the criminals they are supposed to apprehend and participate in burglaries, extortion, etc. This kind of corruption is relatively rare and usually not difficult to eliminate. Seldom does it extend to the top administrative levels. The most common type of police corruption is the payoffs policemen receive (and pass along to their superior officers) from criminals involved with drugs, gambling, or prostitution. This sort of graft is almost impossible to eradicate, partly because the illegal activities involved are so profitable and the payoffs so lucrative, and partly because the activities themselves do not seem terribly immoral to the police, possibly because the crimes have no real victims. Such corruption spreads, moreover, throughout entire departments, from the patrolman on the beat through top administrators and sometimes even to the commissioner, mayor, or other elected officials. Periodic exposés reveal a pattern that has varied little from the pattern laid bare at the turn of the century by Lincoln Steffens in *The Shame of the Cities;* however, the waves of reform following such exposés lead to little more than temporary remissions. No way has yet been found to eliminate this kind of corruption as long as the public wants to gamble, take illegal drugs, frequent prostitutes, etc., and as long as immense profits can be earned by criminals meeting these desires.

Perhaps the most important benefit that would result from the elimination of morals offenses from the penal code would be the relief of the criminal justice system. Prison riots, inordinately delayed trials, crimes committed by defendants out on bail, a clamor for preventive detention—all testify to the dangerously strained conditions of our criminal justice institutions. No one knows how much time is spent by the police, prosecutors, and courts in processing morals defendants, but it has been estimated that as little as 10 per cent of the courtroom hours available in our criminal courts are now devoted to the processing of serious crimes. If we were free to devote the remaining 90 per cent of our courtroom hours to the handling of dangerous offenders or serious crimes of property, we would be able to overcome most of the shortcomings of our present criminal justice system. With fewer offenders to concern them, police work could be more thorough and legitimate. The decongestion of court calendars would reduce the pressure for plea bargaining, as would, incidentally, more carefully prepared cases based on legally gathered evidence. The burden on probation and parole officers would also be lessened, and if the likelihood of arrest were greater due to better police work, then prison sentences might be more likely to act as a deterrent.

At the moment, proposals to repeal morals legislation are neither popular nor acceptable. Such proposals are attacked from both ends of the morality spectrum. On the one hand, guardians of public order are outraged at the prospect of "legalizing" gambling, drug sales, and sexual soliciting. "How would you feel if it were your sixteen-year-old daughter who became hooked on heroin?" "Terrible. But thousands are hooked now, and if she does become hooked, at least she will not have to steal, prostitute herself, victimize other people, or die of an overdose." The response in the imaginary colloquy is correct but probably unconvincing to those who look at the printed word of the law as an amulet to ward off evil. The police, on the whole, do not favor the repeal of morals laws, in part because they see repeal as an admission of their limited role in society, i.e., that they can enforce only those laws the general public is willing to obey. Such an admission is not only ego-bruising but a distinct handicap in the annual race for their share of the public budget.

On the other hand, many people are making a very good living out of dope peddling, gambling, etc., and they are not likely to give up their livelihood without a struggle. What the ties of the underworld to elected and appointed officials are no one really knows, but they exist, and organized crime is certainly capable of exerting pressure behind the scenes to discourage unfavorable legislation.

One can only hope that the uncommitted majority will come to realize the price we pay in corruption, the denial of civil liberties, and the overburdening of our criminal justice system for the luxury of using our penal code to enforce our currently fashionable behavior preferences. We need courage enough to admit that certain kinds of behavior cannot be controlled through the punitive sanction and faith enough to believe that cultural pressure (or innate decency) will suffice to keep us from mass dissipation and self-destruction. And we need political leaders with guts enough to get up and say so.

CHAPTER 13

Prisons and Punishment

Prisons are built with stones of Law, brothels with bricks of Religion.

WILLIAM BLAKE

Inasmuch as ye have done it unto one of the least of these my brethren, ye have done it unto me.

NEW TESTAMENT

To bind up the brokenhearted, to proclaim liberty to the captives, and the opening of the prison to them that are bound.

OLD TESTAMENT

Prison, one enraged reformer, Bruce Jackson, declares, is "the only garbage dump we have that is so repulsive we encircle it with barbed wire and a stone wall."[1] Another knowledgeable party, the Director of the U.S. Bureau of Prisons, confesses that "anyone not a criminal will be one when he gets out of jail."[2] Not to be outdone, President Richard Nixon observed that "no institution within our society has a record which presents such a conclusive case of failure as does our prison system."[3]

Why? Possibly because as part of this hopelessly wrong solution some 200,000 men and women "are caged like animals, they do stupid work and are paid a demeaning wage for it; everything is censored; visits are arbitrarily limited; medical care is wretched; disciplinary procedures are unfair, and the parole system is capricious."[4] Elsewhere, Jackson asks how we expect the 100,000 men we release yearly to be reformed by "being locked for years on end in six-by-nine-foot cages in communities where homosexuality is a norm, mistrust a necessity, and hate a social commodity?"[5]

Much of our plight can be documented by statistics like these from Ramsey Clark:

> Ninety-five per cent of *all* correctional expenditures are for buildings and guards. Such services as health, education, and development of employment skills receive only five per cent.
>
> Eighty per cent of all personnel in corrections employment are used to guard 400,000 prisoners in jails and prisons. Only one in five of all such personnel are available even theoretically to help the 800,000 others on probation.[6]

With possibly 67 per cent of all prison inmates repeat offenders, the Chief Justice of the Supreme Court can find "little evidence that we have improved the situation in the past 30 or 40 years."[7]

No less an insider than James R. Hoffa, ex-head of the Teamsters Union and an alumnus of fifty-eight months behind bars in Lewisburg, Pennsylvania, disturbs audiences across the nation with his impressions of one of the most genteel prisons in the federal system:

> Eighty-five per cent of the guards are characterized as "time-servers," with another five per cent being judged "sadists"; forty-five per cent of the inmates are thought either sexual aggressors, or their victims.[8]

Medical treatment is so bad that a principal fear of the prisoners is that they might require health care, a possibility made likely by prison food that is almost sadistically inedible. In much the same way, Reverend Philip Berrigan, after thirty-nine months in a federal prison in Connecticut, describes the prisoners' plight:

> One can get very subjective about them, having felt their destructiveness in one's bones. . . . Their time has passed . . . they are obsolescent, bankrupt loss . . . laboratories of waste, injustice and desperation, outstanding examples of reciprocal revenge between society and the prisoner.[9]

Or as William Battle, an inmate at the Great Meadows Correctional Facility in New York, puts it:

> I can see no future. No inmate in this institution has a future. There is no rehabilitation to be had. There's nothing to look forward to when you get out except going back to dealing in drugs or knocking some dude over the head who has worked all week for his bread. What's coming in to this place are dudes who have committed crimes. What's coming out are cold-blooded monsters.[10]

Similarly, an inmate of a Maryland prison shook up a 1969 workshop on prison life with his irreverent challenge:

> What's rehabilitation? I've never seen it. We come in laborers and go out laborers. All we learn here is how to make [license] tags, and there ain't no place outside where you can make tags. We're the same guy when we go out, and that's where it's at, baby.[11]

From man to man the tale remains the same—as do the pain and the utter lack of any prosociety gain from "prisons," social arrangements that deform and punish our capacities for freedom.

"Out of sight, out of mind" has poignant application here, and strange observations therefore flow from occasional outside glimpses into prison life. For example, six judges in New York City visited two major upstate penal institutions in the fall of 1972 and urged thereafter four brow-arching reforms on the basis of their mere two days' observation:

1. Wages of 25 cents a day seemed an inadequate work incentive; perhaps this could be raised.
2. A ratio of 300 idle to 1,500 convicts at work seemed excessive; perhaps something constructive could be found for the 300 to do.
3. Inadequate shower and counselling facilities should be improved.
4. More freedom within the institutions might be considered by the warders.

The earnest judges were also perturbed to learn from understandably incensed inmates that wide discrepancies in sentencing was driving men mad. Many sentenced under an old penal law later changed in 1969 were serving twice as long as others convicted since for the same crimes. Thus apprised, the six judges recommended to the presiding justices of their respective judicial districts that such sentences be reviewed.[12]

Similarly, in a major address in January of 1973 Chief Justice Warren E. Burger insisted that it is *not* larger police forces or stricter prison sentences that will stop America's rising crime rate but an improved penal system. Made up of four long-familiar but seldom-enacted reforms, the Burger prescription calls for:

1. Substantial improvement in prison facilities.
2. Better programs in inmate education, job training, and recreation.
3. Intensive training for both prison and parole personnel.
4. Well-supervised release programs to identify those convicted persons who should not be sent to prison at all.

Burger is especially anxious to have inmates tested for potential vocational skills. Then they can be promised that if they use their time to develop salable skills in an area of natural aptitude, they will be released early to seek employment. In this way a vital incentive is available to learn one's way out of confinement in less time than originally decreed.[13]

The rehabilitation component of these suggestions, however, has come in for increasingly critical scrutiny lately from reformers who insist that the Burger goals miss the target altogether. One such critic, Herman Schwartz, pointedly writes:

> Rehabilitation is either a myth or a fraud. If you're talking about parole, it's a fraud, because parole agencies use the facade of rehabilitation to hide the fact that they're almost exclusively exercising a control function. If you're talking about the notion that people might get rehabilitated in prison by going to educational programs or some kind of therapy, that's largely a myth. We really ought to recognize and curb the enormous amount of harm we are doing. Rehabilitation is simply not working.[14]

When asked why rehabilitation fails, Schwartz explains:

> It's not possible because (a) we don't know how to change conduct, if we're talking about changes of personality; (b) we're not willing to spend the money to provide meaningful educational or job training; (c) we're in a recession period and will be for who knows how long, so there are few or no jobs for prisoners when they come out; and (d) there is no indication that we are willing to take even the job-training kind of "rehabilitation" seriously,

> because it costs a lot of money, the unions don't want the competition, and the community apparently wants to keep punishing the offender.[15]

Reasoning in this way, Schwartz insists that we go beyond Burger's "practical" aids and reject tinkering, patchwork solutions and efforts to piece together a crumbling institution (mere rehabilitation is a "very pernicious and expensive delusion").

It is on the better-than-average or exceptional reforms that I want to dwell in this section of the chapter. The first of the items discussed, the new policy of diversion, helps keep men away from prison, and the second, the ombudsman, contributes an outside advocate to the scene. The third, "prisoner power," raises the very controversial issue of inmate rights, and the fourth, abolishment of prisons, takes us as far as reform can logically go . . . and then some.

Diversion Policies. Rehabilitation is seen by some reformers as geared to overdue reductions in prison population ("Probably 50 to 70 per cent of inmates in state prisons could safely be returned to the community"[16]). Popular in this connection are spin-off or rerouting reforms, for example:

> Persons convicted of so-called victimless crimes would no longer receive prison sentences.
>
> Persons convicted of alcoholism, drug mis-use, or mental mis-behavior would receive mandatory treatment in specialized institutions. They would no longer be sent to prisons.
>
> Pennsylvania has a furlough system that, since 1970, has allowed jailers to reward "good conduct" with furloughs of up to seven days. Inmates use the time to seek jobs, take college entrance examinations, visit relatives, or simply go home. Common to 25 other states, Penn. stands out with less than three per cent of the furloughers failing to return to prison.[17]

This new strategy of diverting offenders from confinement is based on four time-proven devices: bail reform, work release, increased probation, and local supervision. The strategy helps to curb input pressures and sharply reduces the contact necessary between the offender and our "correctional" system. Whether or not this reform will gain on the more popular and older practice of primitive imprisonment is unclear—though a hopeful sign or two is well worth calling to your attention. For one thing, it appears significant that the myth of the effectiveness of treatment is being thoroughly discredited at this time. Reformers have finally come to understand that although the system (the courts, probation, prison, and parole) can punish, incarcerate, and try to control, it *cannot* rehabilitate as many and as well as it must. After a hundred years of trying to improve brutal prison regimes so as to use "model" institutions to rehabilitate offenders, progressive reformers now realize the impossibility of this goal, regardless of (rarely available) goodwill or dollars. For the inadvertent *damage* done to the offender through his removal from society at a critical juncture of his life cycle almost always guarantees rampant recidivism and human waste and loss—whatever the other facts of imprisonment.

This realization has helped create an unprecedented anti-internment alliance of like-minded penologists and offenders, including the recently founded National Prisoners Coalition. That organization now champions a "nonviolent approach to the systematic reduction of prison populations" and asks for five programs that minimize deprivation of liberty: work release, halfway houses, expanded probation, early release, and pretrial vocational programs. The alliance also lobbies for novel change mechanisms such as: probation subsidy (paying counties *not* to send offenders to prisons); reversing the burden of proof at parole hearings; speedy-trial legislation; and prohibition of imprisonment for certain classes of property offenders.[18] All of these changes are thought critical in the uphill effort to implement antiprison strategy.

Opposition, of course, is considerable. Hard-liners have cleverly seized the penal reform torch from regrouping reformers who now recognize the futility of "correctional" treatment. With much irony the fundamentalists use the hundred-year-old theme of "inside" rehabilitation as the last line of defense of their old prison systems. The Nixon Administration, for example, has announced its intention to build still more and better prisons—possibly even complete with enrichment items such as vocational training, more psychiatrists, and so on.

But the ultimate outcome is still far from clear, although the Wallace solution ("get the thugs off the streets") is evidence of middle American support for the Nixon Administration's stand ("protection of the public depends primarily on the correction of the offender"—President Nixon). Support *also* builds, however slowly and unevenly, for an alternative to the "same old thing," for relief from the specter of Attica, and for absolution from the guilty knowledge that prisons and reformatories are "universities of crime" (Ramsey Clarke). Diversion as a new policy has a fighting chance —provided that you and I, as potential victims, will trade off a short-term increase in personal risk for a less criminalistic society in the long run. The weight of our private opinion and public influence in the matter is quite possibly "the central problem of the politics of crime in the 20th century."[19]

Ombudsmen. Although the concept of a public defender for prisoners has been tried on a spotty basis across the nation, until recently its success has been minimal. Proponents blame this lack of success on the fact that the office carried little authority or was part of the state department of corrections and therefore could not earn the confidence of inmates.

All the more interesting, therefore, is the improved version of the ombudsman office established in 1971 in Minnesota. An entirely separate entity from the department of corrections, the office reports directly to the governor, thereby presumably gaining both prestige and a certain amount of strategic clout. Designed to offer inmates at all nine state prisons a channel for complaints against mistreatment or unjust loss of rights, the office has received uncensored letters from inmates ranging over such issues as unequal sentences, abuse by a guard, and racial and religious discrimination. As the ombudsman himself explains it, "the fact that we investigate complaints by prisoners probably causes some hardliners to cringe, but this is only a small beginning in over-all reform. Obviously, the public isn't ready for wholesale reform, but if we don't provide some means to deal with inmate grievances, the public is the ultimate loser."[20]

Power to the Prisoners! The main goal of certain reformers is to alter the present distribution of power "inside" by developing more power for the prisoners themselves. These noninmates reason that waves of prison reform directed from outside the walls merely come and go. As Herman Schwartz says, "The kinds of things that people are now talking about one can find in prison-reform statements of 1870, and even of 1930. The problem is that it's from the outside. When the blood fades into the rug, people forget."[21] This is not to gainsay the necessity of securing prisoner rights that already exist in law, for example, the right to have free correspondence and free access to the news media. But it is necessary to go beyond as well to the more controversial and newer issue of "power to the prisoners."

What precisely is at issue here, beyond the rhetoric and the considerable symbolic value of "untouchables" daring to claim a common humanity with their jailers? Schwartz says,

> To gain [some control over their own destiny] they must be able to meet. They need the right to elect representatives. They must be able to make a meaningful presentation of grievances, and to seek support from the outside community in order to mobilize the power that the outside community has. They probably need the right to form a union within prison.[22]

Why? A deputy chief of the Dutch prison administration put it well, if somewhat puzzlingly to the American mind set, when he explained recently of his nation's penal reforms:

> Our aim is to cut down the adverse effects of imprisonment to a minimum. We can do that not by making life pleasanter for the prisoners, but by normalizing it as far as possible. We must stimulate the prisoner's independence, maturity, and sense of responsibility—and believe me, this puts more strain on the prisoners' lives.[23]

Critical in the American struggle is the new role inmates expect the law to play, this time on *their* side:

1. *Cincinnati.* Inmates of the Cincinnati Workhouse sue city officials, contending that the century-old stone jail in which they are incarcerated violates the constitutional prohibition against "cruel and unusual punishment."
2. *Washington, D.C.* Women prisoners charge that the Women's House of Detention is unsanitary and overcrowded. They also maintain that district prison system discriminates against women.
3. *Joliet, Ill.* Statesville inmates sue prison administration. Their complaint: guards will not protect prisoners from assaults by other prisoners.
4. *Lansing, Kans.* A pending lawsuit by Kansas State Penitentiary inmates attacks censorship of mail to lawyers and newspapers.
5. *Stormville, N.Y.* Over half of Green Haven State Correctional Facility's 1800 prisoners organized to form a labor union. In another action, an individual inmate sues for right to marry.[24]

Until recently the courts took a hands-off attitude toward prisoner complaints. Now, thanks to the publicity after Folsom, Attica, Arkansas, Jackson State, and the bloody like, the judges are beginning to listen carefully to inmate assertions of the rights due to all men—and unjustly denied to them.

Details of the suits being filed are fascinating indices of what is missed—and denied. A Pennsylvania prisoner, for example, sued in 1973 for the right to receive *Playboy* magazine, a change of bed linen at least twice a week, and conjugal visits by the wives of prisoners. Other specific demands of his suit included—

1. An end to "random and arbitrary searches" in which guards "ransack the cells and mutilate books."
2. Freedom to receive "newspapers and literature . . . politically to the left" and no more confiscation of literature "that does not coincide with the reactionary-conservative-Neanderthal political viewpoints of the defendants."
3. A full-time medical staff on a 24-hour basis.
4. A diet of at least 2,900 calories and 70 grams of protein per day.
5. Removal of glass windows separating prisoners from visitors.
6. No more "subjecting prisoners in [a block for mental patients] to physical assaults, starvation diets and handcuffs."
7. Two hours of daily outdoor exercise.[25]

Although denied over and over again, such lawsuits continue to come out from behind the bars and may prove less and less easily dismissed with every passing prison riot.

On another front, the Green Haven State Correctional Facility in New York State is watched closely across the nation as it is pressed on the volatile question of prisoner unionization. Inmates at Green Haven want to raise their mean wage above its 59¢-per-day average, obtain better job training on modern machinery, and have some say about work area safety conditions. Over half the inmates have signed union authorization cards, and the thirty-thousand-member District 65 of the Distributive Workers of America has agreed to affiliate with the prisoners' union, subject to ratification by members of both unions (it is not clear, however, whether prisoners actually have the right to bargain over labor conditions, and the question was still before the New York Public Employment Relations Board when I wrote this in 1973).[26]

Also typical of what "power to the prisoner" can mean in practice is the record of the Self-Improvement Coalition, a group of twelve inmates (four white and eight black) that is seeking a bigger voice for fellow prisoners in South Carolina's maximum security prison. In recent months the Coalition has sponsored weekend rock concerts attended by several hundred inmates, organized a law library within the prison, and begun to establish a crafts program with sales outlets. It has also held the first-of-its-kind press conference: with no guards nor any prison officials present two Coalition spokesmen held a news conference inside the walls and castigated the South Carolina prison system and the officials who run it:

In addition to charges that drugs were widely available, the inmates objected to "slave labor" conditions, to what they called racism among officials, lack of adequate medical facilities, harsh discipline and daily threats of intimidation within the prison walls.

But perhaps the most vigorous objection was to being treated without dignity.

Hamilton told of visiting a classification officer to ask for a form to apply for a status change that would allow him more freedom of movement.

His voice rose as he told reporters: "He calls me Hamilton. I'm just as much a human being with right to respect as he is."

Even so, the Coalition representatives stressed their support of an ongoing effort to upgrade the salaries of correctional officers: "Higher pay would at least allow them to get better qualified people."[27]

There is an extraordinary movement now underway to form a national union—like those currently operating in Scandanavian countries—of the nation's 200,000 prison inmates. The movement, whose rallying slogan is "power to the convicted class," claims a membership cadre of some 3,000 California convicts, former inmates, and members of their families (one third of the total are actually in prison, and their names are kept secret). Called the United Prisoners Union, it has drawn up a bill of rights for prison reform as an alternative to what it calls "the certainty of more riots and bloodshed . . .":

The demands include elimination of the "escalating practice of prison brutality," more adequate medical care, the end of segregation of prisoners because of political beliefs, a halt to "imposed racism" on the part of prison officials and guards, and the "warehousing" of convicts by means of determinate sentences, maximum sentences of no more than 10 years and the right of peaceful dissent without reprisals.

Some of the goals set by the union are even more ambitious, such as the payment of prevailing wage rates in prison industries, adherence to Federal and state minimum wage laws, full civil service job rights for parolees and the right of former convicts to hold elective office.

Influenced by a sociologist, John Irwin of San Francisco State College (a San Quentin "alumnus" by way of a robbery conviction), the Union looks upon prison strikes and work stoppages in our "fascist concentration camps" as their best bargaining weapons. Its organizers add, however, that its program is nonviolent and that it is trying to temper the more revolutionary philosophies of such activists as the Black Panthers and the Brown Berets, who are represented in its membership.[28]

Invaluable to the "prisoner power" movement is the newly won right to voice an independent point of view, a First Amendment guarantee that prisoners have long been denied. Typical is the service rendered us all by the right a prisoner now has to publish a letter like this one in a major paper:

To the Editor:

An article in The Times of Nov. 17 has just about capped it all off for me. The article's reference to the project of erecting an indoor recreation building at Attica beats all.

Those of us who are trying to get some changes in Attica couldn't care less about a gym, and many of my fellow inmates feel the money can be used on better things. Of things we consider of greater importance are: expanded educational and vocational programs, decent medical treatment, the release of the hen-pecked guards that work here now and replace these jelly fish with men who will treat us as men.

Many of the changes that are needed don't require a red cent; only an institution that is run to serve its function and not to perpetuate the criminal element of society. Who gives a damn about indoor exercise when you're not getting educated to start another life once outside these walls?

Will the gym replace the petty harassment and ignorant attitudes that inmates have to live with?

Will the gym really serve any other purpose than to sidetrack the real issues and matters that need to be faced squarely in Attica?

Will the new gym get the Warden to come down off his high horse and for once own up to the fact that the institution isn't working, hasn't worked and will never work?

What's sickening about the whole thing is that New York taxpayers will complain about where this money is going and never say anything about a jive project like this.

Give me an education and to hell with the gym.

R. Anthony Schettini
Attica, N.Y. Nov. 18, 1972[29]

For our purposes the issue of the gym is secondary to the gain we all make when the "least" among us is protected in his right to be heard—and to challenge our conventional wisdom!

As hinted at in some of the aforegoing, some, though by no means all, of this current upsurge in prisoner demands can be traced to the politicization of black inmates:

The self-perception of many black felony inmates has changed radically during the past five years. A man may have been a pimp or dope dealer or mugger on the street. Authorities say to him, "You're just a common criminal and you're going to jail," but the new rhetoric permits him to respond, "No, I am not a *common* criminal, I am a black man convicted of a crime. Being black in this society set me in an environment in which crime was the only accessible way to survive or to express my rage. It was the only way I knew to make it, and it even meant I sinned against my black brothers and sisters. Because I was black, you whites dealt with me in a certain way when I was caught, and it now influences the way you treat me in prison. If you considered me the same way as any other offender it wouldn't be so difficult for a black man to get out on parole. No, I am a political prisoner, *not* a common criminal."[30]

Black and white inmates alike harbor fond memories of the late 1960's when students "liberated" buildings and challenged society even as the inmates persist in doing now.

Relevant—and illuminating—are the thoughts of Kenneth Gibson, mayor of Newark, who judges the insurgency behind the walls a testimony of good citizenship for anyone:

> Across the country young men and women in prisons are becoming aware of the forces which have controlled their lives. Many of these people have previously been uninvolved, alienated, without direction. They now attempt to learn how to deal with these forces and institutions so that they might be able to shape their own destiny and that of their children.[31]

Of comparable mind is G. Daniel Walker, a "jailhouse lawyer," who, with the aid of $3,000 worth of legal books in his cell, has placed a number of suits against his prison system—and helped over three hundred fellow inmates with their criminal appeals. Asked to explain his pursuit of prisoner rights he says,

> The prison years are dead years. Men are frozen in immaturity by being deprived of fundamental liberties. Our lives are dominated by petty rules which have no valid security purpose but are great tools of harassment. My aim is to drag Corrections scratching, screaming, and kicking into the 20th century.[32]

Power to the prisoners? Perhaps, especially if you grasp the idea that we are *all* of us prisoners—so long as we need prisons.

Abolishment of Prisons. All other considerations to one side, hard-nosed economics recommends rehabilitative alternatives to our prison-oriented status quo. For example, writer Norman Cousins, when seeking in 1973 to aid the rehabilitation of a hapless thirty-six-year-old ex-convict caught stealing from his car, calculated that the man's eighteen years behind bars had cost taxpayers about $240,000. Released with 25¢ given him as a stake for starting a new life, the skill-less ex-convict went nowhere fast, a prison system scenario that Cousins castigates as "a reprehensible act that calls for correction."[33]

Where to now? After two hundred years of a *failed* experiment with prisons, where might we turn? Two experienced criminal lawyers, Ronald Goldfarb and Linda Singer, in a 1973 assessment of our prison system urged its total abandonment:

> The time has come to forget reforming the prison system and to begin thinking about replacing it. Cleaning it up and improving it will only superficially treat a fundamental problem that needs fundamental change. If we do not act now, as the recent riots have shown, a violent and terribly costly revolution is likely. Social institutions which do not work should not last. They are replaced voluntarily or they are revolutionalized. For obvious reasons, those who believe in the viability of our society and the availability of means for peaceful change of our social institutions must take the lead in this transformation now.[34]

More specifically, what might a reform agenda include if it focused on phasing out our prisons? History professor David J. Rothman urges the following:

A drastic reduction in sentence length; our courts hand out sentences two or three times as long as those in other industrialized countries. Reduction would have little effect on the retributive or deterrent qualities of criminal justice.

A great increase in the use of probation, with a willingness to tolerate many more failures than we do now. Scandinavians use probation four or five times before resorting to incarceration.

An end to discretionary parole; reduced sentences should obviate the need for parole boards.

The classification as "noncrimes" of many acts now punished by prison sentences—especially victimless crimes, such as drug use, drunkenness and the sexual practices of consenting adults.

Pilot programs for the free distribution of heroin. Although there are risks (from "race suicide" to contagion), carefully controlled experimental ventures could evaluate them. The benefits appear considerable: a reduction of drug-related deaths, a decline in street crimes, a decrease by at least one-third in the present prison population.

Improved enforcement procedures. Our criminal justice system relies now upon the symbolic and harsh punishment of a few offenders, rather than on wider enforcement with lower penalties.

The most effective deterrent to crime is the increased likelihood of being apprehended, a goal that could be approached by better use of computers to catch tax evaders and more policemen on the beat to prevent street crimes.

A large order, Rothman insists it is attainable, and in our lifetime.[35]

Indeed, signs of progress are already apparent. Massachusetts has recently abolished all juvenile custodial institutions; Minnesota is not far behind, and both of them, along with California, have managed to close down a number of state prison facilities. The influential Institute of Corrections of the American Foundation is now advising the Justice Department to invest in alternatives to incarceration, not in new prisons. And the National Council on Crime and Delinquency, which has spent decades trying to upgrade penal institutions, recently called for a nationwide halt to the building of jails and detention facilities.

Overseas, alternatives to prison are a preoccupation: Holland relies mainly on fines and is deciding what prisons to close; Finland accents its labor camps; and Sweden makes special use of probation institutions staffed by psychiatrists and sociologists. Belgium allows short-term prisoners to serve their sentences at night and on weekends. British reformers contend that recidivist thieves will often do better in hostels under skilled supervision than they will in jail and that motoring offenders should be set to work on social service projects of various kinds.[36]

All the more provocative therefore is the reform orientation of social critic Arthur Waskow, who, insisting that our prisons are "the bloodiest, most intense, most revolting version of the worst aspects of American society at home," urges us to forget about reform altogether and talk instead about abolishing our jails and prisons.

Even with no alternative at all, Waskow argues, we would create less crime than do our present "criminal training centers." Alternatives, however, *are* available with which to replace our prisons, for example:

1. Parole in the custody of neighbors.
2. Convict- and community-controlled houses where psychiatric help is available, not imposed, and a human eccentricity of life style is permitted, not repressed.
3. Colonies of convicts, as in early Australia, that are separated but allowed to govern themselves and bring volunteers to join them.

Waskow cautions that proponents of such nonprison alternatives must keep two vital points clear—that the public is entitled to separation from persons who pose a threat of physical violence and that the public is entitled to assurances that persons guilty of crimes against property will probably not repeat such acts.

These two minimum legitimate social demands *can* be imaginatively met by nonprison alternatives, provided we collectively agree to abandon our counterproductive goals of punishment and enforced rehabilitation, for these two archaic goals require that a prisoner's whole style of life be controlled, that prisoners be deprived of self-government, and that "undesirables" who want to visit with prisoners be kept away. It is these dehumanizing deprivations that underlie the abominable conditions and high recidivism in our "criminal training centers."

Quite different are the conditions that can follow when we dare to assume that a life as free and normal as possible is more likely to "rehabilitate" the most violent offender than the kind of life he now leads in our prisons. Waskow conjures up a picture of a fenced-off town (or farm) where the gates are closed in one direction only: closed to exit by the initial residents—those who have been convicted of a violent crime—but open to *all* visitors or joiners invited by those residents. The town is self-governing, with full political and religious freedom. Residents work for normal wages, deal in trade and business with the outside world, and have normal relations with any relatives and friends who care to visit or move in. If the residents invite them, the press, lawyers, doctors, and the general public may visit, thereby keeping the town from becoming isolated, like a Siberian labor camp. Escape will be prevented at the borders, not by intense surveillance and policing inside.

Similarly, if we abandon punishment and prisons as protections against property offenders (burglars, embezzlers, shoplifters, vandals, tax evaders, and so on), we can offer these enlarging options to them:

1. Choose living in a self-governing kibbutzlike community, where all participants have equal work and income.
2. Or return to your old home and workplace under careful supervision, not of your whole life but only of the particular role you used in order to commit your crime—a supervision conducted not by parole agents but by your co-workers and neighbors.
3. Or pay a fine that is a greatly graduated income tax.

Many nettlesome matters remain open, of course, for serious reflection:

1. How might such "penal colonies" deal with criminality within their own borders?

2. Will the mayor, town council, and the like have a role in parole decisions—and decisions to reduce sentences for time well spent?
3. How will organized labor reach an accommodation with this new source of possibly competitive job-seekers?
4. Will neighbors or co-workers expect pay for their supervisory efforts, and how will they be chosen—and supervised?

Waskow leaves these for a full public airing *after* the principle of nonprison rehabilitation first wins our general endorsement.

How to get started? While endorsing temporary reforms that help make a prison not a prison (for example, prisoner participation in governance), Waskow cautions against losing sight of the abolishment target. Accordingly he recommends the following reform tactics:

1. Teach-ins on what prisons are now like.
2. The "adoption" of a nearby jail or prison by a particular campus or community group so that together they can use nonprison alternatives in a miniature experimental mode.
3. Legal campaigns based on a belief that all prisons are now cruel and unusual punishment.
4. Securement of totally open visitation by anyone whom the prisoners individually or collectively invite.

Waskow reminds us in conclusion that it is not those who are already in prison who will be the only ones to gain from nonprison alternatives: "The prisons frighten and control us all: Let's end them."[37]

FOOTNOTES

1. Bruce Jackson, "Beyond Attica," *Trans Action* (November–December 1971), p. 7.
2. Lloyd Shearer, "Spotlight: The Nation's Disgrace," *Parade* (October 22, 1972), p. 15.
3. Ibid.
4. Bruce Jackson, "Prison: The New Academy," *The Nation* (December 6, 1971), p. 586.
5. Ibid.
6. Ramsey Clark, *Crime in America* (New York: Simon & Schuster, 1970), p. 17.
7. Jack Booth, "Chief Justice Cites Riot in Urging Prison Reform," *Philadelphia Evening Bulletin* (November 17, 1972), p. 1.
8. James R. Hoffa, *New York Times* (May 16, 1972), p. 86.
9. "Berrigan: The Lessons of 39 Months," *New York Times* (December 24, 1972), p. 2-E.
10. Tom Wicker, " 'Tougher Penalties' for Whom?" *New York Times* (March 6, 1973), p. 39.
11. Richard Hammer, "Role Playing, a Judge Is a Con, a Con Is a Judge," *New York Times Magazine* (September 14, 1969), p. 62.
12. "Judges Who Visited Two State Prisons Urge Improvements," *New York Times* (November 14, 1972), p. 39.
13. Booth, op. cit.
14. Herman Schwartz, "Prison Reform," *The Humanist* (March–April 1972), p. 17.
15. Ibid.

16. David J. Rothman, "You Can't Reform the Bastille: The Attica System," *The Nation* (March 19, 1973), p. 366.
17. H. James Laverty, "Furlough Plan 'Absurd,' Sprague Tells Parley," *Philadelphia Evening Bulletin* (January 14, 1973), p. 20.
18. "National Prisoner's Coalition," *New York Times* (May 16, 1972), p. 86.
19. Robert Martinson, "Crime and the Election," *Dissent* (Fall 1972), p. 562, *passim*. See also Robert Martinson, "The Paradox of Prison Reform," *New Republic* (April 1, 8, 15, and 29, 1972).
20. "Ombudsman for Prisons Is Named by Minnesota," *New York Times* (August 14, 1972), p. 29.
21. Schwartz, op. cit., p. 17.
22. Ibid.
23. Malcolm Stuart, "Prison Phaseout's a Dutch Treat for Prisoners," *Philadelphia Inquirer* (December 17, 1972), p. 3-H.
24. Booth, op. cit., p. 1.
25. Ray Holton, "Prisoner Files Suit for Playboy, Fresh Linen, Wifely Visits," *Philadelphia Inquirer* (March 18, 1972), p. 20.
26. Ilene Barth, "Prisoners Use Legal Weapons in Fight for Rights," *Parade* (October 8, 1972), p. 22.
27. "2 Prisoners Hold News Conference," *New York Times* (March 25, 1973), p. 45.
28. Everett R. Holles, "Convicts Seek to Form a National Union," *New York Times* (September 26, 1971), p. 74.
29. *New York Times* (December 8, 1972), p. 45.
30. Bruce Jackson, "Prison: The New Academy," *The Nation* (December 6, 1971), p. 586.
31. Barth, op. cit., p. 22.
32. Ibid.
33. Norman Cousins, "Our Prison System Doesn't Make Any Sense," *Philadelphia Inquirer* (December 3, 1972), p. 3-H.
34. Ronald Goldfarb and Linda Singer, *After Conviction: A New Review of the American Prison System* (New York: Simon & Schuster, 1972), p. 115.
35. David J. Rothman, "You Can't Reform the Bastille: The Attica System," *The Nation* (March 19, 1973), p. 366.
36. "Crime and Punishment: A New Approach," *The Christian Century* (August 5, 1970), p. 11.
37. Arthur I. Waskow, ". . . I Am Not Free," *Saturday Review* (January 8, 1972), pp. 20–21.

CHAPTER 14

Public Services: Power to the Public!

I know we've come
a long way,
we're changing day to day,
but tell me—where do
the children play?

CAT STEVENS

I hold, with you, that it is only by our each contributing Utopias (the cheekier the better) that anything will come.

HENRY JAMES
TO H. G. WELLS

Our gains in the public service area are nowhere near as many as any of us profess to want, yet often more taxing than many of us can gratefully, much less graciously, accept. As a result, the subject is a difficult one, marked by widespread disparagement of ongoing reforms (for example, Amtrak's efforts to improve passenger rail service; the use of local revenue-sharing allocations to reclaim vandalized public parks, and so on). Consistent with our conditioned admiration of private as contrasted with public achievements, we continue to have minimal expectations of quality in public works (as in public housing, downtown public plazas, public provision for cyclists, and so on), and in the sound and time-honored way of a self-fulfilling prophecy, we get little back on our skimpy expectation (and investment).

It could all be otherwise, if we gravitated toward a different and more demanding vision of the Good City and its various amenities. Jane O'Reilly, a concerned New Yorker, wrote recently after an extended stay in London that:

> the entire city of London appears to be one big amenity. Paris has breathtaking beauties, but London is, well, homey. Civilized homey . . . the perfect suburb—the place for people who would not, could not, consider the suburbs. The trace of Henry James in the air. Civilized. The ultimate Wasp community.[1]

Somewhat more specifically, O'Reilly pinpoints a central defect in our vision:

> In 1890 New York was probably as pretty and humane as London, but we have torn that down and replaced it with alienating towers; we paved what

> little ground remained . . . no amount of effort to persuade me that a block fair is Fun on the Asphalt will convince me that New York is not hideously, pitifully ugly, degrading, and antithetical to humanity. It is impossible to imagine London allowing an area the size of Brownsville to rot, while at the same time a new town is planned for the last great open spaces in Staten Island.[2]

Nevertheless, the journalist finally chooses to return to and reside in New York, for although London is "closer to a cure . . . New York is engaged on a grander search. We are a melting pot, including not only responsible English, but a little of everything else on earth. We are an experiment that has never really been tried before."[3]

How do we improve on our experiment, in New York and everywhere else as well? How do we tackle especially the piece of the puzzle that as taxpayers and voters we have the greatest direct control over, the public services that are ours either to suffer or proudly cite as models for emulation everywhere? ("Londoners," O'Reilly explains, "would never put up with the impenetrable mysteries of our own [mass transit] system, which does manage to get millions of people about, however inefficiently and sordidly."[4])

A few examples are offered in this chapter of stimulating new ideas for reforms for public services, ranging from tinkering with the system (telephone and bicycling aids) to major additions ("bad neighbor" offshore installations) to radical overhauls ("car borrowing" and home building by the poor). Obviously, they only skim the surface of a complex and multifaceted subject and are meant more as mind and mood conditioners, as spurs to creativity and optimism, than as particular items for hastily considered advocacy. Our public services *can* reward more substantially than at present—and *must,* if the social contract that binds us together is to hold our common allegiance and help animate our private vision of the Good Life as well.

Bicycling for Urbanites. In comparison to the auto, the bicycle is a model citizen: it does not kill or maim; it does not pollute; it does not deplete natural resources; it makes no noise; it takes a great deal less space; and it is very much cheaper. What is even more, cyclist Nicholas Johnson continues,

> You ride a bicycle because it feels good. The air feels good on your body; even the rain feels good. The blood starts moving around your body, and glory be, your head feels good. You start noticing things. You look until you really see. You hear things, and smell smells, you never knew were there. You start whistling nice little original tunes to suit the moment. . . . And there's a nice feeling, too, in knowing you're doing a fundamental life thing for yourself: transportation. You get a little bit of your life back.[5]

Bicycles, Johnson concludes, ought to be accorded a preferred position in the transportation systems of American cities (even as they are in Europe). At the very least, they deserve an even break (13.9 million were sold in the USA in 1972, more than new car sales!).

Today, they are the striking losers in a one-sided competition with the auto. America's 80 million cyclists have only sixteen thousand miles of bikeways, or about thirteen inches for each bike rider, as compared with the 3 million miles of paved roads available to 90 million motorists. And most of the existing bikeways are shams. Instead of protective curbing to separate bikes from autos, there are often only white lines or signs along the road's edge, which do little more than lull both cyclists and motorists into a false sense of security (thirty-eight thousand auto-bike collisions were recorded in 1972).

New lobbying groups, such as "Friends for Bikecology," are asking citizen support for a balanced transportation system, including bikeways. More specifically, the "Friends" are promoting a "bicycle community" plan that envisions:

1. Well-defined bikeways, separated from cars, that radiate from residential neighborhoods to schools.
2. On-street car parking that gives way to protected bikeways on key thoroughfares.
3. Bicycle storage facilities that are located throughout the city.
4. Stations for commuters who bicycle to public transportation, store their vehicles, and continue by bus or rail into commercial sectors of the city.
5. Buses, running into the countryside, that have racks to hold bicycles; and adequate bus and rail facilities that play a key role as bike and car substitutes during foul weather.

To secure these changes "Friends" lobbies for a redistribution of public funds in transportation. (In 1972, $22 billion in gasoline and property taxes was spent for roads and highways, whereas less than $1 billion went for public transportation. And practically nothing went for bikeways!) Attention is also called to breakthroughs in Oregon and Washington in hopes that other states will soon follow their example: in 1971, Oregon began to siphon off 1 per cent of gasoline taxes for bicycle paths; Washington followed suit a year later with a 0.5 per cent tax for such paths.

Another objective is to convince planners to "THINK BIKE!" Although the bicycle makes a direct assault on four great problems that plague the modern city—traffic, noise, parking, and pollution—American urban planners have ignored it in their narrow-minded search for solutions to the urban transportation crisis. Yet certain facts encourage substantial consideration of the bicycle:

> Traffic studies show that 43 per cent of all urban work trips made by automobiles are four miles or less; and in nine of ten trips, the driver is the sole occupant. These trips could just as easily be made on bicycle.
>
> A downtown auto parking structure costs approximately $4,000 for each car space—enough to build an enclosed facility that can hold 150 bicycles.[6]

Cyclists call on all of us, bike riders or not, who believe ourselves committed to a safer, more sensible transportation system to support their reform demand for more and safer bicycling and public transit facilities—the better to end soon the tyranny of the auto over all of us.

Car Bans. Cities around the world are tentatively and timorously exploring new ways to halt the gradual encroachment of the auto. Many Italian cities, for example, are extending "blue zones" that completely ban one street or one block to traffic. It was left, however, to the ancient and beautiful city of Florence to become in 1971 the first Italian city to ban cars from its entire city center.

In the spring of 1971 the city fathers drew a blue circle around a forty-block area smack in the middle of the city. Posters went up announcing:

> The historic center does not have room for the horses of your car. . . . The historic center of Florence is still charming, only you do not know it, or do not remember it. Today it is choked by traffic and covered by a cloud of exhaust gas. If you will limit the use of the car and choose public transport, you will discover a new city and restore it to the admiration of the world. Come to the center. Take a bus.

An enlarged picture of a traffic ticket was printed beneath as a gentle persuader to the outraged motorist. The success of the ban was partially affirmed even at the time by the unanticipated efforts made by merchants on neighboring streets to force their inclusion in it. Shopkeepers even struck to press their demand that the car ban be expanded to include their streets.

Elsewhere in Italy experiments that began in Rome in 1968 with "pedestrian islands" continue with unabated enthusiasm. In Rome all vehicles except taxis (which are much rarer in Rome than in New York) are banned from an ever larger number of neighborhood areas. Hundreds of citizens now leisurely promenade while the city's notoriously nerve-racking traffic swirls around their pedestrian sanctuary. One enthusiast has been quoted as exclaiming: "I've rediscovered the small-town joy of strolling up and down a street right in the middle of it."[7] Others similarly inclined press the case for a two-square-mile pedestrian mall in the heart of the city, lest the capital's historic nucleus be fatally damaged by the modern chariots.

In the Far East the Japanese are experimenting with car bans on a more modest but no less effective scale. "Pedestrian Paradise," a program initiated in the summer of 1970 in Tokyo, bans cars from some of the city's major shopping and amusement areas every Sunday afternoon. (Unlike in the United States or Europe, Sunday is usually a busy shopping day in Japan, with department stores and many other shops open all day—and closed on Mondays.) Pedestrians are reported to be ecstatic: "Smell the air, no carbon monoxide." "For the first time in 20 years I can walk where I please." "I feel liberated." Unfortunately, the extremely irregular pattern of Tokyo streets has cut down on the number of "pedestrian paradises" scheduled for opening.

American cities, with their gridiron street pattern, are in a much better position than ancient Italian or Japanese metropolises to take advantage of the contribution that car bans can make to the quality of urban life. At the same time, however, the American reliance on private auto use is unmatched. For example, ours is the only nation where more than half the workers travel to and from work by car (USA, 81 per cent; West Germany, 45; Holland,

38; Japan, 26; Brazil, 26; Finland, 23; Austria, 20; Uruguay, 10). Similarly, few Americans walk to work (Finland, 39 per cent; Austria, 22; West Germany, 22; Uruguay, 21; Japan, 15; Brazil, 12; Netherlands, 9; USA, 6). Not surprisingly then, a spot check in 1970 of major cities by the *New York Times* indicated little but apathy toward the idea of car bans. In St. Louis, for example, the concept had been considered for a decade without action.

In 1971, however, things began to change, and city planners in St. Louis, for one, sought funds to dust off outmoded plans and update them for renewed consideration. Elsewhere, in New York, Philadelphia, and Boston, sections of prime downtown areas have been turned back to pedestrians, but resistance to tampering with America's primary mode of transportation, or America's capitulation to the auto, retains the upper hand. Italy, Japan, and other countries less wed than we are to the automobile continue to show the way.[8]

Car Borrowing. If we could step out of our doors and step right into a waiting public car, the need for you and me to drag about our own private autos would be substantially reduced. Early in 1971 the French began to experiment with just this innovation in Montpellier, a car-clogged city of 350,000.

Their system, TIP (Promotion Coopérative du Transport Individuel Public), boldly and uniquely provides public cars for private use. Painted blue-and-white for easy recognition, the cars are widely available at specially marked TIP stands. For a fee, subscribers receive a key that fits all TIP cars. When a car is desired a subscriber buys a token from cooperating merchants, goes to the nearest TIP stand, inserts the token in a meter on the dashboard, and drives off. (To discourage thefts, a miniature camera in the ignition photographs the driver's key, which has his membership number inscribed on it.) To round out the system TIP service trucks cruise the streets to see that the stands have a sufficient number of cars and that all cars are in working order. TIP designers are excited with the very real possibility that this experimental service may see fifteen to twenty privately owned vehicles replaced by each TIP car.

TIP has worked out a rather clever toll system. A subscriber buys a share in the co-op for $75 a year, reimbursable if he withdraws. To operate a vehicle in the car fleet (numbering 150 in spring of 1972), he purchases a plastic slug for $1.80, good for twelve miles. As the car runs, the meter chews up the rim of the slug; the driver takes it with him from ride to ride until twelve miles' worth of slug is gone and a new slug must be purchased. (One advantage of this system, of course, is that the cars need include no coin box to tempt thieves.)

Not surprisingly, business has gotten off to an uneven start. TIP's thirty-five cabs, lost among the city's forty-five thousand vehicles, are averaging only one slug a day, earning a gross of $1.80 for twelve miles of operation. Traffic jams are apparently discouraging subscribers from using the cars, and TIP cab spaces are grabbed by private cars whose drivers have little reason to fear the summonses they risk—but seldom get from lax local policemen. At the same time, however, about two hundred applicants are waiting for TIP keys, the city continues to provide marked parking spaces without charge, and the transport ministry in Paris subsidizes the experiment with unabashed high hopes.

TIP, thinking big, envisages an international association of co-ops, all of whose cabs would use the same key but differently shaped slugs, so that each co-op would collect its own operating funds. With such a worldwide network of TIP-like vehicles, a traveler could step from his plane or train, buy a slug, and be motorized in minutes.

At present, however, local authorities are frankly perplexed. Trends indicate a staggering increase in private auto use (Marseilles, France, for example, expects to have a doubling of cars in the next ten years, leaving just enough space to park bumper to bumper throughout the area). If TIP, a bold idea, is permitted to fail because of only a halfhearted trial, the result may be an apocalyptic end for the city. Only drastic measures to control cars in the city seem likely to work, and politically vulnerable elected officials are timid about pursuing these. A TIP system and mass-transit support, with a firm ban on private auto use at certain hours and in certain areas, should receive more consideration everywhere.

Urban Transit System. Time and again our progress in promoting the alternative of inexpensive, efficient, safe, and clean mass-transit systems has floundered on the incompatibility of existing systems. Far from complementing one another, the systems of buses, subways, commuter trains, and trolleys in many American cities actually fight each other. A perennial dream of city planners revolves about a transportation system in which all types of mass conveyance would be integrated for the traveler's convenience. Instead of competing with each other for passengers over parallel routes and instead of ignoring each other with headstrong self-serving schedules, the various transit modes would feed into, extend from, and mesh with one another.

Does such a plan exist—anywhere? Has the dream earned realization, or in its failure to do so, does it stand exposed as a hopelessly utopian fantasy? After six years of planning the city-state of Hamburg, West Germany initiated in 1966 a model urban transit system. The world's first integrated transport network, it now draws transportation experts from all over the world to study it.

West Germany's second largest city and largest metropolitan area, Hamburg shares the American phenomenon of a thinning inner city accompanied by rapidly growing suburbs. Before 1966 the subway, railway, and bus operators were cutthroat competitors for the trade of multiplying suburbanites. Commuters placed ever greater reliance on private auto traffic. And as the roads grew clogged, traffic was stalled for longer and longer waits.

Formation of the Hamburg Verbund in 1966 saw eight private transit companies come together under one central public leadership, while retaining their private existence. The one-fare system thus created linked local companies with the federal railroads and buses (comparable integration in the New York City area would integrate the Long Island Railroad and the Penn Central commuter lines with all subways, buses, and ferries, under a joint command).

The guiding principles of the formation of the Hamburg Verbund were essentially three: 1) that none of the Verbund's partners would, at the expense of other members, fare better than before the union; 2) that rail transportation would be retained as the backbone of urban transportation; and 3) that customers should be treated as business partners and wooed with ever more sensible and appealing attractions.

Accordingly, over thirty bus routes were redesigned, twenty were lengthened, and sixteen new lines were opened to get the suburbanite to the nearest train station without time-consuming waits and detours. Fare structures were vastly simplified and substantially reduced. A typical monthly ticket for a suburbanite living eleven miles from the city center costs about $8. The basic price for a single ticket for a section of three miles is 16¢; each additional section costs 5¢ more.

An intensive drive was made to lure suburban motorists back to public transport. Forty new low-cost parking lots were opened throughout the operating area to accommodate five thousand autos at bus and railway stations. Reduced fares were offered for rail journeys made after rush hour, for theater parties, and for weekend use, and season tickets were sold at all banks. (The banks transfer the necessary amount each month so purchasers can have their tickets mailed home.) Well over twenty thousand motorcar owners were won back to mass transit in this way from 1966 through 1970.

Unique in the world is the first-rate plan of division of responsibility in the Hamburg model. The Verbund itself takes care of transport research and planning, the preparation of timetables, the drafting of traffic revenues, public relations, and advertising. For their part, the member transit companies (rail, subway, streetcar, bus, and boat lines) supervise their own individual operations, collect fares, and make technical improvements as these are required.

Is such a plan workable? Hamburg, West Germany's largest metropolitan area, is making it work! The Verbund serves over 2.5 million residents and more than one thousand square miles of territory, linking 233 communities scattered across two political states (Lower Saxony and Schleswig-Holstein). Each of the years since 1966 has brought the joint transport authority an increase in business of 3 to 6 per cent. Other major German cities, including Munich and eleven nearby cities, as well as Frankfurt, are now pressing forward with comparable models. All of these integrated transportation systems, it should be noted, are heavily subsidized by local government shares of a multi-billion-dollar mineral oil tax collected by the federal government (comparable to our offshore oil tax revenue).

A logical model for transportation reform in American cities, the example of the Verbund should close debate on the question of feasibility and shift our attention instead to where, when, and why not?[9]

Airport Linkups. Frankfurt's Rhein-Main Airport, one of Europe's busiest terminals, boasts a new inland transport system that "obviously bears no relationship to what goes on at New York's Kennedy International Airport or anywhere else in the United States—not yet, at any rate."

A few minutes after your jumbo jet has landed you can board an electric train, pay 70¢, and speed in twelve minutes the five-mile distance into Frankfurt. There you can transfer to a 100mph passenger train to any point in Europe. There's no need to worry about your luggage: at the airport's train station you simply check it on to your final destination.

Comparable plane-rail transfer facilities connect airports and the cities of Brussels, Rome (in process), Zurich (scheduled for a 1977 completion), London (in process), and Paris. Meanwhile, despite years of talk and planning, only Boston's and Cleveland's airports of the hundreds of American fields have any rail service, and none offer a direct hookup with Amtrak's passenger lines.[10]

Home Building by the Poor. Dramatic headway *is* possible against the housing shortage for the poor and the decline in central city housing for all. Examples available abroad recommend linking the two problems operationally and facilitating the building of homes by those who actually need them. As logical as this plan appears to be, it is conspicuous by its absence in America. So far have we strayed or progressed from our homestead/log-cabin roots that few living Americans have played any substantial part in the building of their own homes. Although a goodly number exercise considerable craft and creativity in home workshop jobs, few except the desperately poor in Appalachia or the Mississippi Delta and the long hair communalists in the hills and the desert have actually built their own shelter.

Such plans are much more common abroad, especially where the urban poor are concerned. And particularly as an alternative to life in a city public housing project they may warrant a very careful second look. Support comes from many young architects, Peace Corps volunteers, anthropologists, and sociologists who likewise view squatter communities as highly successful solutions to the problems of mass urbanization in the developing nations.

On the other side of the controversy are certain urban planners, politicians, and newspapermen, along with much of the upper, middle, and working classes. Their view, often spelled out in lurid terms by the mass media, the government, and U.S. and U.N. agencies, is that squatter settlements abound with social problems. They are represented as chaotic and unorganized; composed of substandard houses that get worse as time goes on; replete with slum-bred crime, delinquency, prostitution, family disorganization, and so forth; isolated and alienated from the life of nearby cities; high in illiteracy and low in educational levels; and fertile as breeding grounds for radical and revolutionary politics.

It is no wonder, therefore, that squatter settlements are strictly discouraged in the United States and that the most recent model, the "Freedom City" effort of 1968, was bulldozed into oblivion. The case for home building by the poor is intimately interwoven with the case for squatter settlements, and the case rests without champions in this nation of otherwise Jeffersonian "sturdy, independent yeomen."

Our negative view of squatter settlements appears to be grossly inaccurate and bears little relation to reality. Research finds them stable and highly organized; homes are continually improved and invested in; social disorganization is far less than in city slums or public housing; educational attainment is higher than among the poor elsewhere; and politics has a local issue/personality clash orientation. Squatters choose, or fall into, a rational and satisfying relationship with the urban environment that is both cheaper and better for political and social morale than the usual government housing solution.

A key to the difference is the nature of the housing—or the fact that the residents build their own. Their houses involve considerable investments of time, money, labor, and emotion, often revealing great ingenuity and skill. Construction work is a constant feature of life in the squatter settlements. And it explains much of the high morale and self-esteem one can find there that is lacking in government high-rise "dormitories."

When the poor are herded into ready-built city slums or public housing, their families are subjected to a maximum outlay during a period of minimum per capita income. They obtain less space per capita than do the squatters and, eventually, pay twice as much cash (or even more) per unit area. (If they do not pay it, then the state does.) In contrast, the home-building squatter family saves in several ways. It acts as its own general contractor, eliminating administrative overhead and profits. It builds without costly credit and designs and builds without paying professional and legal fees, taxes, and so on. It avoids costly building regulations and uses personal ties in supervision to obtain a higher productivity from the labor hired (which costs less in the first place as no overhead is involved).

To be sure, the home-building poor family must live in a mixture of provisional and incomplete structures for an uncertain period. But this disadvantage is outweighed by certain critical gains: the important issue of family residential security is solved; the more spacious jerry-built home is far healthier than an overcrowded and cramped urban slum; the family has the freedom to build what it most needs in accordance with its changing styles of domestic life; and the self-built house (and neighborhood) makes an incalculable contribution to family and local community integration and development—"Nothing cements relationships more than faith in a common objective and mutual dependence for its achievement."[11] The squatters come to feel that they have some control over their own destinies. They see initiative and creativity rewarded.

At a higher level of generalization the same formula holds: squatter settlements seem genuine solutions, although they are often regarded as problems, whereas government-built housing projects are, in actuality, problems in themselves, not solutions. The paternalistically provided, ready-made housing project is not a vehicle especially well attuned to either economic or social development. Requiring a heavy outlay of scarce and extremely expensive financial capital, the projects invariably conflict with the social needs of low-income people and greatly surpass their material means. Conversely, the home-building poor make a direct contribution to their own housing. By straining their own personal savings capacity and resources for investment in fixed capital, they contribute substantially to the development of the building industry and improve their own living conditions, morale, and productivity. Free to invest their own resources in their own ways, the squatters thrive on personal autonomy, self-esteem, and high motivation.

Can the squatter settlement—a self-help, mass migration community development by the poor—help solve the twin problems of housing for the poor and central-city decay in the United States? Could we soon move to permit, or even encourage, squatterlike communities in this country? The obstacles are formidable. Only public lands could be so used. Zoning codes and local ordinances require that regular construction companies, suppliers, and labor unions be involved in all building. And racial prejudice severely reduces mobility, whatever effort one makes at self-advancement. Add to these problems the narcotizing effect of the welfare dole and the heavy hand of government bureaucracy (which at times operate to keep people poor), and the chances of liberating the poor to build for themselves seem dim indeed.

We forget so quickly that this technique underlies the entire history of the opening up of our own West. And we choose instead only to denigrate it with our mass media caricatures of "Dogpatch" and "Li'l Abner" types. The loss is all ours, and it is considerable. Were we soon to help the poor help themselves into customized self-built housing in new communities of their own design and management, we might make gains in the struggle against poverty that would astonish and honor us all.[12]

"Bad Neighbor" Installations. We want the power, but not the plants. We clamor for more electricity to run our appliances and computers, but in growing numbers we oppose the construction of new generating plants that might pollute the air or nuclear plants that could produce thermal pollution and expose us to the threat of explosion or lethal radiation.

Where to put them—and noisy, dangerous overseas jet airports, and major waste-disposal garbage facilities? With the Dutch as an example, interest is growing in the idea that we begin to group all three "bad neighbor" facilities together out at sea—on one new man-made "island" built by the dike-polder method perfected over three hundred years of use in the Netherlands. After building a huge dike around a designated sea area, engineers pump the area dry and then lay down the desired installation on the reclaimed land. More than 7 million people live on such polders today in the Netherlands.

Proponents in America of the offshore concept are urging Chicago and Cleveland to employ it to build jetports in Lakes Michigan and Erie. The additional location on these sites of power plants and waste-disposal units might make it easier to provide the billions of dollars required to finance the polders. Cost could be further defrayed by the addition of seaport facilities to the new islands and selling off valuable real estate from related mainland jet airports whose traffic is reduced by the new jetport-at-sea. Under serious study in the New York City area, one such polder site could be in operation by 1985.

Opposition to the idea has also developed in New Jersey, where the legislature voted 65 to 0 in the winter of 1972 to impede the $1-billion location three miles offshore of two new nuclear generating plants. New Jersey lawmakers have demanded further studies of the likely environmental impact of the seventeen-story complex and its extraordinary seawall ("the largest and strongest man-made structure ever installed in the ocean"[13]). On the other side of the state line, Albany officials have twice bent to public opposition and blocked the proposed construction of offshore nuclear generating plants near Coney Island and Staten Island.

At the same time, however, the case for offshore installations slowly gains strength as evidence accumulates of their safety, efficiency, and ecological neutrality. "Bad neighbor" installations have to go somewhere, and even with our SST ban, our solid-waste incineration gains, and our efforts at reducing the energy demand, an expansion in the number of such installations is necessary. The power plants probably represent a heat load beyond the cooling capacity of American rivers; the jetports overtax our noise tolerance levels; and our olfactory sense opposes more landfill operations. The obvious answer is the ocean, and as science writer Ralph E. Lapp observes, "it does not take much imagination to foresee by the year 2000 a fringe of low artificial islands along both American coasts almost from border to border."[14]

Another variation, one equally rich in environmental protection merit, is the Nixon Administration's new advocacy of offshore, deep-water supertanker terminals. Priced at $1.3 billion each in 1972 costs and requiring nine years to complete, these islands would substantially reduce the possibility of oil spills by eliminating the major source of such spills, grounding and collison in busy channels and enclosed harbor areas. Although controversial in terms of location, environmental effects, and cost sharing (the Administration is willing to shoulder 20 per cent), the shallowness of eastern ports and the industry's growing reliance on deep-draft supertankers makes an "island" terminal off New Jersey quite likely by 1982.

Far less certain is a proposed lake polder that could alter the entire pattern of air travel in the Midwest. Cleveland's Chamber of Commerce is urging the formation of a Regional Transit Authority to conduct a detailed feasibility study. At issue is the fate of a proposed international jet airport on a diked island five to eight miles offshore in Lake Erie. The study, expected to cost $4 million, will be considered by city and county officials, many of whom have already indicated an unwillingness to subsidize the research, much less go further into the billions of dollars involved in the actual implementation of the plan.[15]

Rail Passenger Service. What might be done to improve our critically ill passenger train service? Americans who have sampled superior train service in Europe, Japan, and Canada are understandably eager to see the low standards here someday match or best those set by the celebrated *Mistral, Rapido, Rheingold,* and *Flying Scotsman* and the New Tokaido line's *Bullet* and Spain's speedy Talgo trains. In the United States, trains can only get better.

Europe seems to improve passenger trains as fast as our rail companies abandon such service. European service offers living proof that railroads can compete with, and often outstrip, airlines and cars. What is more, trains appear to be exceedingly sound ecologically. One track, in Europe or in the United States, can handle as many people as ten to twenty lanes of exhaust-filled expressway. Train boosters boast that the most heavily traveled diesel railroad creates infinitely less noise and pollution per passenger than planes or cars. An electrified railway is pollution free and virtually silent.

How than might our dismal passenger train service be revitalized? Europe's example suggests we might begin by agreeing to underwrite the costs of our entire passenger rail system. In such a case the trains are judged a "public service," a necessary socioeconomic institution, and are kept running no matter what the cost. It was not until 1969, for example, that the British rail system, first nationalized in 1948, finally turned its initial profit. The Japanese National Railways, after running in the black for ninety-two years, lost $2-billion from 1964 to 1971—but is now building or planning thirty-seven hundred miles of additional high-speed railroad. (See Chapter 10, "Producing: Corporate Social Responsibility," for a discussion of the pros and cons of nationalization.)

The experience of other nations recommends extreme, if logical adjustments to the requirements of modernized passenger rail service. The Japanese, for example, reserve one line entirely for high-speed express service. As a result, there are no lumbering freights to beat down the rails or to require that curves be banked less steeply, nor do local trains get in the way of the 131mph expresses. Six hours every night the service shuts down to permit maintenance forces to "manicure" the roadbed back to the desired degree of smoothness. It is not surprising that the resulting system is judged "the world's best maintained, best run, and most heavily patronized railroad passenger service."[16]

In exchange for public support through tax subsidies, the passenger lines abroad offer new "public burden" services. West Germany's trains, for example, offer special social tariffs so that students, blue-collar workers, and so on are charged at a different level. In a similar way, the French strive to offer ever more, within price-control limits. Christened in 1950, air-conditioned in 1969, *Le Mistral* packs a newsstand, an Articles de Paris boutique, a barber shop and beauty salon, dens complete with dictating equipment and ready secretaries, and, of course, a gliding restaurant with epic provisions. Operating between Paris and Nice, the train reaches 100mph over its nine-hour run (American trains average 50mph).

Finally, Europe's example suggests that we should innovate in even more sensitive ways. The Germans, French, English, and others, for example, transport the autos of passengers so they can get a restful night on the train and drive off in the morning. West German railroads have launched a system that permits ticket holders to have their baggage picked up at one hotel and delivered to the next so that they don't have to lug it aboard (the charge is 50¢ for 110 pounds). And the Japanese are building an experimental magnetic levitation line that will operate at speeds up to 310mph. ("My idea is to lay the foundation for the 21st Century railroad in Japan," explains the head of the national system.[17])

At present here in the United States we are carefully assessing the first major experiment we have ever conducted to try to rescue and revitalize the nation's main intercity lines. A complete, if thinned-out rail network run by a public corporation, the National Railroad Passenger Corporation (dubbed Amtrak), has moved since April of 1971 to help the private lines survive their $460 million annual deficit from passenger service.

Contrary to the example set abroad, Amtrak has further reduced service. From 6,000 passenger trains operated a generation ago, the passenger lines fell back to 300 in 1970, and Amtrak reduced this to between 189 and 200 daily intercity trains in 1973 (British Rail runs about 16,000 trains a day). Amtrak has also chosen to buy old rather than customer-capturing new equipment. Of the twelve hundred passenger cars purchased by Amtrak from the railroads for $16.8 million in 1971, the 1965 model is the newest, and most are twenty to thirty years old. And Amtrak putters along on a government subsidy that is paltry in comparison with far more realistic overseas subsidies, whereas Congress has appropriated $40 million a day for highway construction (Amtrak is expected to run a deficit of $130 million annually).[18]

All in all, the Amtrak experiment seems to promise little at best. Some see it as an exercise in first-rate nostalgia—rather than a glimpse of a vital popular transportation medium for a new decade. At its worse, it may play directly into the hands of the railroad executives who frankly want it to fail: many a railway executive secretly cheers because he knows that once the underfunded Amtrak fails, the accursed passenger trains will be banished to museums. So far, then, according to critics, Amtrak is a shadow organization primarily channeling subsidies to the railroads, which, in turn, continue to give priority to their own freight trains, sell tickets under an antiquated formula devised in 1909, and retain both ownership of the tracks and authority for direct supervision of the crews.

Alternatively, we could decide to take the overseas example more fully to heart and use Amtrak to nationalize our private railroads. Then, with Amtrak finally in full charge and no longer grubby and dead-end, it could begin to ensure us the high quality of rail passenger service we merit (and can now enjoy only abroad). New high-speed trains in congested urban areas would be faster and more comfortable than cars, better for our environment, and cheaper and more reliable than airline service. Such a system is costed out at only $1.5 billion a year, one fortieth of our annual highway expenditure. We must fish or cut bait; we must nationalize the railroads and employ Amtrak effectively or, as one quaint railroad president wistfully hopes, "let the intercity passenger train die an honorable death like we did the steamship, or the riverboats and the stagecoach and Pony Express."[19]

At the very least, and possibly as a transitional step toward nationalization, the government should acquire the tracks, the roadbeds, the signal systems, and the other facilities and make the private carriers pay user charges to the government. This would assure the tracks' being maintained at a high standard and help Amtrak gain a critical leverage in its shotgun wedding with the "giants." Amtrak might thereafter move to gain direct control, with the ability to hire the staff of the passenger lines and drive its own locomotives, instead of contracting with the lines as at present. From this changeover from private ownership and private profit-making to the European style of public ownership and public profit-making could be a short and welcomed step. Meanwhile, even as we temporize and putter, in Europe the airlines continue to surrender short-distance routes to more successfully competitive passenger trains: "It's a way of life, taking the train."

We should note, even in closing, that from a socialist perspective, the Amtrak situation at present resembles a classic neocapitalistic solution: the losses are shamefully socialized (passenger revenues), and the considerable profits remain quietly private (freight revenues). What is more, a good number of citizens are deprived of service on the grounds that they are simply not worth the trouble. As socialist leader Michael Harrington explains,

> What was required was a national transportation policy in which the planners would dispose of profits as well as of losses, and could treat the problem in a systematic fashion, taking environmental costs into account in the process. That, however, would have placed the common good above various corporate interests; it demanded encroachment on private rights and the primacy of usefulness rather than of profitability.[20]

Elements of the American public seem to be coming around to a pro-nationalization point of view. A poll by Gallup in 1936 showed the opposition running 2 to 1 against nationalization of the railroads, whereas in 1973 the nation was narrowly divided on the question by 44 to 38 per cent. However, among persons living in cities of a million or more, opinion is 75 to 34 per cent in favor of the government's taking over and running the railroads.[21]

Summary

If, as an architectural critic argues in a related context, we get the cities we deserve, we may also earn the public services we truly merit. The peril to our collective well-being is considerable. As a recent victor in a court case to force better mass-transit service grimly explains, "Rail transport is about 50 times more economical of energy, uses much less land, is 50 times safer than automobile transportation. If the railways continue to fade, we'll see the country paved over with concrete. I'd rather fight."[22]

We *can* do more, beginning, perhaps, in an offbeat way with something as basic as our public telephone system. In most of Europe it is possible to reach an operator from a coin telephone without using a coin. Here it is not. Why? Because the two major companies, the Bell System and General Telephone, resist suggestions that coin telephones be equipped to take emergency calls without requiring the insertion of money. So what? Well, when a few minutes can mean the difference between life and death, perhaps we ought not to lose valuable time in the trivial activity of fishing out the right coin to pay a mechanical pay phone. Agreeing with this idea, the Europeans have long since adjusted their telephone network; indifferent, we remain locked into a life-risking anachronism.

Similarly, we could move on a small but effective scale to replan public spaces for the convenience of the sitting public:

> Throughout the city we can vastly increase the amount of useful space for people, with more plazas, more street space, more nooks and small oases; and for merchants and businessmen as well as everybody else, it would be a lot better if we did. It wouldn't be paradise—New Yorkers would be miserable in such a place. But there'd be more of what gives the city its edge—more shmoozing, more picknicking, more kooks and screwballs and pretty girls to look at.
>
> And there'd be a place to sit. Not a bad test for city planning.[23]

At the same we can think BIG and move to relegate noxious and even dangerous installations out to sea, while opening a rare American dialogue on the pros and cons of the possible nationalization of the American railroad system.

The reasons for action are many, and several are highlighted in this chapter. One in particular, however, merits additional stress: As invaluable as are the primary and direct gains from public service reforms, there is much to welcome as well in the secondary gains we can deliberately secure from particular advances. For example, Senator Philip Hart's plan to let mass-transit users ride *free* could result in the secondary benefit of a one-third reduction in downtown auto traffic congestion.[24]

Similarly, a newly subsidized drop in bus fares in Atlanta in 1972 from 45¢ a ride to 15¢ has proved a major benefit for the black commuters who comprise nearly 80 per cent of the line's passengers. New routes have also begun to bring black residents from their center city homes to jobs in the suburban ring. In all, Atlanta's $1.3 billion, ten-year rapid-transit program, one of the biggest public works ever undertaken in the South, is understandably hailed by whites and blacks alike. White journalist Joseph Kraft, for example, notes that "mass transit works to advance the interests of the poor blacks without raising the touchy subjects of welfare and integrated schools or housing."[25] And a black Congressman from Atlanta, Andrew Young, frankly sees rapid transit as a kind of stopgap for the social programs that are now in trouble all over the country.[26]

We will probably do little however, until we dream differently than at present, until we expect more from the public service section of our daily lives. A clue to the requisites of a new set of citizen expectations may be available in these musings of an old China hand, a former State Department expert on China:

> This new civility may owe something to the example of a state and party that seem to prefer governing by persuasion and propaganda rather than by command and force. One wonders, though, if it does not also have some foundation in the much more comfortable, stable life enjoyed by most people, the broader sense of community that has been created, and the ending of the old, bitterly competitive scramble for a bare existence.[27]

Only as we attain increasingly higher stages of general well-being for all, including our 20 million poor and 20 million near-poor, will we be equal to, ready for, and able to commit ourselves to a new and higher standard of public services.

Alternatively, we will continue to "make do" and "shovel the dirt under the rug" (transfer penalties to less fortunate others, as in the case of inhuman mass-transit conditions, a penalty that falls disproportionately on commuters in the working-class and near-poor sectors of the populace). Our public services, then, like our prisons and mental institutions, reveal much about us—as a civilization and as a citizenry. We have *very far* to go.

FOOTNOTES

1. Jane O'Reilly, "London vs. New York: What Do You Want, Amenities or a Chance to Make it Big?" *New York* (June 12, 1972), p. 24.
2. Ibid., p. 26.

3. Ibid., p. 33.
4. Ibid., p. 27.
5. Nicholas Johnson, *Test Pattern for Living* (New York: Bantam, 1972), p. 113.
6. All statistics in this section are from a "Friends" ad, back cover, *New Republic* (April 28, 1973).
7. Paul Hofmann, "The Pedestrians Have Replaced Traffic Jams on the Via Frattina in Rome," *New York Times* (April 25, 1971), p. 70.
8. See, in this connection, Tabor R. Stone, *Beyond the Automobile* (Englewood Cliffs, N.J.: Prentice-Hall, 1971) and "The Urban Drive to Restrict the Auto," *Business World* (April 14, 1973), p. 27.
9. See, in this connection, Kenneth R. Schneider, *Autokind vs. Mankind* (New York: Schocken, 1972).
10. Edward C. Burks, "Frankfurt Air-Rail Link Called Success," *New York Times* (July 16, 1972), p. 50.
11. William Mangin and J. C. Turner, "The Barriada Movement," *Progressive Architecture* (May 1968), p. 162.
12. See John F. C. Turner and Robert Fichter, *Freedom to Build: Dweller Control of the Housing Process* (New York: Macmillan, Inc., 1972).
13. Carlo Sardella, "Pact Signed for Atomic Plant Off New Jersey Coast," *The Philadelphia Inquirer* (September 19, 1972), p. 1.
14. Ralph E. Lapp, "One Answer to the Atomic-Energy Puzzle—Put the Atomic Power Plants in the Ocean," *New York Times Magazine* (June 4, 1972), p. 90.
15. Helpful in this connection is Edward Cowan, "Offshore Tanker Terminal Gets Administration Push," *New York Times* (July 31, 1972), p. 57. See also Gene Smith, "Contract Signed on Offshore Nuclear Plant," *New York Times* (September 18, 1972), pp. 89, 94.
16. Quoted in "Japan's Troubled Railroads," *Business Week* (April 24, 1971), p. 38.
17. Ibid., p. 42.
18. Alexander R. Hammer, "What Price Amtrak?" *New York Times* (February 18, 1973), pp. 3-1, 3-7.
19. Ibid.
20. Michael Harrington, *Socialism* (New York: Saturday Review Press, 1972), pp. 277–278. See also "Outlook for Rails Called Brighter," *New York Times* (April 22, 1973), p. 63.
21. George H. Gallup, "Opposition to Federal Railroad Takeover Declines," *Philadelphia Evening Bulletin* (March 25, 1973), p. 17-A.
22. Milt Machlin, "One Man's Victory over the Penn Central," *New York* (January 15, 1973), p. 47.
23. W. H. Whyte, "Please, Just a Nice Place to Sit," *New York Times Magazine* (December 3, 1972), p. 32.
24. Michael F. Conlan, "Free Bus Rides Urged to Reduce Pollution Traffic," *Philadelphia Inquirer* (February 25, 1973), p. 9-B.
25. Joseph Kraft, "Atlanta's Mass Transit Story," *Philadelphia Evening Bulletin* (February 21, 1973), p. 11.
26. Ibid.
27. John S. Service, "China's Very Unstarchy Army," *New York Times* (January 27, 1972), p. 37.

READING

*A strategy is outlined in this crackling essay that can be employed in a widely varied range of circumstances, provided only that we choose, as citizen activists, to claim and exercise our right of protest and preference. Unpersuaded of a public service agenda that costs us out of all seeming relationship to any potential gain (as in the shutdown of "unprofitable" passenger rail lines or the routing of a new highway through stable residential areas), we can fight—and win—*if *we have what it takes. And some clues to what that is are contained in this essay, though in the last analysis the mettle we would test is inside ourselves.*

How To Stop A Highway

Daniel Zwerdling

The national mania for highways has made us one of the most mobile nations in the world, but we're fast discovering that the asphalt graying of America contains as much curse as blessing. New highways have disrupted communities—they uprooted 60,000 persons last year. Urban loops and links and crosstown connectors have helped commuters commute but have also hurt the cities—by making it easier for members of the white middle class to keep their jobs in the cities and their bedrooms in the suburbs. More highways have meant more cars, which have meant more noise and air pollution.

So perhaps you are concerned because you've heard that the bulldozers are coming your way, through some part of your community, a favorite park or even your own backyard; or maybe you think there are just too many highways around already and mass transit is a better answer to our transportation problems.

If so, don't stop worrying. There are at least $10 billion worth of new federally funded highways currently on the drawing boards—and with the mammoth auto and highway-building industries pushing them, they have a good chance of becoming concrete in the next few years.

But you needn't be resigned, either. Citizen groups have risen to challenge state highway departments (which do the building, using federal subsidies) in recent years and have stopped a number of highways dead in their tracks. Currently they have some twenty-five highways ensnarled in court suits. Highways *can* be stopped or their impact minimized, and here's how, based on a growing body of successful resistance.

Organize. As soon as you learn that a highway is coming, start getting it together—the opposition. Veteran highway battlers suggest organizing first around existing community groups that are most directly affected by the highway—neighborhood, civic, and church organizations whose members live in the proposed highway's path. Your nucleus group should then select an official-sounding name, order some stationery with a letterhead, and get the use of a duplicating machine. You're in business. Now to broaden your ranks. Among likely allies:

Schools. Increased traffic will jeopardize the children's safety.

Environmental organizations. Most of them are against highway expansion.

Park departments and boards. Highways are often routed through parks.

Kiwanis, Rotary, etc. Groups whose members own small businesses that the highway may displace or isolate behind walls of concrete are natural enlistees.

Apply Political Pressure. In Washington, D.C., Boston and Cambridge, Massachusetts, and Atlanta, Georgia, highway fighters have forged the kind of broad coalitions that politicians dream about—and can't easily ignore. Focus your pressure on key local and state politicians who will be up for reelection soon. What tactics should you use? Antihighway coalitions have tried intensive letter-writing campaigns, personal lobbying, and picketing. In Cambridge and Boston highway opponents marched two thousand strong on the State House and even barricaded a traffic-congested street. In Washington highway foes have disrupted "public" hearings they insisted were fixed.

Study the Regulations. While political pressure may be a first step to halting a highway—and possibly a last, too—it can be an exceedingly difficult route, because the automobile and highway lobbies exercise enormous political muscle in most states, and you will be fighting them, in effect, on their turf. A more generally fruitful avenue these days may be to do battle within the administrative system. Since 1968, state highway departments have been obliged by federal law and administrative edict to follow a spate of complex regulations designed to guarantee a citizen voice in highway planning, and these rules can actually provide such a voice for those who know how to use them. "If anyone wants to stop our highways," a federal highway official reportedly told a conference of highway builders in Washington, D.C., "just make us follow our own regulations." These are some of the broad elements in those regulations and some tactical considerations to heed:

Prepare for Hearings. When a state highway department decides to build a major highway, it must, under the 1968 federal law, hold two public hearings before it can receive federal funds. The first hearing considers the highway's exact location, or corridor, and the second focuses on the highway's design. The state *must* announce each hearing at least twice—thirty days before and five to twelve days before the hearing day—in "a newspaper having general circulation." State highway planners must also send announcements to "public advisory groups" whom the state "knows or believes might be interested in or affected by" the highway.

States often play tricks with these provisions. In Nashville the highway department plastered post offices with circulars announcing the hearing date—but when citizens showed up they discovered the hearing had been rescheduled for the day before. In Seattle state officials held a public hearing on a highway that was to go through a black community. The meeting was held exactly according to the preannounced plan—at an all-white country club, on an island in the harbor, at 10 A.M. Be wary.

At the "corridor" hearing on the highway's location, highway planners will propose several different highway routes, and citizens can testify for or against them.

Federal law requires the state highway planners to consider the "social, economic and environmental effects of those alternate locations"—and the law lists twenty-three specific considerations as a start. For example, the planners must discuss the highway's effects on "fast, safe and efficient transportation . . . residential and neighborhood character and location . . . displacement of families and businesses . . . conservation (including erosion, sedimentation, wildlife and general ecology of the area) . . . multiple uses of space . . . education (including disruption of school district operations) . . . property values . . . maintenance and operating costs of the project and related facilities." Put the highway department on the line: demand hard analysis and numbers, not vague assurances.

Before the highway planners get past the corridor hearing, they must also guarantee in writing that they have already found enough "decent, safe and sanitary" housing for every person whom the new highway will displace—and that means housing with comparable rent that is situated reasonably close to work and in an area with comparable public and commercial services. Highway departments give guarantees readily enough but don't always follow through on them. Demand precise information on alternative housing, and if you don't get it, request an additional public hearing.

Do the Arithmetic. When a state asks the U.S. Department of Transportation to approve its highway location and DOT complies (it usually does), the highway department will announce a public design hearing. This could be held from six months to six years after the location hearing. All procedural requirements at the first hearing apply to this one, too, but now you'll consider minute details on the final design. Some people get scared when they confront all the technical jargon that highway engineers throw at them—but no need. Read a few books, and use your common sense. Skip the explanations about curve radius and bank elevation and cement specifications, and ask: How many cars and trucks will the highway carry per hour, and how will the highway department feed them into the city streets? How much air pollution will they bring, and how will the planners control it?

Once DOT gives final approval for the highway, you've exhausted your administrative channels. But you still have one major weapon left in your antihighway arsenal.

Sue. Highway fighters have discovered that one of their best hopes is to catch a state highway department in a legal procedural mistake and then to drag the highway plans through years of administrative and court proceedings until the highway supporters have given up the fight.

The complexity of highway laws and regulations since 1968 provides fertile grounds for error, but environmental consciousness underlies the law that has nourished most citizen suits and court victories over highway plans. Under the National Environmental Policy Act (NEPA) of 1970, the state highway planners must prepare an "environmental impact statement" for every proposed highway, including possible alternatives to the highway.

NEPA impact statements must consider every conceivable social, economic, and environmental consequence, and you'll want to read the Department of Transportation regulations for guidance. These are some likely weak links to look out for: Does the statement analyze *long-term* effects of the highway, such as land use fifteen years from now as the tax base changes? And does it propose alternatives to the highway, including expanded bus service, mass transit—or building *no road at all?* NEPA requirements are a gold mine of legal activism for citizen groups, because while the courts demand strict compliance, compiling all the information and evaluation required is a mammoth job, and state highway departments trying to get away without doing it properly. Lawyers at the Washington-based Center for Science in the Public Interest have found, for instance, that the exact same NEPA statement, word for word, was filed for two totally different highways in two different states.

Court suits demand a lot of time and can be prohibitively expensive. So a prime requirement is to find a good lawyer who's willing to donate his or her services. Highway fighters in Washington estimate that their counsel, Covington and Burling, has devoted half a million dollars of lawyers' time since they first went to court in 1966. But don't be discouraged. Look around and you'll see that a freeway designed to cut across San Francisco has been abruptly and permanently truncated in midcourse; Chicago's $965 million Crosstown Expressway is currently stalled in court; in Maryland $750 million worth of concrete has been stopped; the $76.1 million Hawthorne-Century Freeway outside Los Angeles isn't going anywhere, either. You definitely can stop a highway.

CHAPTER 15

Promoting Community, Ecology, and Political Gains: Toward a New Habitat

If there is one thing that is clear as we enter the 1970s, it is that the new generation of men and women will make sweeping demands of the institutions they come in contact with.

DAVID BRODER

[We] have at hand great quantities of research findings which clearly indicate what we should be doing. Much indeed we don't know, but we are not doing one-tenth of what we should about what we already do know.

KARL MENNINGER

It is my assumption that images of the future determine present actions. They may or may not determine the nature of the future—that depends on a much more complex set of circumstances. But willy-nilly much of our behavior is postulated upon images of a possible and/or desirable future.

SCOTT GREER

Our three concerns in this chapter—potential reforms in community building, environmental safeguards, and political practices—are alike in that all suffer from a "bad press," public cynicism, and an inadequate appreciation of the gains already made and those reasonably close to securement. Accordingly, this chapter wrestles as much with excessive negativism in all three areas as it does with the case for and against several intriguing reforms that we might weigh.

Overshadowing these three related issues is the paradox that a nation dedicated to social "togetherness," ecological sanity, and democracy seems to be unable to help neighbors remain neighborly, the environment hospitable, and the government credible. We began as co-revolutionaries in the 1700's, drawing strength from a continent blessed with extraordinary natural gifts, and we established what has become the largest democratic governing apparatus in the world. In some ways, we have been steadily losing ground ever since . . . but recently, with the Housing Act of 1968, the Environmental Protection Act of 1970, and public political dialogue (the Watergate spur to governmental reform of the mid-1970's), we may have turned a corner in all three regards.

We have momentum and vision now, thanks in large part to the civil rights protests, Earth Day agendas, and general social unrest of the past decade. With the Vietnam war finally a minor drain on national finances and spirit and with the combination of a Presidential election and a bicentennial both making 1976 a *very* special target year, overdue attention is finally being paid the substantial gains we can secure *soon* on the domestic front.

In the first of the three parts of this chapter, four community-oriented reforms are explored, each more ambitious, complex, and costly than the last, with the lofty challenge of New Towns closing out the section. Thereafter, attention is paid to ecological reforms that pit us against the auto and against our own polluting and wasteful practices, with the deputized citizen "pollution fighters" of Sweden a heartening example of what can be accomplished. Finally, the chapter closes with attention to tax referendums on public policy, the Canadian model of voter registration and executive accessibility, the issue of how a vice president might best be chosen, and the new use we can make of TV in an updating of the old town meeting.

Community Building

Rent-a-Home. Instead of the squalor and stigma of public housing the poor can find better housing of their own choosing in the private market if the government chooses to help pay the rents entailed. A little-publicized Kansas City experiment in 1970 in subsidizing the escape of slum dwellers proved so successful as to encourage its expansion in 1972 into six more cities.

Traditionally, government housing programs for the poor focused on the construction of controversial high-rise units. Often poorly planned and maintained, many degenerated into unsafe and unhealthy perpetuators of human poverty. The reform pioneered in 1970 in Kansas City by HUD experts had the government pay up to 100 per cent of the difference between a decent rental and a welfare client's ability to pay for housing (on a $200 rental of a three-bedroom home a family with an income of $3,000 would pay only $62.50 a month). Some 207 families each cost the government less than $1,500 a year in subsidies. As the price to build low-rent housing for these families was about $25,000 per unit in Kansas City, HUD and city officials hailed the rent-aid plan as a cheaper, better alternative to the "same old thing."

There were problems. Blacks encountered racial discrimination, and almost all chose to move into a corridor of racially changing neighborhoods rather than to pioneer integration in the white suburbs or other hostile areas. Nearly 10 per cent of the low-income families in the experiment found adjustments difficult. High utility bills never before confronted shocked many, as did boosts in travel-to-work fares and the absence of free school lunches for their children in new neighborhood schools. At the same time, however, 150 of the 170 families surveyed in the early 1970's did not hesitate to endorse the direct housing plan over the public housing option always open to them.

In light of the program's success, the approaching 1974 termination of the entire program is most perplexing. Although the government has promised to find housing for the Kansas City families directly involved, the household heads observe worriedly that there is no guarantee of a continuing subsidy.

Whether or not we can somehow still ensure the expansion of this successful effort in rent subsidies everywhere remains unclear.[1]

Homeowners' Insurance in Newly Integrated Areas. Those who express a concern about the effect of neighborhood racial integration on the value of their investment in their homes may only be rationalizing an ugly prejudice against nonwhite neighbors *or* they may be genuinely concerned about what a move-in might do to their largest personal investment—often the only significant repository of their life savings. That the economic dangers these people fear are largely unreal—except in short-run blockbusting situations—does not make their worries any less real to them, or any less costly to race relations in America today.

If this particular source of worry could be removed, reasons law professor Adam Yarmolinsky, three substantial gains are possible:

1. White homeowners might conceivably become less resistant to mixed housing in their neighborhood.
2. Even where economic concerns are pure rationalization by white racists there is something to be said for calling their bluff.
3. There is also something to be said for removing the commercial incentives that lead block-busting real-estate operators to seek rapid turnover in an atmosphere of panic and hate.

Accordingly, Yarmolinsky urges reform attention to a proposed public insurance scheme capable of protecting a homeowner's equity in his residence.

How would it work? Very much like a program the Department of Defense now operates that guarantees up to 90 or 95 per cent of the homeownership equity for DOD civilian employees whose equities are adversely affected by base closings. More specifically, insurance would be made available at modest premiums to homeowners in changing neighborhoods to reimburse them for any loss in investment when they sell their homes. If, after offering his home for sale for a reasonable period at the insured price a homeowner does not find a buyer, he could sell it at the market price and collect the difference from the insurer, or the insurer might take it off his hands for resale and pay him the insured price.

If such insurance were available at a reasonable price, Yarmolinsky points out, this very fact should discourage the depression of property values that may accompany rapid change in the racial character of a neighborhood—and consequently, the cost of the scheme itself would be held down. Which is not to overlook four kinds of potentially costly problems raised in turn by this reform:

1. How to measure the homeowner's equity interest.
2. How to determine the geographical scope of coverage.
3. How to secure an adequate range of risks.
4. How to administer and pay for the scheme.

None of these problems strike Yarmolinsky as particularly difficult, and he suggests alternative answers to each in his writings on the subject.

Overall, the insurance reform speaks directly to the persistent and corrosive demand of middle America: "What has the government done for us lately?" A plan that employs the credit of the federal government to protect the largest single asset that most Americans have might "help reassure these people, and might even begin to knit up the ravelled fabric of the Union."[2]

Social Development Banks. Critical in the prospects of any community project is the realistic question of how to finance it—especially as the risk entailed is likely to be considerable. An interesting and practical model is one pioneered during the New Deal, when under the Farm Credit Act in 1933 thirteen banks were especially established by the federal government to provide capital to new farm cooperatives. From the very start these rural-based banks were viewed as a source of aid (planning, personal, and so on) far beyond mere financial loan services. Acting somewhat like farm extension agents, many representatives of the thirteen far-flung banks spent a considerable amount of time in the field "doing good." Although the federal government has now in effect withdrawn from loaning government money through them, the thirteen banks are now so well established and highly regarded as to receive loanable funds through debenture sales from commercial money markets. They continue to "do good" . . . as many a farm dweller will hasten to attest.

If a good idea is pushed still further, it would appear that such banks could now contribute much to *urban* reconstruction. Mandated by Congress with a substantial capital fund (perhaps $25 billion), and with additional authority to borrow from the commercial market for nonprofit ventures (loans guaranteed through a new federal insurance program), a new national "social development" bank could help fund all kinds of urban consumer co-ops, urban housing co-ops, urban theater co-ops, and local self-rule urban experiments. Directed by a board elected by the borrowers themselves, the policies of the bank branches would be heavily influenced by the will of the neighborhood people. Furthermore, besides being borrowers, urban grass roots ventures could also become shareholders in the bank, with surpluses accruing to them from normal bank ventures for further investment in urban social welfare matters.

How, then, might we finance nonprofit neighborhood projects? Possibly by expanding a successful rural experiment into the city—and letting our "country cousins" teach us a thing or two about getting our show on the road.[3]

New Towns. While the Old America watches—skeptical, occasionally disdainful, more often hopeful—nearly a hundred variations go up across the country on "the Next America" (the boastful title the planners gave in 1967 to Columbia, Maryland, then and now our leading east coast New Town).

An old idea, the "New Town" has nevertheless existed mainly in America only in the wistful minds of architects and planners who admire the examples to be found abroad. Envious of British and Scandinavian successes, the American professionals have long urged adoption of the New Town idea as a desirable alternative to suburban "slurb" and urban blight. Priced, however, at a billion or more development dollars to be laid out over a twenty-year buildup period, the toughest, most trouble-beset land development venture of all attracted few takers—until new federal legislation in 1968 made huge loans available to a wide number of eager urban developers.

Now, however, the always uncertain New Towns seem momentarily on the wane. A tough combination of inflationary building costs and governmental obstacles in the form of zoning and overlapping jurisdictions has taken some of the wind from the New Town sails. The cause also suffers from honest feedback on the inability of new communities magically to transform residents overnight into Camelot-like suprabeings. Whether this dip in public and private interest (and vision) will prove as temporary as I believe or more permanent still hinges in no small part on *your* assessment of the case for New Towns given here.

Awkwardly posed for resolution in America is the far-reaching question: How serious do we intend to be about realizing the enormous potential of a seventy-year-old international idea in community development, that of the New Town (roughly, a self-sustaining community that offers employment and "the best" in urban and rural-style living to people of all economic levels)? Will we soon choose New Towns to help relieve overcrowding in our urban cores and to help house some of the 100 million new Americans expected before 2000 A.D., or will we relegate the idea to obscurity (whatever its considerable success abroad)?

What are New Towns? At their most modest they are unique, self-sustaining, economically viable communities of 150,000 or so enthusiasts on fifteen thousand or more dynamic acres (the size of Manhattan). They are communities of residence and employment, of culture and of recreation, in convenient relation to each other and to existing cities, and guided by certain health and environmental objectives. At their public relations best, they are understandably heralded—in Columbia's case, for example—as "the Next America." At least one academic champion does not hesitate to represent them as "one of the authentic revolutionary ideas of our time."[4] And the sponsors of a leading development insist that its fidelity to the basic characteristics of a New Town make it "not only a place to live but a way to live."[5]

For the past fifteen years, however, the New Town idea has lain dormant in this country. (Abroad it has been promoted with ever-increasing skill and success by the venerable Town and Country Planning Association in England and comparable groups in Scandinavia and Western Europe.) America has chosen instead to explore the possibilities and dynamics of Megalopolis. We were fascinated initially by the sweep and potential of superhighways, mammoth housing projects, FHA largesse, and bold renewal planning. We have only recently been discovering how we have become entangled with a powerful highway lobby, a chain of inhuman housing project disasters, a hopelessly inadequate housing market, and a planless mishmash of nightmare proportions. Slum clearance programs, Model Cities efforts, and Operation Breakthrough successes barely hold their own in combination against the steady erosion of the central city's humanity. Accordingly, our political leaders, planners, and academic urbanologists have begun to look elsewhere, beyond urbanmania, for possible aids.

America's revival of interest in New Towns has been helped considerably by the interest of opinion-shaping elites. Typical is the fact that shortly before his death in the spring of 1968 the late President Eisenhower contributed an essay to *Reader's Digest* urging the creation by private business of planned and integrated New Towns. Soon thereafter Vice President Agnew drew new attention to the subject when, in the summer of 1969, he gave an enthusiastic welcome to the call for ten New Cities and one hundred New Towns over the next thirty years that was issued by the National Committee on Urban Growth Policy. President Nixon joined the discussion later that same summer, criticizing the goal of ten giant cities as far too limited (it would provide housing for only one fifth of the anticipated growth in the number of Americans). It remained for Chase Manhattan Bank President David Rockefeller to pull all the threads together when, in a major address in February of 1971, he called for vast new private efforts to provide for the equivalent of building a New Town of 200,000 every month from now through 2000 A.D.—provided, that is, that vast new federal aid for the private, profit-making endeavor would be soon available. Ten New Cities and one hundred New Towns—all the product of a cooperative, heavily subsidized joint venture dominated and heavily profited from by big business.

Why New Towns at this particular time? Proponents believe we are uniquely positioned now to take advantage of vast tracts of underused land and a manageable nationwide population density—a combination that perilously slips away from us with every passing year. We need to accommodate at least 35 million more Americans (of the 100 million expected by 2000 A.D.) outside of existing cities. If this accommodation were to be undertaken in 350 New Towns, the 3.5 million acres involved would cover a mere one sixth of 1 per cent of our total land area. Any other approach to the goal of doubling our housing stock over the next thirty years would court disaster in the form of suburban sprawl and spoil.[6]

Why New Towns now? Proponents believe that New Towns would encourage the dispersal of the population and its increment from our present urban concentrations. At present we are crowded into suburbs and cities in a planless fashion that may result in America's soon consisting of half a dozen sprawling urban conglomerates separated by vast tracts of underused space (70 per cent of the population is on 10 per cent of the land). New Town proponents urge speedy resort to the creation outside of existing population centers of Columbia-like "magnets."

Why New Towns now? Because little else has any real potential of helping us make progress in the plight of 40 million poor Americans. For several unproductive years now Congress has insisted that the problem of the bad housing of the poor (admittedly fundamental in the perpetuation of poverty) is primarily one of deficient structures and physical decay. The inconvenient fact has been ignored that two thirds of all the poor in 1966 lived in housing deemed structurally sound. This fact demonstrates that bad housing is intertwined with poor schools, high crime rates, and inadequate transportation—in brief, the whole community environment. The (expensive) New Towns would include the poor in meaningful numbers and hold the promise of a healthy and health-restoring community environment.[7]

Typical of the thoughtful and bold plans put forth to relieve urban overcrowding and poverty is a 1968 proposal from two experienced New Town developers who insist that the New Town concept "lends itself admirably to dealing with the critical problems of our urban areas as well as with the race crisis." Their strategy has three key ingredients:

1. A massive ten-year New Town building effort.
2. The construction of 350,000 subsidized New Town housing units a year.
3. The withdrawal of public tax support from suburban developments in favor of the subsidized New Towns.

Pursuit of this strategy for only five years holds out the promise of reducing the size of the urban ghetto by "somewhat more than half," and producing newly desegregated city neighborhoods and outlying New Towns. The plan, of course, cries out for the earliest possible implementation—if it is to have any real chance to succeed.[8]

Why New Towns? Because they appear to be especially well suited to the enormous untapped potential of the technology of mass construction in housing. At present home construction is dominated by scores of small builders, each one responsible for a few-score units a year. The developing of a New Town for 200,000 every month for the next thirty years (à la the Rockefeller plan) would help compel the overdue conversion of the home-building industry from custom on-site to mass on-site and modular techniques. (Former Vice President Agnew noted that "planning for completely new cities allows us to consider the rational distribution of industry on a national scale.")

Similarly, the erection of thousands of housing units within a relatively compact area will compel integration and coordination with the construction of industrial, educational, transportation, health, and other life-support systems. Both major developments—the modernization of home-building techniques and the intensification of coordination in community development—are long overdue in our unevenly advanced nation.

The list could be extended—the reasons that America might intensify its involvement with New Towns *now* are many. They include, in addition to those already cited, the opportunity we currently have to parlay support for proposed New Towns into support as well for a sorely needed national urban plan and the opportunity that New Towns offer especially to help prepare Americans for the postindustrial cybernetic age. If we promote the cause of New Towns in the 1970's we must rationally also promote the cause of coordinated national, regional, and local planning, all imperative and overdue objectives. If we keep the peace and prolong our industrial prosperity we can find few more suitable communities for accommodating the cybernetic age advances that are commonly predicted, such as increased discretionary income, intensified family life, ever-higher standards of living, and expensive cosmopolitan life-styles.

Not surprising, therefore, was the conclusion reached by journalist John Fischer, who in 1969 examined four new books calling on America to endorse the New Town movement. "They are revolutionary documents," he cheered. "They demand nothing less than a reshaping of American institutions, the whole web of local governments, the tax system, the labor unions, the welfare programs, and many other hallowed relics."[9]

Why New Towns at this time? Because America is at another of the special critical junctures in its history (as in 1915, 1933, and 1945, when we joined the modern world, dared to undertake our own planned self-rehabilitation, and ushered in the nuclear age of permanent, if precarious, peace and prosperity). This time the challenge is to reshape American institutions to secure communities for all worthy of a materially well-off nation's highest spiritual potential. We are called on to:

1. Manage our unused land on the public's behalf.
2. Undertake population-response moves of a substantial, democratic character.
3. Offer city dwellers options to urban containment.
4. Fight poverty with the additional tool of possible New Town residence.
5. Tap the enormous potential of mass-technology reforms in construction.
6. Secure the establishment of a national urban policy and its coordination with regional and local plans.
7. Help Americans prepare for the cybernetic age through the provision of prototypes of twenty-first-century-styled New Towns.

In combination with the score of previously cited lessons offered us since 1898, or, more particularly, since the American Greenbelt cities of the New Deal, these seven potentialities of the New Town movement round out an imposing argument in favor of a massive American effort on behalf of New Towns—*now*.

Ecology and Antipollution Moves

Auto-cracy and Victory. Is it possible to reverse the trend, stem the tide, and stop the automobile? Hailed originally as one of the most wonderful inventions of humanity, and currently breaking all sales records annually, the American automobile is nevertheless gaining a new and unflattering image. Of the Chevy Impala, for example, a former editor of a car magazine and ad writer for Chevrolet writes,

> It was an over-size, overweight, over-powered, under-braked, under-tired, dangerously fast (but ponderously slow to respond to any control other than the accelerator), hideously complex, over-decorated, under-engineered, resolutely ordinary, badly assembled, twenty-foot, four thousand pound, front engine, rear drive *thing*. It was very American.[10]

No wonder, then, that Adolf Ciborowski, a UN specialist in urban affairs, indicts the contemporary auto for having "broken apart the orderly ecology of urban living, burdened movement, congested the most valuable places, wasted resources, and killed people."[11] (Approximately 60,000 persons are killed annually in traffic accidents and another 4 million are injured.)

Partial attacks on such specific auto-linked problems as safety, congestion, or pollution are well underway:

1. Regular inspection of all car and truck exhaust systems is a staple of plans sent to the EPA by New York, Chicago, Philadelphia, and Pittsburgh.
2. The "retrofitting" of old cars with catalytic converters to reduce pol-

lutant levels in exhaust emissions is another basic approach—at an average cost of $200 a car.

3. Higher inner-city parking fees and the elimination of many parking spaces are virtually certain.
4. The upgrading of mass-transit facilities, including the reservation of freeway lanes for express bus service and improvement of the rail transit systems, is another almost universal formula.
5. Colorado is considering gasoline rationing for Denver, and the EPA has recommended the same as an answer to the smog problem in the Los Angeles area.

Whether or not the EPA extends its deadlines on pollution control standards, no less a student of the subject than *Business Week* concludes that "some permanent transportation controls in U.S. cities are inevitable."[12] (In Japan, by the way, drivers may soon have to get a license authorizing the *purchase* of a car. Tokyo's Metropolitan Safety Council is asking for traffic and ownership restrictions on "those vehicles for which the social need is not very great." Certain areas of the city will soon be banned to all but essential vehicles. Trucks and other large vehicles will be banned altogether during the day. And, ultimately, some means will be used to curtail sharply the private ownership of "socially superfluous" vehicles.[13])

Journalist William Safire, speculating about what controls in U.S. cities might include, recently advanced this plan:

> *Double the fare on all bridges and tunnels during rush hours, and make the fare free during non-rush hours.* Also, during rush hours, reduce the fare by 25 cents for each additional adult passenger in the car—full cars go free. In this way, economic incentives would be provided to stagger working hours, loosen up the traffic flow, encourage car pools, profit bondholders, and provide a subsidy for the subway.

Characterizing this plan as a "simple, demagogic proposal to solve the traffic solution," Safire caustically notes that "voters don't want speeches that begin, 'There are no easy answers'; they want answers, and the easier the better."[14]

Although some, especially those who are proauto, probably consider Safire's proposals excessive, others condemn them as lax and misleading measures that serve the automobile more than they do people in the end.

One such critic, Kenneth R. Schneider, has outlined a sweeping plan for an overdue rebellion against "the fraudulent claims of technology and enterprise that everything they do underwrites the good life, a rebellion for a civic trust which is at the heart of any civilization." His goals are essentially four:

1. To free man from servitude, the auto must be totally subordinated. Ideally they should be as obedient, silent, and unobtrusive as the city's sewer system.
2. The city will be renewed man-size, with a new efficiency organized for people—their behavior, their bodies, their senses, their associations, and even their casual inclinations.
3. To exercise their renewed franchise the people will first require consid-

erable rehabilitation. For their will has been reduced to buying habits and route planning.

4. For such a rebellion against Autokind to succeed, a revolutionary leadership is required to "purge the motor myths, rebuild the human ideals and social goals, formulate the grand strategy, recruit and organize the cadres, and lead the uprisings."

Schneider, after advancing a detailed, multi-staged plan of attack, concludes on an optimistic note:

> the automobile carries the seeds of its own downfall. . . . All that the car originally had to offer is killed by the car's own excesses. . . . We now set 1994 as our target date to completely overcome society's first mechanical addiction.[15]

To which claim a *Wall Street Journal* columnist, Greg Conderacci, retorts in a related context, "The automakers' production of smaller cars and their frantic push to develop alternate power plants is a good example of their willingness to adapt—if their lives depend upon it."[16]

The question, of course, is victory on behalf of what and for what? Conderacci shrugs off criticism of the automobile complex and points the finger of blame instead at a "wealthy society's search for tinsel, gadgetry, luxury, and status." Schneider, in turn, puts the blame squarely on the "Autokind Complex" and urges us to use a total victory over the car as a foundation for better living: we would not only get relief from accidents, pollution, and congestion, but we would expect to "reduce the cost-benefit calculation of emotion, the monetary pollution of behavior, and the technological congestion of culture."[17] In an America finally in charge of its automobiles, the central characteristics of our environment would have "the excitement of a fair, the discovery of a university, the serenity of a national park."[18]

Ecology as Personal Crusade. Founded in 1970, a Washington citizens group called Concern, Inc., publishes a series of consumer guides called *Eco-Tips* that it mails (on recycled paper) across the nation. Typical of the kind of reform demands we are increasingly asked to make on ourselves, the *Eco-Tips* urge that we immediately:

1. Unplug TV sets with the instant turn-on feature, as they consume electricity twenty-four hours a day.
2. Substitute a switch-operated electric starter for the continuously burning pilot light on gas stoves.
3. Demand returnable bottles for our soft drinks.
4. Buy paper products of recycled material.
5. Avoid frost-free refrigerators and self-cleaning ovens, as both require too much energy to operate.
6. Have the gaskets replaced on our refrigerator doors if we can pull a new dollar bill out easily after closing the refrigerator door on it.
7. Purchase only cars that weigh under two thousand pounds, and drive as close to 50, rather than 60 or 70mph, as possible.

Overall, this nonprofit, tax-exempt group is "determined to harness the vast consumer power of this country to help solve environmental problems."[19]

A similar set of guidelines, called *The Do-It-Yourself Environmental Handbook,* was prepared in 1972 by the Dayton Museum of Natural History. A foreword stated the issue quite strongly:

> From the moment of birth until the hour of death everybody is a polluter. Anyone who takes in food and air also gives off wastes, and is therefore a polluter. This includes, of course, both the writer and the reader of this foreword. It is in the light of this truth that this book has been prepared. Its intended effort is to make all of us balanced polluters who will seek earnestly to reduce our contributions to the environmental crisis before it overwhelms us.

Later, after asking the reader to check the pledges he is prepared to make, the writer urges that these pledges be understood as not being pledges of the reader to the authors or the publisher of the book. Rather, these are pledges "you have made to yourself and to your children, to thus help the world survive."

Specifically, the *Handbook* includes hundreds of tips on conservation that anyone can use in the home, the backyard, the car, the school, and the supermarket, or while traveling. For example:

1. Reduce or eliminate the use of household pesticides; most are more dangerous to you than the pests.
2. If your community does not have a recycling center, take steps to start one.
3. You can save eight to ten trees per year if you see that all reusable paper is returned for recycling.
4. Avoid the use of plastics; until biodegradable plastics are widely available it is best to avoid them entirely.
5. Put all organic matter into a compost heap.
6. Do not throw away something that can be fixed.
7. Buy organically grown foods.
8. Select all the items you buy with durability in mind.
9. Convert your car from gasoline to propane gas.

The reader is also urged to examine new school construction to make certain that every possible environmental consideration is made:

> For example, there are in existence today sewerless toilets that use the same water over and over, producing no sewage. There are heat-recovery techniques, incredible insulations, solar energy traps, rainwater conservation practices, and trash and garbage pulping and composting machines that can enrich school lands with waste materials schools now throw away.

Here, as elsewhere in the *Handbook,* the name and address of a specialist is offered for further consultation.

Over and over the recommendations reach deep into our personal lives: limit the size of our families ("population growth is our most frightening problem"); quit smoking; raise the question of securing a clean environment in your religious group; and so on. The authors urge readers to adopt new ways of living, and deny that they deal only in trifles:

> But what is a trifle—like leaving a newspaper in a restaurant in fit condition for someone else to read—if a million people do it? Then that trifle saves a small forest of trees.
>
> Is it a trifle when, on going to dinner, you switch off 300 watts of lighting in the living room? Perhaps. But, when 10,000,000 families do it, enough electricity is conserved to provide the needs of a city of 10,000 for 15 days.

This concept, the *Handbook* authors conclude, involves our trust in collective action. As they interpret the data, one of the happier signs of our troubled times is the fact that more and more concerned people—millions of them—are beginning to do many of the things that this handbook recommends. Joining this particular "army" finally makes it possible to "enlarge the satisfaction you earn by happily doing what you know to be right . . . urgently needed . . . and critical to the future of all you hold dear."[20]

Pollution Control. What if Earth Day had really succeeded beyond our wildest hopes and had taken firm and deep hold in America? What kind of antipollution program might we have developed? And, to come down a bit from the clouds, what kind of program must we continue to strive for—given the sad failure of Earth Day efforts to survive our apparently insatiable appetite for quickie crusades of empty moral uplift and deceptive programmatic flim-flam.

Sweden, in particular, sets us an example well worth emulating in spirit and in detail. Crisp legislation is a key ingredient in an attention-commanding program initiated in 1969. At that time Sweden became the first nation in the world to impose a total ban on the use of DDT, Aldrin, Dieldrin, and other chlorinated hydrocarbons. As one official explained, "It wasn't very difficult to do. Very little if any of these are manufactured here, and besides, we made the farmers realize that they are the first to suffer from exposure."[21] The law also established a fund of about $50 million to be spent over five years to pay 25 per cent of the cost for providing antipollution equipment. (Industry has no excuse for inaction. A new government-aided company, Swedish Waste Conversion, has been formed to market antipollution equipment.) To help move things along a time limit was set in 1969 for the cleanup: by 1972 all factories had to meet the new, tough antipollution standards.

As if this were not enough, the Swedes went further to shift the responsibility for policing to industrialists where plant expansion is concerned. Now a company cannot build a new factory unless it can prove to a government antipollution commission that the proposed installation will not muck things up. Similarly, the fifteen or so nuclear energy plants proposed for construction by 2000 A.D. must be sited in conformity with a new comprehensive master plan designed to minimize their ecological effects, although this means additional cost and construction difficulties. Swedish factory owners can take some comfort, however, in the sure knowledge that the government enforces its antipollution measures across the board: a mill that cleans up is assured that no other mill can gain a competitive advantage by continuing to pollute.

To help ensure that the new law's various provisions are safeguarded, the nation has taken a bold and imaginative step: *it has "deputized" a quarter of a million citizens!* A sizable adult education program aims at creating in each community a corps of well-informed citizens who can organize public hearings and confront industrial and civic officials on what they are doing about pollution. In 1969 some 250,000 people attended a few evenings' instruction on the technical and legal aspects of pollution. Some 10,000 took an additional two weeks' instruction, and 1,000 of these were picked to conduct public inquiries and, in general, to agitate in behalf of pollution control. Similarly, in 1971 the national school system put more than 1 million students into a week-long action program on the conservation of the environment. This highly coordinated effort involved field trips, laboratory work, and classroom experiments—all focusing on pollution. The program was set up as a "good foundation for continued and more basic study."[22]

Overseeing the entire program is a new government body, the National Swedish Nature Conservation Office, the only organization of its kind in the world. With a staff of about 175 and a budget of about $50 million, the Conservation Office has branches for nature conservation, water and air control, and research. Special attention is paid by staffers to the consulting Board for Environmental Problems, an Office-related national policy-making body for antipollution activity. Its twenty-four influential members include ten scientists and representatives of labor, industry, finance, and the press. Fortuitously located in the Ministry of Agriculture the NSNC Office is the coincidental beneficiary of a decline in agriculture's importance in the Swedish economy. Interest in pollution is on the way up, and "the Ministry is delighted to have a new and expanding responsibility."[23]

Of greatest value is the tenet that guides the entire operation: the Swedish antipollution effort reflects foresight rather than an emergency response to an intolerable situation. For example, though few, if any, of Sweden's inland waterways have reached the stage of being too thick to navigate and too thin to cultivate, there are plans to have sewage purification plants serving all built-up areas within a few years. Communities will be eligible for grants of 30 to 50 per cent to meet the cost, and backing up this assistance is a new law that states that municipal waste may not be discharged without a permit. The systems approach to the pollution challenge underlies all of this planning and contrasts sharply in its no-nonsense stance with our own haphazard and uneven strategy.

To recapitulate then, how does one conduct a model pollution-control effort? Firm legislation, complete with reasonable government subsidies to help business meet the costs of correction, is combined with a target date that is in the near future and a master plan for the entire nation's ecological well-being. Enforcement is shared with informed citizen volunteers, and the national school system strives to infuse the young with conscience and craft in the matter of pollution and ecology. High-level government support is assured through the careful positioning of the antipollution program in the bureaucracy, and the main effort is preventive, obviating remedial programs at a later, sadder time. How, then, does one conduct a first-rate environmental control program? Possibly as the Swedes have.

Political Reforms

An Economic Vote. We are all accustomed to paying taxes and thereafter leaving allocation decisions to the politicians (and their mandarin-class staff advisers)—even when we know that the outcome is likely to displease us greatly (for example, even as we prepare to pay this year's federal income tax many of us are troubled by the constancy over decades of the 80 per cent figure that represents our federal expenditure on military and defense items).

It could be otherwise—if you and I gained the right to turn in our own advisory allocations of tax dollars to specific cabinet departments, agencies of the federal government, and so on. Our decisions could be predicated on our own estimates of the needs and our own judgment as to whether or not a particular department was doing a useful or necessary job for the country.

For example, assume that your total tax bill came to $2,500. You might advise the allocation of $1,000 to HEW; $250 to Defense; $750 to Urban Development; $300 to foreign aid; and $200 to mass transit. Proponents of this reform expect that cabinet officers might compete for funds either through the President or by individual appeals to the people for these advisory allocations. As a result, government officials might become more responsive to the people. But critics are quick to posit three far less desirable outcomes: many might "vote" close to 100 per cent of their taxes for military and defense expenditures; the tabulation of tax data could become overwhelmingly complex; and finally, "uninformed" voters could undermine the government. Yet we already spend heavily on defense; we could use new computer technology to keep the "voting" straight; and we *should* predicate our dynamic democracy on creating an ever-better-informed citizenry.

In my classes I often ask students to write down the percentages of present and future tax dollars that they would prefer to see allocated among the various federal budgetary items. When I later fill the blackboard with a record of current Congressional practice, a chorus of surprise, dismay, and, more rarely, pleasure underlines for us all an alarming "softness" in our system of representative government. Current defense spending, for example, represents $1,200 in taxes for every American family—or twice what we spend on pre-college education and eight times what government and industry together spend annually to reduce air and water pollution.[24] Economic advisory voting, anyone?

Voter Registration and Executive Access. It is sometimes argued that a country that professes to be the most democratic nation on earth, that is committed to helping solve problems through the ballot box, ought to move heaven and earth to find each voter and convince him to participate.

In Philadelphia, however, where I am writing, the responsibility for registration is a partisan political football—and 25 per cent of the eligible voters remain unregistered. Reformers urge a three-point agenda of national relevance:

1. Permit volunteer registrars to sign up voters—as in Pittsburgh and New York—instead of restricting the task to the paid, patronage-picked registrars.

2. Open permanent registration sites at more convenient locations with more convenient hours (Philadelphia has two sites that are open only during business hours).
3. Repeal laws that strike voters from the lists for failure to exercise their franchise in a set time period (two years in Pennsylvania). Instead, rewrite the laws to aid rather than hamper voting.

Still more provocative is the suggestion that we convert our entire system to the Canadian model, where registration is the sole responsibility of a federal civil-service agency manned by conscientious and talented careerists. Totally impartial and committed exclusively to boosting the number of eligible voters, the Canadian pros help account for a 75 per cent turnout in the vote for Prime Minister—as compared to our 45 per cent Presidential turnout in 1968.

Similarly, Canadian access to the chief executive might warrant emulation. The first hour of each day in Parliament is put aside for unrehearsed questions the Opposition puts directly to the Prime Minister and his aides. When answers appear evasive, the Opposition does not hesitate to employ desk thumping, cat calls, and cries of "Shame." ("Imagine the scene in Congress; dream about it; Mr. Nixon being asked about Vietnam; or John Mitchell about the Watergate bugging!"[25]) In contrast our President is never directly challenged, and in his first four-year term, Mr. Nixon chose to meet the press in only twenty-seven formal conferences.

Choosing a Vice President. Although the Vice President has many functions (ceremonial, political, and the like), his main purpose is probably his immediate availability to succeed to the suddenly vacant office of the Presidency. Accordingly, some reformers urge that the Vice President be selected with as much public scrutiny or voter participation as the President gets.

For example, the Vice President could be elected in the middle of the President's tenure, both officials serving overlapping four-year terms. This might help assure that the Vice President would be selected on his own merits and not to complement the political attributes of the Presidential candidate. The change should also enhance the office and make it more attractive for men of Presidential stature to seek (similarly, the Vice President might be made a Senator-at-Large with full voting rights).

There is the controversial possibility in this reform that the Vice President might come from another party or might not be personally or politically compatible with the incumbent President. However, the President would remain free to secure personal and confidential advisers from anywhere, and it does not seem imperative that one of them be the Vice President. And the occasion for a mid-term vote of confidence (or no confidence) and a substantial upgrading of the office are two special strengths of this modern rearrangement of a shopworn relationship.[26]

A radically different reform takes off from the novel premise that the real problem is the very office itself and that no new procedures to reform the process of selection will do as much good as abolishing the office altogether!

The office is sharply faulted for the fact that its nonelected holder is chosen in a "cavalier and unrepublican manner":

> The Presidential nominee designates his choice of a running mate for *pro forma* approval of the convention. This practice in effect amounts in case of a vacancy to selecting a President of the United States by appointment, a procedure flagrantly at odds with the republican spirit of the Constitution.

All that can now be done to counter the intolerable danger posed by the traditional procedure is to eliminate the office and, in time of emergency, provide instead for an interim Acting President to serve for perhaps three months until a new President can be elected.[27]

Still a third variation on the theme endorses retention of the office but would eliminate the "cavalier" role of political convention delegates in the designation process. Instead, the President would designate his successor *after* the election from among his Cabinet members. This procedure would presumably,

> do away with the low political bargaining that in every campaign stains the access to the offices of President and Vice President. Also—and this is of cardinal importance—the choice by the elected President would be motivated by considerations calculated to provide the country with the best man and not one who could bring votes to an elective ticket.[28]

Which, however, is precisely what still a fourth reform holds up for praise and high valuation. From this perspective it is high time that the Vice Presidential candidates actually counted for something and could make or break the election. This could be simply accomplished if each voter were allowed to pull down two levers, one for a Presidential candidate and the other for a Vice Presidential candidate. Although voters could split their votes, only one party would gain both offices. A hypothetical example appears in Table 15–1. In this fashion, proponents suggest, the Vice President arrives in Washington with a healthy sense of his own independent appeal, as he actually ran and contributed substantially to the party's win.

Which plan do you prefer—and why? This much is clear—we can and ought to do better than we do now in the critical matter of putting a successor a "heartbeat" from our Presidency.

TABLE 15–1. 1972 Election (000,000 Omitted)

Nixon	21	McGovern	18
Agnew	16	Shriver	20
	37		38
Democrats win.			
Nixon	21	McGovern	16
Agnew	16	Shriver	18
	37		34
Republicans win.			

Town Meeting—TV Style. The promotional poster was headlined "GUT ISSUES" and carried six illustrated case studies of an unprecedented TV series of "20th Century Town Meetings." Viewers would be asked their opinions about the following dilemmas:

1. Should attractive mobile home parks be allowed to come into more of the New York Urban Region? Is there a *better* way to lower the cost of housing?
2. Should job relocation, or the moving of whole companies, be endorsed as an answer to our exploding population problem?
3. Should new superhighways be built, or, should driving be discouraged?
4. Should mass transit gains be supported by higher tolls on auto roadways?
5. Should all citizens be guaranteed employment? If not, how should unemployment be cured?
6. Should some children be bussed to different schools for a better racial balance and a better education for all? Is there a better solution?

The poster concluded by urging readers to tune in six hour-long TV "specials" on these matters and mail the ballots they could find in local newspapers to the Gallup polling organization. One week after each debate Gallup would report the vote tabulations to cooperating papers, and the sponsoring organization, the Regional Plan Association (RPA), would bring the "Back to the People" results to the attention of local, state, and national decision-makers.

Organized in a project called "Choices for '76," the TV series was designed to use the technology of television and the computer to enable 20 million people to participate in twentieth-century town meetings. Hailed by its RPA sponsor as "possibly a major advance in American democracy," the TV series was unveiled in 1971 with publicity directed at five potential gains:

1. To lift a mood of growing gloom with new hope as people discover that there *are* solutions to many problems, and that every citizen *can* be heard on what ought to be done.
2. To reverse the present drift and stalemate by getting a broad public consensus on major issues.
3. To generate a new level of citizen involvement.
4. To help cities and suburbs, blacks and whites, young and old, Republican and Democrat, to discover and begin working together for their common destiny.
5. To improve the democratic process itself by giving people a voice on issues which are seldom openly debated and, if they are, almost never by the public as a whole.

As time went by the fifty-year-old, citizen-based, nonpartisan RPA saw two additional gains:

1. Media cooperation was extraordinary: Every TV channel plus all radio stations and 25 newspapers participated! Every program was broadcast 12 different times over the weekend period, mostly in prime time, and twice in Spanish. Never before had the mass media participated so overwhelmingly in a public service project.

2. 500,000 viewers were organized into small-group viewing and discussion audiences by churches, unions, schools, and businesses.

Especially appealing to many were the bona fides of the solutions or remedies reviewed, predicated as most were on more than $50 million in funded government research reviewed over a two-year period by RPA staffers.

The TV shows themselves taxed viewers as only real-world dilemmas can. For example:

1. Should more private unsubsidized middle-income housing be built in the Region? (To do that will require changing present zoning laws on vacant lands.)
2. Should neighborhood parkland be acquired free? (To do that will require "cluster" zoning—giving up some private yard for public open space.)

Despite the fact that, or perhaps because, the issues required such earnest reflection, an average of thirty thousand viewers mailed ballots in after each TV special.

Especially hailed was evidence the series produced that polarization (by income, race, location, and so on) has real limits: a two-thirds majority of viewers agreed on what reforms were worth support without regard to race, income, or residence. As Francis Keppel reported,

> For example, in the Town Meeting on housing, people voted 2 to 1 to replace local school taxes with state-wide taxes. Three-quarters favor greater public investment in rehabilitation and maintenance. Only 16 per cent wanted to continue the Federal freeze on housing subsidies.
>
> In the Transportation Town Meeting, 92 per cent favored encouraging more reliance on public transportation. And they were willing to pay the bill, with 86 per cent in favor of subsidies for public transportation and 75 per cent wanting to continue highway construction. And by a vote of 3 to 1, they favored building highways where the need, cost and controversy is greatest—in cities.
>
> Eighty-two per cent of the Environment Town Meeting participants voted for creating a tristate agency which would make all major decisions on how to combat pollution.[29]

Comparably exciting was evidence that over 1 million people viewed the first of the six programs.

Questioned about what might happen after the TV series was over, "Choices for '76" made two points in justifying the $1.5 million experiment (twenty foundations and sixty corporations co-sponsored the effort equally with HUD):

1. When RPA pioneered a much smaller TV project, "Goals for the Region," in 1963, the results led to several major public parks, and alerted public officials to far stronger support for public transportation and air pollution control measures than most planners or officials knew existed.
2. RPA planned a Fall 1973 final Town Meeting to review the choices

made by TV viewers and examine changes in governmental structure and finance the voters could support in future elections in order to accomplish the stated goals of the region's residents.

RPA also cited the support given their novel effort by six U.S. Senators from the region: "It addresses two of the nation's most critical needs: improving the way our largest urban areas are developing and improving the democratic process itself. . . . This project could thus be a major advance for all of urban America."

As far as the balloting itself was concerned, an editorial in the *New York Times* of November 28, 1972, expressed a view held by many in and outside of the project:

> The polling itself can hardly be conclusive, since there is no real way to prevent a stacking of the vote, but that is the least important aspect of the scheme. The ferment that it should stir up, the focusing of public interest, the informed discussion of pressing problems—these are hopeful products to be expected from what promises to be a constructive and creditable project.

In 1973, with the TV shows behind them, RPA remained convinced that "it *is* possible to adapt the Town Meeting concept of Revolutionary times to exploration of contemporary issues such as housing, poverty, environment." Moreover, RPA insists that this experiment to promote full citizen involvement is no frill but a necessity if planners are ever to know *our* values, on which we citizens, and *not* the planners, are experts.

Support of such projects is evident in the question Alvin Toffler poses in *Future Shock:* "We need to initiate . . . a continuing plebiscite on the future. . . . On the edge of a new millennium, on the brink of a new stage in human development, we are racing blindly into the future. But where do we *want* to go?" Hopefully, RPA concludes, "Choices for '76" will show some directions. And, as RPA President John A. Keith explains, the TV project, although an "imperfect step to participation in a region of 20 million people, is a first step. What we are trying to do is loosen up the system so things can change."[30]

Project 76. We can go little further than we dream, for we pursue only what we can imagine. Pierre Bertaux writes in this connection,

> Every culture has just the future that is contained in the dynamic force of its image of the future. The future of a culture can be predicted by the power of its thinking about the future. No culture can maintain itself for long without a positive and generally accepted image of the future. A culture which shuts itself up in the present or what amounts to the same thing, in a short-sighted perspective of the future, has no future.[31]

All the more exciting, therefore, is an extraordinary blueprint for an urban renaissance, a detailed plan for a remarkable future for our cities, advanced recently under the code name "Project 76." Aimed at finally freeing us from ineffectual pilot programs and counterproductive peripheral "wars" on urban social problems, Project 76 is understandably heralded by its creator, Stewart Udall, as "the most exciting national enterprise since the founding of the republic . . . a task so spacious, a goal so intimate yet universal, that our people will be unified by the endeavor it compels."

Project 76 is nothing less than a vast project "to make all our cities fair, and all our human relations amicable." It draws especially on secondary lessons gained from the nation's space program: "One thing it *has* done is prove beyond doubt the prodigious value of total planning, of goal-setting, of multidisciplinary systems analysis and action, and this is the great contribution of the space effort." The first step envisioned is the President's calling together a well-publicized commission of eminently talented citizens (including the entire Congress) to devise detailed goals, priorities, and realistic budgets to permit the Project's completion by the year 2000. Every community in the nation is next expected to draft a compatible master plan to achieve its own redesign and renovation no later than the year 2000. In this way the Project rejects the shopworn project-by-project approach in favor of sweeping planning at every level, addressed to the total environment of entire regions—and the nation as a whole.

At the local level of the city Project 76 could give to the public life of many communities a creative excitement now largely unknown in this country. Each mayor could convene a "council to recreate the city," with a representative and revolving membership of artists, designers, labor leaders, businessmen, professionals, politicians, and community spokesmen. "Developers" would finally have to share the power to shape the city, and there would be a flowering of opportunities for engineers, architects, sculptors, muralists, painters, landscape architects, and local leaders in culture and recreation.

Local planning might draw especially on the lessons in democracy available in the Model Cities experiment, possibly the single most significant Great Society program of the 1960's. Many planning innovations warrant special use, including advocacy tactics (whereby professional planners espouse the will of community residents), block grants to local authorities, comprehensive planning (cultural and social, as well as economic), and the planned sharing of facilities to eliminate costly duplication and to preserve open space. The local focus of such work should also help municipalities promote and enhance their individuality. Indeed, the creative promotion of authentic local tradition (farmscapes in rural Ohio, pueblos in Santa Fe) could help check the deadening trend toward alikeness and "encourage the diversity and style that are the distinguishing marks of a genuine civilization."

While initial planning was proceeding during the first two or three years, immediate priority could be given to job-creating cleanup work, which might be done by the hard-core unemployed in the worst slums. Such an urban cleanup corps could roll back blight, reclaim public beauty, and begin the training of the work force required for large-scale blight-removal projects. This phase could lead to a new public appreciation of a man-centered "urban ecology" and a novel love for the man-made and man-arranged lineaments of the cities—the historic houses, vistas, bridges, and spires—much like the naturalist's appreciation of nature.

Federal grants to cover at least half the cost of initial planning and cleanup are indispensable. Indeed, in the first year we should spend on Project 76 at least as much as we have been spending on the exploration of outer space—

and we should increase our annual grant level from that $5-billion amount to $50 billion no later than 1985. Funds should be channeled directly to the cities under a distribution formula that gives a first-phase priority to slum renovation but that guarantees ultimate participation by each community on the basis of its population size and its willingness to invest matching money (perhaps 20 per cent).

Now, as the action accelerates, solutions can be sought for such regional problems as the provision of mass transit for each megalopolis, the encouragement of New Towns in appropriate areas (in and outside of existing cities), and the renewal of towns and cities of less than thirty thousand in population (to slow down the migration of people into the big cities). Fresh and unfettered teams of campus and off-campus enthusiasts—architects, engineers, sociologists, anthropologists, philosophers, economists, lawyers, and managers—could be drawn together around a common commitment to the humanizing of the urban milieu.

Something of a snowball effect can be expected in short order. Each advance—each new beautiful subway, each introduction of an open square from which a new neighborhood could radiate, each downtown mall or minipark, each altering of the urban fabric—should lead to new demands for larger and better solutions. Streets, for example, might be partially reclaimed for people as malls, open space, and greensward. Surface superblocks might be tried out, with high-speed vehicles and their noise and fumes confined underground, only human-scale movement being welcomed overhead. Whatever the particulars, the campaign itself will finally help us all to reject the idea that urban mediocrity is our natural and unavoidable fate.

Does Project 76 have a chance? Skeptics are quick to scoff at its price tag, but we have paid more (and gotten less?) for our highway, space, and nuclear development programs. These critics amplify the whispers heard that the burgeoning suburbs will be favored over cities left to wither into further decline, and they reluctantly concede the indispensability of uniquely urban functions (commerce, culture, even crowds) and the heady capital investment at stake in anything less than a Project-like urban renaissance. Above all, the skeptics, shaking their heads over the Project's value-laden implications—as starkly set out in Table 15–2—doubt our national will, our ability to find the inner strength and determination necessary to carry it off.

TABLE 15–2. Project 76

Prevailing Practice	*Proposed Reform*
Timid, preconceived planning	Bold, sweeping planning
Centralist, elitist approach	Integrated (local and central), democratic approach
Short-term commitment	Long-term (2000 A.D.) commitment
Primacy of profit; economic rule	Primacy of "poetry"; humanistic rule
Stringency in funding; less for less	Adequacy in funding; more from less
Disregard of urban heritage and history; homogenization thrust	High regard for city heritage and uniqueness
Skepticism regarding the future of cities	Faith in the special proud destinies of cities

Former Secretary of Interior Udall, the Project's author, never falters for a moment in his faith in the nation's ability to make Project 76 the key to "the era of greatness that has eluded us for so long."[32] Could he know something we (skeptics) don't . . . about ourselves, about the nation, and, in a very special way, about an America finally equal to the vision (and blueprint) of Project 76?

Bicentennial as Breakthrough? Futurist Robert Theobald, almost alone among public figures in the early 1970's, remained enthusiastic about the bicentennial celebration's ability to help strengthen the nation: "It is possible for all of America to reconsider its values during the next four years. The models exist. The necessary technologies exist. All that is lacking is the will." To help stiffen our resolve, and stir our imagination, Theobald offers examples of several potential gains:

> Today we live in a global culture. One way to symbolize the worldwide significance of the Bicentennial would be to launch three synchronous satellites to provide free people-to-people communication throughout the world.
>
> One central feature of the Bicentennial could be a travelling idea fair which would visit each state for a week during the Bicentennial year. Each state would also plan its own exhibits which would be on display for the whole summer season illustrating how people can get involved in improving their own communities.

As for the official American Revolution Bicentennial Commission (ARBC), Theobald worries that it "seems to be caught in the gray pall which descends on all bureaucratic bodies—it is an effort to read any of the material which they put out for there is no excitement and no spark."[33]

A third approach, far to the political left of both Theobald and the ARBC, is that of the People's Bicentennial Commission, a twenty-three-person non-profit group formed in 1971 to change American society radically by subtly radicalizing the people. Jeremy Rifkin, its twenty-seven-year-old founder, insists that

> people are looking for real alternatives. None of the politicians are talking to the common sense changes that need to be done. But the handwriting is on the wall. By 1976, every alienated constituency will start demanding what's due them. The Bicentennial is a ray of hope.[34]

More specifically, the People's Bicentennial Commission (PBC) urges support for "revolutionary alternatives" for the bicentennial years. Typical is a call for PBC's on a local level that, formed around the bicentennial motif, will analyze, expose, and combat contemporary injustices in the local community. For example, in a factory or mining area, industrial health and safety may be a volatile issue, whereas for suburbanites, air or noise pollution may be the most visible of many problems.

The local PBC campaign can take many forms:

> Recognizing the important contributions made by local activists in the day-to-day struggles for justice in the community can be an important way to

> forge a new sense of the meaning of patriotism among the citizenry. Public acknowledgement of the work of activists concerned with the real issues of human dignity and freedom, especially when given mass visibility through press conferences, can be a very important educational tool. PBC's might even want to time such ceremonies to correspond with the hollow award ceremonies of the local chamber of commerce or American Legion, where a bank executive is invariably praised for his great humanitarianism and goodwill. The contrast can be a powerful experience for people watching the evening news, and is a way of getting people to reflect upon their own social and political identifications.

The possibilities, PBC explains, are "limitless. To commit ourselves to each other; to plan a birthday the world will never forget; to fulfill the American dream; to create a world of peace."[35]

Now, how the bicentennial will finally shape up is very unclear from the vantage point of the summer of 1973, when I write. The possibilities, however, are exhilarating, whether on Theobald's or the ARBC's or the PBC's terms. For the bicentennial, from *any* perspective, calls our attention back to our nation's origins and challenges us to examine the quality of life within our communities, along with the various futures we can choose among. This synergistic planning exercise (past, present, future) itself is a rare opportunity to reorient (rededicate?) the entire nation.

Perhaps Theobald is correct in quietly contending that "the years from 1973 to 1976 will be as crucial for the long-run development of the world as the years from 1773 to 1776 were for the future of America."[36]

Summary

The reforms discussed in this chapter are something of a sampler, an index or representation of what is "out there" awaiting your scrutiny—and hopefully, your support. Many, many other items could have been reviewed, for example:

1. To spur the development of more economical cars and help alleviate the petroleum shortage, a bill has been proposed to set a tax rate on gasoline sales that declines as mileage improves; an auto getting 20 miles or more would be exempt.[37]
2. To provide a voice for the consumer in highly technical proceedings on the merits of proposed utility-rate requests, the State of Indiana alone among the 50 pays a full-time attorney to act as an *Ombudsman;* the concept of a people's advocate in utility proceedings has gained support as the emergency energy crisis and new environmental priorities heighten the public's stake in how a utility runs its business.[38]

In any case, the point throughout this chapter has been our common obligation to exercise conscientious scrutiny, hard-nosed realism, and creative application, all as part of our own decisions about a *very* personal investment in the prospects of the one planet, Spaceship Earth, we all share.

FOOTNOTES

1. Homer Bigart, "U.S. Helps Poor to Rent Own Homes," *New York Times* (July 9, 1972), pp. 1, 38.
2. Adam Yarmolinsky, "Reassuring the Small Homeowner," *The Public Interest* (Winter 1971), pp. 106–110.
3. Marcus Raskin, *Being and Doing* (New York: Random, 1971), pp. 279–280.
4. M. Lieberman, "New Communities," *Saturday Review* (May 15, 1971), p. 20.
5. Gulf Reston, Inc., *The Reston Story* (1970), p. 7. Available through the Gulf Reston Corporation, Reston, Virginia.
6. *Time* (March 7, 1969), p. 26.
7. "Living Room," *New Republic* (December 19, 1970), p. 8.
8. B. Weissbeard and H. Channuk, "An Urban Strategy," as discussed by Neil Gallagher, *AIA Journal* (January 1969), pp. 31–37.
9. John Fischer, "Planning for the Second America," *Harper's* (November 1969), p. 23.
10. Quoted in Greg Conderacci, "Hanging Crepe on Old Detroit," *Wall Street Journal* (February 5, 1973), p. 10.
11. Adolf Ciborowski, "Foreword" to Kenneth R. Schneider, *Autokind vs. Mankind* (New York: Schocken, 1972), p. 12.
12. "The Urban Drive to Restrict the Auto," *Business Week* (April 14, 1973), p. 27.
13. "Restricting Car Ownership," *Parade* (July 16, 1972), p. 6.
14. William Safire, "Selected Shorts," *New York Times* (May 31, 1973), p. 41.
15. Schneider, op. cit., p. 200.
16. Conderacci, op. cit., p. 10.
17. Schneider, op. cit., p. 267.
18. Ibid.
19. Harry B. Ellis, "Energy—How Much Is Your Share?" *Philadelphia Inquirer* (May 27, 1973), p. 8-F.
20. E. J. Koestler et al., *The Do-It-Yourself Environmental Handbook* (Boston: Little, Brown, 1972).
21. D. S. Greenberg, "Pollution Control: Sweden Sets Up an Ambitious New Program," *Science* (October 1969), p. 200.
22. Mike Michaelson, "Sweden's Youth Says 'Nej' to Pollution," *Today's Health* (January 1971), p. 22.
23. Greenberg, op. cit., p. 201.
24. "White Flags and Whitewash," *New Republic* (October 7, 1972), p. 5. See also Marcus B. Raskin, *Being and Doing* (New York: Random, 1971), pp. 310–312.
25. "Can Government Govern?" *New Republic* (September 16, 1972), p. 6.
26. Irving B. Kravis, "Separate Election for Vice President," *New York Times* (October 2, 1972), p. 34.
27. Sterling D. Spero as quoted in the *New York Times* (September 9, 1972), p. 73.
28. Dudley Lunt and Voleny Righter, *New York Times* (September 9, 1972), p. 73.
29. Francis Keppel, "Town Meeting: An Approach to Urban Problems," *New York Times* (May 14, 1973), p. 30.
30. All quotations in the section on "Choices for '76," including those from Toffler and Keith, are from W. A. Caldwell, ed., *How to Save Urban America* (New York: Signet, 1973, an RPA book).
31. Quoted in Daniel Bell, "Notes on the Post-Industrial Society," *The Public Interest* (Winter 1967), p. 34.
32. Stuart L. Udall, *1976: Agenda for Tomorrow* (New York: Harcourt, 1968), p. 38.

33. Robert Theobald, "Bicentennial Countdown," *Futures Conditional* (March 1973), p. 13.
34. Quoted in Eugene L. Meyer, "200 Anniversary Offered Alternative by People's Group," *Washington Post* (January 21, 1973), p. A-6.
35. PBC, *The Bicentennial Era, 1972–1976* (Waterloo, Wis.: Artcroft Press, 1972), p. 39. Available from PBC, 1346 Connecticut Avenue N.W., Washington, D.C. 20036.
36. Theobald, op. cit., p. 12.
37. "Business Notes," *Wall Street Journal* (May 9, 1973), p. 1.
38. Patricia F. Bode, "Ombudsmen Challenge Utility Rate-Hike Requests," *National Observer* (February 17, 1973), p. 5.

READING

As architect and writer Ellen Perry Berkeley explains in this essay, a very special contribution to the challenge of home environs is beginning to come from women architects and planners. The perspective and values they bring to bear on the "man-made" mess is unique and invaluable . . . we need all the help we can get here, especially that which has been unjustly frozen out in years past: we advance now together, or not at all.

Women and the Man-made Environment

Ellen Perry Berkeley

The "man-made environment" is indeed man-made. Of some thirty-three thousand licensed architects at work in 1970 in the United States, only 4 per cent were women, according to the Bureau of Labor Statistics. Perhaps because urban planning is a newer field, it is more open; of some eight thousand planners, about 20 per cent are women (clustered, however, in the lower jobs). To the modest extent that these professionals, men or women, have any real say in deciding what gets built (and where and how and for whom), men do most of the talking.

For years, the rare woman in these fields generally tried to be "one of the guys," avoiding other women in an office, professional and clerical alike. The women professionals assumed an isolated toughness ("I've made it on my own") and were reluctant to question whether, in fact, they had made it at all. But recently, with women everywhere coming together in new ways, women in these professions are revealing to each other the mild insults and gross injustices that have plagued all levels of their begrudged careers.

Despite efforts to blend in—to be Architects and not Women Architects—women stand out distinctly from men: women architects and planners get lower salaries (often for similar work) and have lesser responsibilities (often

This material is adapted from an article by Ellen Perry Berkeley commissioned by *Ms.* magazine.

with similar experience). Also, while men enjoy unquestioned recognition as "serious professionals," no matter how mediocre or self-serving their individual work may be, women must constantly prove their dedication no matter how competent their individual work may be.

Last year, almost simultaneously, two groups arose to change all this: in New York, the Alliance of Women in Architecture, and in Boston a group called WALAP (for Women in Architecture, Landscape Architecture, and Planning). An older, and less active, group exists in Los Angeles, and a newer group is forming in the San Francisco Bay area.

One of the major goals, among women working in these various groups, is to increase the number of women professionals. Another goal, stemming from a growing awareness of the injustices suffered by professional women, is to have women choose the work that suits them in these expanding fields—not be relegated automatically to roles as professional helpmate or to jobs typically considered "woman's work" (like interior design in architecture or research in planning).

There is a growing awareness, too, among a few women involved in environmental design, of *the need to design for women in a new way—the need to design buildings and communities that respond to the changing roles and needs of women.* This important new emphasis has already resulted in a score of ideas about new forms of environment and new forms of working. Even more important to a few women is the idea that *all women, professional and nonprofessional, have a part to play in this quest for a better environment for women.*

What follows, then, is a report on these new ideas and on the women who are actively pursuing them, with a few observations on where it all could lead.

The Women's Design Program at California Institute of the Arts (in Valencia) grew from the need of one School of Design faculty member "to relate feminism to design." Design acts as "an introduction to your own consciousness," says Sheila de Bretteville, who lists her name alphabetically among the dozen students.

The group has looked at the environment. "When our male-dominated institutions give physical expression to themselves, the environment is anonymous and cold (men call it rational); the female (emotional) traits are devalued and reserved for the private realm." The group has also looked at history, digging up some remarkable women designers from the past and present. Any woman now working "in a design field" is asked to send her name to their Registry of Women Designers.

Sheila de Bretteville's own graphic design has drawn much from the new feminism. Forms repeat— "it's a kind of woman's time, not one thrusting climax but several climaxes." In an issue of *Everywoman,* she made each two-page spread similar, much as consciousness-raising groups give each person equal validity. In a "menstruation project" done by the Women's Design Program, students made videotapes of conversations among women (and men), giving new validity to subjective experience on this subject. The tapes may be distributed for educational use.

This year the group was studying utopias, past and present. "Utopias are authoritarian, hierarchical, certain, logical," says de Bretteville. "What if we as women designers were to project a utopian vision based on the female tone?" There was much talk, few drawings.

She and two others—Judy Chicago and Arlene Raven—now have plans to form a Feminist Studio Workshop unattached to any institution. "Our purpose is to develop a new concept of art, a new kind of artist and a new art community built from the lives, feelings, and needs of women." If the workshop grows, an architect might be on the "faculty" in its second year.

Two master's theses on "environments for birth" have come from the College of Environmental Design, University of California, Berkeley. In a course called "Rites of Passage" (given by psychiatrist Arthur Colman), students probe the "physical and social structures designed for three human crises"—birth, pairing, and death.

One student, Wendy Bertrand, defines childbirth as "a biological and social event distinct in itself"—not a sickness—and removes it from the hospital. In her proposed "Family Birth Center," midwives stay with the mother in one room, since the current practice of moving through many rooms mainly serves the status needs of staff. A pleasant room accommodates the father (perhaps in a double bed), the newborn (perhaps in a hanging cradle), and older children, when not in the child-care facility. Two families share a bath/kitchen, as they share the whole experience. An emergency room is unobtrusively available.

Research for an actual "environment for birth" was proposed by several Berkeley professors, including Arthur Colman and Roslyn Lindheim, the school's only full professor of architecture who is a woman. No funds yet. One observer says the project was misunderstood as "a return to home birth"; another blames the medical profession's resistance to midwives.

The Women's Commonwealth in Texas is one of six case studies in collective participation in design, in a book on nineteenth-century utopias that Dolores Hayden is writing on a fellowship at Berkeley:

> It varied whether women were as active as men in design, but the Shaker women were fully as inventive. And at Oneida, where everyone was concerned with interior design (things like the effect on people of the positioning of chairs), women were considered experts. Today we're doing the same thing but our approach is scientific; theirs was intuitive and personal.

Also at Berkeley, students have excitedly discovered Julia Morgan (designer of Hearst's San Simeon) and want to find other women architects of the past.

Some students are thwarted. A planner at Harvard wanted to do a paper pointing out that traffic counts are made when most travelers are men, but her professor wanted "a more technical subject." A planner at Hunter reports that 60 per cent of the students in the master's class are women, "but there is virtually no mention of the role of women planners coming from an educational program dominated by men."

More women professors would help, especially those with the need to bring their work into focus with the rest of their lives. Phyllis Birkby, an architect new to teaching (at Pratt) but long aware of women's issues, speaks of "the inner environment of the mind." In her teaching she tries to use design to explore ideas on alternative life styles. (An Amazon commune strikes her as an interesting project.) She tried to start a women's workshop but saw the women "struggling just to survive as students; their identity as women was not top priority."

Women students do more community work at Harvard than men, relative to their numbers. "And many groups asking us for help are women, they're the ones in community activities," says Mania Seferi, director of the Urban Field Service at Harvard's Graduate School of Design.

Recent UFS projects: helping a community stop a school until the architect agreed to redesign it with the community; devising space standards for day care; and designing a place for homeless women. (It isn't true that all homeless women are prostitutes, says Ms. Seferi, but housing programs don't cover flophouses anyway. "How do you provide alternative housing for people who aren't even recognized to exist?")

The UFS and other such centers are struggling financially—and dying—getting less and less aid from the design schools. Perhaps Ms. Seferi's description of UFS explains why:

> We're trying to break down discrimination by professionals against nonprofessionals, trying to get through a male-oriented bureaucracy. These women wouldn't call it "women's lib" but it really is women against men, since the nonprofessionals are mostly women and the professionals are mostly men.

A comprehensive analysis of what the planning profession has done to women as a distinct subgroup will be done by the American Society of Planning Officials, under a grant from the U.S. Department of Housing and Urban Development. ASPO sees a two-fold problem:

> 1) planning has not given proper consideration to the needs associated with the traditional roles of women as wife and mother and as individuals within the nuclear family, and 2) planning has failed to be cognizant of and therefore to consider properly the changing roles of women and emerging life styles.

Karen E. Hapgood, co-developer of the project proposal, elaborates:

> Since it was always assumed that a woman's place was in the home, transportation to take her out of the home was never a real concern. Lack of community facilities reinforced her isolation. The New Towns provide greater variety, but the nuclear family bias remains. And now zoning commissions are coming down hard on communal arrangements everywhere.

The study will look at women's needs and roles, and at various "planning tools"—zoning ordinances, subdivision regulations, renewal policies, transportation models, capital resource allocations, building standards, housing types, and location standards. It should be an impressive work.

A small group has already started this kind of analysis. Bay Area Women Planners meet once a month to produce "a feminist perspective on suburban design."

From their first paper:

> The woman maintains the house, not for herself, but for her husband, her children, and her friends. . . . Her children go to school and to classrooms where they belong, her husband goes to an office or factory or job site where he belongs, and she stays in the house where she belongs. The rest of the family has two significant spaces in which to function, but she has one primary space, her house. . . . But even to say that the house is hers is misleading, for in fact, in most houses, the woman has little or no space that she can really call her own. . . . She is cut off from her peers by living in the house, yet she is also cut off from herself by not having a place to maintain a life apart from her family.

Ruth Friedlander and June Baker, members of the group, add: "Planners (men) forget about women alone there all day; they think only of the League of Women Voters 'input' to the general plan."

Cedar-Riverside is no imitation suburb; it is the first federally designated "new town in town" and is located in the center of Minneapolis. If all goes well, thirty thousand people will enjoy a personalized small-transit system, a service-by-phone system, a twenty-four-hour environment, the acceptance of many life styles, a rich urban life.

Gloria Segal is vice-president/treasurer of Cedar-Riverside Associates, Inc. —"not a planner but a nonprofessional with a great deal of naïve tenacity." She is the only woman in the League of New Community Developers (the fifteen or so approved under the federal New Communities Act). "Women do have a sensitivity to human needs, because we're put in the role of caring for the young and for the arts." She recalls feeling utterly isolated when her children were small, and she wants more women to be on planning and redevelopment commissions: "men just can't know the frustration and loneliness of women's lives."

Because it is so tied up with "life style," housing is of major interest to environmental feminists.

Some are repulsed by the cell-like cubicles suggested for the future (even though there are equal cells for women). Housing should support people instead of technology, they say. One architect, Phyllis Birkby, speaks of "a movable focus within shelter, not pinning down functions so precisely—people shouldn't have to eat only around the kitchen table, or talk only around the hearth."

One feminist wants housing "where the two spouses have the same chance for living; the family should be a nucleus open to society." Mariadele Michelini, president of Italy's Committee for the Assertion of the Rights of Women, proposes that groups of four hundred to five hundred units—for individuals, not families—have access to complete services such as day/night nurseries and kitchens serving meals or takeout foods. (This goes further than the "service house" or "family hotel" existing in Sweden in small but growing numbers.) Ms. Michelini asks architects to design such communes and guarantees that Bologna's officials, of which she is one, will exhibit and discuss them.

"The better a site plan fulfills the needs of small children, the happier the mothers are with their housing," says Clare C. Cooper, who is an urban geographer teaching at Berkeley and doing "user research" in housing. There were other factors, of course, in her detailed comparative study of two housing projects, "but I think this is a key one." Outside space is used almost entirely by children (80–90 per cent), she finds, and it needs far more thought than it now gets from designers. As a new mother herself, she is looking analytically at her new perceptions and needs concerning the environment.

Another close observer of environment is Yolé G. Sills, a sociologist teaching at Ramapo College (Mahwah, New Jersey) who returned from a visit to Asia with observations like this: "What can the Indian woman do with her pessary when she is lifting her sari—she has to put it on the dirt floor." And: "When Japanese houses began to have doors that could be locked, no one had to stay at home any more." Sills and Naomi Tor, a planner, are studying retirement communities from a feminist perspective.

Do women bring something special to the design professions? Lulu Stoughton Beem thought so, in 1884: "Women are naturally better judges of color, better in the blending of fabrics, besides knowing intuitively what is wanted about a house—wants too small for men to perceive."

Women today resent being stereotyped and are hesitant to create new stereotypes. In a meeting of women planners, the idea that women are more "life-conserving" brought this reply from one woman: "I've found as many men who *are* life-conserving as I've found women who *aren't*."

But women have long been in the "serving" and "caring" roles. To what effect, in these professions? Elaine Dow Carter, who teaches in Columbia's Urban Planning Division, believes that "women have been pushed into the very professions that will be most important to planning—learning, health, all the human service fields. And the roles traditionally given to women are the ones that really count in planning, in the long run."

A similar view appears in Doris Cole's interesting history, being published by *i press*. An architect herself, Ms. Cole traces women's involvement in American architecture from Indian times to the present. Women *practiced* architecture long before they were *in the profession;* they have consistently cared about the practical and useful, while men have chosen (or been chosen for) the philosophical and monumental. Ms. Cole explains that the woman's concern for her environment has expanded from home to community: "The national environment is her home today, and it is perhaps most distinctly her challenge to put this 'home' in order."

Others, too, believe that women have a distinct outlook. "Women tend to empathize more with the people who will use a building," says Mimi Lobell, "whereas men tend to see a building as a chance to project something about *themselves*." Regi Goldberg adds, "The approach is conceptually different. Our concern is with people and their relation to form and space; men often make the space and try to fit the people into it." Regi Goldberg, Marjorie Hoog, and Mimi Lobell have just formed a "feminist architectural design office" in New York. In their Women's Architectural Alternative, "women will learn to work together without competition; women will learn to trust each other," says Ms. Goldberg. "An understanding of women, of each other, will be at the very basis of our work." About separatism, she says, "We don't want to go back into the universities and offices to try to change the men. We want to generate something that's *us,* and from there we can feed back into society." It will be a "floating office"—any architect can bring in a job, can stay for a short or long time. The office will give women experience in working drawings (if this is lacking) and will thus give women "a better chance in the male structure." The office has nonprofit status, with profits going into scholarships for women architectural students and into a school to make people more aware of their environments. Two of the early members are already teaching: Mimi Lobell is at Pratt doing a seminar on alternatives for the professional, and Regi Goldberg is at Queensborough Community College (part of the City University of New York) teaching paraprofessionals and heading a "feminist environmental design studio."

Another all-woman office exists in Cambridge, Massachusetts, five women in search of a work arrangement freeing them from previous constraints. Schedules are flexible (some members are part time), and structure is nonhierarchical. "I'm interested in working with, rather than for, people; I don't like either giving or receiving orders," says Joan Forrester Sprague. We formed the Open Design Office to be "people," she says; women in architecture are often "appendages." (The group was interviewed by a newspaperwoman not exactly on their wavelength; when one architect answered that her husband's work wasn't pertinent, the reporter snapped, "I can find out anyway, you know.") This office, too, is nonprofit ("no one climbs to fortune over the backs of others"), based on its intention to research and promote the role of women in the environmental professions. Says Lois Stern about the office, "I never had an outlet for the idealism I'd developed in school, but this office is really an alternative—where people care about each other and want to work with clients in a new way." Emilie Buck Turano continues, "Clients always bring an architect pictures of what they want, and the architect always throws the pictures away. We really *care* about what the client wants. This may be a female response, and one of the most important things a woman can offer in a profession where the architect often dictates to the client."

A growing number of women will be entering these professions. But "if women planners are to make any difference at all," says Frances Fox Piven, a planner who teaches at Boston University and has written incisively on many social problems,

> it will only be because they have been moved beyond their immediate self-interest in jobs and status, and if that can happen, it is probably only by forming alliances with women outside the profession. Most women, after all, will not be planners, no matter what the outcome of struggles within the profession. Most women will have to live and work in the battered slums and sterilized suburbs shaped by planners. Maybe connecting with their experience can make a difference.

Mimi Lobell believes this too. "Architects have to find ways to get in touch with nonprofessionals," she says, but her suggestion of an all-day session between professionals and nonprofessionals was not picked up by the Alliance of Women in Architecture. (In fairness, the idea needed more people and funds than the AWA had at the time, but the idea itself wasn't fully appreciated: "What would you tell them?" asked one woman. "You wouldn't *tell* them anything," said Ms. Lobell.)

"A major part of making change is who decides," says Nancy Slavin, an architectural designer in San Francisco; "it shouldn't be educated types like me." She studied at Harvard but was recently involved in the kind of low-key architectural problem rarely assigned in school—she converted a thirty-seven-foot school bus into a mobile health clinic (operated by the New York Women's Health and Abortion Project).

"Aren't there really two different questions," asks Lynda Simmons, vice-president and director of development at Phipps Houses, "the power of women in the profession of architecture, and the power of women to change the environment?" (She is an architect herself, handling the financial/legal aspects of development as well as supervising the architects who design this foundation's low- and middle-income housing.) She believes architects as a class are relatively ineffective in changing the environment; the bigger question is the effectiveness of women:

> If the State of New York could be persuaded to change its standards on open space, or build day care with its housing, it would be a tremendous victory for women—or women in their present roles. We all work for the day when not only women will be homemakers. But it's no wonder men don't want to be in the windowless kitchens being built today.

It will take a tremendous effort—a women's lobby—to make changes, Ms. Simmons says:

> But by changing even one set of federal housing standards you affect thousands of people. Whatever anyone wants to do is needed—more women in housing agencies, more women going down to the Board of Estimate, more women telling men that a pleasant play space near the laundry machines *makes sense* to a young mother in a housing project.

Women have to do more thinking on the whole subject: What *specifically* are the bad aspects of high-rise housing (and how might they be modified)? What *specifically* does it take to build "community" instead of "housing"? And what *specifically* should be changed in the living environment to make women's lives not only easier—but also richer?

"Continuing education" programs (and the university-level women's studies) offer two places to begin studying "women and the environment." Consciousness-raising groups offer another ready-made mechanism for looking at the subject.

"Doing something about the environment" has come to mean using a non-polluting detergent. Women need to do something about the buildings, rooms, towns, roads, and cities that are called the "man-made" environment. The term is unfortunately apt.

READING

Uncontrolled growth and the misuse of the environment, according to Senator Vance Hartke, "may well be the primary source of the social problems that confront the nation." Accordingly he outlines a national growth policy that makes possible the planning, coordination, and foresight we need if we are "to restore our ecological system to its balance." The relevance of this program to the prospects of our cities, old and new, is so obvious as not to require comment, except to suggest that without reforms like those that the Senator champions we will continue to lag rather than lead in community distinction. His recommendations warrant every possible consideration.

Toward a National Growth Policy

Vance Hartke

America is beset by a number of problems that continue to grow more rapidly than the government's ability to limit or contain them. Since 1900, the country has undergone something of a demographic revolution. In terms of total numbers, our population has increased from 76 million in 1900 to almost 205 million in 1970. This represents an additional 129 million people that our society has been called upon to accommodate over the past seventy years. By the end of the year 2000, the population will soar to between 270 million and 320 million.

More alarming, America, as a metropolitan nation, will see an even greater population increase in the urban areas. By 2000, present trends will concentrate 70 per cent of the population in the twelve largest urban regions occupying one tenth of the national land area.

Can our society cope with these enormous increases in population and the resulting changes in settlement, land use, and resource consumption?

These massive increases and concentrations of population will press dangerously the nation's ability to preserve the quality of the environment and almost completely deplete our natural resources.

Along with the increase and concentration of population, however, will come an even more serious threat—the increasing separation of black and white citizens in the nation's cities. By 1985, three out of every four urban blacks will live in the central city. By contrast, seven out of every ten whites in metropolitan areas are expected to live in the suburbs. Thus, the basic conclusion of the Kerner Commission Report—that "our nation is moving toward two societies, one black, one white—separate and unequal"—will have been proven true.

However, the vast national expansion into the suburbs—which is generating racial polarization in our metropolitan areas—is not due solely to population increases but also to migration. This migration is reinforced by the relocation

Reprinted by permission from *The Futurist* (December 1972), published by the World Future Society, P.O. Box 30369, Bethesda Branch, Washington, D.C. 20014.

of many corporations and governmental facilities—and jobs—to the suburbs.

Local governmental units have also contributed to the disjointed growth of our metropolitan areas into an increasingly segregated and financially unbalanced society by exclusionary zoning, which precludes lower-income people and blacks from moving into suburban areas.

These social and economic imbalances are also, in a large part, the result of the heavy dependence of local public services on locally applied taxes, principally the property tax.

Land use in our urban areas is another example of tremendous waste and mismanagement. Even though land is our most valuable natural resource, long-term decisions in this field have been made largely on the basis of expedience and short-term economic considerations. Mountains have been carved by strip mines, wet lands dredged and filled, suburban sprawl allowed to proliferate. Once land is committed to a specific use—be it social, economic, or environmental—it may be impossible to use it differently in the future.

Today, the effects of uncontrolled growth and the misuse of the environment are just beginning to be felt and understood and may well be the primary source of the social problems that confront the nation today. Controlling the nation's growth is not only an end in itself but the key to understanding the future of American domestic policy. We have to act now to adopt a national growth policy which will both protect our heritage of irreplaceable values and provide guidance for future national development.

Bill to Set Up National Growth Policy

In May of this year, I introduced in the Congress the National Growth Policy Planning Act of 1972, S.3600. This act calls for the creation of a national growth policy to bring about economic development, population control, housing distribution, the use of natural resources, the protection of the environment, and the location of government and private facilities so as to increase the odds that our nation will continue to prosper. The act establishes a national growth policy planning board to help coordinate the efforts of federal, regional, state, and local governments to control and manage growth. It is hoped that out of this an effective research, planning, and coordinating body on the national level can (while emphasizing a large measure of state, local, and public participation) formulate goals and guides for the nation's growth in the next half century. The bill also would establish a program of federal assistance for state and interstate agencies so that they can develop statewide and regional growth planning as elements of a national growth policy.

I have introduced such comprehensive legislation because I believe the nation faces problems of such magnitude and complexity that a concerted national effort is necessary to guarantee our very survival. The nation's population continues to grow and concentrate in our urban areas; the effects of pollution become more alarming; we continue to deplete our natural resources; industry continues to proliferate uncontrollably and to stimulate excessive and artificial demands. This nation must be brought to realize the prospect of ecological disaster and the need for an urgent and sufficient response. And yet the social problems that we face today only portend more enormous ones in the future. A recent report of the Club of Rome, an internationally distinguished group of businessmen, economists, and scientists, documented the immediate need for controlling growth. The report forecast ecological collapse on our finite world resource base sometime in the next century.

I believe the National Growth Policy Planning Act of 1972 develops a framework for an efficient policy to manage and control growth in both our urban and rural areas. However, the problem of controlling national growth is tremendously complex and interrelated with our other social problems and deserves more attention from our nation's leaders.

I have come to realize that we need even broader legislation than S.3600. Planning for the growth of the country encompasses a myriad of complex and interrelated problems that must be addressed by an even more comprehensive legislative effort to develop an effective national growth policy.

Reorganizing Government to Deal with National Growth

Any truly constructive legislative effort must call for the development of a national growth policy at the highest level of government. Such a policy must be developed within the Executive Office of the President and must replace the presently inefficient Domestic Council. The new, restructured council would combine the responsibilities of the Council on Environmental Quality, the old Domestic Council, the Advisory Commission on Intergovernmental Relations, part of the Office of Management and Budget, the Department of Housing and Urban Development's comprehensive planning assistance program, and two defunct bodies, the National Goals Research Staff and the Advisory Commission on Population Growth and the American Future.

The Council would do the following:

1. Set national goals for growth and development, including specific population policy goals.
2. Coordinate federal programs.
3. Review regional, metropolitan, and state growth policy initiatives for compliance with federal guidelines.
4. Develop depressed areas of the country.
5. Administer incentives to and sanctions on local units of government to plan and manage growth.
6. Prepare an annual report on national growth and development.

Such "constructive" legislation should also provide grants-in-aid for the creation of federal but decentralized regional planning bodies much like the Appalachian Regional Commission.

While it is extremely difficult to limit or stop growth in certain areas, a more critical problem is the development of desolate areas and the redevelopment of areas that have been subject to national neglect. A proposed national growth policy and development bill would provide for the creation of a National Development Corporation (NDC). The NDC would have two main functions: 1) to coordinate the activities of metropolitan, regional, and state development corporations; and 2) to act as the developer of last resort where federal incentives have failed to spur action toward what needs to be done for the public good.

This Congressional growth policy would also concentrate on consolidating and simplifying a number of complex and overlapping programs of federal financial assistance to communities and neighborhoods.

A special emphasis should be placed on federal incentives for setting up state and metropolitan housing agencies. This would provide not only a sufficient supply of housing for people of all incomes and life styles but also a means to racial integration of suburban and rural areas by the dispersal of housing opportunities.

A National Development Bank Is Needed

To broaden the sources and decrease the cost of capital funds for state and local governments, an essential element of a "cost possible" national growth would be the creation of a national development bank, to be modeled after central banks throughout the world and similar to the World Bank. It would, however, differ from current central banking practices in that its primary emphasis would be on uplifting depressed areas rather than on making a profit.

Also as an integral component of a national growth policy, a metropolitan land bank should be created to provide metropolitan authorities with federal assistance in acquiring, managing, and disposing of land according to the preconceived metropolitan plan. The key benefits derived from this affirmative role would be the advance acquisition of land for public purposes, avoidance of the expenses of urban sprawl, and improved management and control of the land market. By providing an infrastructure for orderly urban development, this land bank would mean that the increased value of land, caused by government activities, could be recaptured and applied to the costs of the program.

Location of Government and Business Facilities

Another area of tremendous potential concerns the location of federal and corporate facilities. Before the location of any federal facility is decided, or an activity affecting national development is begun, federal departments and agencies should be required to file a report with the new, restructured Council of National Growth and Development. The report would be similar to the environmental impact statements required by the National Environmental Policy Act. The report would establish the proposed activity's consistency with a balanced national growth policy—its environmental and economic impact and its general effect on regional development and the costs involved. Private corporations would also have to comply with these standards.

Finally, federal procurement policies should be integrated into a scheme of national growth management. Regulations could be issued by the Council on National Growth and Development to assure that, in any federal procurement above certain prescribed amounts, consideration would be given to balanced national growth and development policies. And the regulations would also provide for the use of alternative sources of procurement if costs are not excessive. In this manner, the purposes of the act would be promoted and the criteria for determining such considerations would be established.

In the Ninety-third Congress, I plan to introduce legislation which follows these guidelines.

Why Foresight and Planning Are Necessary

In *The Limits of Growth,* an interesting riddle is offered to illustrate the danger of inaction in developing a realistic growth policy:

> Suppose you own a pond on which a water lily is growing. The lily plant doubles in size each day. If the lily is allowed to grow unchecked, it would completely cover the pond in 30 days, choking off the other forms of life in the water. For a long time the lily plant seems small, so you decide not to worry about cutting it back until it covers half the pond. On what day will that be? On the twenty-ninth day, of course. You have one day to save your pond.

Planning, coordination, and foresight are urgent and mandatory if we are to restore our ecological system to its balance.

The sole hope of the future lies in a complete national commitment, from the highest level to the lowest. The early "benevolent" history of land use policy failed miserably. In the same way, local sanctions were grossly inadequate. Confusing structures and a myriad of committees have been created to combat a dilemma that should have received the highest possible federal priority. But a federal effort is not enough by itself. Nor can action on the state and local level abate the crisis by itself. National action, and only national action, will prove successful in devising and implementing a viable growth and development policy. Otherwise, we may have only one day to save ourselves and our country.

PART IV

Pulling It All Together

Where do we go from here? And where is here? Or, to put it somewhat more formally, how does a reader of this book keep up the reform momentum engendered or enhanced by its reading? And just what kind of foundation or launching pad has the book sought to provide?

CHAPTER 16

From Launching Pad to Orbit

And always remember: getting there isn't half the fun—it's all the fun.

ROBERT TOWNSEND

The letter killeth, but the spirit giveth life.

ST. PAUL
New Testament

The reasonable man adapts himself to the world: the unreasonable one persists in trying to adapt the world to himself. Therefore all progress depends on the unreasonable man.

GEORGE BERNARD SHAW

Launching Pad

Where is *here?* Well, to begin with, I advised you at the beginning that this "cookbook" or "recipe collection" of reforms for social problems would prove incomplete, would suggest solutions that are expensive, and would tax your thinking and your feelings with the very novelty of its proposed solutions. Its incompleteness, however, should spur your own research efforts, even as your wrestling with cost-cutting strategies is a critical part of anyone's "coming of age" as a citizen and a reformer of significance. As for the "future shock" of reform novelty, what with college students' having survived exposure to over 350,000 TV commercials before their nineteenth birthday, it is reasonable to expect both growing resiliency and *savoir faire* where novelty is concerned—a hard-earned and invaluable ability to see through the spangles and the glitter to whatever of real merit there may be underneath.

I have explained that I am committed to the idea that "a man is not free to do that which he cannot imagine doing."[1] Accordingly, the entire book has sought to expand your range of options, to enlarge your repertoire of possible responses to ever more change-resistant and time-honored social problems, and to put you in touch with choices possibly unknown to and undreamed of by you.

It is well to recognize that in a very special way this type of exposure does not relieve our anxieties about our "situation" or calm our misgivings about trends in this "Age of Anxiety." Rather, this exposure to reform possibilities rarely thought of before can exacerbate tension and strain as it challenges us to reassess prior unexamined assumptions and convictions in many reform matters. In the place, then, of the corrosive "escape from freedom" that Erich Fromm warned against nearly thirty years ago, we gain a new mental freedom—through heightened imagination—to help us all move America closer to our heart's desire.[2]

At the same time, the preceding fifteen chapters compensate somewhat for their taxing toll by spreading the comfort of knowledge of new allies. Drawing on overseas examples of ongoing progressive reforms, and highlighting the less well known among small-scale or very young American reforms, the chapters help us gain the impression of more out there of worth than we ever previously imagined. This enlarging perspective should also help you as a student traveler to become a collector of reform insights when you are abroad. And it should help direct classroom discussion of potential reforms to experiments elsewhere, as well as backward in history and forward to the drawing boards and blueprints of hard-headed dreamers. (I am reminded of Kurt Vonnegut's prescription for an ideal President—someone whose entrance is greeted by the strains of "Beautiful Dreamer," rather than "Hail to the Chief.")

Finally, there is the matter of where *you* are coming from and why. Do you operate from a conservative base? A liberal orientation? A radical perspective? A visionary worldview, or, as a student of mine described it earlier in the book, from a bedrock *Weltanshauung?* As you figure this out, you should gain new strength in understanding others, for although we all come from very personal orientations that are at one level unique to ourselves, on another level we can all be usefully classified by a B-C-L-R-V typology. As well, your exposure to the identification of these different points of view should help you to appraise the consistency and merit of the stands that others take on various issues (for example, a radical plan for income redistribution, or a conservative design for a criminal justice system).

Moreover, the fact that many of us unwisely settle into one of the five dominant political viewpoints and lose our faculty for independent and open-minded opinion formation does not obligate *you* to do so. On the contrary, the material in this book on the B-C-L-R-V perspectives makes all the more possible the creation by you of your own proud amalgam of seemingly disparate reform ingredients and plans . . . that suit *your* well-informed proclivities in the matter.

Is this study finally, however, only an academic exercise, another "ivory tower" vanity of little real-world significance? In these mid-years of the 1970's nothing so exasperates me, as a teacher and "veteran" of social problems and social reforms, as having students and colleagues express with unbecoming, world-weary cynicism that "it does not matter, any of it, very much at all." My own contrary position makes me contend that:

1. We do not have social "problems" so much as we have social "opportunities," or leverage for making substantial gains on our mutual behalf.
2. We are not confined to altruistic or humanitarian motives for implementing reforms; we have hard-nosed, businesslike reasons to reform also.
3. We do not "solve" problems once and for all with any particular faddish panacea that captures our fickle enthusiasm; rather, we generate

new challenges with every partial reform we apply—in a spiral that can take us to new heights or undo us all together.

These propositions have me convinced that our reform agenda in the second half of the 1970's can and must be built on exhilaration rather than ennui, realism rather than piety, and persistence rather than sporadic forays.

"All Signals Are Go"

Where do we go from here? First, a large number of overseas reforms have been "lost in the shuffle" and merit your own research and study. For example:

1. Canada's "baby bonus" is a monthly payment to all families, rich and poor, of $6 for each child under six, $8 for a child six to sixteen, and $10 for youths sixteen to eighteen if they are in school. In 1972, the government sent checks totaling $640 million to 3.5 million families with 7.5 million children. In 1973, the government moved to raise the bonus to an average of $20 a month.[3]
2. Switzerland has let its top executive authority reside in a seven-man federal council since 1848. A switch from our style of presidency to a multiple executive might be best suited to new American responsibilities, as in the case of triggering off nuclear missiles—which would require a four-person majority.[4]
3. "We are the only major nation on earth that permits air time to be sold to political parties and office seekers," explains Fred W. Friendly, former president of news for CBS and now broadcast consultant to the Ford Foundation. He recommends instead that the federal government pay for political air time at special low rates and turn it over free to major candidates.[5]
4. Arabellas, or legal "eros centers," are now open in West Germany, with others planned for five more European countries. Complete with such amenities as tennis courts, bowling alleys, beer cellar, nightclub, sauna, solarium—and a fully equipped room for sadomasochists—each of the four seventy-two-woman brothels are lauded by investors (guaranteed annual return of 9 per cent) for having raised houses of prostitution to a "socially more human level."[6]
5. A tax on automobile horsepower, as in Europe, might help discourage our acceptance of the gas-guzzling, high-horsepower dandies that Detroit believes we cannot live without.
6. The United Auto Workers urges the United States to emulate a Swedish law that requires that any investor who is going to get government guarantees of his overseas outlays must prove first that his action will not hurt U.S. workers and, second, that his money will not be spent in a racist, antiunion, or gouging fashion abroad.[7]
7. The French, in Brittany, can boast "one of the most forward-looking engineering feats of our time—the harnessing of the ocean tides to produce power without pollution . . . an unusual example of man's wise use of natural resources while protecting his environment."[8]
8. European construction workers are switching to a *silent* jackhammer.

An eighty-five-pound model costs $175 less than its unmuffled American counterpart.[9]

More such innovations can be cited, but the point is already clear: go west, young man, and east, and south, and north . . . go everywhere in the search for still better clues to a still richer life for us all!

Second, as noted earlier in this chapter, several domestic reform issues are slighted in this volume, often because of the considerable attention they already receive elsewhere. Whatever the explanation, each is owed your *own* independent investigation and the identification of your personal reform platform in every case. Attention, for example, should be paid to:

1. The use of Methadone as a heroin substitute.
2. The abandonment of the draft in favor of a modern volunteer (professional) army.
3. The revival of interest in vocational education via the career-preparation effort of the government.
4. The New Federalism effort at the heart of our revenue-sharing experiment.
5. The use of chemotherapy to return previously institutionalized mental patients to out-patient care in the community.
6. The large-scale government experiments now underway with a "guaranteed annual income" for welfare recipients.
7. The new efforts to curb noise pollution.
8. The revival of interest in replacing our antiwar movement with a peace movement.
9. The use of "benign quotas" in education and employment issues influenced by governmental fiat, on behalf of currently underrepresented minorities.

Case studies of recent reform efforts that have allegedly failed, such as performance contracting in education and "black capitalism" in entrepreneurial aid to a minority group, are also relegated to discussion elsewhere, although the temptation to plunge in right here is considerable. Similarly, the efforts of the Gay Liberation movement, and of the Gray Panthers on behalf of the aged, warrant your constructive appraisal, as does also the remarkable reform movement now underway to help the terminal patient prepare for his impending death.

Third, it is incumbent upon us to practice and improve our skill in creative thinking about reforms. Our task is not one of cut-and-dried acceptance or rejection of any social reform we come across. Rather, our task is one of contributing to the *further* development of each one. A good example is provided in the mini-essay I borrow from a recent student of mine, James Parise. When I drew his attention to hydroponics, or the process of growing high-quality, giant yields of foodstuffs without using soil, he reflected on the matter for several weeks and came up with this exciting adaptation:

> Given the freedom and capital to design a city-oriented hydroponic farm I would do the following. For a small-scale operation I would choose a building the size of the Acme Foodmarket building at Forty-third and Locust Streets,

to which I will arbitrarily assign the dimensions of 70 feet square. Utilizing optimal design procedures, I would orient the growing tanks so that tank surface area would be maximized and energy utilization would be minimized.

An inverted pyramid design would provide 120 square feet of growing area over straight rows parallel to each other. This pyramid would offer 3,225 square feet of growing area, whereas a step system of two parallel beds would offer only 3,105 square feet of growing area. This extra 120 square feet would mean at least an extra 74.4 pounds of vegetables produced annually. The peripheral tank and walkway would be elevated to a height of 8 feet with each successive tier being lowered by a foot. This plateau effect would serve a twofold purpose: 1) nutrient solutions could be pumped to the highest tank and then allowed to drain to each successive tank, saving pumping energy from tank to tank and aerating the solution in one step; and 2) elevation of the outside tanks would provide area for equipment to be stored, that being the area underneath each row of tanks.

Being the adaptive-system freak I am, I would leave most of the environmental control up to a computer, probably a PDP-8 or equivalent minisystem. It would be equipped with sensors to measure environmental parameters, such as temperature, humidity, nutrient solution content, pH, and so on, along with growth detectors and data concerning produce yield. The computer would be given control over all system parameters, including the choice of music played to the growing plants. The computer would also be instructed to perform search operations around accepted nominal parameter values in an attempt to maximize yield and minimize energy. Further, the computer would handle replanting schemes determining where new plants would be most effective and just what plants would be most effective. By allowing the computer to play this search game I would expect yields to become increasingly large.

The function of people within this system would be to handle such things as deciding when vegetables were ripe, handling system repair work, double-checking the computer to safeguard against malfunctions, cleaning up the area, and, of course, keeping the plants company. I would also urge community participation by allowing community members to purchase membership tickets that would entitle them to discounts on the goods being grown in exchange for work done to maintain the farm. As a special unplanned bonus, ventilation equipment would bring carbon-dioxide laden air into the farm and, at no extra cost, pump out oxygen-laden air (plants take in carbon dioxide for use in photosynthesis and expel oxygen as a photosynthesis "waste" product).

As cities continue to grow, food will have to be shipped in from greater distances, resulting in higher prices and older vegetables. The use of city-based hydroponic farms would eliminate transportation prices and middle men; in fact, farm members would be encouraged to pick their own vegetables if they so desired. Thus hydroponics could become an important method of feeding the cities' population.[10]

Regardless of the particular details of Jim's hydroponic project, the point of making a *personal* contribution should be clear—and self-vindicating.

I am reminded in this connection of a reform dividend of the Watergate affair often lost sight of in the din and roar of that matter: Citizens of every political persuasion and social class profile overnight became students of political reform in widespread discussions of how politics might be rehabilitated, offenders punished, and so on. Typical is this engrossing list:

1. Adopt a single six-year term for the President.
2. Require the President to submit to a yes or no vote of confidence every two years by national election.
3. Provide a place for a "no" vote on the Presidential ballot, so as to enable the public to deprive all candidates of the necessary 50 per cent for election. "We should not be required to vote for the lesser of several undesirable candidates."[11]

Again, as with hydroponics, the particulars are nowhere as important for my purpose here as the general point that we are *all* of us potential architects of change!

Fourth, in this heady question of "where do we go from here?" there is much to do where behind-the-scenes, low-profile controversies are concerned. Again and again, certain strategies for reform leave our ranks divided, as reasonable minds find reasonable cause for heated disagreement—and call on us to take a position. Typical "hot spots" include the following:

1. "blacks and other minorities at many companies now are getting favored treatment. . . . 'There are some real injustices perpetrated in the name of antidiscrimination,' says the personnel vice president of a Midwestern manufacturing company, 'but the overall thrust of the program is certainly in the best interests of the country.' "[12]
2. California permits continued corporate takeover of its farm land, but the 1972 legislature in Minnesota chose to fight strongly against this in favor of "the family farm." It has passed a law that permits only family farm corporations and corporations with less than ten shareholders to acquire new land in the state.[13]
3. "Legalized gambling seems well on its way to becoming a fact of American life as legislators throughout the country advocate lotteries, horse and dog racing, and even cock fighting as a relatively painless way to get new revenues to stem rising state and local taxes."[14]
4. Business hails the 1973 creation of the Society of Consumer Affairs Professionals in Business. However, Betty Furness, Consumer Affairs Commissioner in New York City, scoffs at such "cosmetics" and suggests "it was a great compliment to consumers. The companies have to get together to fight the increasing strength of the consumer."[15]
5. Apropos of calls for the establishment of iron-clad spending limits on political campaigns, journalist Tom Wicker dissents: "the question really is whether enough is spent on political education, the discussion of issues, the disclosure of a candidate's plans and views."[16]
6. An effort is underway to put U.S. arts programs on a par with art subsidies in Europe; proponents hope Americans will be willing to spend one dollar per capita by 1976 to foster "culture." Critics of a proposed

$840 million authorization (1974–1976) demand to know why the arts should prosper while the OEO is being dismantled and the poor "sacrificed."[17]

7. PEP (the Public Employment Program), our first major effort of the kind since the New Deal, survived a Presidential veto to provide almost 200,000 jobs in its first two years. Proponents would like to see funding raised to create 500,000 jobs on a more or less permanent basis. The Nixon Administration wants PEP ended.[18]
8. Many liberals now doubt whether further school desegregation is worth fighting for. Journalist Walter Shapiro retorts: "Busing may not exude radical chic and may seem naive in this justifiably cynical age, but it has the rare virtue of being right. Busing has far less to do with the education than with whether we want an integrated or segregated society. Nineteen years after the *Brown* decision, I still choose integration."[19]

In addition to these matters of disputation we are obliged to find our position in the controversial issue of the Equal Rights Amendment, the Consumer Protection Agency Bill, the Worker Alienation Research and Technical Assistance Act, and other pending (1973) pieces of major legislation.

Fifth, it would be well for us to work at sharpening our technical skills, our how-to-do-it abilities in matters increasingly marked by a hard-edged component of facts and figures and their manipulation: basic accounting techniques, computer programming, Delphi polling, input-output analysis, modeling, PERT-systems, PPBS, social audits, social indicators, statistics, systems analysis, and questionnaire design and implementation. Relevant here is the story told of the 1972 HEW use of PPBS to examine eight alternative methods of reducing motor-vehicle injury. The study showed that a nationwide driver training program would cost $88,000 for each death averted, whereas a seat-belt program would cost a thousand times less for the same benefit, or $87 for each death averted.[20] Here again, it is the larger issue I would stress: Any serious contribution by us to the nation's social reform agenda requires increasing knowledge of mechanical aids and tools.

Similarly, we are well advised to search out new allies and assess their potential role in a multifaceted reform scenario for the 1970's:

1. John Gardner's Common Cause organization has grown since its 1969 founding to include 215,000 dues-paying members funded entirely from $3,225,000 in annual dues. It is dedicated to "opening up the system" through the reform of campaign financing, open meeting laws, disclosure laws, and so on. In 1973, its principal legislative issues included making highway trust funds available for mass-transit use, an unequivocal press shield law, and "tax equity."[21]
2. VISTA, founded in 1964, is engulfed in controversy. Although it had a record number of applicants in 1973, the agency is putting 6 per cent fewer volunteers in the field in 1974. Moreover, the director has proposed assigning volunteers to social programs run by fraternal lodges, labor unions, and ethnic groups. Critics blast this proposal for diluting the original antipoverty aspects of the agency.[22]

3. ACTION, a federal program, enrolled over a thousand students in twenty-four colleges during 1973 in various community aid activities. Many counseled prison inmates, worked with the elderly, organized local recreational programs, and, at the same time, earned up to a year's academic credit for "relevant" activities off campus.[23]
4. Across America the court volunteer movement grows impressively: an estimated one out of five adult courts and half of all juvenile courts offered a variety of volunteer services in 1973. These included predisposition and presentencing investigations, marriage counseling, tutoring of juvenile offenders, helping to find jobs for probationers, and so on.[24]
5. Ralph Nader's organization, Public Citizen, Inc., published a unique *Action Manual* in 1973 rich in reform strategies for consumer protection, governmental reform, tax justice, job safety, equal opportunity, and government bureaucracy: "Such small projects are the building blocks of a larger citizen movement."[25]

Many other potential allies—including the Alternatives Pursuits project of the National Institute of Mental Health and the remarkable reform design of Synanon—belong in such a list.

Above all, however, attention is owed to the Public Interest Research Groups (PIRG's) that now, after only two years of organizing, include over 400,000 student members at over fifty schools in fourteen states. Modeled on Nader's organizations, though independent of him, a PIRG is a student-funded and -directed organization composed of a professional staff (lawyers, scientists, and organizers) backed up and aided by hundreds of student researchers.

Typical of their accomplishments since the 1970–1971 academic year are the following:

1. The Minnesota PIRG has filed suits against the Forest Service to stop timbering in the Boundary Water Canoe Area along the U.S.-Canada border; to require police to wear visible identification badges at all times while on duty; to permit 19-year-olds to not only vote in Minnesota, but to run for office; and to require the Republican and Democratic parties to comply with the law and publish the locations and times of the precinct caucus meetings.
2. MPIRG also has prepared a handbook on tenants rights in Minnesota and reports and studies on subjects as diverse as discrimination against women by Minneapolis employment agencies; snowmobiles; the hearing aid industry in Minnesota; the state clean air plan, and about forty other subjects. Altogether during its first year of operation MPIRG's 14-person staff worked on more than 60 separate projects.
3. OSPIRG, the Oregon Student PIRG, is funded by students at 12 Oregon campuses. OSPIRG recently conducted a major study of advertising fraud in the Portland area which uncovered widespread use of illegal "bait and switch" tactics. Ford dealerships and Sears stores, among others, were charged with illegal activities and some agreed to cease this practice. Thorough critiques of a proposed mass transit system for

Portland resulted in the city's plan being scrapped and new plans following guidelines laid down by OSPIRG being drawn up. OSPIRG also has issued reports on utility rate setting procedures; water pollution in the Willamette River and Coos Bay, and the effects of clear-cutting practices on Oregon's forest reserves. Thirty-two courses are being offered on nine Oregon college campuses in which students can receive academic credit for OSPIRG-related research.

4. The Vermont PIRG has issued studies on conflicts of interest among Blue Cross directors, the impact of the ski industry on Vermont, and the effects of new highway construction around Burlington. VPIRG sponsored a state-wide conference on Vermont health care, and has formed a state-wide citizen lobby with offices at the state capital in Montpelier. VPIRG staff also have testified before legislative committees on the Equal Rights Amendment and health care and have urged broader interpretations of the Vermont "right to know" law.
5. In New Jersey the PIRG spearheaded the successful fight to defeat a 650 million dollar transportation bond. NJPIRG is supervising over 100 students on 10 research projects.
6. The Western Massachusetts PIRG has filed a major law suit to overturn state procedures for setting utility rates. The attorney general has filed an amicus brief joining the PIRG suit and the case is pending before a 3-judge federal court in Boston. WMPIRG has issued a study on prescription drug prices showing that the cost to consumers varied by more than 400%, depending on where the drug was purchased. WMPIRG has drafted and will lobby for laws requiring the posting of prescription drug prices and for the free substitution of generic equivalents in place of higher priced name-brand drugs.
7. The Missouri PIRG drafted a new consumer code to protect poor people in St. Louis and has produced and distributed a model tenant lease for use by renters. MOPIRG also participated in a study of Educational Testing Service and is working with St. Louis area unions to secure better enforcement of the occupational safety and health laws.
8. The Texas PIRG issued a major study of the Austin Capital Improvement Plan, pointing out its weaknesses. Voters subsequently turned down a bond issue to finance the plan.
9. PIRGIM, the PIRG in Michigan, uncovered an old law imposing criminal sanctions on landlords for gross housing code violations. PIRGIM presently is suing to have this law enforced.[26]

Especially impressive is the fact that the average age of the PIRG's cited is under six months!

Already, however, the combined annual budget of PIRG's exceeds $1 million, and this figure will climb as more colleges join existing programs and new PIRG's are formed. (Tax PIRG, for example, operated in 1972–1973 on less than $50,000, a figure that rose in 1973–1974 to over $250,000. Note also that less than 5 per cent of the student body on most campuses chose to withdraw that portion of their student fees that goes to a campus-voted PIRG.)[27]

It would seem that with this particular social "invention" a new quality of campus-based social reform effort is possible. Or, as the PIRG at the University of Northern Iowa has explained in the campus paper:

> Its basic philosophy is to combine student action with student idealism. Too often people cite that students are quick to criticize public policies or institutions, but slow in proposing effective solutions. The PIRG now organizing on 22 Iowa campuses will suggest well thought-out solutions when it offers criticism."[28]

Summary

Where do we go from here? A helpful guide in the matter was offered some years ago by J. B. Priestley:

> We should behave toward our country "as women behave toward the men they love. A loving wife will do anything for her husband except to stop criticizing and trying to improve him. That is the right attitude for a citizen. We should cast the same affectionate but sharp glance at our country. We should love it, but also insist on telling it all its faults."[29]

I would take this statement further to contend that we have a responsibility as well to help our country sort through the many reform options available to it and choose those that especially honor us all. In the spirit of the late Pablo Picasso's effort to find "answers that ask questions," I urge an effort on our part to help America choose reforms "that ask questions."

Where then do we go from here? Why, to work, of course:

> We are making some progress. In fact, victory is inevitable. The very fact that we have to fight today for what the Declaration of Independence demanded two hundred years ago is itself a radicalizing phenomenon. We either win an individual skirmish, or the fact that we lose to the forces of greed and repression is so outrageous that more and more people are turned on to the need for change. The blind insensitivity of many of our nation's institutional leaders, their preposterous reactions to the mildest of sensible suggestions, is the best guarantee of change.[30]

FOOTNOTES

1. Snell and Gail Putney, *The Adjusted American: Normal Neurosis* (New York: Harper Torchback Edition, 1964), p. 3.
2. See Erich Fromm, *Escape from Freedom* (New York: Avon, 1971).
3. Jay Walz, "Canada to Raise the 'Baby Bonus,'" *New York Times* (April 29, 1973), p. 10.
4. W. B. Lloyd, "Switzerland's Example," *New York Times* (May 20, 1973), p. 16.
5. "Friendly Bids U.S. Pay for Politicians' Air Time," *New York Times* (May 25, 1973), p. 59.
6. "Sex *mit Herz*," *Time* (April 23, 1973), p. 104.
7. Michael Harrington, "Prospects for a Peace Movement," *The Nation* (June 11, 1973), p. 744.
8. Karl Keyerleber, "The Tidal Dam at St. Malo," *The Nation* (June 11, 1973), p. 755.
9. Harriet Van Horne, "Rock-Ridden City," *New York Post* (June 11, 1973), p. 34.

10. Written by James Parise and used with his permission.
11. Robert T. Clark, Letter to the Editor, *Philadelphia Inquirer* (May 22, 1973), p. 10-A.
12. Ralph E. Winter, "Changing Bias," *Wall Street Journal* (June 6, 1973), p. 1.
13. Randall Halvorson, "Family Farms," *New Republic* (June 23, 1973), p. 32.
14. Robert E. Tomasson, "More States Look to Legal Gambling to Raise Revenue and Stem Tax Increases," *New York Times,* (April 10, 1972), p. 28.
15. Gerald Gold, "Betty Furness Finds Myriad Things to Do, but Not Much Time to Do Them," *New York Times* (June 11, 1973), p. 33.
16. Tom Wicker, "Subsidizing Politics," *New York Times* (June 8, 1973), p. 39.
17. "Help for the Arts," *New Republic* (June 23, 1973), p. 9.
18. "Public Employment," *New Republic* (June 23, 1973), p. 7.
19. Walter Shapiro, "Black and White Together Is Still the Point," *Washington Monthly* (June 1973), p. 42.
20. As referred to in G. E. Berkley, *The Administrative Revolution* (Englewood Cliffs, N.J.: Prentice-Hall, Spectrum ed., 1971), p. 101.
21. Paul R. Wieck, "The John Gardner Brigade," *New Republic* (June 2, 1973), p. 21.
22. "VISTA, Despite Travail, Is Optimistic in 9th Year," *New York Times* (June 12, 1973), p. 24.
23. John P. Roche, "Matter of Academic Credits," *Philadelphia Evening Bulletin* (February 6, 1973), p. 25.
24. Theodore Irwin, "Volunteers Help Lawbreakers Go Straight," *Parade* (December 10, 1972), p. 18.
25. Donald Ross, *A Public Citizen's Action Manual* (New York: Grossman, 1973), p. 253.
26. From materials mailed to me from PIRG, P.O. Box 19404, Washington, D.C. 20036.
27. Ibid.
28. Bill Koch, "ISPIRG, Highland Appear at UNI," *Northern Iowan* (September 28, 1971), p. 3.
29. Quoted in James Reston, "The Personal Tragedies," *New York Times* (June 15, 1973), p. 35.
30. Nicholas Johnson, *Test Pattern for Living* (New York: Bantam, 1972), p. 121.

Annotated Bibliography

I consider my entire work an instrument of education. I am displeased with the current set-up, the categories we instill in children. We must change the concepts, we must begin by humanizing man. We must instill transitive concern—concern with the non-self. Our degree of being human stands in direct relation to our concern with others.

If I am able to convince people that being human is important, that concern for the other is part of being human, I've established a norm.

ABRAHAM HESCHEL

To believe in something not yet proved and to underwrite it with our lives is the only way we can leave the future open.

LILLIAN SMITH

Prepared by Susan Marker, Gerald L. Pocius, Heather Reeves, and Arthur B. Shostak, the last of whom assumes full responsibility for its final format.

Alinsky, Saul, *Rules for Radicals* (New York: Random, 1971).

This practical primer for "realistic radicals" is aimed at those who are committed to changing the system under its own rules. "Make the enemy live up to his own book of rules. . . . You can kill them with this . . . for they can no more obey their own rules than the Christian church can live up to Christianity." A classic text for organizers and activists.

Bakal, Yitzhak, ed., *Closing Correctional Institutions* (Lexington, Mass.: Lexington Books, 1973).

The case for deinstitutionalization is forcefully presented in this volume of alternatives to the correctional system that currently exists. The Massachusetts experiences are also closely examined by the editor, a member of the Massachusetts Department of Youth Services.

Baumol, William A., Rensis Likert, et al., *A New Rationale for Corporate Social Policy* (Lexington, Mass.: Lexington Books, 1971).

A work dealing with corporate philanthropy and the influence of social research on corporate responsibility. Will the stockholder determine the course of America's social reforms?

Becker, S. J., Joseph M., ed., *Guaranteed Income for the Unemployed: The Story of SUB* (Baltimore, Md.: Johns Hopkins, 1973).

Advertised as "A valuable addition to the limited information on the development and operation of private income-maintainance programs."

Benveniste, Guy, *The Politics of Experience* (Berkeley, Calif.: The Glendessary Press, 1972).

Advertised as "a penetrating foray into the wilderness of systems analysis, planning, and policy making. Who are the planners? Whose interest do they serve? How does the new breed of advisors influence policy in the corridors of power? . . . Joins theory with practical experience to challenge the images of expertise, especially those created by experts themselves."

Biddle, William W. and Loureide J., *Encouraging Community Development: A Training Guide for Local Workers* (New York: Holt, 1968).

A training guide written to meet an unusual challenge in a period of rapid social change and consciously planned development. It stresses the local worker who will live with the people he is involved with. Deals with everyday specifics.

Cohen, Harold L., and James Filipczak, *A New Learning Environment: A Case for Learning* (San Francisco: Jossey-Bass, 1971).

Report on a new money-for-learning hope for reaching dropouts and unemployables via a learning approach that can be applied in public schools and reformatories anywhere. Used at the National Training School for Boys in Washington, D.C., the approach uses operantly formulated contingency systems and the design of a special environment to produce remarkable behavioral and attitudinal changes.

Colman, McCarthy, *Disturbers of the Peace* (Boston: Houghton, 1973).

A collection of profiles of people who have refused to adjust to standards they believe are wrong. Some of the most successful "mad blind men who see" are from Appalachia, and it is heartening to read of a new pallet-making factory in Clairfield, started with no grants from regional commissions or any lobbying from any trade association in Washington.

Committee for Economic Development, *High Employment Without Inflation: A Positive Program for Economic Stabilization,* C.E.D., 477 Madison Ave., New York, N.Y. 10022, 1972.

This policy statement presents a basic reappraisal of the causes of economic instability in the American economy and proposes a new positive program for achieving high employment without inflation, incorporating necessary structural reforms. It recognizes that monetary and fiscal policies alone cannot achieve the nation's stabilization objectives.

The Drug Abuse Survey Project; Foreword by McGeorge Bundy, *Dealing with Drug Abuse, A Report to the Ford Foundation* (New York: Praeger, 1973).

Probably the best review we have of the entire drug problem. This important survey, compiled by experts in medicine, psychiatry, law, and economics, describes the extent and nature of drug abuse. It also evaluates current and proposed efforts to control the problem through education, treatment, and law enforcement.

Etzioni, Amitai, and Richard Remp, *Technological Shortcuts to Social Change* (New York: Russell Sage Foundation, 1973).

What part can technology play in reducing social problems? Can technological services, by bypassing the complexities of social engineering, deal more efficiently and effectively with major portions of social problems than the currently used human services? These questions are explored in terms of four areas: Methadone in controlling heroin addiction; Antabuse in treating alcoholism; gun control in reducing crime; and the breath analyzer in highway safety.

Goodman, Robert, *After the Planners* (New York: Simon & Schuster, 1971).

Argues that fundamental political, social, and economic change must take place before planners and architects can make any significant contribution to the whole community process. Advocates a system of "community socialism" in which people in actual communities "determine their own objectives, select their own environmental criteria (and social and economic, as well), and, in general, arrange their lives together."

Grosser, Charles F., *New Directions in Community Organization: From Enabling to Advocacy* (New York: Praeger, 1973).

Changing community organization is surveyed. The antipoverty war, the civil rights movement, changes in social philosophy, activities of organized religion, and the shifting urban scene of the 1950's and 1960's give way to new activist methods of organizing and new settings. The author concludes with informed speculations as to the nature of future organizing.

Harberger, Arnold C., ed., *Project Evaluation: Collected Papers* (Chicago: Markham, 1972).

Focuses on the theory of project evaluation and its applications, with emphasis on public-sector investments designed to promote economic development. Offers measures of key parameters needed for the social evaluation of projects in transportation, electrical power, and irrigation.

Holt, John, *Freedom and Beyond* (New York: Dutton, 1972).

Ranging from early childhood to adult education, Holt discusses the existing alternatives to conventional schooling, such as open schools and free schools. Children are educated much more by the whole society around them and the general quality of life in it than they are by what happens in schools. "For all the talk . . . most of our schools have changed very little."

Horn, Robert E., and David W. Zuckerman, *The Guide to Simulation Games for Education and Training* (Lexington, Mass.: Information Resources Inc., 1970).

A list of over four hundred games and simulations for education in schools and colleges and training in graduate schools and business. Advertised as "the most complete and authoritative source of information on currently available educational games and simulations."

Kahn, Herman, and B. Bruce-Biggs, *Things to Come: Thinking About the Seventies and Eighties* (New York: Macmillan, Inc., 1972).

From the possibility of a new "missile gap" to the impact of technology on the performing arts, from the realignment of international power blocs to the prospects for further polarization in U.S. society, the authors analyze the most important developments—where, when, how, and why major changes might occur and what significance these events would have for America and for the world at large.

Klein, Carole, *The Single Parent Experience* (New York: Walker, 1973).

A complete guide for the woman or man who wishes to raise a child outside of marriage: adoption, pregnancy, and legal counseling; child-care and communal living arrangements; advice on dealing with family, school, and community problems.

Kostelanetz, Richard, ed., *Human Alternatives: Visions for Us Now* (New York: Morrow, 1971).

"The crucial question confronting us now is not whether we can change the world but what kind of world do we want, as well as how to turn our choices into realities." This lively collection of essays deals with scenarios available to us in the not-so-distant future. It is valuable for its emphasis on the "human" in reforms. Kostelanetz begins with alternative forms of knowledge and covers fields as diverse as politics and planning, economics and education.

Kwee, S. L., and J. S. R. Mullender, eds., *Growing Against Ourselves: The Energy Environment Tangle* (Lexington, Mass.: Lexington Books, 1972).

The effects of a rapidly developing technology on the environment are problems our leaders endeavor to ignore. This book presents an analysis of environmental-technological problems and policies, as well as sound recommendations for strategies against environmental waste in the private and public sectors.

Levitan, Sar A., *The Great Society's Poor Law: A New Approach to Poverty* (Baltimore, Md.: Johns Hopkins, 1973).

Advertised as "The first independent objective evaluation of OEO's accomplishments and failures," this book is an authoritative reference work on this first stage in the long war on poverty.

Moffet, Toby, *The Participation Put-On* (New York: Delacorte, 1971).

The twenty-five-year-old ex-head of the Office of Education's Office of Students and Youths recounts the sources of his disenchantment with social action efforts in HEW. Promoted as a "gallows humor account of bureaucracy, in inaction, and a forceful narrative of a young man's disintegrating hopes for doing 'constructive work' within the government."

Morris, Norval, and Gordon Hawkins, *The Honest Politician's Guide to Crime Control* (Chicago: U. of Chicago, 1970).

"Spurning 'the war on crime' and other law-and-order nostrums, two distinguished criminologists have thrown away the rule book in this witty, highly readable volume." The authors present a program that covers the amount, costs, causes, and victims of crime, the reduction of violence, the police, juvenile delinquency, and other specific problems.

Nader, Ralph, and Donald Ross, *Action for a Change: A Student's Manual for Public Interest Organizing* (New York: Grossman, 1971).

Addressed to the question of "What can I do to improve my community?" and "How do I go about doing it?" Explores the mechanics of taking a serious abuse, laying it bare before the public, proposing solutions, and generating the necessary coalitions to see these solutions through. Especially urges students to form public interest research groups to help promote "initiatory democracy."

Orlans, Harold, *Contracting for Knowledge: Values and Limitations of Social Science Research* (San Francisco: Jossey-Bass, 1973).

Summarizes and evaluates empirical evidence and expert opinion on social scientists' biases as well as on the nonexistent ethical standards of most social science associations. Explores the private scholar's responsibility to government and the kind of knowledge needed to solve social problems. Assesses the dubious quality of much sponsored research and the evaluation of government social problems. Outlines the kinds of social research for which universities, nonprofit institutes, and profit organizations are best suited. Finally, the book analyzes government controls over private research publication and the meaning of "utilizing" social research.

Pohlman, Edward, ed., *Population: A Clash of Prophets* (New York: Mentor, 1973).

Presents all sides of today's urgent debate on the future dangers of overpopulation. Included are the opinions of leading scientists and demographers, spokesmen of the West and the Third World, ecologists, and politicians.

Rivlin, Alice M., *Systematic Thinking for Social Action* (Washington, D.C.: The Brookings Institution, 1971).

An attempt to give a "midterm report card" on the progress of the analysts in improving the basis for public decisions on social action programs. Urges systematic experiments with different ways of using the social sciences and analyzing the results.

Ross, Donald, *A Public Citizen's Action Manual* (New York: Grossman, 1973).

Provides practical and imaginative suggestions for consumer action, ranging from the correct procedures for filing noise pollution complaints to advice on checking local property tax assessments.

Rossi, Peter H., and Walter Williams, *Evaluating Social Programs: Theory, Practice, and Politics* (New York: Seminar Press, 1972).

The obvious question to ask about any social program is "How effective is it?" This book deals squarely with this question and its relationship to social action. Why has so little high-quality evaluative research been done on social programs? What should government and social scientists do to foster soundly conceived and executed evaluative research? This book touches on these questions and others in a challenging and much-needed collection of essays.

Satir, Virginia, *Peoplemaking* (Palo Alto, Calif.: Science and Behavior Books, 1973).

"Family life is something like an iceberg. Most people are aware of only about one-tenth of what is actually going on . . . and often they think that is all there is." This book examines the other nine tenths of family life, drawing on the author's thirty-five years as a family therapist. Her main concerns are self-worth, communication, and system and family rules, all presented in human terms relying on case histories and "communication games."

Sharp, Gene, *Exploring Nonviolent Approaches* (Boston: Porter Sargent, 1971).

A basic introduction to the technique of nonviolence and noncooperation, its previous uses, and its need for further study. Includes an argument for national defense without armaments, a course program in civilian defense, and an extensive bibliography.

Walzer, Michael, *Political Action: A Practical Guide to Movement Politics* (Chicago: Quadrangle, 1971).

Twenty-five chapters that deal in careful detail with how to solicit for funds, how to organize democratically, how to provide effective leadership, and many other questions, including the psychological satisfaction to be gained from active participation in a movement.

Weinberg, Martin S., and Earl Rubington, eds., *The Solution of Social Problems* (New York: Oxford U.P., 1973).

Examines the many sociological theories that are used in understanding social problems and how these perspectives can be used in formulating problem-solving action. Contributors include Philip Slater, Desmond Morris, Charles Reich, Alvin Toffler, Stokely Carmichael, and R. D. Laing.

Williams, Walter, *Social Policy Research and Analysis: The Experience in the Federal Social Agencies* (New York: Am. Elsevier, 1971).

Drawing on his OEO experiences, the author analyzes flaws in both the social science research community and the federal social agencies that help explain why social science research is seldom relevant to major policy decisions. His reforms include a call for "some mechanism (a staff office) . . . that can work in a peer relationship with the social science researchers and the federal bureaucracy."

Index